Person, Place, and Thing

in Henry James's Novels

Person, Place, and Thing
in Henry James's Novels

CHARLES R. ANDERSON

DUKE UNIVERSITY PRESS

Durham, North Carolina

1977

For

Mary Pringle Anderson

Eugenia Blount Anderson

Gertrude Roberts Anderson

— *my heroines*

Table of Contents

Acknowledgments

Few authors have been as much written about as Henry James. There are more than one hundred books, and probably as many as a thousand articles, of criticism, biography, personal and literary relations with contemporaries. Over the years I have tried to read as many of these as I could and to profit by them in every way possible. My debt to previous commentators is large, too large for more than a general acknowledgment here, but those who have been specifically useful are acknowledged in the notes at the end of my book. It has not been my purpose to make a compilation of everything important that has been said about my chosen subject, nor even to append an annotated bibliography, but to offer my own critical interpretations of certain novels.

My largest debt is to the great shelf of James's own writings, some sixty-five volumes, which are surveyed briefly in my introduction. The pleasure and enrichment I have derived from a lifetime's immersion in these books have persuaded me that I have something to say about James's fictional art; and I have tried to say it straight out, only bringing in what others have said when it seemed indispensable. The chapters that follow are simply one person's reading of a half-dozen novels by Henry James, with grateful thanks to those who have paved the way and a hope that this selection will prove to be representative of his monumental achievement as a creative artist.

For permission to draw on two of my previous articles, I would like to thank the Duke University Press ("Person, Place, and Thing in James's *Portrait of a Lady*," in *Essays in Honor of Jay B. Hubbell*, 1968), and the University of Georgia ("A Henry James Centenary," *Georgia Review*, Spring, 1976). I would also like to express my gratitude to the Guggenheim Foundation for a year's fellowship, which enabled me to launch the study and research that has resulted in *Person, Place, and Thing in Henry James's Novels*.

C. R. A.

Person, Place, and Thing

in Henry James's Novels

Experimenter

Henry James's achievement has a threefold distinction. He was a brilliant creator, an international novelist in his grasp of the "great tradition," and a radical experimenter who transformed the art of fiction. By common consent he is the commanding figure for students of the novel as it developed from nineteenth- to twentieth-century modes.

One of the basic problems for a creator of fictions is how to put his characters in relation with one another so they can achieve communication and understanding. As long as the convention of the omniscient author prevailed, this problem was sidestepped. The gradual disappearance of the all-knowing and commenting author has marked a transition from the Victorian to the modern novel. As the conviction has gained ground that in real life every individual is a kind of "isolato"—imprisoned in the capsule of his own self—so the responsible novelist has assumed the same difficulty for his fictional characters in their struggle to make meaningful relations with one another.

Henry James began his career just when this issue was coming to loom as crucial for the writer of fictions. His awareness of the problem in his own life, even with close friends, is testified to in a letter of 14 January 1874, just as he was starting to compose his first novel. Concerned with the difficulty of actually "answering" the letter of a long-time intimate, he asks: "But do we, in talk or in writing, ever really answer each other? Each of us says his limited personal say out of the midst of his own circumstances, and the other one clips what satisfaction he can from it." As a novelist James accepted this challenge, knowing it was one that could be met only by developing adequate techniques. His best known device is the use of a major character, who is also a semidetached narrator, as the consciousness through which all is seen and understood. As James experimented with this technique during a quarter century, he brought the novel a long way from the loosely constructed fictions of his predecessors to the tighter forms we know today. The use of such a new point of view has many advantages over the convention that allows the novelist to speak in his own voice, even when this central consciousness is not carried to its ultimate development in the narrator whose vision virtually creates the fictional world. But this device does not solve all the technical problems. How can the other characters, whose story is being told, really achieve communication and understanding? How can they penetrate the appearances, façades, masks, and masquerades by which people conceal their secret selves from each other?

It has been a commonplace of Jamesian criticism to say that his characters exist only in their relations with each other. But the crux of the matter is: How do they arrive at any real relations at all? It is my purpose to show that they do so only indirectly, and that the process of their doing so is the whole of their story. It is not until one character understands some associated object which he assumes is symbolic of another character that he comes to understand him, or thinks he does—the inherent ambivalence of the symbol being a chief complicating factor. I use the term "object" for convenience, to include places and things of all sorts: a house, estate, or rural landscape; the vista presented by a boulevard, the interior of a favorite café, a box at the theater, or a street scene; a teacup, painting, statue, or other work of art.

Such a symbolic relation between people and things can be observed in real life, of course, at least on special occasions. James's originality consists in his adopting this as a principal mode of characterization in his fiction. A hint as to the possibilities that lay in this direction came from his first master. Early in 1875, at the beginning of his own career, James wrote an essay surveying the whole achievement of the *Comédie Humaine* in which he praised Balzac in three ways: "There is nothing in all imaginative literature that in the least resembles his mighty passion for things—for material objects, for furniture, upholstery, bricks and mortar,...towns, houses and rooms.... This overmastering sense of the present world was of course a superb foundation for the work of a realistic romancer.... It gave him in the first place his background—his *mise-en-scène*.... The place in which an event occurred was in his view of equal moment with the event itself; it was part of the action." In his most effective writing Balzac passed almost imperceptibly "from the portraiture of places to that of people." Person, place, and thing! Clearly Balzac was the novelist from whom James first derived the suggestion for his own basic technique of rendering character in terms of place and thing —their transformation into symbols being the younger artist's great contribution.

A short passage in *Roderick Hudson* (1875), completed in the same year as the essay on Balzac, proves that James was projecting thus early the technique he used to such advantage in his later novels. (One of his fictional people says to another that his *things*—his apartment and its furnishings—are indicative of his *character*.) Though formulated in his first novel it was not used there, except this once. In his second, *The American* (1877), James carried the experiment a bit further by providing characterizing images for the five main characters, but these images do not really help to establish relations among them. The mode was fully developed a few years later. It functions with striking effect in his first masterpiece, *The Portrait of a Lady* (1881)—and from then on to the end of his career.

For Henry James one of the most rewarding situations was the American in Europe, an apparently simple character projected against a complex background. But persons, places, and things are never exactly what they seem. It is their ambivalence that gives the novelist his opportunity to suggest multiple meanings, matching our uncertainty about meanings in real life. All art forms based on creating an illusion of truth-to-life—painting, drama, fiction—make elaborate use of the difference between appearance and reality. One of James's chief methods of doing so is in his distinction between Europe and "Europe." *Europe* stands for the realities of Italy, France, and England, recorded by the novelist with ever greater precision over the years. *"Europe"* stands for the various American preconceptions of those countries, assigned to his fictional characters with increasingly subtle discrimination. But the contrast between Europe and "Europe" is, happily, not quite so simple. Preconceptions may be false in one sense, but they also contain some psychological truth.

What *is* Rome, for example, after all? The sum total of the statistical data in Baedeker? or what we feel and believe about Rome? Certainly there are vast differences between what it means to a religious pilgrim, to a lover of art and history, to a journalist writing a column on "Rome Today" for an American newspaper. Which view of Paris is nearer the truth: the glittering metropolis that both attracts and repels the moralist, or the perfect symbol of Civilization conjured up by romantic expatriates? Again, England is Our Old Home to the sentimental pilgrim, the last stronghold of feudalism to the assertively democratic critic from the New World—and both pictures differ greatly from that of the visiting business man. An American novelist who would deal with Europe convincingly must master all these perspectives and discriminate among them clearly, even while he creates his own myth of Europe / "Europe" which adds the suggestiveness of poetry to the whole.

Everything conspired to make Henry James an international novelist. Europe was dominant in his early education. By the end of his adolescence, he had spent a third of his young years abroad. This was followed by a decade at home, finishing his desultory years at Harvard and deciding on a career. When he was twenty-six he began his adult explorations of Italy, France, and England, absorbing all that Europe had to offer and at the same time trying to choose the ideal post for a novelist. Finally, after one more attempt at making a go of it in America, he left there for good at the age of thirty-two, spent 1875–76 in Paris, then settled permanently in London. This was his home for the remaining forty years of his life—with frequent, all but annual, visits to the Continent, lasting from several weeks to as many months.

During these long residences in foreign parts James was keenly observant of places and things European, also of English and French and Italian people, especially of the American abroad. These observations filled his letters and spilled over into a long series of travel essays—six volumes of them, and enough uncollected ones to fill a couple more. Though undertaken as a means of supporting himself by his pen, these sketches are highly relevant to his fictional art. He drew on them in much the same way that other authors have made use of their journals and notebooks. Readers interested in the creative process can watch with fascination as the traveller's impressions are transformed into the very fabric of his novels. Written over a period of three decades, the essays vary widely in quality. James knew even at the outset that writing such travel pieces was not as simple as one might think. "It's a complex fate, being an American," he warned himself in 1872, "and one of the responsibilities it entails is fighting against a superstitious valuation of Europe." Some of his earliest sketches fall in this category—touched as they were by the sentiments of a pilgrim from the New World to the Old and colored by his enthusiasm for the picturesque. That the author realized this is indicated by his assigning them to certain characters in his novels as American preconceptions of "Europe." On the other hand the narrator of the fictions, whether James himself or a surrogate consciousness, could find in the travel essays much to suit his own purposes—many passages that portrayed Europe with scrupulous realism or with deliberate heightening. The range is from trial flights for capturing the essence of places and things to those symbolic descriptions that give his later fictions a poetic dimension.

Two other kinds of essays grew out of James's observations of Europe—essays on the theater and on painting, the art forms other than literature that drew him most. Knowing he had no real talent as a drama or art critic, he never published them as books. Journalism they may be, but they have important bearing on his fictional techniques, as indicated by the titles supplied editorially for two posthumous volumes: *The Scenic Art* and *The Painter's Eye*. From his intimate knowledge of the theater, and from his own disastrous attempts to write plays, James learned how to adapt the scenic method from drama to novel and worked out a new technique for his presentations of setting or *place*. From his abortive efforts at trying to become a painter when a young man, and from his lifelong devotion to art galleries and exhibitions, he learned to apply to his fiction the "painter's eye" which his early teacher prophesied would give a special distinction to his real talent. Pictures are probably the most effective symbolic *things* in his novels because they too are mirrors of reality, a second art form that creates the illusion of truth-to-life used to reinforce that of the fictionist.

The largest number of essays Henry James wrote are in the field of his second great talent, literary criticism—approximately ten volumes of them covering most of the great nineteenth-century authors of Europe, as well as of England and America. More than any of his other writings they throw light on his own art of fiction. For a creative writer he was unusually widely read. He learned from many masters, and to follow his elaborate commentaries on novelists from Hawthorne to Dickens and George Eliot, from Balzac to Flaubert and Zola, from Turgenev to Maupassant and Daudet, is to be privy to the development of many of his own techniques. For, like most writers who are both creators and critics, his literary criticism tells us as much about himself as about his chosen subjects. Many of the things he learned from his predecessors and contemporaries are touched upon in my book: the right balance between fiction as art and as a story of morally interesting characters, the shift from loose chronicle to tight dramatic form, the concern with portraiture rather than plot, the creation of a style in which language and imagery are inseparable from the novel's meaning. But my chief emphasis is on how James evolved his own fictional mode over the years by what he learned from the realistic romances of his earliest masters on down to the symbolic realism of his latest, shifting the center of interest from external action to the dramas of consciousness. In this way the study of James's literary criticism illuminates my thesis, that the symbolic relationship of person-place-and-thing is a basic technique in his fiction.

There are two other strictly literary volumes in the shelf of James's writings that round out his critical commentary. First the *Notebooks,* which record the germs or *données* of most of his fictions, frequently expanded into "scenarios" planning in advance many details of characters, situations, and scenes to be worked out. The other is the late Prefaces, written for the collected edition of his works but also available as a separate volume entitled *The Art of the Novel,* in which the master recapitulates the problems he faced when writing his novels and tales and the techniques he created to solve them.

Finally, there are the relevant biographical materials. James wrote three volumes of biography, dealing with Hawthorne, the one novelist offering a native tradition on which he could build, and with the sculptor W. W. Story, and the American artist colony in Rome. Much more pertinent are the three volumes of James's autobiography, a "history of the imagination" as he called it, replete with all the persons-places-things that haunted his mind from childhood to maturity as bodied forth in his reading and his observations at home and abroad. Last comes the voluminous correspondence, some fifteen thousand surviving letters. Only a fraction of them have been published so far, but more are now forthcoming in a multivolume selection of James's best letters under the editorship of Leon Edel, to supplement his five-volume official biography. James was a superlative letter writer, and his correspondence is an indispensable source for students of literature since it is concerned above all with his creative life: his evolution as a professional writer, the influences that were most important for him, the plans and problems connected with his innumerable writing projects, vignettes of the persons-places-things that went into his fictions. This brings the miscellaneous writings of James to a total of more than thirty volumes. I have chosen a representative selection of his novels and will interpret them in the widest of contexts, confident that this will enrich our understanding of them.

The shelf of James's fiction is so large—thirty-six volumes in all—it was necessary to decide on some selective process in order to keep within bounds my choices for close reading. One way to this goal was to bypass the shorter fictions, however tempting, and stick to the novels. Of these I wanted some laid in Italy, some in France, some in England—person-place-and-thing varying so greatly in these three countries. Then since James's techniques for interweaving these strands evolve gradually over the years, along with his development of the scenic and symbolic modes and other aspects of his fictional art, it seemed desirable to choose some novels in his early manner, some in the late, and some from the period in between. The half-dozen of my final choice not only answer to these requirements but also have the seal of the master's approval. Near the end of his life when asked to draw up a list of his best, or rather a list that would best lead a young admirer into the heart of his fictional world, James unhesitatingly named the following: *Roderick Hudson, The American, The Portrait of a Lady, The Princess Casamassima, The Tragic Muse, The Wings of the Dove, The Ambassadors, The Golden Bowl*. It would have been a pleasure to include them all, but space forbade. I have reluctantly omitted two: *The Tragic Muse* as too "special," *The Golden Bowl* as too limited in reader appeal—at least so it seemed to me. The remaining six illustrate all the points of my thesis. And each of them has a basic form or mode that is highly distinctive as well as a theme that is uniquely different, all challenging to the critical analyst.

For those who maintain that a good story is sufficient unto itself and needs no interpretation, James himself made answer. In "The Lesson of Balzac" (1905), one of his major pronouncements on the art of fiction, he declared: "Criticism is the only gate of appreciation, just as appreciation is, in regard to a work of art, the only gate of enjoyment." This is my warrant for the chapters that follow.

The Heady Wine of Rome

RODERICK HUDSON

Here I am then in the Eternal City.... I've seen the Tiber hurrying along, as swift and dirty as history! ... At last—for the first time—I live! It beats everything: it leaves the Rome of your fancy—your education—nowhere.... I went reeling and moaning thro' the streets, in a fever of enjoyment. In the course of four or five hours I traversed almost the whole of Rome and got a glimpse of everything—the Forum, the Coliseum (stupendissimo!), the Pantheon, the Capitol, St. Peter's, the Column of Trajan, the Castle of St. Angelo—all the Piazzas and ruins and monuments. The effect is something indescribable. For the first time I know what the picturesque is.... To crown my day, on my way home, I met his Holiness in person—driving in prodigious purple state—sitting dim within the shadows of his coach with two uplifted benedictory fingers—like some dusky Hindoo idol in the depths of its shrine. Even if I should leave Rome tonight I should feel that I have caught the keynote of its operation on the senses.

Such was the ecstatic report of Henry James, age twenty-six, sent to his brother William back in America at the end of the first day he had ever spent in Rome, 30 October 1869. The letter is clearly self-dramatizing—"I went reeling and moaning thro' the streets"—deliberately done for the audience at home. (A week afterward he wrote to his sister, "The excitement of the first hour has passed away and I have recovered the healthy mental equilibrium of the sober practical tourist.") Another purpose was to capture his present emotional experience in words for authorial use later. It was such letters as this that he had in mind when he asked his family to keep them: "They will serve me in the future as a series of notes or observations—the only ones I shall have written."

First novels tend to be autobiographical, no life story being better known to young writers than their own. It is no surprise, then, to find parallels between *Roderick Hudson* and some of Henry James's experiences, especially in the early chapters (though nothing of his personality or character). Some five years before beginning his first full-scale novel the author, like his fic-

[9]

tional hero, had left America for Europe in search of a milieu better suited to an artistic career—though as novelist rather than sculptor. Since James already knew England and France well, his real objective this time was the discovery of Italy. Early in September 1869, taking the dramatic route over the Alps, he entered the golden land that was always to symbolize for him Romance and Passion. Everywhere he felt "the aesthetic presence of the past." As he made his way through the lake country and the old ducal towns of north Italy, then to Venice and Florence, he exhausted his vocabulary in letters to the family, trying to capture what he could only call "*the Italian feeling,*" underscoring the phrase for emphasis. The climax came with his arrival in Rome on a day in late autumn. After "a wash and breakfast [I] let myself loose on the city"—so begins the letter quoted in full above.

Papal Rome and Provincial America

By arriving in 1869 Henry James had the good fortune to see Papal Rome in all its splendor, with its processions and ceremonials, and he never forgot it. In another year the Risorgimento had taken over and Papal Rome had shrunk to what is today Vatican City. In "A Roman Holiday," an essay written during James's next visit in 1873, he said: "Something momentous had happened—something hostile to the elements of picture and color and 'style.' " The impressions of his first immersion in Rome were indeed so vivid that they came back in a flooding memory more than thirty years later when he was writing his biography of the expatriate American sculptor, William Wetmore Story. There, once again, he recorded his vision of the august procession of the Pope in his "great black-horsed coach," rumbling through the streets of the city. "The canvas then was crowded, the old-world presence intact," his eloquent reminiscence concludes: "The saints, the processions, the Cardinals, all the Catholic pomp, have [now] retired from the foreground."

When James began writing *Roderick Hudson* in 1874, he could have laid his novel in the more secular "modern" Rome that was then emerging as the capital of a newly unified Italy. But he chose instead as his setting the spectacular Papal Rome he had known in its last hours, several years before. The time scheme of his fiction is indicated by the glimpse of Pius IX in a state progress through the city streets granted to his hero Roderick in an early chapter:

In Rome his first care was for the Vatican; he went there again and again. But the old imperial and papal city altogether delighted him; only there he really found what he had been looking for from the first—the complete antipodes of Northampton. And indeed Rome is the natural home of those spirits ... with a deep relish for the artificial element in life and the infinite superpositions of history. It is the immemorial city of convention.... And in that still recent day the most impressive convention in all history was visible to men's eyes, in the Roman streets, erect in a gilded coach drawn by four black horses. Roderick's first fortnight was a high aesthetic revel. He declared that Rome made him feel and understand more things than he could express.... He had caught instinctively the keynote of the old world. He observed and enjoyed, he criticised and rhapsodized. (84–85, 82)

Roderick Hudson's reactions to Rome are strikingly similar to those of Henry James in the letter of 30 October 1869, the vision of the Pope in his coach serving as a symbol of the lost splendor.

Papal Rome was the milieu chosen by the author, with a sure instinct, for the career of his artist-hero. With its emphasis on picture and scene, it might appear to be more appropriate to a painter—in words or pigments—than to a sculptor. James makes it clear, however, that his protagonist was not a narrowly specialized artist, but was more like the many-sided Renaissance man: "Roderick's quick appreciation of every form of artistic beauty reminded his companion of the flexible temperament of those Italian artists of the sixteenth century who were indifferently painters and sculptors, sonneteers and engravers" (91). This deliberate choice of a rich setting and a richly responding temperament gave a more universal meaning to the young American sculptor's European career and made it easier for the young novelist to identify with him.

The Italian section of *Roderick Hudson* (beginning with chapter three and occupying three-fourths of the whole novel) opens in late autumn, the year being clearly 1869, though not so named. The hero and Rowland Mallet, his companion and patron—after two months in England, Paris, Venice, and Florence—have now been in Rome for several weeks, drinking in all it has to offer. "I have an indigestion of impressions; I must work them off before I go in for any more," (78) Roderick declares, lying idle on the grass in the Ludovisi gardens. He will not look any more at the works of others until he has some of his own to show. After a long pause he pursues:

What becomes of all our emotions, our impressions, ... all the material of thought that life pours into us at such a rate during such a memorable three months as these? There are twenty moments a week—a day, for that matter, some days—that seem supreme, twenty impressions that seem ultimate, that appear to form an intellectual era. But others come treading on their heels and sweeping them along.... I want to pause and breathe;

[11]

I want to dream of a statue. I have been working hard for three months;
I have earned a right to a reverie. (80, 81)

After three months in England, during his sojourn of 1869, Henry James had
written William that the purpose of his trip was to study the art and history
of Europe, and so to acquire an education "which may be of future use to
me." Then he added: "My present business is simply to be idle."

The immediate source of Roderick's meditation on the process by which
experience is transformed into art can be found in the final paragraph of
James's early travel sketch entitled "A Roman Note-Book." During a second
long residence of more than two years in Europe, he had spent another rap-
turous period in Rome from January to June 1873. As he packed his bags to
leave, he tried to sum up its significance for his artistic career—in words
strikingly similar to those he was to put in his hero's mouth a few months
later:

> One would like, after five months in Rome, to be able to make some gen-
> eral statement of one's experience, one's gains. It is not easy. One has the
> sense of a kind of passion for the place, and of a large number of gathered
> impressions. Many of these have been intense, momentous, but one has
> trodden on the other, and one can hardly say what has become of them.
> They store themselves noiselessly away, I suppose, in the dim but safe
> places of memory, and we live in an insistent faith that they will emerge
> into vivid relief if life or art should demand them.

Within a few months of Roderick's meditation, his Italian experiences had
resulted in the creation of his first two statues, Adam and Eve. In a similar
length of time James's "impressions" had begun to emerge in the form of his
first novel. Writing to a friend from Florence, where he was hard at work
on *Roderick Hudson*, he confided: "I have been hugging my Roman memories with extraordinary gusto." To a fellow novelist in America he explained
why he had left the Italian capital: "Rome, for direct working, was not good
—too many distractions and a languefying atmosphere. But for 'impressions'
it was priceless." Was James thinking of his hero-in-the-making? Certainly
"too many distractions and a languefying atmosphere" had something to do
with the tragic conclusion of the young sculptor's career after his brief hour
of triumph. What were the "distractions" of Rome for the novelist became,
when translated into his fiction, the *hazards* of a career in that city for his
hero. It is true that Roderick was an extreme case of the unstable artistic
temperament and that a century ago Rome, in the popular mind, was a place
of romance and mystery where anything could happen. James realized that
it might strain the credulity of readers to make a mere place responsible for

a tragic fall, even if only in a contributory way. Though he had warned himself against "a superstitious valuation of Europe," still this is one of the undeniable themes of *Roderick Hudson*.

Hawthorne's *Marble Faun* (1860) offered an example, and a warning. All four characters in that novel, centered on the artistic circle in Rome, were obsessed with the Eternal City as the epitome of beauty and evil; one of them, Donatello, as a reincarnation of Praxiteles' "Faun," became a symbol of the mysterious power of the past over the present; another, Hilda, turned from original work as a painter to making copies of the Old Masters, because of her experiences in Rome. Two of James's earliest fictions set in Italy were overly romantic embodiments of these themes: "Adina" and "The Last of the Valerii," both conventional stories with stereotyped characters. When his brother William visited him in Rome in 1872 he complained of the burden of history there, and suggested that if one remained in Italy long he would cease to use his own creative powers. A much more original story by Henry written shortly thereafter, "The Madonna of the Future," is an elaboration of this idea. The relation of this story to *Roderick Hudson* is made clear in a letter to Howells from Florence in the spring of 1874. "My story is to be on a theme I have had in my head a long time and once attempted to write something about," James said. Then, hoping to persuade the editor of the *Atlantic Monthly* to accept his new novel for serialization, he added by way of prevue: "The opening chapters take place in America and the people are of our glorious race; but they are soon transplanted to Rome, where things are to go on famously. *Ecco.*"

Now for a word about the American launching. The author makes careful preparation in his preliminary chapters, the two laid in a small New England town, for the coming impact of Rome. There, as the story is set in motion and the characters are introduced, all of their preconceptions of Europe—of Italy in particular—support the idea of its being a dangerous place for an innocent American to begin his career as an artist. "Rome is an evil word in my mother's vocabulary," Roderick says of the widowed Mrs. Hudson; it stands for benighted heathendom just as Northampton Mass represents for her the center of Christendom (26–27, 40). She has a "holy horror" of sculpture as a profession anyway, especially for a young man of "a passionate disposition." The family solicitor is scornful of imitating antique models, which he describes as pagan deities with "no arms, no noses, and no clothing." Mary Garland betrays the most valid concern of all when she asks, in reference to her fiancé's second step of working from living models, "Are the Roman women very beautiful?" (54, 55).

Roderick's own preconception of Europe is a compound of romance and

[13]

poetry, as symbolized by his breaking out into a snatch of song from Tennyson's *Princess*, "The splendor falls on castle walls," on the very night when
he decides to accept Mallet's offer and go to Italy. His moods alternate between
exhilarating dreams of his future and violent anger over his past deprivations.
But he must be prepared to work hard and discipline his impetuous nature,
his wealthy sponsor warns; otherwise his Roman life may become "a sort of
idealized form of loafing, thanks to the number and quality of one's impressions" there (6, 63). These varied preconceptions help to characterize the
actors in James's drama and to prepare his readers for a number of possibilities
in the unfolding action, once patron and protégé arrive in Rome.

Another purpose of the opening chapters had been to present Roderick's
"native scene" in all its barrenness, as "the antithesis to a state of civilization
providing for 'art.' " So the mature artist says in his late Preface, but as he
looks back over his first novel he sees how pathetically his evocation "fails of
intensity." The fault lay in his being drawn at that time to a school of realism
not properly suited to his own evolving fictional mode. "One nestled, tech-
nically, in those days, and with yearning, in the great shadow of Balzac,"
James confesses: "his august example towered for me over the scene." Ad-
miring his unforgettable representations of French provincial towns, he says:
"I remember how, in my feebler fashion, I yearned over the preliminary
presentation of my small square patch of the American scene." But Balzac's
high practice was unsuited to one who was "not in the least emulating his
systematic closeness." Besides, the French master, who always required "a
due density in his material," would have found little enough in Northampton
to engage his pen. At any rate, the young American novelist's presentation
of his New England town is far too thin and diffuse; in spite of a dispropor-
tionate amount of space, nearly one-sixth of the whole book, too much of it
is devoted to plot, too little to picture.

A more mature Henry James would probably have begun *Roderick Hudson*
with the first scene laid in Rome. His later theory and practice support such
a conjecture. In this same Preface to his first novel, he makes one of his most
important formulations about the art of composition. He has been remarking
on the endless relatedness of people and events, stretched out in time, and
their ramifications in all directions spatially. Then, in a memorable metaphor,
he resolves the novelist's dilemma as he faces the question of selection from
such unlimited possibilities: "Really, universally, relations stop nowhere, and
the exquisite problem of the artist is eternally but to draw, by a geometry of
his own, the circle within which they *appear* to do so." This technique, if
applied to *Roderick Hudson*, would have meant drawing the circle so that
the story would be contained within Italy. Then the "American scene" could
have been worked in by a brief flashback, early in the narrative. Such was the

resolution of a similar problem in *The Portrait of a Lady*, written just five years later; there the heroine's native background is sufficiently evoked by the symbolic rendering of a single place, the family home in Albany.

When the characters in *Roderick Hudson* are transplanted to Rome "things are to go on famously," James had promised his publisher. Not only did the European scene provide the requisite "density" of material, but the young American novelist began to experiment with new techniques for "evoking" it, instead of describing it in the older manner of Victorian realism. And his travel essays, written at the time of the novel, served as a kind of laboratory for him. One reviewer of *Transatlantic Sketches* (1875) remarked that the author not only describes objective scenery but also puts into his writing the "scenery of his own mind." James himself declares that his purpose in these sketches is to write *à la Gautier*, and his major critical article on this French-man (written early in 1873) makes his meaning clear. He praises Gautier's travel essays for the very qualities that were to distinguish his own *Trans-atlantic Sketches*, and later his fictions—"the vivid, plastic image," the multi-colored picture, "the masterly evocation of localities." Since one of the main concerns of my book is James's development from conventional description to the extraordinary skills of the mature novelist in rendering picture and scene, *Roderick Hudson* is the appropriate place to begin. From that brave "first attempt at a novel" (his phrase in the Preface) to the masterpieces of his major phase we can trace the evolution of two of the basic techniques in modern fiction: the use of scenic presentation instead of narrative, and of symbolism rather than realism in the descriptive parts. By means of them James gave a new significance to the relationships of person, place, and thing.

Italy: Scene and Symbol

The Italian section of *Roderick Hudson*, begins with the sculptor-hero and his patron, Rowland Mallet, stretched out at leisure in a large garden on the Pincian Hill talking about art and the artist's life. Just three months had elapsed since they left America, on September 5 (1, 74), but these had been filled with "impressions" for Roderick—impressions that were all but over-whelming. The purpose of James's first Roman scene is to evoke the golden air of Italy:

> One warm, still day, late in the … autumn, our two young men were sitting beneath one of the high-stemmed pines of the Villa Ludovisi. They had been spending an hour in the mouldy little garden-house, where the colossal mask of the famous Juno looks out with blank eyes from that

dusky corner which must seem to her the last possible stage of a lapse from Olympus. Then they had wandered out into the gardens and were lounging away the morning under the spell of their magical picturesqueness. Roderick declared that he would go nowhere else; that, after the Juno, it was a profanation to look at anything but sky and trees. (77)

So he remained lying on the grass while Rowland wandered off to look at a fresco of Guercino in the casino nearby. Returning, he refrained from praising this painting which, though a favorite with visitors at this period, Roderick (without having seen it) had declared "couldn't be worth a fig." Instead, Rowland talked of the view from the belvedere which, he suggested, "looked like the prospect from a castle turret in a fairy tale" (74). These words echo Roderick's romantic song on one of his last nights in Northampton, "The splendor falls on castle walls," as he dreamed of the glories of Europe in store for him (59). He had indeed heard "The horns of Elfland faintly blowing!"

When James was composing this chapter of his novel during the early spring of 1874, he was able to draw on his own impression of the same scene as recorded in "The After-Season in Rome" and "A Roman Note-Book," two travel essays written during a visit to Italy the year before. The first one is devoted to the gardens:

> The Villa Ludovisi . . . is really a princely place. . . . The stern old ramparts of Rome form the outer enclosure of the villa, and hence a series of picturesque effects. . . . The grounds are laid out in the formal last century manner; but nowhere do the straight black cypresses lead off the gaze into vistas of a more fictive sort of melancholy. . . . [Nature leaves you] nothing to do but to lay your head among the anemones at the base of a high-stemmed pine and gaze crestward and skyward along its slanting silvery column.

The second essay, after more details about the immense gardens, contains an account of the villa itself and its art treasures, directly suited to the novelist's needs:

> A morning [walk] at Villa Ludovisi. . . . There is surely nothing better in Rome; nothing perhaps exactly so good. . . . The sculptures in the little Casino are few, but there are two great ones—the beautiful sitting Mars and the head of the great Juno, thrust into a corner behind a shutter. These things it is almost impossible to praise. . . . If I don't praise Guercino's Aurora in the greater Casino, it is for another reason; it is certainly a very muddy masterpiece. . . . Besides, it is unfair to pass straight from the Athenian mythology to the Bolognese.

[16]

For the scene in *Roderick Hudson* the impressions of this famous garden, recalled now from his two essays, are merged by James into a single setting of supreme romance with just the "right style" to awake a burgeoning artist.

The visitor to Rome today will look in vain for the vast grounds of the now vanished Villa Ludovisi (which occupied the site of the famous classical Gardens of Sallust), for they were sold off in 1883 to make way for more than twenty-five blocks of the modern quarter around Via Veneto, now one of the chief centers for tourists. The casino, with its seventeenth-century fresco by Guercino, still survives surrounded by a small garden; the Juno, along with the other antique sculptures collected by Cardinal Ludovico Ludovisi (many of which were unearthed at the villa), can be seen in the Museo Nazionale Romano, housed in the ruins of Diocletian's Baths. James leaves it to his more inquiring readers to discover the particular appropriateness to his story of these two works of art. "Aurora" is the subject of Guercino's painting, but Roderick refused to look at it since this was to be the glorious dawn of his own career. The colossal head of Juno, which he admired extravagantly (as Goethe and Schiller had before him), is actually a Roman copy of the first century after a Greek original of the fourth century B.C. This antique sculpture becomes a clue to the kind of statues the young American will make.

As Roderick took out a notebook and began a rough sketch of the impression made on him by the great Juno, what had been mere scene-setting develops into an actual scene, however brief, with dialogue and action. Suddenly, hearing a noise on the gravel walk and looking up, he saw three persons advancing. Ignoring the elderly couple, he stared in wonder at the young girl strolling behind them: "She was tall and slender, and dressed with extreme elegance. . . . A pair of extraordinary dark blue eyes, a mass of dusky hair over a low forehead, a blooming oval of perfect purity, a flexible lip, just touched with disdain, the step and carriage of a tired princess—these were the general features of his vision" (87). Since the strangers passed by without a word, dialogue is confined to the two young men. "What a movement, what a manner, what a poise of the head! I wonder if she would sit to me?" the sculptor exclaimed. Rowland, serving as a check to his eagerness, observed that though indeed beautiful she looked dangerous. "If beauty is immoral, as people think at Northampton," said Roderick, "she's the incarnation of evil" (88). Ten minutes after this "glimpse of ideal beauty" had disappeared, he handed the completed sketch of Juno to his patron for admiration. On the head of the goddess he had superimposed the features of the *femme fatale*, whom he came to know as Christina Light. (James certainly knew, and presumably his hero too, that Juno stands for the female principle in life, and that her name is supposedly derived from *juvenis*, "a marriageable young woman.") "I have been wanting a subject," said Roderick; "there's one made to my hand!" (89). But it was some months before he met Christina and persuaded her to pose.

In his best fictions James is more interested in his heroes' reactions than in their actions, in rendering the quality of a lived life than in recounting its events. Even in this early novel, overloaded with action though it is, he is less effective when attempting to unfold his plot than when he concentrates on picture and scene. Besides the initial one at Villa Ludovisi, there are two others indispensable for establishing the *ambiente* of Rome in which the American sculptor's rise and fall are to take place. His studio is one, the apartment of his patron is the other. After his vision of two ideal models (one antique, one living), Roderick was so taken with an idea that he found a studio, shut himself up in it, and went to work:

> He had established himself in the basement of a huge, dusky, dilapidated old house, in that long, tortuous and pre-eminently Roman street which leads from the Corso to the Bridge of St. Angelo. The black archway which admitted you might have served as the portal of the Augean stables, but you emerged presently upon a mouldy little court, of which the fourth side was formed by a narrow terrace, overhanging the Tiber. Here, along the parapet, were stationed half-a-dozen shapeless fragments of sculpture, with a couple of meagre orange-trees in terra-cotta tubs, and an oleander that never flowered. The unclean, historic river swept beneath; ... opposite, at a distance, were the bare brown banks of the stream, the huge rotunda of St. Angelo, tipped with its seraphic statue, the dome of St. Peter's and the broad-topped pines of the Villa Doria. The place was crumbling and shabby and melancholy, but the river was delightful, the rent was a trifle, and everything was picturesque. (89–90)

Roderick's sleeping quarters were a fifth-floor lodging in nearby Via Ripetta. But when he was not working or rambling through streets and churches and gardens, absorbing the spectacle of the papal city, he could be found lounging in his patron's luxurious rooms:

> Rowland had found a convenient corner in a stately old palace not far from the fountain of Trevi, and made himself a home to which books and pictures and prints and odds and ends of curious furniture gave an air of leisurely permanence. ... In the evening, often, under the lamp, amid dropped curtains and the scattered gleam of firelight upon polished carvings and mellow paintings, the two friends sat with their heads together, criticising intaglios and etchings, water-colour drawings and illuminated missals. (90–91)

It is interesting to compare these fictional settings with two factual ones recorded in James's letters from Rome during his long residence there in the winter of 1873, when he saw a good deal of Luther Terry and W. W. Story, the American painter and sculptor who spent most of their mature lives in the Eternal City. After a visit to the former he wrote:

> His studio is one of those delightfully odd nooks which constitute the superiority of Europe to America. A squalid house in a squalid street, promising gross darkness within. You ring and the door is opened by an invisible agency; you ascend a long stone staircase and find yourself in a delightful little second story court or hanging garden, open to the sky and bedecked with verdant bower and trellis. Straight out of this opens the large still studio.

Terry's place is a more typical corner of Rome's Bohemia—the "squalid street" probably being Via Margutta, near the Piazza di Spagna, a favorite area for artists' studios since the seventeenth century. But Roderick's dilapidated quarters are more picturesque and command a grander view across the Tiber to St. Peter's.

The wealthy Story, who considered himself a patron as well as an artist, had installed himself in a sumptuous suite in the Palazzo Barberini (now the National Gallery), where he entertained lavishly. After attending a reception there James wrote:

> An apartment in a Roman palace is a very fine affair, and it certainly adds a picturesqueness to life to be led through a chain of dimly lighted chambers, besprinkled with waiting servants, before you emerge sonorously announced, into the light and elegance of a reception-room with a *roof*, not a ceiling.

This palace, apogee of the splendor of life in baroque Rome, was just right for the somewhat ostentatious Story. An apartment in a more stately palace, several blocks deeper into old Rome, was chosen for the fictional patron, who preferred a simpler kind of elegance.

James knew the habitats of the American colony intimately and could have recorded them with precision. But he also knew that he must create rather than transcribe his settings if he wanted them to symbolize his characters. By playing up the romantic aspects of Roderick's studio and playing down the grandeur of Rowland Mallet's chambers, he achieved a pair of complementary pictures that reveal much about the temperaments as well as the tastes of sculptor and patron, especially when they are opened out into scenes dramatized by characters in conflict. These latter developments take place in a sequence that accords with James's planned emphases.

"My subject," he says in the late Preface to *Roderick Hudson*, "had defined itself—and this in spite of the title of the book—as not directly, in the least, my young sculptor's adventure, [but his] patron's view and experience of him. . . . The centre of interest throughout *Roderick* is in Rowland Mallet's consciousness, and the drama is the very drama of that consciousness—which I had of course to make sufficiently acute in order to enable it, like a set and lighted scene, to hold the play." (This famous Jamesian technique is not as effective in his first novel as his retrospective Preface claims.) The first fully developed scene takes place in Rowland's apartment, a dinner party honoring the early success of his protégé. (The first one laid in the studio does not come until several months and many pages later, and even then is concerned less with showing the artist at work than with setting the stage for his falling in love.) The early period of Roderick's career as a sculptor—clearly not the novel's subject—is reported, not rendered, and in a few sentences. By the end of six months abroad he had completed a life-sized marble of Adam and another of Eve. The most talked of young man in Rome, he was "flushed with triumph." In May, Rowland staged his little party by way of celebration.

The select group invited to the dinner for Roderick was small enough to be manageable scenically yet at the same time diversified enough to make a fair representation of both the foreign colony and the artist colony in Rome, overlapping here as usual. But they are introduced to the reader by the old-fashioned method of piling up descriptive detail, rather than in James's new experimental manner by evocation in a few symbolic strokes. Rowland's apartment, as a scene-setting hospitable to art, had already been brought to life vividly in seven or eight lines. Now as many pages intervene, devoted almost exclusively to a presentation of the four guests, before the scene itself materializes. Since only one of them plays a role of any importance in the novel, he alone calls for commentary.

Gloriani, an American sculptor of French and Italian extraction, is the dominating figure on this occasion. He is also an ambiguous character. A man of forty, whose works brought huge prices, "he now drove a very pretty trade in sculptures of the ornamental and fantastic sort," but these had no appeal for Rowland. "What he relished in the man was the extraordinary vivacity and frankness, not to call it the impudence, of his ideas, [and that he was] unlimitedly intelligent and consummately clever" (97–98). It is possible that the artist groups gathered round Terry and Story offered composite models for Singleton and Miss Blanchard, the minor American painters at Rowland's dinner, as James's biographer assumes; even that Gloriani was an Italianate version of Story (who in 1869, at age fifty, was a popular success). From casual asides in James's letters of that time it is clear he thought of them all as warnings for himself—amateurs, imitators, at best mediocre talents—examples of the "artist-failure" in Italy. And one comment to a friend, an art historian widely travelled in Europe, suggests a reasonably close parallel for Gloriani: "So you're acquainted with Story's Muse—that brazen hussy—to put it plainly. I have rarely seen such a case of *prosperous* pretention as Story. His cleverness is great, the world's good nature to him greater." Similarly one might propose as a model for Roderick the sculptor Hiram Powers, who came from a similarly unpromising American background and, with the aid of a patron, had made a sensation in Italy during the preceding generation with his statues of the ideal and the abstract, at least two of them bearing names later used by Roderick, "Eve" and "America."

Source hunting of this sort has a special appeal to biographers, but James has clearly stated his own opinion of its limitations. "There is no strictness in the representation by novelists of persons who have struck them in life," he declared. "From the moment the imagination takes a hand in the game, the inevitable tendency is to divergence, to following what might be called new scents. The original gives hints, but the writer does what he likes with them, and imports new elements into the picture." The end product is what interests students of literature, the created characters and their functions in the fictional construct: here Singleton and Blanchard as foils to Roderick's genius, Gloriani as the gauge of his potential and the prophet of his fall. These functions are revealed in the scene at Rowland's dinner party.

It is appropriate at this juncture to consider Stephen Spender's analysis of what he considers to be Henry James's greatest contribution to fictional techniques. "What James did in fact revolutionize is the manner of presenting the scene in the novel," he declares, "and the relation of the described scene to the emotional development of the characters." With Balzac, Flaubert, and Dickens, according to Spender (one may add Hawthorne, to complete the list of James's early masters), the reflective and descriptive parts of the novel were threads leading to certain dramatic scenes: "In the description, we see the alignment of characters; in the scenes we witness the release of emotions, the expression of passion." But James reversed all this—Proust, Joyce, and others following his lead. Spender thus sums up the "Master's" transformation of the novel-as-form:

The scene, with accompanying dialogue and action, is used mainly as a means of aligning the characters: explaining what are the reactions of each to the other.... The descriptive parts of the book, which are mainly monologues, are used to reveal the growth of passionate feelings, of love, of hatred. There are, of course, scenes which are highly dramatic, but the emphasis of these is not revelatory: they are the climax of what has already been revealed.

This is a sweeping pronouncement that may indeed hold for *The Golden Bowl*, which is cited by way of illustration. It will also be interesting to bear in mind Spender's thesis, watching for the development of such a revolutionary technique, as we follow James from the early to the late novels.

The first full-scale scene in *Roderick Hudson*, Rowland's dinner party, will serve admirably for our initial example. James allows himself ample space, some ten pages in addition to the detailed presentation of characters. There are numerous touches that create the illusion of a full social evening. But the scene proper grows out of two pictures partially superimposed, as in a stereopticon, achieving the effect of coming to life in three dimensions. The first takes place at Rowland's circular dinner-table, with the whole company assembled. Roderick plays his role as hero of the feast, drinking freely and talking eloquently. Singleton gazes open-mouthed, as if listening to Apollo, but Gloriani has a twinkle in his eye. Having begun with Adam and Eve, the older sculptor chides, "I suppose you are going straight through the Bible." The brash younger man replies that though he may do a David in the posture of a Greek athlete, he is ready to turn to the New Testament: "I mean to make a ripping Christ." To this Gloriani quips, "You'll put nothing of the Olympic games into him, I hope" (104–105). The discussion then turns to theory, Roderick's weak point. Though insisting he is a Hellenist, his commitment to the idealistic shows his confusion of schools. "I mean to go in for big things," he boasts. "I mean to do things that are simple and vast and infinite.... Excuse me if I brag a little; all those Italian fellows in the Renaissance used to brag." The others join in, but the burden of the debate is taken over by Gloriani. Roderick's early successes are due to his lack of self-consciousness, "But, my dear young friend, you can't keep this up"—so runs his prophecy. Tossing off a tall glass of champagne, Roderick declares: "I mean to make a magnificent statue of America! ... My 'America' shall answer you!" (107–111).

The second picture-into-scene comes when the two sculptors continue their battle of wits after dinner. Through the host's consciousness we see and overhear: "They were standing before Roderick's statue of Eve, and the young sculptor had lifted up the lamp and was showing different parts of it to his companions. He was talking ardently, and the lamplight covered his head and face. Rowland stood looking on, for the group struck him with its picturesque symbolism" (112–113). The young genius, radiant in the circle of his admirers. (This composition, with its special use of lighting to focus on the central figure in a group, is strikingly reminiscent of paintings by the Venetian "Realist" Caravaggio.) As Rowland strolls up, Gloriani points to the statue with some words of praise, then: "He can do it once, he can do it twice, ... *but!*" With some irritation Roderick demands, "In a word, then, you prophesy that I am to fail?" When the muse deserts, the older man says with a paternal pat, come to me for consolation instead of meditating suicide. "If I break down," the young American replies passionately, "I shall stay down."

The first important scene in *Roderick Hudson* is evidence enough that James, at such an early point in his career, had gone only a small way in revolutionizing this aspect of the novel-as-form. Though the scene is used here partly as a means of "aligning the characters" and explaining their reactions to each other, what we chiefly witness at Rowland's dinner party is "the release of emotions, the expression of passion"—certainly in the case of Roderick— which had not been revealed in the previous descriptive parts of the novel. Such a dramatized scene is more nearly in the manner of Balzac or Dickens than in that of the later James, whose legacy to the modern novel was scenic presentation made compact by symbolism. Here, the use of narrative realism makes the scene more discursive in the presentation (and, unavoidably, in the critic's re-presentation).

Whatever its technical limitations, the celebration in Rowland's apartment advances the plot effectively. Bearing in mind Roderick's performance so far, in the studio and in the drawing room, the reader is sufficiently alerted by the older sculptor's prediction that "passion burns out," and that in compensation he may find himself resorting to romanticism, even violence. There is a further suggestion in the comic anecdote told by Mme Grandoni, the fourth dinner guest, of a *femme fatale* who was the possible cause of an artist's decline. At any rate, a week after the party, when Rowland found Roderick sitting before an unfinished piece of work with his head in his hands, "He could have fancied that the fatal hour foretold by Gloriani had struck" (114).

There is even more implied preparation for Roderick's abortive career in the humbuggery and amateurishness of the other fictional artists in the Roman colony around him—for so, from any strict point of view, one must define their discussion of art at Rowland's dinner. In his biography of W. W. Story (1903) James recaptures all the romance, all the pretentiousness and dilettantism of the artist circle surrounding that American sculptor, as he had come to know it in the early 1870s. To these expatriates, he recalled in his backward glance, Rome had seemed like "the aesthetic antidote to the ugliness of the rest of the world." Americans had the naive idea that in Italy "art hung in clusters and could be eaten from the tree," but their ambition to pursue their careers dissolved all too quickly in "the golden Roman air." Instead, he continues in an elaborate baroque conceit, what Italy produced for them was "a sense of the sterner realities as sweetened as if, at the perpetual banquet, it had been some Borgia cup concocted for the strenuous mind. But the sensitive soul in general drained it, and, for the most part, at first, in innocent delight, without a misgiving or a reserve. Moreover, as most of those who sickened or died of it never knew they were ill or dead, the feast had never the funeral air, and the guests sat at table to the end."

To the extent that this describes the circle around Story it is a matter of history, though there is no evidence to indicate that these particular painters and sculptors would have become great artists anywhere else. The theme of the American "artist-failure" in Italy is clearly a romantic one, but the legend was believed in widely enough to make it acceptable in nineteenth-century fiction. The hero in James's early story "The Madonna of the Future" seems almost a case history of one of those sensitive souls drugged by the "Borgia cup," in the extravagant metaphor quoted above—the American painter whose "masterpiece" remained a blank canvas for twenty years, while he dreamed of becoming a modern Raphael and the model he loved as the ideal "Madonna" grew old and fat. The sculptor Roderick Hudson, conceived two years later, was of a different breed, one of the more "strenuous minds." Though the atmosphere of the Roman art colony was not a healthy one for him, both his rise and his fall were spectacular in comparison with the unrealized careers of the others. The remaining three-fourths of the novel are devoted to his disintegration, following his short-lived triumph.

The Fatal Woman

The first episode illustrating Roderick's "fall" is not successfully rendered. Near the end of May sensing that the young sculptor was depressed because his muse had deserted him, Rowland packed him off for a long rest, with enough money to last through the summer and bring him back to Rome, where he would find the golden mood again awaiting him. From one ambiguous letter written at Baden-Baden, calling for more funds, and from a generalized confession when they meet at Geneva several months later, the patron learns all that is ever known about his protégé's holiday at the famous German resort. Roderick's story is summarized for the reader's benefit: he fell in with the idle rich, got involved in flirtations and various expensive diversions, took to roulette and found himself up to his knees in debt.

The banality of sowing wild oats by gambling and affaires is all the more insistent by reason of being presented only as exposition. Everything is done by past narrative, lacking even the quasi-immediacy of a present-tense flashback. Tempters and temptresses are faceless and nameless and so they fail to come alive. Since there is no dialogue nor action there could be no dramatization of an emotional crisis. In a word there is no scene at all, in James's earlier or later manner. When Rowland, all tolerance, urges that the whole unfortunate episode should merely serve to teach his protégé the basic importance of willpower, the latter pleads destiny. "One conviction I have gathered from my summer's experience," he admits, "is that I possess an almost unlimited susceptibility to the influence of a beautiful woman" (128). To Rowland this has an ominous meaning. But the reader must take it all on faith. Baden-Baden and Roderick's first disintegration simply have failed to materialize.

The mature James, rereading *Roderick Hudson* in order to revise it for inclusion in the definitive edition of his fiction, singled out the handling of the time-scheme as its chief fault, one that "just fails to wreck it." Roderick's disintegration should have been a gradual process, but it "swallows two years in a mouthful" and thus appears to present him "as a morbidly special case." It was a fault of composition, not of conception, James concludes. Even while composing the novel, he admits, "I felt how many more adventures and complications my young man would have had to know, how much more experience it would have taken in short, either to make him go under or make him triumph." Truth to life demands fullness of treatment; art requires compactness. This was the problem to be solved: "It didn't help, alas, it only maddened, to remember that Balzac would have known how."

As James matured, he developed his own techniques for coping with the formidable time question that always confronts the novelist. The Preface to *Roderick Hudson* contains a hint of how he was to do it later: "To give the image and the sense of certain things ... without all the substance or all the surface, and so to summarize and foreshorten." But this technique was not used in his first novel, nor had he yet conceived the extension of this which served him so brilliantly in *The Portrait of a Lady*. There a complex of scene-like symbols, reflected in Isabel's midnight vigil, give the *sense* of certain key episodes in her early married life that are bypassed in the actual narrative. The fault in James's first novel is more in the handling of scene than of time. Two years is indeed a small space in which to present so great a fall as Roderick's, but it sufficed for the tragedy of Hyacinth Robinson in *The Princess Casamassima*. There the foreshortened narrative is made convincing because it is rendered by adequate scene and image.

[25]

Some scenes do function significantly in *Roderick Hudson,* to be sure, especially the first three. The one in the Ludovisi gardens had provided the young sculptor's initial inspiration. The second, at Rowland's apartment, showed him in the full flush of early triumph, the cynosure of the little Roman art colony. The one that opens out before us now, carrying his rise one stage higher, even as it introduces the prime agent of his fall, takes place in Roderick's studio. At least it begins there. For this is not a static *mise-en-scène* but a multiple exposure. Shortly after the ominous summer at Baden-Baden, Christina Light's mother brought her to the young sculptor for a possible "sitting." "By Jove!" cried Roderick as the beautiful girl strode in majestically, "it's that goddess of the Villa Ludovisi!" (136–137). The setting is sketched in with the fewest possible strokes, his sparsely furnished studio on the Tiber being just what an artist's workshop should be. The visitors are characterized just as deftly, Mrs. Light's comments on his clay models revealing her as fatuous in the extreme. To Roderick's impassioned plea, addressed to her, "I *must* make your daughter's bust," it is the young sophisticate herself who replied: "I might sit to Phidias, if he would promise to be very amusing and make me laugh." The whole first phase is Dickensian (138–144).

When the scene shifts to Rowland's rooms, a few days later, the exposure is only a flash but it highlights two of the characters. "I like looking at people's things," Christina said after wandering around his apartment: "It helps you to find out their characters.... You have too many things; one seems to contradict another." Then her frank conclusion: "You have what is called a 'catholic' taste, and yet you're full of obstinate little prejudices and habits of thought, which, if I knew you, I should find very tiresome. I don't think I like you" (151–152). The reader will be struck with Christina's astuteness in analyzing people; the critic with James's, in being able to project thus early the technique he used to such advantage in his later fictions. As for the absent sculptor, when she saw his *things,* his sculptures "in the marble," she admired them enough to yield. She would sit to him.

The next setting, an improvised studio in Mrs. Light's saloon, carries the story forward with a vivid tableau. As the bust neared completion, Rowland was called in for an opinion. He found the model standing before a mirror to readjust her coiffure, Roderick directing the operation with sharp disapproval. At that moment Christina lost patience: " 'Do it yourself, then!' she cried, and with a rapid movement unloosed the great coil of her tresses and let them fall over her bare shoulders.... She looked like some immaculate saint of legend being led to martyrdom" (161). The simile at the end gives just the right ambiguous touch to a picture primarily emphasizing the sensuous appeal of Christina's beauty. When her mother takes over the role of hairdresser, this emphasis is renewed. Rowland feels as if he were looking at "a sketch of an old slave-merchant, calling attention to the 'points' of a Circassian beauty" (162). (A submerged reference here to Hiram Powers' *Greek Slave*, a full-length nude that made something of a sensation when exhibited in America a generation earlier?)

The finished bust is put on show in Roderick's studio, and the scene shifts back to where it started, all the parts being so interlinked thematically as to give the effect of a single scene, dramatizing Roderick's infatuation with the beauty of Christina and his embodiment of it in his finest sculpture. When the foreign colony came to admire, Gloriani's praise was especially pertinent. "I would have put her into a statue in spite of herself," he declared: "She would make a magnificent Herodias!" (171–172). When James revised his first novel he spelled out the parallel, followed by a vision of Christina with Roderick's head on *her* charger. Here it is merely implied that he *may* lose his head to her—his head rather than his heart. This is one of the questions that keeps asking itself throughout the novel: Is his infatuation a matter of love, or is it merely egotistical and esthetic? Roderick's own comments are ambiguous. In the marble she is perfection; in the flesh, "She is a creature of moods; you can't count on her." To Rowland she is simply a dangerous woman, a "willful, passionate creature" with a "capricious temper" (169–170).

This multiple scene, spread out over thirty-five pages, the later James would probably have encompassed in a single exposure. More compactly, first, by using scenic presentation to establish the relations among characters so as to render his theme, with only minimal use of discursive narrative; secondly, by putting into operation the principle, only stated here, of things symbolizing characters. What was it that Christina perceived about Rowland's character, symbolized by his apartment and its furnishings, that made her instinctively dislike him? Was it the complex of traits that led him eventually to block her incipient love affair with Roderick?—surely the chief complicating factor in the plot and the chief cause of the hero's "fall." But though James caught a glimpse here of his new technique he failed to carry it through, and we are left with only vague clarification of the relations between the three main characters. In *The Portrait of a Lady*, just a few years later, a comparable though quite different triangular relationship (between Ralph Touchett, Gilbert Osmond, and the heroine) is worked out almost exclusively by the symbolism of person-place-and-thing. But to expect all that of *Roderick Hudson* would be asking too much of a first novel.

Even so, the studio scene does bring out several new alignments: the two young men confronted with Mrs. Light and her beautiful daughter; next the patron with Christina; then the latter modelling for the sculptor; finally Rowland and Roderick face to face with the new element in their lives—the *femme fatale*, rendered by a series of exotic similes. Its chief function, however, is the old-fashioned use of scene: to advance the plot by "release of emotions," notably those of the temptress and the tempted man. The primary mode of *Roderick Hudson* is that of the early James, as he recognized in the late Preface. "I was dealing, after all, essentially with an Action," he recalls of the compositional problem presented by his first novel. Then he adds: "Since one was dealing with an Action one might borrow a scrap of the Dramatist's all-in-all, his intensity." Just how small a scrap it was will appear shortly. The studio scene is the last important one in the novel—at least in terms of any experimentation with those techniques by which the mature artist was to revolutionize the novel-as-form.

The Romantic Genius

From this point the story moves forward by action, by episodes that are mostly narrated. Of the few that are dramatized, several of those most fully developed as scenes can only be described as "throw-aways," since they are irrelevant to the novel's real concerns. One example will suffice. The scene occurs near Florence, where Rowland has gone for a rest, disgusted with his protégé's behavior. If Roderick was determined to fizzle out, he found himself thinking, why not give him a push? For two days there swam before his eyes "a vision of the wondrous youth . . . plunging like a diver into a misty gulf" (a rather too-obvious prevue of the novel's tragic ending). When this vision was followed by another, of Roderick's Northampton fiancée holding out her hand to Rowland himself, the patron realized that this wishful thinking was sinful, and that his growing love for Mary Garland might make him willing to sacrifice the friend whose career he had committed himself to.

In this state of mind he walked out to the old Franciscan monastery at Fiesole. The setting is admirably done. Its romantic beauty and otherworldly solitude made it the ideal retreat for a harassed man. And the little drama of imagined guilt and penitence enacted there is striking. But the whole subplot is simply a lame contrivance to serve as a foil to the main one. The novel's center of interest may be less in the young sculptor's adventure than in Rowland's "consciousness" of it, as James says in his Preface; but Rowland's own "adventure," his undeclared love for Roderick's fiancée, is a distraction rather than a main concern. Actually, this novel offers only two lines of interest for the reader—the fall of a precarious genius and, as its corollary, his infatuation with a fatally beautiful woman. This being so, to devote one of its best scenes to such an unconvincing side issue is to throw it away (283–288).

There are several other scenes, or rather scene-settings, drawn from the author's travel essays written a year or two before, that remind one of the "paste-ons" so often used in conventional novels—descriptive passages that serve well enough for local color but are not really essential to the particular story. The critic may be excused for looking over the novelist's shoulder as he scans his "notes" for usable material. In one of Roderick's moods of depression he had gone to Frascati, out in the Alban Hills some miles east of Rome; Rowland followed, finding him lying under the trees of Villa Mondragone and reading Ariosto. James had spent several days in this region during the spring of 1873, looking at the shabby provincial palaces there, imagining one to be a haunted house, another "sinister" with its secrets of the past. In his essay "Roman Neighborhoods" occurs the following, beginning with Villa Aldobrandini:

> I should like to confound these various products of antiquated art in a genial absolution; and I should like especially to tell how fine it was to watch this prodigious fountain come tumbling down its channel of mouldy rock-work, through its magnificent vista of ilex, to the fantastic old hemicycle where a dozen tritons and naiads sit posturing to receive it. The sky above the ilexes was incredibly blue and the ilexes themselves incredibly black.

Then he turns to the Villa Mondragone:

> The great Casino ... stands perched on a terrace as vast as the parvise of St. Peter's, looking straight away over black cypress-tops into the shining vastness of the Campagna. Everything, somehow, seemed immense and solemn; there was nothing small, but certain little nestling blue shadows on the Sabine Mountains, to which the terrace seems to carry you wonderfully near.

In *Roderick Hudson* the two descriptions are fused to form a setting in which the artist-hero delivers himself of a melancholy prophecy as to his own future:

> If I had only been a painter— ... I should only have to look up at that mouldy old fountain against the blue sky, at that cypress alley wandering away like a procession of priests in couples, at the crags and hollows of the Sabine hills, to find myself grasping my brush.... But a sculptor now! ... You can't model the serge-coated cypresses, nor those mouldering old Tritons and all the sunny sadness of that dried-up fountain; you can't put the light into marble—the lovely, caressing, consenting Italian light that you get so much of for nothing. (206–207)

[29]

With a simple twist from gloomy past to gloomy future, James has turned his travel notes into a picturesque setting for a "speech"—Roderick's discourse on the precariousness of genius, especially that of the sculptor who must work from human models.

At its conclusion, almost too aptly, the model accountable for Roderick's fall appears—Christina Light—with her mother, her prospective fiancé Prince Casamassima, and the Cavaliere Giacosa. The picnic on the vast terrace at Villa Mondragone that follows, with its successive pairings of the characters, is an admirably managed episode (210–231). But it is not a scene in the sense of being related to the elaborate setting indicated above. It could have happened anywhere. Sometimes, as here, James seems to have been so attracted by a picturesque description in his own travel essays that he could not resist the temptation to work it into his novel, regardless of any relevance to the action. (The reverse process was a more valid way of working. Having conceived a scene essential to his purpose, like the one at Villa Ludovisi that opens the Italian section of the novel, he was able to refresh his memory of the setting by rereading his description-on-the-spot in an earlier travel sketch.)

The next "paste-on" illustrates another problem in composition. It is an ambitious attempt at a scene planned as preparation for two climactic scenes at the end of the novel. It takes place, about a month after the Frascati episode, in the Coliseum (James's spelling of the *Colosseum*), which Roderick's patron often visited:

> It was a long time since Rowland had ascended to the ruinous upper tiers of the great circus, and, as the day was radiant and the distant views promised to be particularly clear, he determined to give himself the pleasure.... There are chance anfractuosities of ruin in the upper portions of the Coliseum which offer a very fair imitation of the rugged face of an Alpine cliff. In those days [1870] a multitude of delicate flowers and sprays of wild herbage had found a friendly soil in the hoary crevices, and... they bloomed and nodded amid the antique masonry as freely as they would have done in the virgin rock. (232–233)

From his perch Rowland finds himself unexpectedly privy to a rendezvous between Roderick and Christina. After a heated exchange, in which she chides him for being weak and vacillating, this foolhardy young man starts climbing the vertical wall of the Coliseum to prove her wrong, by plucking a blue flower she had admired growing on a ledge high above them. Rowland, though it means revealing his presence as a kind of spy, intervenes to stop him: "My dear Roderick," he cries: "That's an exploit for spiders, not for young sculptors of promise" (237–241). His protégé's act of bravado may seem a bit silly, though it is not inappropriate to such a temperamental genius. But in comparing the upper reaches of the Coliseum to the Alps James may seem guilty of contrivance to dramatize his episode.

Yet he had described them in just such terms, before even conceiving of *Roderick Hudson*. "One never passes the Coliseum, of course, without paying it one's respects," James wrote in a travel essay of 1873:

> The upper portions of the side toward the Esquiline seem as remote and lonely as an Alpine ridge, and you look up at their rugged sky-line, drinking in the sun and silvered by the blue air, with much the same feeling with which you would look at a grey cliff on which an eagle might lodge. This roughly mountainous quality of the great ruin is its chief interest; beauty of detail has pretty well vanished, especially since the high-growing wild-flowers have been plucked away by the new government.

The novelist of 1875 apparently seized upon the Alpine simile in his earlier travel note as exactly suited to his purposes in *Roderick Hudson*.

Both of the "scenes" that this one was to prepare for take place in the Alps. In the first it is Rowland who scrambles up a little peak to pluck a wild flower for Roderick's fiancée, Mary Garland: "Suddenly, as he stood there, he remembered Roderick's defiance of danger and of Miss Light, at the Coliseum" (427). In view of the weaker "love affair" of the subplot and the stronger character of Rowland, this reenactment does indeed seem silly. The other part of the dual sequel is Roderick's plunge to death from an actual Alpine cliff in the last chapter of the novel, an ending that has been universally criticized as melodramatic. The failure of the whole sequence is not so much due to the inadequacy of the initial scene—though that is a scene only in the older novelistic mode—as it is the result of a young novelist's ambition outstripping the resources of his art at the moment. The first part of this "paste-on" is not an exact fit. And the edges show where it is scissored for two later impositions. It takes a master's command of techniques to make a complex of interlocking scenes so convincing that there is no hint of contrivance—convincing because based on the symbolic rightness of the original one. With the "vista" and the "frame" symbols of *The Portrait* and *The Ambassadors* it was achieved. But *Roderick Hudson* came too early for such sophisticated art.

Closely allied to the "paste-on" descriptions are the ones that can be designated quite simply as "scenery," rather than scenes. One example from near the end of the novel will serve. When Christina's marriage to the Prince throws Roderick into a deep depression, Rowland decides to take him on an extended trip to see if a summer purged of the memories connected with Rome will bring his protégé back to his senses and to his chisel. On the way out of Italy they pause briefly at Como. In describing the beauty of this famous lake James lets himself go as a painter of romantic scenery, only to check himself at the end with a sly aside to the reader: "It was all confoundingly picturesque; it was the Italy we know from the steel engravings in old keepsakes and annuals, from the vignettes on music-sheets and the drop-curtains at theatres" (423). In a similar description of Lago di Como two years before, the author of *Transatlantic Sketches* gives just such a wink to his audience: "I wondered," he concludes, "where I had seen it all before—... Where, indeed, but at the Opera, when the manager has been more than usually regardless of expense." The scenery of picture books and stage sets! Roderick's speech on beauty and disintegration, delivered to Rowland in this setting, is itself operatic. But there is no action, no scene (422–426).

Another matter related to the problem of "scenery" must be glanced at now, if only to clear James of an undeserved criticism—that he all but turned his first novel into a guidebook to Rome. On three occasions he does name places that are well-known tourist spots, identifying them in a few lines, then using them as settings that are only mildly appropriate to the incidents that follow: Santa Cecilia in Trastevere, as an out-of-the-way meeting place where Rowland can beg Christina to let Roderick alone; Saint Peter's and the Palatine, as two of the Roman sights he took Mary Garland to see. Aside from the really important scenes at the Villa Ludovisi and at the Coliseum, these are the only traces of a Roman "guidebook" in *Roderick Hudson*. One need but compare this novel with the half-dozen travel essays on Rome that form the core of James's *Transatlantic Sketches* (1875) to have a measure of the real thing. In one of these alone, "A Roman Holiday," there is a page or more devoted to each of the following: the Corso in carnival time, the Campidoglio, Forum, Coliseum, Palatine, churches on the Caelian Hill, Saint John Lateran and the Santa Scala, Santa Maria Maggiore, Saint Peter's, and Saint Paul's Outside the Walls—all in the course of eighteen pages. This essay and its companion pieces were written, of course, quite intentionally for visitors to Rome.

His travel writings were also experiments in the art of description, and the author of *Roderick Hudson* drew upon them extensively, as has been shown. But for every bit of *Transatlantic Sketches* transferred to his fiction ten times as much remains untouched, primarily those very aspects that made them like a guidebook. The charge that James's first novel was also turned into one should more properly be levelled at Hawthorne's last, *The Marble Faun* (1860). The younger writer was one of the earliest to make this criticism, calling it "a manual of Roman sights and impressions." The point is elaborated in James's critical biography, some twenty years after *The Marble Faun* was published: "It is part of the intellectual equipment of the Anglo-Saxon visitor to Rome, and is read by every English-speaking person who arrives there, who has been there, or who expects to go." Even more interesting is the suggestion of a relationship between Hawthorne's *Italian Notebooks* and his novel: "The Note-Books are chiefly taken up with descriptions of the regular sights and 'objects of interest,' which we feel often to be rather perfunctory and a little in the style of the traditional tourist's diary. They abound in charming touches, and every reader [of *The Marble Faun*] will remember the delightful colouring of the numerous pages in that novel, which are devoted to the pictorial aspects of Rome."

This linking of journal and novel, in terms of their guidebook qualities, is in fact quite valid. Reading *The Italian Note-Books* and *The Marble Faun* in sequence, one is struck by the quantity of the former that is unloaded on the latter, till the fiction sags under the weight of its nonfictional elements. These addenda almost always take the form of scenery rather than scene. As James phrased it elsewhere, though the "drama in *The Marble Faun*" has lost its appeal, "the breath of old Rome, the sense of old Italy, still meet us as we turn the page." The master's hand that had rendered the meaning of *The Scarlett Letter* in a succession of dramatic scenes, only a decade before, had indeed lost its skill. James, a great admirer of Hawthorne's American novels and tales, took a lesser view of the writings laid in Italy. The notebooks he likened to a tourist's diary, the novel to a picture book. When he began the composition of *Roderick Hudson*, set in Rome and dealing with the foreign artist colony like *The Marble Faun*, he was well aware how closely he was following in Hawthorne's footsteps and was particularly anxious to avoid the faults in his later writings.

The major technical problem that James wrestled with in his first novel was, beyond question, how to relate scene to character and action. If descriptions of settings had been too prominent in the European fictions of his predecessor, they were not important enough in the American fictions of his contemporary Howells. And in neither case were they effectively assimilated. In the very period when *Roderick Hudson* was gestating, James's groping toward his own solution is clearly what prompted the long commentary on his friend's first novel. Though finding much to admire in *A Chance Acquaintance*, he complained of "a want of interfusion between the 'scenery' element in the book and the dramatic." "Your people and your story," he wrote to Howells, "are intrinsically more interesting than your background—that is, the American scene." Then, in conclusion, a generalization that might apply to the kind of novel Howells wanted to write: "Vivid figures will always kill the finest background in the world." James's own development was to be altogether in a different direction, one in which fusion of the "scenery element" with the dramatic would be a principal mode of rendering character.

Although James had little to learn from his young contemporary, he still had much to learn from his American "master," especially in the use of symbol and scene so admirably exemplified in Hawthorne's early fictions. It was six years before James brought these techniques to a high finish in *The Portrait of a Lady* (1881), but the Roman scenes in the first half of *Roderick Hudson* are remarkably effective. The other scenic materials in the rest of this novel have now also been surveyed: simple pictorial sketches used as backdrops; scenes in embryo that never progressed beyond the status of scenery; those that materialized as vignettes, good in themselves but inadequately fused with dialogue and action; finally, fully developed scenes that must nevertheless be counted as thrown away because irrelevant to this novel's main themes. The significant use of scenic method comes in the first half of the story.

Toward the New Novel

In the last half of *Roderick Hudson* the reader finds himself concerned with plot rather than scene. Actually the story is quite interesting in its own right —a fact that must not be obscured by the critic's temptation to find fault with the techniques of this early novel, because James set such high standards of performance in his best fictions. The sharpest criticisms of all are made by the author himself in his late Preface; but he is generous enough to conclude that "the interest of the subject" compensates for the "flaw in the treatment." To indicate briefly the place of *Roderick Hudson* in James's shelf of fiction and in the contemporary novelistic tradition is the critic's only remaining function.

It is chiefly in the matter of plot and characters that commentators have found James indebted to his predecessors for various aspects of his first novel. The influence of Balzac and Dickens and Hawthorne, as regards the techniques of setting and characterization, has already been pointed out. But it was Turgenev who taught James "realistic portraiture" rendered by dramatic means, which he contrasts with Dickens's method "of specializing people by vivid oddities." In his essay on the Russian novelist (1874) James goes on to describe two of his heroes in terms that show their kinship with his own young sculptor; but this falls short of the exaggerated claims of borrowing that have been made. Different investigators have dug out of Turgenev's fictions—*Spring Freshets, Rudin, Smoke, On the Eve*—models for Roderick and Christina in all the complications of their entanglement. As for plot, Georges Sand's *Jacques* provided the source for the final tragedy, according to one; *L'Affaire Clemenceau* by Dumas fils served as model for the story as a whole, according to another. If one accepted all these charges of borrowing at face value, he would begin to fear that James's first novel was at best a poor pastiche. The young author had in fact studied these writers and learned much from them. But when the reader actually turns to the novels that have been suggested as sources, he is more struck by their differences from *Roderick Hudson* than by their likenesses to it.

Indeed, the number of possible plot structures is so limited, in life as well as in fiction, that it is easy to find broad similarities between one story and another; and so it is with the basic aspects of characters, to the extent that they are types rather than individuals. The results of all this source hunting are of small use to the critic. Concerned primarily with the texture of language, the relation of manners to morals, the involvement of person-place-thing with these, and with each other, he is inclined to find the deliberately extravagant claim of T. S. Eliot more suggestive: "James owes little, very little, to anyone." (The other half of Eliot's meaning can be found in his dictum that a real artist never "borrows," he "steals"—since what he takes he makes his own and cannot return.) Henry James was one of the most widely read creative writers of his time, but he assimilated what he learned from other novelists so that he might make it into something entirely new. As early as *Roderick Hudson* he was beginning to show signs of breaking from the conventional novel in many ways.

Far more important than any possible borrowings of mere details is the undeniable relation of James's first novel to a major literary tradition, extending throughout the nineteenth century from the early Romantics to the late Decadents. What is most interesting is the originality with which he turns an old tradition in a new direction. Mario Praz in *The Romanic Agony* has surveyed literally hundreds of poems and novels centered on the dual themes of the "Fatal Man" and the "Fatal Woman," interlinked, but one of them dominant in the first half of the century and the other in the second half. There are many variations on both themes, and *Roderick Hudson* (not mentioned by Praz) has only tangential kinships with each of them.

As for the former, the Fatal Man, bypassing the demonism of the Byronic hero and the sheer madness of the protagonist in Poe's Gothic tales, James settled for the erratic genius—impetuous and fascinating but self-destructive. Lord Byron, according to his grandson, behaved in real life "as if he believed himself to be destined to wreck his own life and that of everyone near him." And one of Poe's saner artist-heroes could easily have made such a speech as the following by Roderick, in mid-career: "The whole matter of genius is a mystery.... Do I succeed—do I fail?... I'm prepared for failure. It won't be a disappointment, simply because I shan't survive it. The end of my work shall be the end of my life. When I have played my last card, I shall cease to care for the game. I'm not making vague threats of suicide" (207, 208). In the revised version this reads: "threats of the dagger or the bowl." Roderick does indulge in drunken sprees, like the madder of Poe's heroes, but we only hear about them indirectly. The final tragedy is ambiguous—whether he falls, or jumps, to his death from a cliff during an Alpine storm. Was it accidental or suicidal? Both of these methods of self-destruction, by "the dagger or the bowl," would have led to melodrama, and they were wisely kept to one side.

James wanted a more dramatic agent for the young sculptor's disintegration and he found one in the Fatal Woman, the other traditional theme to which his novel is related. It is she, dominating the central story, who draws the precarious genius to his downfall, wrecking the happiness of all around him. Two passages, previously quoted separately, take on new meaning when brought together in this context—especially in the revised version. One of the results of his wild summer at Baden-Baden, Roderick admits, is the conviction of his "unlimited susceptibility to the influence of a beautiful woman." (This was changed radically: "I'm damnably susceptible, by nature, to the grace and the beauty and the mystery of women, to their power to turn themselves 'on' as creatures of subtlety and perversity.") A few months later, as his infatuation with Christina Light rises to its first climax, Rowland fears her as a dangerous woman, "a complex, wilful, passionate creature who might easily engulf a too confiding spirit." The metaphor became more frightening in the revision: to draw him down "into some strange underworld of unworthy sacrifice, not unfurnished with traces of others of the lost." The Fatal Woman was already there in the early version; but in the revised edition the very language brings to mind, as James probably intended, Keats's well known lines,

> I saw pale kings, and princes too,
>   Pale warriors, death-pale were they all;
> Who cried—"La Belle Dame sans merci
>   Hath thee in thrall."

The author has invoked, for readers acquainted with the tradition, the very type of the fatally beautiful woman, she whose beauty is supreme for the very reason that it is accursed. Roderick is Christina's first victim; the "others of the lost"—Hyacinth Robinson and the Prince—come only after she has been "resurrected" in a later novel, *The Princess Casamassima*.

There are phrases scattered through *Roderick Hudson* that echo the dual tradition of the Fatal Man and the Fatal Woman: Christina's "infernal coquetry and falsity," "I have suffered damnable torments," I have "a restless demon within" (391, 461, 462). Though James is silent as to the germ of his first novel, the creative impulse for it probably came more from a conventional plot—the precarious genius lured to destruction by a fatally beautiful woman —than from a conception of the characters who illustrate it. His very real contribution to this romantic tradition was to drop all the extravagant melodrama, the satanism and vampirism, so he could make something viable out of it for the new novel. Recognizing egotism as the basic evil in traditional Fatal Women and Fatal Men, he makes Christina and Roderick quite realistically "exploiters"—egotists who use other people, ruthlessly, for their own selfish ends—as opposed to "appreciators," like Rowland and Mary, who want to help others fulfill themselves. Thus early did James begin to formulate his dichotomy of "good" and "bad" characters, elaborated over the years into more and more subtle categories (notably in *The Portrait of a Lady* and *The Wings of the Dove*), as a key to the moral meaning of his fictions.

The very terms by which James transformed the older novel meant a shift of emphasis from external to internal action. This was carried so far by the end of his career that many readers complain of works like *The Golden Bowl*, "Nothing ever happens in a James novel!" He was aware of his tendency, and its danger, from the beginning. In the midst of composing *Roderick Hudson*, he wrote to a friend: "The fault of the story, I am pretty sure, will be in its being too analytical and psychological, and not sufficiently dramatic and eventful." But it was only in terms of competing with popular rivals of the day that James could have thought of his first novel as "too analytical and psychological." His concern in this letter was simply anticipatory of the mode of his major fictions—from *The Portrait of a Lady* (1881) to *The Ambassadors* (1903)—in which the developing, shifting, reversing relations of the characters comprise most of the "action." By comparison with them, one of the faults of *Roderick Hudson* is that it is *too* "eventful."

Once James had committed himself to action in this early novel, he had on his hands quite as big a problem in stopping the chain of events as he had been faced with originally in getting it started. E. M. Forster, a kindred spirit, has bemoaned the necessity that compels a novelist to have a story at all, whether he wants one or not. He must pull it out of himself endlessly, like a tapeworm, until the time comes when he has to snip it, in two places, so as to have a beginning and an end. Much earlier in this chapter—on the strength of James's own formula for limiting a story (since really "relations stop nowhere" the artist must draw "the circle within which they shall *appear* to do so")—I suggested that *Roderick Hudson* would be more compact if it had begun with the first scene laid in Rome, omitting the opening chapters in which the action takes place in an American setting. Now to make a further suggestion: perhaps the novel should have ended with the last chapter laid in Rome, omitting the concluding ones in which the story dribbles away through northern Italy into a melodramatic finale in Switzerland. By drawing the circle so, a somewhat discursive story would have been cut by one-third and all would take place in the "golden air" of Rome. More important, such limiting would make the novel begin when Christina Light enters and end when her marriage carries her offstage; by the same stroke the extraneous subplot of Rowland's love for Mary Garland would be cut to a minimum.

As is frequently true of a richly promising first novel, *Roderick Hudson* has a little too much of everything. It is not only over-plotted but over-peopled, not by having too many characters but too many competing centers of interest. To the extent that James is already experimenting with the "analytical and psychological" mode of his major fictions, his conception and grouping of characters in *Roderick Hudson* is of interest as the starting point for later developments. Instead of the usual triangular structure, however, there are five points here, five figures in a patterned relationship. On either side of Roderick are Christina and Mary, though the cosmopolitan girl who is to marry Prince Casamassima plays a far more active role than the hometown girl. Even when the latter is sent for (having been absent in America for nearly half the story) interest centers quite as much on her unfolding relation with Rowland, who has fancied himself in love with her all along, as on her collapsing engagement to Roderick. This is a cumbersome vehicle to set in motion, and it takes a good deal of plotting to keep it going. The Prince is clearly the fifth wheel, the triangle he makes with Roderick as the rival suitor of Christina being transparently a plot contrivance.

Roderick and Christina are the two characters who hold the center of the stage, and one of James's problems was to "work in" the others sufficiently to enable them to sustain their roles without distracting the reader's attention. With Prince Casamassima this was a minor matter, since he was a stereotype and his role purely perfunctory. The real complication is that the two young women were conceived as antithetical, representing corrupt Europe and innocent America in a tug-of-war over the hero. But as James recognizes in his Preface, to make this antithesis effective, Mary had to be "plain," Christina being so "colored." As a consequence, neither Rowland, torn between love of Mary and loyalty to Roderick, nor Mary, torn between the two men, is of much concern to readers because they are not convinced of any real emotional involvement. Even the three-sided relationship involving Roderick with the two women lacks intensity for the same reason. All of these triangular patterns give way, in reader appeal, to a far more original one—the two-way pull the artist hero feels toward the patron who has made his career possible and the "heroine" who provided both inspiration and fatal infatuation.

Christina Light, indeed, is the great success of the novel. She illustrates what James really borrowed from Turgenev—a method of portraiture, rather than a model to follow. Such a creation, stepping right out of the page into life, could have taken the spotlight from Roderick except that everything *she is* lends itself exclusively to bringing out all that *he is*. This makes not two rival centers but a single one, of considerable intensity. Knowing that "wound up with the right silver key" she would keep going by her own motion, James limited her participation in the story to its central half—the part from which Mary Garland is largely absent. Then, having played her fatal role, she is whisked offstage into the waiting arms of the Prince (or rather into his title and fortune), leaving the hero to his ineluctable fall.

Both Christina and Roderick are in their "presence and action … all firm ground," as James rightly claimed in his Preface. The passive third member, Rowland, is equally effective but in a special sense, as will be seen. *Roderick Hudson* would have been a stronger and more compact novel if it could have been chiefly concerned with this triangle, the reader's interest focussed on a single center rather than diffused over several. As the author's practice worked out, over the years, such a three-figured pattern proved to be his most successful and varied novelistic structure—two actively engaged characters and a semidetached one. What accounts for this success was James's perfecting of a new technique. By making his semidetached character an observer, a center of consciousness through which the reader understands all, he created a point of view for controlling and justifying the story. Such an observer, to function convincingly, must fulfill two sets of requirements. First, he should be sufficiently detached to be able to see and judge, while at the same time sufficiently involved so as not to seem like a contrivance. Closely related is the second set of requirements. In conception he must be simple and clear enough to serve as a lens through which we see the others and participate in the action, yet complex enough in intelligence and sensibility to be interesting in his own right. Rowland Mallet, though he does not measure up to all these specifications, was James's first experiment in using the observer as a point of view.

At the time of composing *Roderick Hudson* James was not aware of just how revolutionary a mode of accounting for a story this might prove to be. The technique, capable of many and subtle variations, was elaborately explored in the later fictions. Extended by writers who followed him—such as Conrad, Joyce, Fitzgerald, and Faulkner—it became one of his major contributions to modern fiction. As a first novel *Roderick* was rich in promise for James's future career. Here one finds his earliest experimentation with the observer as a center of consciousness; his creation of the mode of scenic presentation as a substitute for discursive narrative, to establish relations among characters; his discovery of the principle that things can be made to symbolize characters and to render themes visually. And the reader may add (as if the critic had forgotten it) that *Roderick Hudson* is also a remarkably good novel in the older sense of being an absorbing story.

Walls of Separation

THE AMERICAN

Of all Henry James's novels dealing with the international theme—the contrast of cultures and ways of life—those most centrally concerned with it are the two laid in France, *The American* (1877) and *The Ambassadors* (1903), written a quarter-century apart. What sets them apart even further is the shift of emphasis from a novel of sociological significance to one of humanistic significance. In *The Ambassadors* the contrast between America and France becomes the metaphor which illustrates the hero's "education." He moves from a preconception that the differences are simple to an understanding of their complexity. And the reader's interest is always centered on Strether's education. In *The American* the hero's experiences are used to illustrate the contrast between the two civilizations. Newman never actually gets "educated," never changes inside; he just becomes more and more aware of the differences between America and France. Our main interest is always centered on the contrast. The earlier novel lacks subtlety in its theme and in the techniques of rendering, to be sure. But it has a great advantage in that its dominant mode (despite the ending) is one of broad and genial comedy.

The ending, as a matter of fact, was criticized by William Dean Howells in a letter written just before the last installment of the novel appeared in the *Atlantic Monthly*, prior to its publication in book form. James was quick to take issue with his best literary friend in the States. On 30 March 1877 he wrote:

> I quite understand that as an editor you should go in for "cheerful endings"; but I am sorry that as a private reader you are not struck with the inevitability of the *American* denouement.... It was cruelly hard for poor N. to lose, certainly; but there are tall stone walls which fatally divide us. I have written my story from Newman's side of the wall, and I understand so well how Mme de Cintré couldn't really scramble over from her side! If I had represented her as doing so I should have made a prettier ending, certainly; but I should have felt as if I were throwing a rather vulgar sop to readers who don't really know the world and who

don't measure the merit of a novel by its correspondence to the same.
...I suspect it is the tragedies in life that say more to my imagination.

James's defence of *The American* raises several issues. First, there is the problem of the "inevitability" of the novel's conclusion, which will be treated later. Then there is the implied contrast between these two leading American novelists of the day, in fictional theory and practice, a point touched on here and there in the present book. Finally, there is the clear statement of James's theme, "walls which fatally divide us," that makes the letter to Howells an ideal starting point for my interpretation of *The American*. At the end of the story, a Carmelite convent within which the French heroine has been immured by her family symbolizes the "wall" that separates her from her American fiancé, an ending that is "tragic" not in the classical sense but in marking the hero's defeat, at least on the practical side. And there are other walls of separation between the New World protagonist and the Old World he wants to enter, predominantly comic in tone, beginning with the first chapter and running throughout. The "walls which fatally divide us," Americans and Europeans, is what this novel is about.

Language, Art, and Manners

The opening scene is a memorable one, and for a very good reason: it was James's own first "vision" of his hero. Thirty years later in the Preface to *The American* he recalled how in the fall of 1875, at the beginning of his French year, an earlier idea for a novel had been resurrected in Paris (the idea having come to him before the conception of the character). It was to be about an American who was "cruelly wronged" by a foreign aristocratic society, and the famous city had "offered" him ever so promptly the situation and the main character, everything that was needed to make his conception concrete: "It was all charmingly simple, this conception, and the current must have gushed, full and clear, to my imagination, from the moment Christopher Newman rose before me, on a perfect day of the divine Paris spring in the great gilded Salon Carré of the Louvre."

This scene, set in the year 1868, begins to unfold on the very first page of the novel, with the hero expanding in the presence of a typically Parisian "offering," largely unaware of the walls of separation (language, art, manners) between the splendor symbolized by the Louvre and his understanding of it: "He had looked out all the pictures to which an asterisk was affixed in those formidable pages of fine print in his Bädeker; his attention had been strained and his eyes dazzled, and he had sat down with an aesthetic headache." But out of the side of his eye he was caught by the playacting of one of the ever-present army of copyists—"if the truth must be told, he had often admired the copy more than the original"—and he went over to inspect her "masterpiece." Drawing on the full strength of his French vocabulary, "Combien?" he abruptly demanded (1, 3–4). This is also the only language he is really fluent in, the language of money. It makes a brilliant opening, the assumption that art also has its price, symbolizing one aspect of the American in Europe.

In the exchange that follows, Christopher Newman's failure to grasp what is going on comes more from his misunderstanding of manners than of language. Though he suspects that the price Noémie Nioche writes down (2,000 francs) is high, he never dreams it is ten times the usual one. By her skill in acting he is completely taken in: "Beauty, talent, virtue; she combined everything!" The one talent she does have—histrionic—blinds Newman to her lack of all the others. He buys her botch of a copy on the spot and promises to buy others. She sees a chance for more of the American millionaire's money and quickly arranges for her father to give him a series of French lessons, at an exorbitant fee. To round out his theme James now returns to the esthetic barrier. As the Nioches leave, Newman wanders back to the divan and seats himself before Veronese's great canvas of the marriage-feast at Cana: "Wearied as he was he found the picture entertaining; it had an illusion for him; it satisfied his conception, which was ambitious, of what a splendid banquet should be." When he notices a copyist at work here too, he begins to think of "art-patronage" as a fascinating pursuit: "Suddenly he became conscious of the germ of the mania of the 'collector'" (6–12).

As a launching scene in the traditional nineteenth-century mode, this one introduces us to the hero, sets the stage for his adventure, and sounds the theme—the three walls of language, art, and manners that separate the American from the Old World he has come over to discover. The comedy, and the charm, derive from Newman's unawareness of these barriers. They continue throughout the novel to stand between him and his experience of Europe, especially the separating wall of manners. These constitute James's theme, and, after a brief aside, they will furnish the main topic of this chapter.

There is an attractive sequel to the opening scene, which sets the plot in motion. As he is leaving the Louvre, the hero encounters Tom Tristram, an old friend who is now part of the American colony in Paris, and they sit down together at a cafe table in the great quadrangle of the Palais Royal: "The place was filled with people, the fountains were spouting, a band was playing, clusters of chairs were gathered beneath all the lime-trees.... Newman felt that it was most characteristically Parisian. He would like to spend six months like this, just enjoying himself" (16–20). It is obviously settings like this that James had in mind when commenting in the Preface that Newman's adventure was to have taken place "on a high and lighted stage"; and the "many-tinted medium by the Seine, with the life of the splendid city playing up in it like a flashing fountain in a marble basin," offered just that. But this is one of the few vignettes of Paris to be found in *The American*. When he tried to write of places "under too immediate an impression," James explained, it gave him neither time nor space for perspective. That is why the novel achieved no very large "transfusion of the immense overhanging presence."

Wary of letting too much of his Parisian life during 1875–76 flow into *The American*, James siphoned off most of the daily incident into a series of "letters" to the New York *Tribune*, written simultaneously with the composition of his novel. These were potboilers pure and simple, a journalistic mixture of current events and personalities as well as local color sketches. Even the latter had little relevance to his fiction since they lacked the esthetic purpose of his earlier *Transatlantic Sketches*, which were serious practice pieces in the art of description—"images and pictures à la Gautier" he had proudly called them. Consequently we cannot watch the author transforming travel essays into scene-settings in this novel, as proved so revealing of his method in *Roderick Hudson*.

In one sense this was all to the good, since what James needed for *The American* was not a cluster of decorative pictures of Paris but a few carefully selected scenes. The small one at the cafe was for the purpose of advancing the plot. When Tristram asked why he had come to Europe, Newman replied that, having made his fortune, he wanted to change the pattern of his life altogether:

> I want the biggest kind of entertainment a man can get. People, places, art, nature, everything! I want to see the tallest mountains, and the bluest lakes, and the finest pictures, and the handsomest churches, and the most celebrated men, and the most beautiful women.... [I want] to look about me, to see the world, to have a good time, and, if the fancy takes me, to marry a wife. (23, 17)

Only two of the *Tribune* "letters" are relevant to *The American*. The first one, written just ten days before James sent off the first installment of his novel, contains a passage remarkably like Newman's declaration to Tom Tristram of his plan of attack on Europe:

> The American who comes to Paris for the first time receives, of course, a multitude of impressions; he takes to the French capital, generally speaking, as a duck to water, and he is not slow in maturing his opportunities for diversion.... We wander about Europe on a sensuous and

esthetic basis,... staring at picturesque scenery, listening to superior music, watching accomplished acting.... The average American in Europe, traveler or resident, makes up the substance of his life out of these things.... They are offered him in Paris in a fashion which enables him to lay down his money with one hand and take with the other in perfect security.

James deliberately modelled his hero on the typical American-in-Europe, as this comparison indicates. But there are variations within the type, and Newman differs in important ways, as revealed at his meeting with Tom's wife.

Mrs. Tristram is the first in a long line of *confidantes* in the novels, invented by James to help him get his story going or, more important, to serve as a sounding board against which the hero can try out in advance his plans of action and later evaluate his experiences. Having told Mrs. Tristram about his designs on Europe, now that he has made his pile in America, Newman agrees with her pronouncement that it is high time for him to marry. "There must be a beautiful woman perched on the pile, like a statue on a monument," he declares characteristically: "I want to possess, in a word, the best article in the market" (33, 34). She met his specifications at once with a candidate, Claire de Cintré, her friend from school days. Daughter of the aristocratic Bellegarde family, Claire had been the victim of a *mariage de convenance* but is now a widow of twenty-eight, with no particular desire to marry again. The high value of the prize and the difficulty of acquiring it make this young lady seem like just the right challenge to Newman, but he cannot pursue his chances until she returns to Paris in the fall. Meanwhile the reader must wait to see whether or not the hero will win in marriage "the proud and beautiful Madame de Cintré, the loveliest woman in the world" (39). The plot of *The American*, to its great advantage, could have been just as uncomplicated as that.

The critic's real concern, however, is the novel's theme and James's techniques for rendering it. Of the walls separating Newman from an understanding of Europe, that of language plays the smallest part. To have made it more than minimum would have been farcical, the kind of thing indulged in by Mark Twain in his clowning moods. On the social or intellectual level a language barrier can be serious indeed. Wishing to avoid the banal, James simply made the whole Bellegarde family (the only foreigners with prominent roles in the novel) proficient in English. The old Marquise is English by birth; of Claire and the younger son Valentin, friends declare that they are "anglaise"; the older son, the Marquis Urbain, may be stiff in his speech as in everything else, but there is no evidence of a language difficulty (126,

150, 256, 324). Newman's failure to communicate because of his limited French is confined to his dealings with the "low" or peripheral characters, as a tourist, hence is part of the comedy.

The esthetic barrier is more prominent in the novel, and in an indirect and symbolic way it is related to the really fatal dividing wall, that of manners. But it begins in the comic vein, as Newman offers to buy Noémie's copy of the Murillo Madonna at the Louvre. When the picture is delivered, covered with varnish and put in an elaborate frame at least a foot wide, he is delighted. Though this greatly increased the cost, he pays without a murmur and orders a half-dozen more copies at the same price. The sequel is a caricature of the hero's innocence, when Noémie confesses that she does not know how to paint at all. Newman is less shocked by his ridiculous blunder than baffled by the deviousness of her new line of conduct: "She was playing a game; she was not simply taking pity on his aesthetic verdancy" (57). In the Nioche episode the dividing walls of art and manners are only tangentially related, but this is merely a comic prelude to later episodes where the relation becomes symbolically important.

By 1877, when James's novel was published, the other "game"—making the American abroad prefer copies to the Old Masters—was a standard joke, well used but far from worn out. Since James was quite aware of it, one must assume that he knew what he was about artistically when he attached his novel to this tradition. A brief look at three embodiments of it, all familiar to him, will prove rewarding. Evidence that the joke was already popular a decade before can be found in *Italian Journeys* (1867), where Howells recorded an anecdote about a fellow countryman who refused to look at the original of Raphael's *Transfiguration* until he had studied all the extant copies. The fear of appearing culturally ignorant, James's friend commented, is "the worst form of American greenness abroad." This is a variation on the basic story, but not beyond the range of Newman's esthetic activities if he had only thought of it.

The book that gave widest currency to the general comedy of American confrontation with European culture, as every one knows, was Mark Twain's *The Innocents Abroad*, published in 1869—the very year of James's first adult sojourn in foreign parts. The *locus classicus* for present purposes is the incident in the little chapel on the outskirts of Milan as Twain's comic persona is exposed to Leonardo's *Last Supper*. But he was chiefly attracted by the dozen or more copyists, working against time, "transferring the great picture to their canvases" before it disappears altogether: "I could not help noticing how superior the copies were to the original, that is, to my inexperienced eye. . . . Maybe the originals [of the Old Masters] were handsome when they were new, but they are not now."

[46]

As a professional humorist, Twain knew how to provide laughs for all comers. Europeans were sure the satire in *Innocents Abroad* was directed against American vulgarity and ignorance. On the other hand, American readers thought they recognized the reverse, satire of the dead hand of the past in Europe. The real object of Mark Twain's satire, however, was not the people on either side of the Atlantic but the traditional American travel book—the sentimental and reverential pilgrimages to the Old World recorded in a long series of volumes stretching over half a century from Irving's *Sketch Book* (1819) right down to 1869. Though modern readers are unaware of this, contemporaries were certainly alert to the parody and must have relished Twain's shift to comic realism. By linking *The American* (in its early chapters only) to *The Innocents Abroad*, James had the additional advantage of suggesting that his book was part of the newest direction of a very old tradition. And since he was knowledgeable about painting far beyond Mark Twain or any of the literary fraternity in America at that time, he was able to give another turn of the screw, making the comedy more subtle and complex—broad as it may seem today to devotees of his "later manner."

James stands quite alone among American novelists of the nineteenth and early twentieth centuries as an appreciator of the fine arts, and he was the only one who used them as a significant part of the texture of his fictions, with one exception. We need merely call the roll: Hawthorne, Melville, Howells, Twain, Hemingway, Faulkner, and the rest. Hawthorne, the only one James felt a real kinship with, is an instructive example. More than any of the others he used art and artists as subject matter in his stories, notably in *The Marble Faun*. The same thing is true of the *French and Italian Note-Books*, which record his impressions of the European museums and galleries he visited. Yet a reader of these two works would have no difficulty in subscribing to James's own reluctant conclusion: "Hawthorne was a good deal bored by the importunity of Italian art, for which his taste, naturally not keen, had never been cultivated." Then specifically as to pictures: "The 'most delicate charm' to Mr. Hawthorne was apparently the primal freshness and brightness of paint and varnish, and . . . the new gilding of the frame"—which explained his preference for the works of American artists then plying their trade in Italy over the Old Masters in museums. Is it too much to suggest that Nathaniel Hawthorne supplied one brush stroke for the portrait of Christopher Newman?

By 1877 there was no danger of the great American joke having worn thin. But was James running the risk that readers a century later would find this aspect of *The American* dated? The answer is that comedy of this kind will probably never grow hackneyed. Besides, the bright new copy of the Old Master, heavily varnished and framed in gold, is an effective symbol of

[47]

Newman's "aesthetic verdancy"—one of the barriers that separated him from an understanding of Europe. Jokes of this sort have been a part of American humor so long as to become part of a cherished tradition. James was both clever and lucky when he linked *The American* to it.

If Newman experienced a certain drop when Noémie's frankness exposed his esthetic ignorance it was only temporary, and he was quite his old assured self by the time he began his summer tour of the Continent. With fine economy James confined this to a ten-page chapter, yet gave an adequate sense of his initiation into Europe without losing the sense of Paris as the novel's unifying center. More important, the author wanted to save further examples of the separating wall of art until they could be related to the wall of manners, presented scenically rather than by travelogue summary. The combination was first achieved in an exchange of visits early in the fall between Newman and Valentin de Bellegarde, Claire's younger brother.

A warm friendship developed between the two young men, spontaneously and by very reason of their differences—symbolized by their chosen places of residence. Newman had established himself in a suite of rooms on one of the new and rather pretentious avenues opened up during the reign of Napoleon III. (In an essay of 1877 James spoke of the "huge, blank, pompous, featureless sameness" of the boulevards laid out by M. Haussmann, that have "gradually deprived the streets of Paris of nine-tenths of their ancient individuality.") Newman had a relish for luxury and splendor, but his idea of it was satisfied by an apartment with rooms "so brilliant and lofty ... you wanted to keep your hat on." Tom Tristram found one to fit the hero's specifications: "It was situated on the Boulevard Haussmann, on a first floor, and consisted of a series of rooms, gilded from floor to ceiling a foot thick, draped in various light shades of satin, and chiefly furnished with mirrors and clocks. Newman thought them magnificent" (74).

It was into this glittering apartment that Valentin was ushered when he paid his visit. Newman found him standing in the middle of the drawing room, eyeing it from cornice to carpet, with a sense of lively entertainment on his face. When he begged his new friend to sit down and have a cigar:

> "Surely I may not smoke here," said M. de Bellegarde.
> "What is the matter—Is the room too small?"
> "It is too large. It is like smoking in a ball-room, or a church." (87)

Newman was really baffled. Some of the comedy of this novel consists of such sophisticated spoofing by the French aristocrats, which by going over the American's head underscores his limitations. But Valentin's part in this was always kindly.

The difference between the two bachelors, reflected so clearly in their esthetic tastes, can best be brought out by juxtaposing James's description of the other's apartment. It was in the basement of an old house in the rue d'Anjou St. Honoré:

> When Newman returned Bellegarde's visit, he hinted that *his* lodging was at least as much a laughing matter as his own. But its oddities were of a different cast from those of our hero's gilded saloons on the Boulevard Haussmann: the place was low, dusky, contracted, and crowded with curious bric-a-brac. Bellegarde, penniless patrician as he was, was an insatiable collector, and his walls were covered with rusty arms and ancient panels and platters, his doorway draped in faded tapestries.... Newman thought it a damp, gloomy place to live in, and was puzzled by the obstructive and fragmentary character of the furniture. (96–97)

The old and the new, taste and the lack of it, could hardly be more sharply contrasted. The two settings with their detailed furnishings, are then developed by dialogue into minor scenes which effectually render the difference between the two characters and the paradoxical basis for their friendship. Both *place* and *thing* are used in James's new mode: to aid Newman and Valentin in understanding each other and in establishing a meaningful relationship. The reader will find these matters spread out before him in chapter seven. But the critic must summarize.

Valentin, as the younger son of an ancient noble family, had to be content with the role of a *gentilhomme*: "To Newman, Bellegarde was the ideal Frenchman, the Frenchman of tradition and romance.... Gallant, expansive, amusing; a master of all the distinctive social virtues" (86). The disparate characteristics of the two companions made the basis of their capital friendship. One form their difference took in Newman's summing up was a generalization on the international contrast: Frenchmen of that age seemed to have "young heads and very aged hearts" whereas in America "lads of twenty-five and thirty have old heads and young hearts" (93). The results rather than the qualities of their difference interested Valentin. "You, evidently, are a success,...a financial, commercial power," he said with a mild kind of envy: "I couldn't go into business, I couldn't make money, because I was a Bellegarde. I couldn't go into politics, because I was a Bellegarde—the Bellegardes don't recognize the Bonapartes....I couldn't marry a rich girl, because no Bellegarde had ever married a *roturière*" (93–94).

Innocently amusing as this recital sounds, it strikes an ominous note for the hero. In listing the barriers he faced as a young nobleman trying to find a suitable career, he is unwittingly naming the principal barriers Newman will face, with a fortune made in business and no rank to ennoble his name, in seeking the hand of Valentin's sister in marriage. Yet the American struck him as a natural aristocrat. "It's a sort of air you have of being thoroughly at home in the world," said Valentin. Newman attributed this to "the privilege of being an American citizen.... That sets a man up" (95, 98).

The Making of "The American"

A graphic description of this New World protagonist who was capable of making such an impression on the young French aristocrat is given in the opening pages of *The American*: "He had the flat jaw and sinewy neck which are frequent in the American type," he was long and lean and muscular, his posture and carriage were "relaxed and lounging," his suit and cravat a bit gaudy. In sum: "An observer with anything of an eye for national types... might have felt a certain humorous relish of the almost ideal completeness with which he filled out the national mould" (1, 2). Having presented his hero as a "typical American," James then hastens to add some ambiguous brush-strokes to give him individuality and make him credibly human: shrewd yet credulous, confident yet shy, an eye in which innocence and experience were strangely blended—and at the same time he was extremely intelligent and extremely good humored (3).

The portrait of Newman as we see him in Paris gains another dimension by being set against his past life in America. It is Tom Tristram who first draws out of him his "intensely Western story": a meteoric career in mining, manufacturing, and speculating on the stock market, finally winding up in San Francisco as the scene of his happiest strokes of fortune (18–20). To Mrs. Tristram he admits that up to his thirty-fifth year his sole aim in life had been to make money, but now he has different plans. "I am not cultivated, I am not even educated; I know nothing about history, or art, or foreign tongues," he says: "But I am not a fool, either, and I shall undertake to know something about Europe by the time I have done with it." Then she adds a finishing flamboyant touch to the portrait: "You are the great Western Barbarian, stepping forth in his innocence and might, gazing a while at this poor effete Old World, and then swooping down on it" (31). When the literal-minded hero protests, she explains that she does not mean he is "a Comanche chief," and that by "swooping down" she is only referring to her marriage-plot—which is launched in the remaining pages of the chapter.

In his late Preface to *The American* James confesses that the "germination process" of his fictional characters is "almost always untraceable" and that this is notably true of Christopher Newman. Fortunately, the evolution of his paradoxical hero can now be traced quite convincingly, and in the author's own words.

During his travels in Europe, beginning with his first adult trip, James was sharply observant of the American abroad. Writing to his family in 1869, after several months each in England, Switzerland, and Italy, he began his commentary on his travelling compatriots:

> There is but one word to use in regard to them—vulgar, vulgar, vulgar. Their ignorance [of] everything European—...and then their unhappy poverty of voice, of speech and of physiognomy—these things glare at you hideously. On the other hand, we seem a people of *character*, we seem to have energy, capacity and intellectual stuff in ample measure. What I have pointed at as our vices are the elements of the modern man with *culture* quite left out. It's the absolute and incredible lack of *culture* that strikes you in common travelling Americans.

A similarly unfavorable opinion of his countrymen in Europe remained with James at least a decade longer, as recorded in an essay entitled "Americans Abroad" a year after the novel was published: "The great innocence of the American tourist is perhaps his most general quality," and Europeans take this as a sign of his vulgarity, since he is also "ill-made, ill-mannered, ill-dressed."

Such a picture of the American abroad if treated seriously in fiction would have seemed fatally snobbish, but James was too wise for that even as a young author. Treated comically, and sympathetically, it could make a smash hit, as proved by Twain's *Innocents Abroad* (published the very year of James's letter). No reader needs to be told how successful a fictional antihero our greatest humorist made out of the "vulgar American" in Europe. James himself made clever use of the type by assigning it to a minor character in his novel, who serves as a foil to the hero, thus helping to picture him by showing what he is not. Tom Tristram shows enough similarities to the persona of *The Innocents Abroad* to indicate where James found his model.

Another foil for Newman is the young Unitarian minister he travels with for a few weeks during his summer tour of Europe. The Rev. Mr. Babcock, a dispeptic and serious-minded man, finds the hero "an excellent, generous fellow" but with a very grave fault, "a want of moral reaction" to the churches and galleries and ancient monuments they were visiting together, because he cared only for the pleasure of the hour. The original of this minor character was prompt to reveal himself. William James, writing of his delight in reading *The American*, said of "the morbid little clergyman" in a letter to his brother (recalling their travels in 1874): "I was not a little amused to find

[51]

some of my own attributes in him—I think you found my 'moral reaction' excessive when I was abroad." This helps to define the hero, once again by showing what he is not. By implication William may have recognized some of his brother Henry's attributes in Christopher Newman, slight though they may be.

James's first fictional use of the typical American abroad—the heroine's father in "Travelling Companions," a short story composed just after his return from Europe in 1870—is an extension of the favorable postscript to his tirade against American vulgarity in the letter to his family of the year before: that his countrymen are a people of *character* even if they are lacking in *culture*. We are told:

> Mr. Evans ... was in many ways an excellent representative American. Without taste, without culture or polish, he nevertheless produced an impression of substance in character, keenness in perception, and intensity in will, which effectually redeemed him from vulgarity. It often seemed to me in fact, that his good-humoured tolerance and ... fearlessness of either gods or men combined in proportions of which the union might have been very fairly termed aristocratic.

This is a preliminary sketch for Christopher Newman, "Nature's nobleman," but there are still important aspects of the portrait to be added.

Some of the more attractive ones are echoed in James's tribute to a famous American whom he came to know well during numerous meetings in Paris and in Florence, just a few years before writing *The American*. This friend is characterized as "inveterately, in England or on the Continent, *the* American abroad," extraordinarily youthful, and with a robust love of life:

> His America was a country worth hearing about, a magnificent conception, an admirably consistent and lovable object of allegiance.... The sign that, in Europe, one knew him best by was his intense national consciousness....
>
> He was fond of everything human and natural, everything that had color and character, and no gaiety, no sense of comedy, was ever more easily kindled by contact. When he was not surrounded by great pleasures he could find his account in small ones.

This character sketch is so appropriate to Newman that it will come as something of a surprise to readers to be told that it is a description of James Russell Lowell.

Two other American authors, notable for their reactions to Europe, enter the picture also. Nathaniel Hawthorne's lack of sophistication in esthetic matters has already been suggested as one element in Newman's preference for bright new copies instead of dusky Old Masters. This lack, according to James, was the result of his provinciality. The point was so insisted on in his critical biography, *Hawthorne* (1879), that it brought forth some strictures from another American friend who had "an intense national consciousness" but did not have Lowell's wit to temper his patriotism. William Dean Howells, in his review of the book, complained that the charge of "provincial" was overused, even abused. He went further and voiced his objection to James's "theory, boldly propounded, that it needs a long history and 'a complex social machinery to set a writer in motion.'" His patriotism was offended by the expatriate author's clear preference for Europe as the novelist's "ground."

James's reply to Howells was full and strong: "It is on manners, customs, usages, habits, forms, upon all these things matured and established, that a novelist lives." The "paraphernalia" representing them are found most richly in an old civilization: "I shall feel refuted only when we have produced [in America] ... a novelist belonging to the company of Balzac." It was unquestionably his own ambition to be such a novelist, but Howells he feared was just as provincial as Hawthorne. James's controversy with his friend about American provincialism and the richer texture of "manners, customs, usages, habits, forms" in European society comes several years after publication of *The American*, to be sure, but it is relevant to the character and situation of Newman since these matters were very much in the author's mind at the time of composing his novel. (He had known Howells well for a full decade.)

Such an account of the hero's diverse origins may seem to present him as a thing of shreds and patches. But to the extent that he is a typical American he has to be a composite figure, since the "type" never exists in any single individual. The traits attached to Christopher Newman are certainly various: innocent and provincial, patriotic and culturally ignorant, youthful and robust in the enjoyment of life, strong-willed and forceful in character, genial and open in personal bearing. Contributions to the portrait have come from many models: Hawthorne and Lowell and Howells for positive traits, Mark Twain and William James for foils, above all the author himself in his experiences and observations of the American abroad over a period of years. A final ingredient must now be added, to restore the balance with a little more weight in the scale of comedy, by linking *The American* with another literary tradition.

The relationship of James's novel to the popular native genre of the comic hero and the tall tale—in which the humor derives chiefly from exaggeration and the grotesque juxtaposition of opposites—was pointed out long ago by Constance Rourke in *American Humor* (1931), but that account needs to be supplemented. The relationship does not have to rest on conjectured parallels, for James himself has provided the clue: "Newman had sat with Western humorists in knots, round cast-iron stoves, and seen 'tall' stories grow taller without toppling over, and his own imagination had learned the trick of piling up consistent wonders" (98). This anecdote is given in connection with Newman's narrating his past career to Valentin, with the author's comment that "it amused him to heighten the color of the episode" whenever his companion's credulity seemed on the point of protesting.

James was too sophisticated a writer to turn his hero into a Western boaster, however. With a clever shift he puts the tall tales in the mouths of the French aristocrats, for the most part. When the Bellegardes—probing Newman's background to see if he is acceptable as a suitor for Claire's hand—use subtle mockery to make sport of him as an American dupe, he in his innocence laughs at the wrong thing while the reader finds himself laughing at the verbal play of the aristocrats, thus producing comedy on a double plane. This was the new turn James gave to "American humour," with the European being the jokester and the American the butt of the joke. Yet Newman also has some of the characteristics of the American comic in his appearance, posture, and speech, as previously shown; and in addition to being likened to a "Western Barbarian," he is twice compared to Benjamin Franklin in a humorous context (19, 158).

As a concluding touch the name-game should be treated as part of the comic symbolism of the genre. (The very title, *The American* bespeaks the naive aggressiveness of the national type, a novel by a Frenchman called *Le Français* being unthinkable.) James himself gives sufficient warrant for playing this game. At the very beginning, in introducing himself to Noémie, Newman calls attention to the fact that he was named for a famous Christopher, leaving the reader to bear it in mind as he reads on through to the end this tale of a Columbus-in-reverse—the new man from America coming over to rediscover the Old World. The pattern, obvious enough in the hero's name, can be extended to many of the characters. *Valentin*, the younger Bellegarde who favors Newman's suit, has for his name-saint the patron of young lovers. *Claire* ("Light") is the ideal of all that is pure and lovely, but after her unhappy marriage to the Comte de *Cintré* she had been left, in her widowed state, bound ("girdled") by her family's will. The older brother, *Urbain*, is the embodiment of a formal civility so extreme as to suggest that it is merely a superficial ornamentation or veneer. Finally, the family name *Bellegarde* sums up all the "walls" that separate Newman from his heart's desire. It may be freely translated as Finecastle (or great house, as in *The Princess Casamassima*). More literally *garde* signifies the castle "keep" or innermost fortress, where the very existence of the family can be protected against intruders. Some readers may find these comic names too broadly farcical. But they are only showy when the critic pulls them out for examination; allowed to slip back into place in the novel, they are unobtrusive. The name-game, added to the other evidence, makes it clear James was conscious of the native tradition of humor when writing *The American*. But that tradition accounts for only part of its comedy.

In *The Comic Sense of Henry James* (1962) Richard Poirier offers his own interpretation of *The American*, linking it to a much older and more literary tradition—classical comedy as filtered through the Renaissance. His theory is that most of the comedy in *The American* results from dramatizing the conflict between the "free" and the "fixed" characters, representatives respectively of "open" and "closed" societies. The terms, as he points out, are James's own, set forth in one of his Prefaces:

> For the spectator of life,...the fixed constituents of any reproducible action are the fools who minister, at the particular crisis, to the intensity of the free spirit engaged with them. The fools are interesting by contrast, by the salience they acquire...; and the free spirit, always tormented, and by no means triumphant, is heroic, ironic, pathetic, or whatever,...'successful' only through having remained free.

Applying this theory of comedy to *The American*, Poirier finds that the "free" spirits are Newman, Valentin, and Claire, people who are still open to experience; and that the two principal "fixed" characters are Urbain and the old Marquise de Bellegarde, people who are contented with their place in a conventionally ordered society. The comedy in this novel exposes and evaluates the difference between the two types of characters, since it is almost entirely social satire. The hero himself, even when made fun of affectionately, is never satirized by the author; the villains are never grotesque as individuals, though their society is. And since the "fixed" are associated with Europe and the "free" with America (in this sense Poirier classes Valentin and Claire as "imprisoned Americans"), his interpretation becomes an essential part of any study of the international theme. It is also supplemental to my own particular thesis: that the theme of *The American* is to be found in the walls of separation between the New World protagonist and the Old World he wants to understand and "possess," rendered by symbol and scene. Accordingly, Poirier's interpretation of the comedy will be referred to from time to time when relevant to my own approach to the novel.

Another way of defining Newman, therefore, is by contrast with his antagonists—later by confrontation with them—and this will serve as an introduction to both the comedy and the theme of the "walls which fatally divide." The American hero is beyond question the epitome of the free and open character. In the second paragraph of the book we are told by the author that Newman gives the impression "of standing in an attitude of general hospitality to the chances of life." A hundred pages later Valentin summarizes his reaction to his American friend by exclaiming, "Happy man, you are strong and you are free" (98). The young Frenchman's account of the limitations on his own freedom in finding a career would seem to make him one of the fixed characters. As a Bellegarde he was seriously affected on the practical side of his life by the restrictive family code, it is true, though even here he managed to escape from the irksome daily pressure of it by establishing himself in an independent apartment. Far more important is the fact that he has remained free in spirit. Hence he can serve as Newman's confederate in dealing with the other Bellegardes, the really "fixed" ones.

It is Valentin who provides what help the hero gets. In answer to queries, he gives sketches of the elderly marquise and of his brother Urbain, fifteen years his senior, in which the satire is only partially veiled by decorum. The Bellegarde of chief interest to Newman is the sister, but Valentin, who adores her, confesses he cannot talk about her without rhapsodizing. After two pages of this she is "half a *grande dame* and half an angel," and so on; for all his palaver we learn nothing of her except that she is perfect, that is, *ideal* (102–103).

It is in recounting the story of what his family had done to Claire, ten years before, that the veil of decorum is dropped. She had been betrothed at eighteen, against her wishes, to "an odious old gentleman" aged sixty. The only redeeming feature of this marriage was that he lived only a few years. But he bequeathed no more wealth to Claire on his death (the purpose of the family's scheme) than he had brought happiness to her in life. When Newman complains bitterly of "your horrible French way," Valentin breaks down and responds with an anecdote of this *mariage de convénance* that clearly divides the Bellegardes into the "fixed" and the "free": "It was a chapter for a novel. ... The evening before the ceremony [Claire] swooned away, and spent the whole night in sobs. I declared it was revolting and told my sister publicly that if she would refuse, downright, I would stand by her. I was told [by my brother] to go about my business, and she became Comtesse de Cintré" (104–105). Urbain and the marquise are rigid in their adherence to the conventions of their "closed" society and ruthless in applying them, when necessary. Valentin is enough of a free spirit to rebel against one of its most time-honored traditions, when pushed too far. Claire wishes to be free but quickly surrenders when her elders put the pressure on, and in the end resigns herself to becoming literally immured in their closed world.

One final point about Valentin's revelation of the family's cruelty in enforcing their code. When he says, "It was a chapter for a novel," what comes to mind is not the new realism of a Flaubert or Daudet but the old-style melodrama of a Dumas *fils* or the romances of George Sand. (James had written essays on both of them during the first half of 1876, while *The American* was in progress.) The reference gives Valentin a way of talking about the Bellegardes' past behavior, and gives the author an "out" for their possible future doings. Much of Newman's European experience struck him as being like a novel, or like a play.

A Comedy of Contrasts

At the time of Newman's early visits to the Hôtel de Bellegarde he did not have the benefit of Valentin's analysis of the family. All he had to go on was the description of the Bellegardes thrown out irresponsibly by Mrs. Tristram: "They are terrible people—her *monde*; all mounted upon stilts a mile high, and with pedigrees long in proportion. It is the skim of the milk of the old noblesse" (37). As for Claire, after a one-sentence summary of her miserable marriage, "She suffers from her wicked old mother and her Grand Turk of a brother. They persecute her" (75). Such histrionics need much toning down, of course. But exposition, even at its best, is a far less effective mode of presenting characters than action, with fully developed scene and dialogue. This is especially true of those major confrontations in *The American* where the setting is symbolic as well as dramatic.

The Hôtel de Bellegarde is the most elaborately and effectively worked out *mise-en-scène* in the novel. On the occasion of Newman's first visit there, the house itself is described in terms of an actual wall of separation, the symbol of a fixed and closed world, which he intuitively feels to be difficult of access by outsiders like himself:

> He walked across the Seine, late in the summer afternoon, and made his way through those gray and silent streets of the Faubourg St. Germain whose houses present to the outer world a face as impassive and as suggestive of the concentration of privacy within as the blank walls of Eastern seraglios. Newman thought it a queer way for rich people to live; his idea of grandeur was a splendid façade, diffusing its brilliancy outward too, irradiating hospitality. The house to which he had been directed had a dark, dusty, painted portal, which swung open in answer to his ring. It admitted him into a wide, graveled court, surrounded on three sides with closed windows.... The place was all in the shade; it answered to Newman's conception of a convent. (41)

(The last sentence is one of James's careful—too careful?—preparations for his conclusion, in which the Bellegarde family force Claire to break off her engagement to Newman and take refuge in a Carmelite convent.)

Though the hero was admitted through the outer gate, the portress gave him no satisfaction except to tell him to apply at the farther door. There he presented his card to a young gentleman, who, with a frank reassuring smile, responded that he would deliver it to his sister. At this point an older man appeared, wearing evening dress, who took the card, looked at Newman from head to foot, and then "gravely but urbanely" said, "Madame de Cintré is not at home" (42). The wall of separation takes several forms here: the closed outside portal, the noncommittal portress, the blank façade of the house, the marquis who administers the polite snub. Even this brief glimpse makes clear which of the brothers is fixed, which free.

Newman's second call was successful, though the barriers of art and manners are added even as the actual separating wall yields. Late one autumn afternoon he was conducted through a vast dim vestibule, up a broad stone staircase, to an apartment on the floor above:

> Announced and ushered in, he found himself in a sort of paneled boudoir, at one end of which a lady and a gentleman were seated before the fire. The gentleman was smoking a cigarette; there was no light in the room save that of a couple of candles and the glow from the hearth.... He had an unusual, unexpected sense of having wandered into a strange corner of the world. (78)

In this formidable mansion Newman finds himself, in spite of his disposition to take things simply, facing a situation that is complex and puzzling: Claire and Valentin Bellegarde seemed "enveloped in a sort of fantastic privacy." It was some time before their graciousness put him sufficiently at ease to perform that movement so frequent with him as to be his characterizing image —extending his legs, "a sort of symbol of his taking mental possession of a scene."

Even so, the conversation remained rather formal and on the surface. For example, to Newman's question, typical of a visitor from the New World, "Your house is tremendously old?" his young host responded by pointing up above the eighteenth-century chimney piece to a carved panel with an armorial device and the date 1627: "That is old or new, according to your point of view" (80–81). The American hero finds the faded and tarnished decor of the interior as esthetically baffling as he had found the architectural exterior forbidding. But he finds the brother and sister to his liking. Count Valentin is pleasant and friendly, though his habitually ironic tone is somewhat perplexing. Claire measures up to Mrs. Tristram's extravagant claim of "perfection"—a term which previously had presented only a blurred image to him. The Hôtel de Bellegarde, which on the first visit had served only as a setting for Newman's rebuff, has this time developed into a small-scale scene for the alignment of characters (83–84).

The story moves along smoothly through the next few chapters—from Newman's decision to seek Claire's hand, through his courtship and proposal of marriage—with no need of a cicerone. The critic's only function is to point out two aspects of the barrier of Old World "manners, usages, forms" that still exists even with the friendly young. What chiefly emerges in the long talk when Newman confides his plan to Valentin is the difficulty these two have in understanding each other, despite their sympathy and good will. Even with Claire there is room for puzzlement. "Newman wondered where, in so exquisite a compound, nature and art showed their dividing line.... Where did urbanity end and sincerity begin?" (114–120). These episodes, essential to the plot, are presented by simple narrative or by exposition. It is by scenic presentation that the separating wall of manners is most effectively rendered.

If Newman's meeting with Claire and Valentin was the first real scene taking place at the Hôtel de Bellegarde, the occasion of his introduction to Urbain and the dowager marquise is the second. (The "rebuff" and the "proposal" are scenes only in the older sense of dramatized episodes for advancing the plot.) His pleasant reception by the young Bellegardes and his confrontation with the older ones are both scenes in James's newly developing mode for establishing relations among characters. Valentin's formal presentation of the hero to his mother and older brother is the most important scene in the first half of the novel because it is the first confrontation of the protagonist with his formidable antagonists. James's extravagant use of language, especially his imagery, produces some of the comic evaluations of character and situation. Most of the comedy, however, results from the actual dramatic conflict between free and fixed characters, between open and closed social behavior.

The blank façade of the Hôtel de Bellegarde and its esthetically baffling interior have been described on previous occasions as barriers to understanding. This time Newman is ushered into an apartment he has not penetrated before, one that strikes him as "rather sad and shabby," the salon of the dowager Marquise de Bellegarde:

It was a vast, high room, with elaborate and ponderous mouldings, painted a whitish gray, along the upper portions of the walls and ceiling; with a great deal of faded, and carefully repaired tapestry in the doorways and chair-backs; a Turkey carpet in light colors, still soft and deep, in spite of great antiquity, on the floor; and portraits of each of Madame de Bellegarde's children, at the age of ten, suspended against an old screen of red silk. The room was illumined, exactly enough for conversation, by half a dozen candles, placed in odd corners, at a great distance apart. In a deep arm-chair, near the fire, sat an old lady in black. (125–126)

When Newman is introduced, he cannot help recalling by way of contrast the "range of expression as delightfully vast as the wind-streaked, cloud-flecked distance on a Western prairie" to which he likens the face of the absent Madame de Cintré. "But her mother's white, intense, respectable countenance, with its formal gaze, and its circumscribed smile, suggested a document signed and sealed; a thing of parchment, ink, and ruled lines" (127). Newman said to himself that here was "a woman of conventions and proprieties" who lived in a world of things "immutably decreed."

A few minutes later Urbain de Bellegarde entered, kissed his mother's hand gallantly, then "assumed an attitude" before the chimney piece. When presented to this "perpendicular person," the American hero realized he had "never yet been confronted with such an incarnation of the art of taking one's self seriously; he felt a sort of impulse to step backward, as you do to get a view of a great façade" (130). Characterizing images are as old as literature itself. All depends on what is done with them. The three here are striking, especially the last, and they are explicit in differentiating the fixed Bellegardes from Claire, whom Newman (with his image of American openness) hopes to set free. They constitute only a small beginning compared to the brilliant use James was later to make of the characterizing image; yet they are good examples of the extravagant language used to enhance the comedy of *The American.*

From these characterizations it is clear that the chief wall of separation in this scene will prove to be that of manners. The marquise's opening gambit seems simple to the point of ingenuousness. It is an apparently random anecdote about the only other American she has ever met, but with the implication that an American is some odd kind of anthropological specimen that exists outside of civilized society (127). In its vagueness it is the exact opposite of her customary idiom, as we hear it for example at the end of the interview when Newman asks her directly if she will favor his suit for her daughter's hand. She responds "with impressive brevity" a softly spoken "No!" When he reminds her that he is very rich, her reply, "How rich?" is equally brief, and as straightforward as he had been. "You are very frank," she says finally. "I will be the same" (136–137). Her linguistic skill is a mark of her subtlety of mind, and as an adversary Newman respects her.

Just as the mother brought out his best "American" traits, so the most un-
attractive ones are called into play by the stiff formalism and condescension of
her elder son. In the brief exchanges with the marquis here, Newman loses
his customary poise. As a result he falls into slang, into boasting about being
self-made, and into tactless remarks to leisured aristocrats about how hard it
is for a business man to learn how to be idle (131–133). They respond by
subtly mocking him—the marquise herself playing the leading role by creating
one of those inverted American tall tales, mentioned earlier in this chapter.
The occasion ends in a social victory for the Bellegardes, who have the weight
of a long tradition behind them, but a moral victory for Newman, who is
guided solely by his humanity. Yet James, by making the marquise entertaining, persuades the reader to suspend judgment on her treatment of
Newman.

The sequel takes place three days later when Newman receives a formal
invitation to dine at the Hôtel de Bellegarde. This is another scene symbolizing
the wall of manners that separates the American hero from his understanding of Europe. When dinner is announced, his venerable hostess takes his
arm to be led down:

> The dining-room, at the end of a cold corridor, was vast and sombre; the
> dinner was simple and delicately excellent. . . . Once seated at table, with
> the various members of the ancient house of Bellegarde around him, he
> asked himself the meaning of his position. Was the old lady responding
> to his advances? Did the fact that he was a solitary guest augment his
> credit or diminish it? . . . Whether they gave him a long rope or a short
> one he was there now, and Madame de Cintré was opposite to him. She
> had a tall candlestick on each side of her; she would sit there for the
> next hour, and that was enough. The dinner was extremely solemn and
> measured; he wondered whether this was always the state of things in
> "old families." (149–150)

The settings for the three scenes of confrontation with the Bellegardes are
alike in that all give Newman the sense of having wandered "into a strange
corner of the world." But James has modulated them carefully to suit the
differences in the three meetings and to symbolize the several characters: the
dim but friendly sitting room of Claire, the cold high-vaulted salon of the
marquise, and now the vast and sombre dining room.

The talk, mostly between Newman and Urbain, was formal and cautious.
It continued in this vein when the three men retired to the smoking room
after dinner, the marquis more and more circuitous, the American feeling
himself increasingly in opposition to this "man of forms and phrases and
postures, a man full of possible impertinences and treacheries" (150). Fi-

nally the younger brother comes to the point and tells Newman the good news: "You are accepted as a candidate for the hand of our sister":

> "There has been a family council," the young man continued.... "My mother and the marquis sat at a table covered with green cloth; my sister-in-law and I were on a bench against the wall. It was like a committee at the Corps Legislatif. We were called up, one after the other, to testify. We spoke of you very handsomely.... At this point I was ordered to sit down, but I think I made an impression in your favor." (151–152)

Urbain's response to this is to apologize to Newman for "the deplorable levity" of Valentin. But the younger brother has deliberately assumed the role of the wise clown:

> "In the good old times," said Valentin, "marquises and counts used to have their appointed fools and jesters, to crack jokes for them. Nowadays we see a great strapping democrat keeping a count about him to play the fool. It's a good situation, but I certainly am very degenerate." (152)

Now we have a characterizing image for the fifth and last of the major characters. Who but a real fool would resent the clownings of the court fool? This is exactly what the marquis does. He is infuriated when his snobbish insinuations of superiority are translated by the younger brother into language plain enough to expose their essential vulgarity, at least to make them seem comic.

Newman's limited understanding needs to be supplemented at many points. This is most skilfully achieved when Valentin's ironic voice comes to the reader's aid. But sometimes the author finds it necessary to step in with a confidential aside, as happens when the men rejoin the ladies in the salon of the marquise. "I am afraid the picture was lost upon Newman," James says, commenting on the striking image of social dignity and the habit of unquestioned authority exhibited by the "little time-shrunken old lady" as she tells Newman that they were doing him "a great favor, ... stretching a point," in accepting his suit (159–160).

During the weeks that followed, in spite of the patronising hauteur with which he had been accepted as a suitor, Newman conducted his official courtship with tact as well as with great joy. On both sides it seems to the reader less a matter of their falling in love than of mutual admiration and of envisioning the happiness they could give each other—he by possessing such a prize, she by being rescued into life. The hero's chief attraction for her was his *difference*, that very cluster of "American" characteristics which Urbain and the Marquise could not swallow. When Claire gave her answer his sense of triumph went to his head, and step by step his ingenuous enthusiasm led him to his fall. He would give a gala announcement party, he declared, with all the great opera singers and actors from the Comédie providing the entertainment. The Bellegardes stared. *They* will give the fête, a formal reception: "We want to present you to our friends; we will invite them all" (190).

The ball at the Hôtel de Bellegarde is the most memorable scene in the book. It reminds the reader, in its charming presentation of the hero, of the opening scene that took place at the Louvre on a spring day just a year before. The tone on this occasion is set by Newman's naive enjoyment of himself. His confrontation with an alien culture (for comedy or otherwise) has receded into the background, at least for the moment. The walls of separation are now down, in the sense that the portals of this normally inhospitable mansion are thrown wide, though the barrier of manners is never more impenetrable than when most invisible. The American fiancé arrived early, was greeted with majestic formality by the marquise, and took his place in the receiving line beside Claire and the whole Bellegarde family. Soon the grand occasion was under way:

A stream of people had been pouring into the salon in which Newman stood with his host, the rooms were filling up and the spectacle had become brilliant. It borrowed its splendor chiefly from the shining shoulders and profuse jewels of the women, and from the voluminous elegance of their dresses. There were no uniforms, as Madame de Bellegarde's door was inexorably closed against the myrmidons of the upstart power [Napoleon III] which then ruled the fortunes of France. . . . [But Newman was introduced to several] elderly gentlemen, of what Valentin de Bellegarde had designated as the high-nosed category; two or three of them wore cordons and stars; . . . [among their number were] three dukes, three counts, and a baron. (210, 208)

At this point the Marquis de Bellegarde offers to present Newman to more of his distinguished guests and, taking his arm, escorts him to the far end of the suite of reception rooms, where he begins by introducing him to "The greatest lady in France," (clearly modelled on a princess James had met at the Duke d'Aumale's reception in January 1876). This is the fat Duchess d'Outreville, whose exchange with the hero is another one of those tall-tales-in-reverse by which James gives a new twist to the traditional mode of "American humor," though this sally is a good-natured one. Then Urbain presents his prospective brother-in-law to a score of other ladies and gentlemen, selected for their typically august character. Here the author whispers in the reader's ear: "If the marquis was going about as a bear-leader, if the fiction of Beauty and the Beast was supposed to have found its companion-piece, the general impression appeared to be that the bear was a very fair imitation of humanity" (214).

The reader, if he is alert, will recall another piece of animal imagery, the one used by Valentin months before when telling how one of the Bellegardes in the Middle Ages had married a beggar-maid—"it was like marrying a bird or a monkey; one didn't have to think about her family at all" (106)— the relevance to the hero's courtship being clear though the mismating is reversed as to sexes. Newman is not privy to his creator's aside at the ball, of course, but his present situation in the Hôtel de Bellegarde apparently brings back to mind the young count's family anecdote. "Am I behaving like a d———d fool?" he asks himself. "Am I stepping about like a terrier on his hind legs?" (214). The menagerie assembled here may seem too miscellaneous to have any special meaning as applied to Newman, but all the images have one important thing in common. They refer to animals who have been trained to perform like human beings: dancing at the end of a rope, singing in a cage, aping the master who calls the tune, or prancing upright at his heels— most allegorical of all the allusion to the Beast yearning for Beauty's womanly love to redeem his humanity. Such is the risk a Bellegarde would run in marrying "outside."

The self-assured American hero is too happy on the night of the ball to be held more than a moment by any apprehensions of this sort, however: "The lights, the flowers, the music, the crowd, the splendid women, the jewels, the strangeness even of the universal murmur of a clever foreign tongue, were all a vivid symbol and assurance of his having grasped his purpose.... Just now the cup seemed full" (215). With his elation at this pitch Newman seeks out the old marquise to tell her how magnificent her party is. To her noncommittal reply, "My desire was to please you," he responds by asking her to please him still more by taking his arm for a promenade among the guests. "People made way for her as she passed.... But though she smiled upon every one, she said nothing until she reached the last of the rooms, where she found her elder son. Then, 'This is enough, Sir,' she declared with measured softness to Newman, and turned to the marquis" (218).

To call the ball scene brilliant is to refer not to the social event as such (though in an ironic way it *is* brilliant), but to James's techniques in using it to render his theme. It is the finest example in his fiction prior to *The Portrait of a Lady* of what Stephen Spender calls his revolutionary mode of using the scene mainly as a means of aligning the characters and explaining what are the reactions of each to the other; also of what Peter Garrett calls James's pioneering use of scenic presentation rather than narrative and of symbolism rather than realism as principal modes in the modern novel.

The occasion of the ball at the Hôtel de Bellegarde offers a concentrated moment for recognition of differences, and serves as the climax of what has been previously revealed. Newman is presented to the reader in his most attractive guise, even when his spontaneous enjoyment of success leads him to breach the forms of decorum; but in the eyes of the French aristocrats he is at best the comic hero of a western tall tale, at worst an alien in the civilized world. The Bellegardes and their circle appear in their most attractive form as a mannered society of grace and sophistication, expressing themselves in skillful gesture and witty exchange, with only a hint of condescension toward the American outsider. The basic theme of international contrast, on the other hand, is symbolized by the animal imagery, with Newman only faintly aware of how it implies the permanence of the dividing walls between the two cultures. This is all very different from the old-fashioned use of scene as a confrontation between opposing forces for the release of emotions or for forwarding the plot by dramatic action. The chief link with plot here comes at the very end when Newman, wishing to bid farewell to his hostess, is told that she has left the ball feeling faint, having "succumbed to the emotions of the evening" (218). It is the only preparation we have for what follows.

Romance and Melodrama

From this point on the author of *The American* is in trouble. A few days after the ball when Newman calls at the Hôtel de Bellegarde, somewhat unexpectedly, he finds Claire dressed for travel, flanked by the Marquise de Bellegarde and Urbain in rather formidable pose. Asked what is the matter, "I cannot marry you," she says quite simply; "I am ashamed. I am afraid of my mother." (She is going to Fleurières, the family château in western France near Poitier, she concludes, to be alone.) The hero is taken completely by surprise—but no more so than the reader (241–244).

As one reads along in this chapter, it becomes clear that something has gone wrong with the storytelling as well as with the story. The action is awkward, the characters strike postures, the dialogue is limp or theatrical. Urbain equivocates, the marquise is evasive. When the hero challenges her to be more specific, the only reasons she gives for making Claire break the engagement are unconvincing. "We really cannot reconcile ourselves to a commercial person," is her first point, quite inconsistent with their carefully weighed acceptance of him several months before. Then, somewhat more plausibly, she declares that the American's behavior at the ball, making her "parade" with him before "the eyes of the world," was what broke her down. Newman is baffled and outraged by what has been done to him—these emotions rather than the grief of a stricken lover (247–250). But though he feels there is some evil behind this sudden reversal of his fortunes and is determined to find the "key to the mystery," he seems unconvinced by the whole episode—as the reader is also.

The trouble goes far deeper than the fact that instead of a happy ending the novel has an unhappy one, the point complained of by Howells and defended by James in the quotation at the beginning of my chapter. Something is seriously wrong with the entire last third of *The American*. What has been a realistic comedy of manners turns into a romantic tragedy of manners. As plot takes over and the theme of international contrast recedes, the story mires down in melodrama—with villainy and dark secrets, sensational incidents, and violent emotional appeal—all the trappings of popular Victorian fiction. Each attempt James makes to retrieve gets him in deeper. In order to provide Newman with his "key" to the family mystery, for example, he invents the subplot: Valentin's affaire with Noémie—which results in his clash with another of her lovers, the challenge, the duel, and a fatal wounding. The author tries to make this liaison serve as a foil to the main plot by having the young Count say to the hero, "It's a striking contrast to your noble and virtuous attachment" (203), and by carefully synchronizing the two romances. (Valentin's occupies the chapters just before and after chapter eighteen, where Newman's collapses.) The subplot also serves a small purpose by providing two more examples of the separating walls of French custom, the *affaire* and the *duello*, that the American has difficulty penetrating the real meaning of. But since young Bellegarde on his deathbed furnishes the hint of "foul play" in the family's past, it seems clearly a romantic extravaganza to forward the plot: "At Fleurières. You can find out. Mrs. Bread knows. It will avenge you" (267–268).

The conclusion of the first subplot leads to the beginning of the second: Newman's rendezvous with Mrs. Bread in the village of Fleurières and her revelation of the family secret. There he learns that Claire's father had opposed the scheme to marry her off to the old Comte de Cintré; the violent family quarrel that resulted had broken his frail health; then his wife and son, to get him out of the way, had "murdered" him by withholding the medicine on which his life depended. This lurid story is spelled out in all its details, including the inevitable "incriminating document," the old man's deathbed note accusing the marquise and Urbain of killing him. It helps very little that James tried to "plant" a preparation for this piece of melodrama by having Newman say to Mrs. Tristram of the two elder Bellegardes, jokingly, much earlier in the novel: "I shouldn't wonder if she had murdered some one—all from a sense of duty, of course" and "If he has never committed murder, he has at least turned his back while someone else was committing it" (165–166). Fleurières itself—where Newman rattles the skeleton in the

[66]

closet under the noses of the elder Bellegardes and pleads with his fiancée not to retire to a convent, both in vain—seems like a "Gothic" château, a French version of Monte Bene, the ancestral house of Donatello in Hawthorne's *Marble Faun*. But surprisingly it had a real-life original.

An interesting sidelight on how the romantic and melodramatic came to color the setting for this episode can now be found in descriptions of two actual châteaux in the Île de France, just south of Paris, that were combined to furnish a model for Fleurières (which is located, in the novel, some two hundred miles to the west). In August 1876 James paid a visit to the Lee Childes at Varennes, a few miles from Montargis, "*au cœur de l'ancienne France,*" where he was entertained in baronial style. "The little chateau itself I wish you could see, with its rare and striking picturesqueness," he reported in a letter to his mother: "It stands on a little island in a charming little river [the Loiret] which makes a wide clear moat all around it, directly washes its base, and with its tower, its turret, its walls three feet thick (it's of the 15th century!) ... it is as pretty as a *décor d'opéra.*" The romantic tone here can be explained by the fact that Varennes was James's first experience of a château. And his excursions to several neighboring villages, with the châtelaine, immediately suggested literary parallels to the young American author: the peasants at one place were "as good as a chapter in *La Petite Fadette,*" a novel by George Sand; the old curé at another was "like a figure out of Balzac" (two favorite French fictionists whose works James had been rereading in recent months).

A more specific model for James's fictional château, which can now be certified by a newly published letter, was a second one that he visited nearby. "Don't imagine that in the description of the Fleurières in *The American* I have betrayed the Childes by reproducing Varennes," he reassured his family a few months later. "*Nullement.* It is another and much finer place in that country—Chateau-Renard." His comments on Renard have not come down, but a description by the historian Soulange-Bodin is strikingly like that in the novel. Of Fleurières James says that its "immense façade of dark-stained brick" was framed in "a mass of elms and beeches," an impressive pile dating "from the time of Henry IV" (1589–1610): "The building rose from an island in the circling stream, so that this formed a perfect moat. ... The dull brick walls, which here and there made a grand, straight sweep; ... the deep-set windows, the long, steep pinnacles of mossy slate, all mirrored themselves in the tranquil river" (270). Of Châteaurenard, reconstructed in 1609, the art historian says: "Le miroir d'eau, encadré de verdure, s'harmonise avec la construction où le jeu savant des briques et des pierres est coupé par les grandes fenêtres à petits carreaux, et sommé d'énormes toits d'ardoise à peintes raides."

Fictive Fleurières was thus a composite of two real châteaux, well known to the young American novelist but transformed by his romantic imagination into a perfect exemplum of the picturesque. In its melancholy disrepair and its gloomy interior, we are told, it looked to Newman like "a Chinese penitentiary" (echoing his earlier likening of the Hôtel de Bellegarde to "a convent"). This theatrical vision and the melodramatic episode that takes place at Fleurières in *The American* came from the author's immersion in popular French fiction and contemporary plays at the Comédie Française, as will be seen. But first, one more clue from the Île de France. During his stay with the Childes family, James may also have heard of Château Bellegarde, even if he did not visit it. The same historical authority cited above lists it in his *Châteaux Anciens de France, Connus et Inconnus*, as among those in the Department du Loiret—the neighborhood where James was visiting—adding that its name derived from its purchase in the eighteenth century by the Marquis de Bellegarde, later guillotined during the Revolution. Whether this information came to the novelist in time to provide him with the name for his aristocratic antagonists is not known, but at least it offers a remarkable coincidence! A month later, September 1876, James was back in Paris writing the concluding chapters of *The American*. That he did not discover the châteaux that inspired the "Gothic" setting for his lurid Fleurières sequence until so late in the game suggests that this part of the plot was being spun out by improvisation, another trait of the melodramatist.

Readers of *The American* do not need the services of an interpreter in following out its melodramatic plot to the end. They can take it at their own pace, entertained by it or not according to their tastes in fiction. The critic's only valid function in relation to the last third of this novel is to discover, if he can, what went wrong, why such a promising comedy of manners broke down into melodrama. The problem has engaged the attention of many commentators; but Henry James is the best, as well as the first, critic of his own novel. In his Preface, written some thirty years later, he offers a detailed discussion of the flaw in *The American*. The conclusion does not correspond to the way things happen in real life, he says: "The great house of Bellegarde ... would positively have jumped at my rich and easy American, and not have 'minded' in the least any drawback—... taking with alacrity everything he could give them, only asking for more and more, and then adjusting their pretensions and their pride to it."

Such a conclusion would have called for a different theme and a complete reworking of the plot. In preparing his fictions for the collected edition, 1907–1909, James simply excluded those that needed such drastic revision. When revising *The American* he did what he could to remedy its fault, but he was artist enough to confine himself to retouching the surface, using the "painter's sponge and varnish bottle" as he aptly described it. Though the changes made in this novel are more elaborate than those in any other except *Roderick Hudson*, they are mostly concerned with pointing up the contrast between the informal, even gauche, behavior of the American hero and the mannered life of the French aristocracy, between New World "innocence" and Old World "experience" in the moral realm. The aspects of Newman's character that were offensive to the Bellegardes are increased, while they, in turn, are made more intemperate and intolerant.

With these revisions the old master felt that his early novel deserved to be included in the New York Edition. But in the Preface he had more to say about the flaw in it, which prompted his famous distinction between romance and realism:

> By what art or mystery, what craft of selection, omission or commission, does a given picture of life appear to us to surround its theme, its figures and images, with the air of romance while another picture close beside it may affect us as steeping the whole matter in the element of reality? ... The balloon of experience is in fact of course tied to the earth, and under that necessity we swing, thanks to a rope of remarkable length, in the more or less commodious car of the imagination; but it is by the rope we know where we are, and from the moment that cable is cut we are at large and unrelated.... The art of the romancer is, "for the fun of it," insidiously to cut the cable, to cut it without our detecting him.

Further defining the *real* as those things "we cannot possibly *not* know, sooner or later," and the *romantic* as "the things that, with all the facilities in the world...we never *can* directly know," he indicates how all this relates to his own career as a novelist by saying that authors "of the largest responding imagination before the human scene" (naming Balzac and Zola) do not settle for one mode or the other but commit themselves in both directions.

Then James applies his definition to a specific consideration of *The American.*

> I had been plotting arch-romance without knowing it, [he confesses]. I had dug in my path, alas, a hole into which I was destined to fall. I was so possessed of my idea that Newman should be ill-used—which was the essence of my subject—that I attached too scant an importance to its fashion of coming about.... So where I part company with *terra-firma* is in making that projected, that performed outrage so much more showy, dramatically speaking, than sound.... I should have cut the cable without my reader's suspecting it.

[69]

This is the real clue to the novel's fault, as furnished by the Preface. James did not begin his novel with the conception of a character, his hero, but with an "idea" about him. The Preface makes it clear that the original *donnée*—which had come to him in America "some years before" he began composing his novel in Paris (autumn 1875)—had to do with "the theme of a 'story,'" of an American made to suffer at the hands of persons pretending to represent a civilization in every way superior to his own: "What would he '*do*' in that predicament?"

Writing to Howells on 3 February 1876, when his second novel was under way, James said: "The story is *The American*—the one I spoke to you about (but which, by the way, runs a little differently from your memory of it." This tantalizing fragment of a reference is the only external evidence we have—corroborating what is clearly evident in the text itself—that Christopher Newman's "story" (the plot) was originally thought of one way, then worked out "a little differently" in the process of composing. But there is considerable indirect evidence that the realistic observation of the American abroad and the comedy inherent in the international contrast were brought together by James from his long experience of Europe to illustrate the story he had had in mind for some years of a "betrayed and cruelly wronged compatriot," and that the plot took its unfortunate turn into "arch-romance" and melodrama during the Paris year, 1875–76, after the writing was under way. The former aspect of the novel, the comedy, has already been set forth fully in my tracing of Newman's evolution as the typical American in confrontation with a foreign culture. Now for the latter.

My diagnosis of how *The American* got turned aside from being a comedy of manners is that it was too "literary"; the young novelist was influenced too much by other writers. Early in this story when Valentin told Newman about Claire's forced marriage to the old Comte de Cintré and declared it was like "a chapter for a novel," my comment was that this brought to mind a writer such as George Sand, rather than the younger realists such as Flaubert. The relevance is even clearer when near the end of the story, after the whole fantastic plot has been unfolded, the hero declared: "it was like a page torn from a romance, with no context in his own experience" (319). James had read Sand with considerable interest since the beginning of his career. Now, in June 1876 when he was about half way through *The American*, came news of her death. This prompted him to write a memorial to her in one of his "Letters" to the New York *Tribune*, with a fairly full commentary on her fictional mode, based on a rereading of her novels. She was "a born romancer," he says, differentiating her at the outset from the realistic school. Most to the point is his account of her storytelling method: "She was an *impro-*

visatrice, raised to a very high power.... No novelist answers so well to the childish formula of 'making up as you go along.' "

These comments apply almost equally well to the freehanded inventiveness with which James spun out his own plot in the last third of *The American*. During the year in which his novel was published in book form, he published a critical essay surveying George Sand's whole career. There another matter is taken up, related to her improvising, the fact that many readers who enjoy her fictions still find themselves saying: "It is all very well, but I can't believe a word of it!" James then expands this pleasantry with some very pertinent comparisons:

> We believe Balzac, we believe Gustave Flaubert, we believe Dickens and Thackeray and Miss Austen. Dickens is far more incredible than George Sand, and yet he produces much more illusion. In spite of her plausibility, [she] always appears to be telling a fairy-tale.... During the last half of her career, her books went out of fashion among the new literary generation. "Realism" had been invented, or rather propagated; and in the light of "Madame Bovary" her own facile fictions began to be regarded as the work of a sort of superior Mrs. Radcliffe.

In this second essay, written less than twelve months later, James is clearly taking a sharper view of a former favorite. How account for the sudden change? The answer is that he was becoming one of the "new literary generation" himself.

Between 1875 and 1877 James had gone through the most remarkable period of growth in his life so far—the two years from his arrival in Paris (and beginning *The American*) to the publication of his long essay on George Sand. The period included not only his Paris year, when he came to know Flaubert's circle with some intimacy, but also his first English year, in which among other things he began to absorb into his own fictional mode the new French realism. This had some effect on Christopher Newman's story, though only a slight and indirect one. It was not until several years later that the influence of Flaubert and the other French realists—an influence always confined to techniques—had its full impact on the novel that marks the great turning point in his career, *The Portrait of a Lady* (1881). But Isabel Archer's story had already been conceived by the summer of 1877, when he was announcing that George Sand's books were being driven out of fashion by *Madame Bovary*. In a letter to his mother James wrote that when he found the time and serenity for composing his new novel, "it would be to *The American* 'as wine unto water.' " Looking back from this height, no wonder he saw the "facile fictions" of Mme Sand as the work of "a sort of superior

[71]

Mrs. Radcliffe." And maybe his own lurid inventions for the Fleurières chapters now seemed uncomfortably like a superior kind of *Mysteries of Udolfo*. But this is not to suggest that James found a specific source for his plot in the novels of either of these ladies—merely that *The American* was influenced in a general way by Sand's romantic mode of improvisation. The theme James began with (an American cruelly wronged by French aristocrats) called for writing an "arch-romance," but that was not a flaw in itself; the flaw was in working it out *à la* Sand to a conclusion that was more "showy" than "sound."

As for the plot, it is quite probable that James found his model at the Théâtre Français. If Valentin and Newman thought of the most melodramatic parts of the book as being like a romance, the author also plants enough clues to warrant treating the whole story as a stage play and the characters as actors. For example near the beginning, when the hero had only seen the outside of the Hôtel de Bellegarde but had heard sensational hints about the family from Mrs. Tristram, he said to her: "It is like something in a play;...that dark old house over there looks as if wicked things had been done in it, and might be done again" (76). At strategic points throughout, theater imagery reappears, usually with a shift from tragic implications to pleasant comedy. At the very end there is a reversion to the tragic when Newman confronts the old marquise with his knowledge of the family secret and she carries off her part like "a veteran actress."

For a devotee of the theater like Henry James these references cannot be accidental. He was not only an ardent playgoer but a voluble commentator on what he saw. During the Paris season of 1875–76 at least ten critiques on the French theater, its playwrights and actors, came from his pen. His passion for the "Parisian Stage" had begun three years before, as reported in an essay by that title written after a visit to the French capital in the fall of 1872: "To an ingenuous American the Théâtre Français may offer an aesthetic education,...a copious source of instruction as to French ideas, manners, and philosophy." Another sentence in this essay—"An acted play is a novel intensified; it realizes what the novel suggests"—when added to the above, seems prophetic of the way in which the theater came to influence *The American* several years later. The same uncritical enthusiasm marks James's next brief essay, with the same title, written in January 1876 near the beginning of his French year. A third general piece, written at the very end of this formative year, entitled "The Théâtre Français," pronounces it "an institution which...I passionately admire." This last is the longest of his early dramatic criticisms, and he thought well enough of it as a "literary" essay to include it in *French Poets and Novelists* (1878).

It is not surprising that such admiration for the French theater might result in an important influence on the impressionable young novelist. At the top of living dramatists he ranked Dumas fils. "He sprang straight from the lap of full-grown romanticism," James wrote in a memorial essay of 1896. Inheritor of the tradition of his father, of Hugo and Sand, the younger Dumas also dealt with the passions as illustrated in the complex relations between men and women but from a new point of view, that of the professional moralist. Because of his originality he was beyond imitation, James said, even in the theater world where "helping ourselves from our neighbor's plate" was the rule. Consequently, "We picked our morsels from the plates of smaller people." The playwright whose works may be put forward most convincingly as a model for *The American* is Émile Augier. A commentator on the whole shelf of his plays says that for the most part they follow a formula, which he calls the "Intrusion-Plot," and his summary seems strikingly pertinent: "Into a group [usually a family] there comes an intruder whose presence is resisted by one or more persons and accepted by one or more, with resulting conflict, until someone's eyes are opened to the true situation, to the danger, or to a possible solution. Different outcomes are possible, but the most frequent is the elimination of the intruder." Though this commentator apparently did not have James's novel in mind, his formula covers *The American*; further, the same source could have served for other aspects of its plot besides the intruder theme, since Augier's plays frequently involve a compromising scrap of paper, a duel, and violent evil—such as the "murder" of the old Marquis de Bellegarde.

James not only saw nine of Augier's plays, for the most part during his Paris year, but in the following year from London he wrote an essay for the New York *Nation* summing up his opinion of the author of "these masterly dramas." He placed Augier second only to the younger Dumas among French playwrights, saying that both are dedicated to social and even didactic, rather than simply entertaining, drama. Then, pertinently for the present thesis: "M. Émile Augier, on his social side, is preoccupied with the sanctity of the family, as they say in France; ... [for] thanks to a variety of causes, it is in terrible danger of falling apart ... [from] misplaced gallantry and the encroachments of mercenary wiles." At just about the same time, 1 May 1878, James wrote to his brother of his long cherished ambition to "astound the world" by writing plays himself: "My inspection of the French theatre will fructify. I have thoroughly mastered Dumas, Rugier, and Sardou"—melodramatists all. It was more than a decade before he actually began playwriting. Then, interestingly enough, his first venture was a dramatization of Christopher Newman's story, with the melodrama greatly enhanced and a happy ending substituted which pleased contemporary audiences, but not subsequent literary critics. When William James heard of the play's success he wrote, "Keep at it and become a Dumas *fils*." (But in the next few years Henry's high hopes as a playwright collapsed.)

"Walls which fatally divide"

George Sand and Émile Augier seem clearly the most important influences responsible for the shift to romance and melodrama in the last part of *The American*. But even if James had happily kept to his original mode, a comedy of manners, his theme of the international contrast might well have turned him to the French novel and drama for help in filling a large gap in his knowledge. Three of his travel essays of this period are retrospective of the problem and so are pertinent here. In the fall of 1877, a year after completing *The American* and settling permanently in England, James returned to "the most brilliant city in the world" for the purpose of looking at it again, this time with different eyes. Then he recorded his reactions in "Paris Revisited," written for an American magazine:

> It is hard to say exactly what is the profit of comparing one race with another, and weighing in opposed groups the manners and customs of neighboring countries.... There comes a time when one set of customs, wherever it may be found, grows to seem about as provincial as another. ... This is especially the case if we happen to be infected with the baleful spirit of the cosmopolite—that uncomfortable consequence of seeing many lands and feeling at home in none. To be a cosmopolite is not, I think, an ideal; an ideal should be to be a concentrated patriot.

James's irony here should not mislead the reader. When he says that the "ideal" is to be "a concentrated patriot" one must remember that this is the perfect phrase for Christopher Newman, whereas "the baleful spirit of the cosmopolite" is the necessary requisite of the novelist who, like himself, needs to see both sides so as to present the international contrast convincingly.

The second essay appeared just one year later, when James decided to enter a journalistic debate that had been going on in the New York *Nation*, with many repercussions in American "colonies" abroad. The question raised was whether his countrymen appeared to advantage, or otherwise, in Europe. The novelist's first point was that no European would ever concern himself with such a question in reverse. If an Englishman or a Frenchman were made aware that foreigners were criticising him, he would be quite indifferent about it: "He would comfortably assume that the standard of manners—the shaping influences—in his own country are the highest, and that if he is a gentleman according to these canons he may go his way in peace." Then comes the central passage in "Americans Abroad" that is highly relevant to all James's international fictions, though it has been overlooked by most previous commentators:

> Americans in Europe are outsiders: that is the great point, and the point thrown into relief by all zealous efforts to controvert it. As a people we are out of European society; the fact seems to us incontestable, be it regrettable or not. We are not only out of the European circle politically or geographically; we are out of it socially, and for excellent reasons. We are the only great people of the civilized world that is a pure democracy, and we are the only great people that is exclusively commercial.

The argument is very close to his thesis in *The American*. The final sentence of the essay is aimed directly at his hero, Christopher Newman, whether as indictment or defence: "On the whole, the American in Europe may be spoken of as a provincial who is terribly bent upon taking, in the fulness of ages, his revenge."

In the first of these essays James assumes the role of the cosmopolite, who understands two or more civilizations; in the second he classes himself with other Americans in Europe as one of the "outsiders," at least by implication. In the privacy of his *Notebooks* he gave this as a major reason why at the end of 1876 he chose London for his permanent residence. "I couldn't get out of the detestable *American* Paris," he moaned: "I saw, moreover, that I should be an eternal outsider." James's uncertainty—was he enough "inside" French society to risk drawing major fictional characters from its aristocracy?—may lie at the root of the trouble with *The American*. A final travel essay entitled "Italy Revisited," written in this same retrospective year (1877), has a comment that is equally applicable to France: "Our observation in any foreign land is extremely superficial, [but] our remarks are happily not addressed to the inhabitants themselves, who would be sure to exclaim upon the impudence of the fancy picture." Knowing that he was a complete outsider in Italy, the author of *Roderick Hudson* had limited his foreigners to a few minor characters.

How much more did James know of French life? To his brother he wrote by way of summing up his year in France: "A good deal of Boulevard and third-rate Americanism." And to his friend Howells: "Of pure Parisianism I see absolutely nothing." James's biographer spells this out. He had very stimulating literary relationships that meant much to him as an artist, but only glimpses of French society that could serve his needs for subject matter in *The American*.

[75]

James's most rewarding attachment in Paris, both personally and professionally, was with Ivan Turgenev, an expatriate like himself but one who had lived there much longer and was able to help him understand the French, in general ways at least. It was he who introduced the American to Flaubert, at whose *salon* he met the most interesting writers of the day. James had published a long appreciative essay on Turgenev shortly before coming to Paris, and as their intimacy deepened now he found the Russian's theory and practice of fiction more appealing than ever. Though Turgenev also cared much for questions of form, he was a valuable antidote to the French realists. With his large openness of mind he was free of their restricting esthetic formulas. Also he wrote stories that were "morally interesting"; he believed in the value of renunciation and often endowed his heroes with that virtue. These points James certainly had in mind when composing Christopher Newman's story. The Russian novelist was influential in many ways, but more on *The Portrait of a Lady* and *The Princess Casamassima* than on *The American*.

A specific service Turgenev rendered in connection with the earlier novel was introducing James to a young Russian compatriot, Paul Zhukovsky, with whom he struck up a warm and easy friendship. A genial dilettante, a good talker, and a lover of camaraderie, he may well have sat for the portrait of Count Valentin, as has been suggested. This would account for his being the one really convincing Bellegarde: as another "outsider" Zhukovsky would have been easier for the American to understand than a French aristocrat. The other friendly Bellegarde, Claire, called for no detailed delineation: she was simply an "ideal," a precious prize to be sought and lost.

It was Urbain and the old Marquise, the typical French aristocrats, who gave the American novelist real trouble. James's biographer has suggested that he learned most of what he knew about the Faubourg St. Germain from Balzac. This hint can now be confirmed in James's own words by quoting pertinent comments from his critical essay on the author of the *Comédie Humaine*, published in December 1875, at the beginning of his French year. It is a full-scale review of Balzac's achievement, prompted by a recent complete edition of his novels and tales, many of which James reread for the occasion. His familiarity with the *oeuvres* is manifest in the detailed references to illustrate his points, but his general commentary is most relevant here.

Balzac's ambitious program in the *Comédie Humaine* was to illustrate every phase of French life and manners during the first half of the nineteenth century, "a complete social system—an hierarchy of ranks and professions." But James wonders how, in view of the French novelist's plebeian origins, he gained his knowledge of aristocrats: "Did he go into society? did he observe

[76]

manners from a standpoint that commanded the field?" The critic then answers his own question:

> He began very early to write about countesses and duchesses; and even after he had become famous the manner in which he usually portrays the denizens of the Faubourg St. Germain obliges us to believe that the place they occupy in his books is larger than any they occupied in his experience. ...There is sufficient evidence...that he was more familiar with what went on in the streets than with what occurred in the *salons*.

How then did Balzac create convincing aristocratic characters? His knowledge may have been encyclopedic but his imaginative powers were equally impressive. "The things he invented were as real to him as the things he knew," James concludes. "This is certainly a proof of the immense sweep of his genius—of the incomparable vividness of his imagination."

For the American novelist, an "outsider" for different reasons, this was encouraging. Though his own observation of character and scene in the aristocratic *monde* of Paris was limited, his knowledge of Balzac aided by his own imagination might suffice. But there was one serious lack in what his French master could teach: "Balzac's figures, as a general thing, are better than the use he makes of them; his touch, so unerring in portraiture and description, often goes woefully astray in narrative, in the conduct of a tale. Of all the great novelists, he is the weakest in talk." For dialogue and action James had to turn elsewhere. The *Comédie Humaine* had to be supplemented by the Comédie Française. If the Bellegardes are melodramatic, at least they were modelled on characters in contemporary French plays and novels.

As long as *The American* sticks to the mode of a comedy of manners, its French aristocrats, for all their borrowed "literary" finery, function quite well in their traditional roles. When the plot turns to melodrama they are, at best, about as convincing as the stage villains of Augier and the romantic antagonists of George Sand; at their worst, they are an outsider's imitation of these conventions rather than an "imitation" of life, in the Aristotelian sense. Such were the risks James ran in working out his theme of international contrast by direct confrontation on a serious level. He never again went so far in trying to represent continental Europeans as major characters in his novels. After *The American* his European characters are usually confined to minor roles, and for major figures their places are taken by American expatriates who have become Gallicized or Italianate. In rare cases a European may function as a major character by being turned into a cosmopolite. With a culture nearer his own, that of England, the problem was easier; after long residence there, James learned to portray English characters as convincingly as Americans. But as late as 1899, when his last great period as a novelist was just beginning, he made a sweeping indictment of those fictionists who attempt the portrayal of foreign characters that is clearly meant to include himself: "There are multitudes of tales by English and American writers, which profess to deal with French and Italian life, yet probably not one of which . . . has any verisimilitude or value for Frenchmen or Italians."

The evidence is undeniable that several hands took part in the making of the conclusion to *The American*. This is not too surprising for a novelist who was extraordinarily well read in the literatures of several nations and who was still in the process of finding his own voice and his own distinctive mode. But only the five chapters of the Fleurières sequence were damaged by this literary borrowing. By the time the action has shifted from the gloomy château back to Paris James has regained some control of his story. The two scenes that bring the novel to a close are, by comparison, real and convincing.

The first of these is the final confrontation between Newman and the elder Bellegardes, his abortive attempt at revenge by threatening to make public the deathbed letter of the late Marquis accusing them of "murder." The setting is the formal Parc Monceau, with its clipped shrubbery and trim allées, now "full of the freshness of spring." But the marquise and Urbain deflect him from his purpose by their hauteur, especially the mother's superior style of brazen assurance, in one of the most effective bits of dialogue in the whole novel. There are theatrical touches here, but no melodrama. This is a scene in James's new experimental manner; not for the release of emotions or to advance the plot, but to present a final alignment of the major characters; it does not offer a revelation of new meanings but serves as the climax of what has previously been revealed, in the preliminary encounter at Château Fleurières. And its deeper significance is revealed symbolically. As the confrontation takes place, Urbain's little girl (Claire's beloved niece), in one of the allées nearby, "attended by the footman and the lap-dog, walked up and down as if she were taking a lesson in deportment"—the traditional discipline being passed on to the youngest generation (324, 326–331). The "Fine Castle" of the Bellegardes will continue to be defended against intruders by the wall of manners.

The final renunciation is presented by picture rather than by scene. When spring came round again, hearing that Claire had finally finished her novitiate and taken the veil, Newman came back to Paris—just two years after his first arrival there. He went straight across the city, over the Seine, and to the Carmelite convent where the woman he had yearned for was immured. It was located on the rue d'Enfer, the name echoing the hell he had been through for the past twelve months:

[78]

Newman found himself in a part of Paris which he little knew—a region of convents and prisons, of streets bordered by long dead walls and traversed by few wayfarers. At the intersection of two of these streets stood the house of the Carmelites—a dull, plain edifice, with a high-shouldered blank wall all round it. From without Newman could see its upper windows, its steep roof and its chimneys. But these things revealed no symptoms of human life; the place looked dumb, deaf, inanimate. The pale, dead, discolored wall stretched beneath it, far down the empty side street —a vista without a human figure. (356)

It is striking how similar this description is to his first impression of the Hôtel de Bellegarde ("it answered to Newman's conception of a convent"). The difference lies in the fact that the excluding barrier now functions absolutely on the actual level, and the symbolism of "walls which fatally divide us" is complete. Though there is no dialogue, Newman's unspoken soliloquy constitutes a debate between his two selves—the winner and the loser, the avenger and the renouncer—so that picture virtually becomes scene.

That night he burned his scrap of paper in Mrs. Tristram's fireplace. Then he went home again to the New World, presumably never to return to the Old—sadder but not really wiser and largely an unchanged Newman. His experience of Europe was over. Though it did not afford the hero any education, it does offer the reader entertainment and some understanding of the international contrast, of the walls that can separate the people of two different cultures.

The American is a remarkable novel, despite its flaw. Determined not to be caught up in the sentimental Victorian convention of a happy ending, James fell into another trap, the romantic "tragedy" of French melodrama. The problem of how to bring his novels to an end was resolved, from *The Portrait* on, by shifting the emphasis from outward plot to internal action. But to write this kind of drama-of-consciousness meant creating characters of greater psychological depth than those in his first two novels, characters that are "morally interesting" as he said of Turgenev's protagonists. Whatever the limitations of *The American* it marks a high point in the author's long apprenticeship and the promise of much finer things to come, especially in terms of those revolutionary techniques by which we recognize the genius of Henry James: using scene, image, and symbol to reveal character—a radical new relationship of person-place-and-thing.

Vistas Opening and Closing

THE PORTRAIT OF A LADY

Henry James's *Portrait of a Lady* enjoyed the advantage of being his first major novel. Two years previously he had summed up his admiration for Hawthorne's masterpiece by saying: "[*The Scarlet Letter*] has about it that charm, very hard to express, which we find in an artist's work the first time he has touched his highest mark—a sort of straightness and naturalness of execution, an unconsciousness of his public, a freshness of interest in his theme." Similarly, *The Portrait* has that spontaneity as well as confident strength which are possible only when an author first lets himself go, after holding back his full powers until he felt ready for a really "big" subject.

This was also James's first artistic triumph with a subject and a theme that had occupied him increasingly during his long apprenticeship: the American "innocent" involved in the international situation. In his late Preface he recalled of his early years in London that "the 'international' light lay, in those days, to my sense, thick and rich upon the scene"; and of *The Portrait* especially that this was "the light in which so much of the picture hung." Now in 1881, after many years abroad (the last six in continuous residence), he was able to record the observed reality of Europe with precision and to discriminate it from various American preconceptions. More important was his shift from the argument of a thesis to the creation of characters, the proper business of a novelist. By placing his emphasis on the "education" of Isabel Archer through her experience of Europe, he makes the cultural contrast merely a means to this end.

Such are the attractions of this novel in theme and subject matter. Previous commentary has been largely concerned with them. But *The Portrait* also marks James's first real break with the traditional novel and his pioneering of new techniques. It is with these problems of fictional art that the present chapter is concerned.

New Directions in Fiction

One of James's best known devices for discovering a new novelistic method is that of using a major character as the central consciousness through which all is seen and understood. In *The Portrait of a Lady* he does not use this new point of view in any strict sense, but he does achieve something of the same effect by "seeing" as much as possible through the heroine's viewing consciousness. Although the author-narrator often "goes outside" to supplement her limited understanding and point out what she does not see, the method in this novel can be described as a sort of middle stage between direct authorial presentation, such as George Eliot had used, and presentation entirely through one character's perceptions, the mode that transformed *The Ambassadors* into a marvel of dramatic structure.

Another new technique, however, is first fully developed in *The Portrait of a Lady*, and it functions with striking effect in this early masterpiece. This is the mode of using places and things to symbolize people, so that the fictional characters come to understand each other (or think they do) and are able to establish meaningful relations—the principal thesis of my book, as set forth in the introduction. This new method of reading symbols is described with great explicitness about one-third the way through *The Portrait*. The worldly Madame Merle, twice Isabel's age, has been lecturing the younger woman on the art of understanding people:

> "When you have lived as long as I you will see that every human being has his shell and that you must take the shell into account. By the shell I mean the whole envelope of circumstances.... What do you call one's self? It overflows into everything that belongs to us.... I have a great respect for *things*! One's self—for other people—is one's expression of one's self; and one's house, one's clothes, the books one reads, the company one keeps—these things are all expressive." (I, 259–260)

The heroine disagrees violently, declaring, "Nothing that belongs to me is any measure of me." But this is merely the protest of youth, whose self-esteem has been wounded. For more than two hundred pages people have been judging Isabel Archer by her "shell," the whole envelope of circumstances surrounding her. And she, who lacks a rational and analytical mind, has been understanding people chiefly by what she *sees*—places and things which she takes to be symbolic of those she has been forming relations with ever since her arrival in England.

The Portrait of a Lady is pervaded by a network of imagery—the objects that fascinate the heroine as possible keys to the meaning of Europe and its people, those used by her friends when characterizing one another in their conversations with Isabel, and occasional symbols offered unobtrusively by the author himself. For example her uncle, a successful American banker living in England, is pictured as an old man contentedly drinking his tea (that is, what life has brewed for him) from an "unusually large cup, of a different pattern from the rest of the set, and painted in brilliant colors." His wife, Mrs. Touchett, is described as a contemporary of the Medici who must have been present at the burning of Savonarola: "I can show you her portrait in a fresco of Ghirlandaio's." Madame Merle, Isabel's principal confidante, is compared to a rare and lovely piece of porcelain, but with a crack in it. Of her newspaper friend Miss Stackpole—sent over to Europe by the New York *Interviewer* to write a series of articles on the inside life of the aristocracy— Ralph Touchett saw at a glance: "From top to toe she carried not an ink-stain" (I, 2, 106, 249; II, 69). A large number of images are applied to the four men who center their lives on the heroine: Ralph Touchett, Lord War-burton, Gilbert Osmond, and Caspar Goodwood. The most elaborate series is inspired by Isabel herself, used by friends and suitors as they try to char-acterize what she means to them. All this richness is justified on the natural-istic level (and so is not mere ornament) by the fact that these characters are unusually sensitive to their milieu, especially the heroine.

The first to attempt an understanding of Isabel Archer through imagery was her cousin Ralph Touchett, relegated from the active role of suitor to the passive one of appreciator by his disabling invalidism. "A character like that," he said to himself, "is the finest thing in nature. It is finer than the finest work of art—than a Greek bas-relief, than a great Titian, than a Gothic Cathedral." The extravagance of these metaphors may mark his awareness of the irony of his own position, but they also suggest that he has found in the newcomer from America much to enjoy, to admire, and to wonder about. "Isabel's originality was that she gave one an impression of having intentions of her own," he mused. Then he asked himself a very special question: "She was intelligent and generous; it was a fine free nature; but what was she going to do with herself?" (I, 77, 78). He was not long in deciding that in addition to normal desires for love and marriage, she also wants an education. She has come over to observe Europe (or "Europe"?), to absorb the beauty and knowledge it has to offer: its art treasures, its storied past, its traditions, cities, and institutions, as well as its people and way of life—all chiefly under-stood through what she *sees*. Ralph's question "What was she going to *do* with herself?" suggests that here at least he is serving as the author's mouth-piece.

In his Preface to *The Portrait* the mature James says of his early master-piece: "The germ of my idea, I see, ... must have consisted not at all in any conceit of a 'plot,' nefarious name, ... but altogether in the sense of a single character, the character and aspect of a particular engaging young woman, to which all the usual elements of a 'subject,' certainly of a setting, were to need to be super-added." He then goes on to say that he learned this mode of creation from the lips of Turgenev, as the "usual origin of the fictive picture" in his own experience:

> It began for him almost always with the vision of some person or persons, who hovered before him, soliciting him.... He saw them ... vividly, but then had to find for them the right relations, those that would most bring them out; to imagine, to invent and select and piece together the situations most useful and favourable to the sense of the creatures themselves, the complications they would be most likely to produce and to feel.... "To arrive at these things is to arrive at my 'story,'" he said ... "—to show my people, to exhibit their relations with each other; for that is all my measure."

Returning to the problem of the inception of *The Portrait*, James recalls that in order to make a "subject" out of the "slim shade of an intelligent but presumptuous girl" affronting her destiny, it was necessary to organize an "ado" about her. He thought her out thoroughly as a complex figure and then woke up one morning to find himself in possession of the "situation," the people, and the "relations" in which she would have to be placed in order to bring out her potential: "It was as if they had simply, by an impulse of their own, floated into my ken, and all in response to my primary question: 'Well, what will she *do*?'"

One may wonder how James, writing his Preface in 1907, could remember so precisely what he had heard "fall years ago from the lips of Ivan Turgenieff" that so influenced his approach to fictional composition. But he had recorded the Russian novelist's words as long ago as 1883, in a memorial essay at the time of his death—a slightly different version of the statement above that is actually closer to the language James uses in his Preface for the origin of his own novel, *The Portrait*. It begins: "The germ of a story, with him, was never an affair of plot—it was the representation of certain persons,... being sure that such people must do something special and interesting." It ends: "The story all lay in the question, What shall I make them *do*?" A perfect parallel! The tribute, in this warmest of his critical essays, ends on a personal note. For "certain writers," clearly implying himself, "the manner in which Turgenieff worked will always seem most fruitful." The most important lesson James learned from him was this particular mode of creation, the one that is dominant in his novels from *The Portrait* on.

He was also a great admirer of Turgenev's heroines, as witnessed in an essay of 1874. James's description of Hélène, protagonist of what he considered the Russian's masterpiece (*On the Eve*), suggests that she supplied some of Isabel Archer's traits: "Hélène's loveliness is all in unswerving action...; a young girl of a will calmly ardent and intense,...[with] spontaneity and independence, quite akin to the English ideal of maidenly loveliness." A general commentary on his other heroines suggests what some critics feel to be another of Isabel's traits: "Russian young girls...have to our sense a touch of the faintly acrid perfume of the New England temperament—a hint of Puritan angularity." But that is all. The charge that James borrowed plot and characters from Turgenev is without substantiation. The influence was real, but it was confined to creative techniques and to his emphasis on human values—his "power to tell us the most about men and women," notably those lovely heroines who appealed so strongly to the author of *The Portrait of a Lady*.

The same is true of other supposed sources for *The Portrait* · Another novel, *Madame Bovary*, that was very much in James's mind at the time he was composing his own early masterpiece, is also concerned with an unhappy marriage, but it would be hard to imagine any story further removed from Isabel's. What drew James to Flaubert was not his subject or his theme, neither of which he found "morally interesting," nor the heroine of his greatest novel, who was "really too small an affair." What made Flaubert for all serious modern novelists the one who carried "the flag of the guild" was his complete dedication to art. In the first of three major essays, 1876, James praises him as the great continuator of Balzac, *Madame Bovary* as the "last word" in realism. Then he summarizes Flaubert's theory of fiction as exemplified in that novel:

> Human life, we imagine his saying, is before all things a spectacle, an occupation and entertainment for the eyes. What our eyes show us we are sure of....We will "render" things—anything, everything, from a chimney-pot to the shoulders of a duchess—as painters render them....We care only for what is—we know nothing about what ought to be. ...The accumulation of detail is so immense, [James comments] the vividness of portraiture of people, of places, of times and hours, is so poignant and convincing, that...the reader himself seems to have lived in it all, more than in any novel we can recall.

The influence of such a theory on the composition of *The Portrait of a Lady* needs no comment. A dozen years after that novel was published James calls attention, in his second essay (1893), to a more subtle aspect of Flaubert's art, modifying the earlier emphasis on realism. "Just as subjects were meant for style, so style was meant for images," he says of this French master: "Significance was measured by the amount of style and the quantity of metaphor thrown up....If you pushed far enough into language you found yourself in the embrace of thought." The finishing touch comes in the last essay, an introduction to a new translation by James of *Madame Bovary* (1902). The form is perfection itself, he declares of this novel, inseparable from the subject so that the story and the style are one, genuine and whole: "The work is a classic because the thing, such as it is, is ideally *done*." As a novelist who mediated between realism and symbolism, he was for James the artist who pointed the way to the modern mode.

Those aspects of Flaubert's theory most admired by him were, quite naturally, the ones that most influenced him as a practicing novelist. His eloquent praise of form and style in *Madame Bovary* can with equal justice be applied to *The Portrait of a Lady*; there could scarcely be a better description of the extraordinary development of James's fictional art in the four years following publication of *The American* (1877). Writing to his brother William in 1879, he said that all his writing to date had been merely a series of "experiments of form," the first stage of what he expected to be "a step-by-step evolution." *The Portrait* was a leap, rather than a step. Again, in the matter of style his advance in these years was swift and sure. True his search for the *mot juste* was never as passionate and persevering as Flaubert's, which he caught in a memorable image: "His life was that of a pearl diver, breathless in the thick element while he groped for the priceless word, and condemned to plunge and plunge again." But in the sharpness of his verbal wit and the suggestiveness of his poetic language James by 1880 (the date of Flaubert's death) had outstripped any novelist writing in English. In *The Portrait*, as truly as in *Madame Bovary*, "significance" can be measured by "the amount of style and metaphor thrown up." The lesson of Flaubert was of prime importance for the young American writer. Yet there was something seriously lacking in him and the other French realists—something hinted at in such prases as the one buried in eulogy above, that they care only for what *is* and "know nothing of what ought to be."

At first George Eliot seemed the one who could teach him how to fill this lack, a novelist whose characters were morally interesting and whose themes were deeply concerned with what ought to be. By the spring of 1876 James was searching for a corrective to the French realists by reading with considerable eagerness her recently published *Daniel Deronda*. His essay on this novel was a companion piece to the one on *Middlemarch* of three years before, as a matter of fact, so that this critical activity was not the result of a new discovery but the revival of an old admiration. James's deep and abiding interest in George Eliot was recorded in no less than eight reviews and essays over a period of two decades, 1866–1885—more criticism than he lavished on any other novelist. Though he covered her whole shelf of fiction, his most significant commentary is applied to her last two masterpieces, and these are the novels that have been singled out as major influences on *The Portrait of a Lady*.

A contemporary review in *Blackwood's Magazine* (March 1882) compared the marriage situation in James's new novel with that in *Daniel Deronda*; one in the *Century Magazine* (November 1882), by his staunchest American defender Howells, called attention to the close kinship of the two novelists, notably in the similarity of Isabel Archer to the heroine of *Middlemarch*. These claims of indebtedness have been echoed by a number of critics down to the present. There is certainly more general resemblance between James's novel and both of George Eliot's—in plot-situation and character-relations, less so in theme—than is true of any of the other reputed sources for *The Portrait*. But the differences quite outweigh the likenesses. Curiously enough, James's own commentaries on the stories of Dorothea Brooke and Gwendolen Harleth, though written before that of Isabel Archer was even conceived, make both the likenesses and differences clearer than any other commentator has succeeded in doing. This is not to suggest that he was clairvoyant, but simply that as a practising novelist he was alert to all fictional possibilities.

In his 1873 critique of *Middlemarch* James said of the heroine: "An ardent young girl was to have been the central figure, a young girl framed for a larger moral life than circumstance often affords, yearning for a motive for sustained spiritual effort and only wasting her ardor and soiling her wings against the meanness of opportunity." But this is followed by his caveat, the creative artist talking to himself: Dorothea was such a superb conception she deserved a weightier drama. Then there is the pertinent reference to Casaubon and the heroine's grievous alliance with him: "She marries enthusiastically a man whom she fancies a great thinker, and who turns out to be but an arid pedant. Here, indeed, is a disappointment with much of the dignity of tragedy." This also is followed by the critic's reservation: Dorothea's tragic situation "never expands to its full capacity."

In his next essay, "*Daniel Deronda*: A Conversation" (1876), James takes an equivocal stance by using the form of a debate among three allegorical figures, which may be taken as representing his own inner debate about the merits of George Eliot and of this novel in particular. "Theodora" (T) defends the English moralist, "Pulcheria" (P) attacks from the side of the French realists, "Constantius" (C) may be thought of as James in the role of mediator between the two schools of fiction. Of the heroine T says: "Gwendolen is a perfect picture of youthfulness—its eagerness, its presumption, its preoccupation with itself, its vanity and silliness, its sense of its own absoluteness. But she is extremely intelligent and clever, and therefore tragedy *can* have a hold on her." In the matter of characterization C agrees: "Gwendolen's whole history is vividly told.... It is so deep, so true, so complete, it holds such a wealth of psychological detail, it is more than masterly." But P objects, the author's need to moralize has interfered with her realism: "When [Gwendolen's marriage to Grandcourt] turned out ill she would have become still more hard and positive; to make her soft and appealing is very bad logic."

The relationship of these characterizations and marriage situations to those of Isabel and Osmond, both in their likenesses and differences, is clear enough. And there is sufficient evidence that James had these two novels and their author very much in mind during the gestation and composition of *The Portrait*. But it should be borne in mind also that James was writing on a well-known theme from life. Marriages are universal; they can be happy or unhappy, successful or tragic. The former are preferred by participants, to be sure, but the latter are more viable for writers of novels and plays, since the successful life has no "story" in it.

It is only when novels such as *Middlemarch, Daniel Deronda,* and *The Portrait of a Lady* are reduced to skeletal summaries that they seem alike; fleshed out to their full dimensions what loom are the differences. Once again James's own words have all the force and clarity that could be desired: "Each is a tale of matrimonial infelicity, but the conditions in each are so different and the circumstances so broadly opposed that the mind passes from one to the other with the supreme sense of the vastness and variety of human life, under aspects apparently similar, which it belongs only to the greatest novels to produce." James here is actually contrasting two marriage stories, of Dorothea and of Lydgate, both of which are in *Middlemarch*. But the same words can be applied to the relationship between his own novel and either *Middlemarch* or *Daniel Deronda*. At most one might say that *The Portrait*, in certain aspects of its central characters and situation, is a variation-on-a-theme by George Eliot. How little this affects the originality or merit of James's masterpiece can be illustrated by reference to a less complicated art form, that of the musical composition. Mozart, for example, quite frankly labelled one of his pieces "Variations on a Theme by Haydn." Such a composition provides the additional interest of letting us recognize echoes of one of his masters, but it is nonetheless a creation by Mozart. What holds our absorbed attention is the originality in both substance and techniques of the younger artist, who has become a master in his own right. The variations are what count.

The most interesting parts of James's essays on George Eliot relate to her techniques, or lack of them. Of *Middlemarch* he declares that it lacks a sense of design and construction, it is too discursive and contemplative, too expansive and panoramic. "It sets a limit, we think, to the development of the old-fashioned English novel," he says in conclusion: "If we write novels so, how

[87]

shall we write History?" The matter of her deficiencies is continued in the "debate" on *Daniel Deronda*. Constantius admits that the English novelist has an "admirable intellect," but with her tendency to philosophize "She has come near spoiling an artist." "She has quite spoiled one," Pulcheria replies: "She has no sense of form," and then proceeds to praise Flaubert and Turgenev instead. The rejoinder attempts to mediate: "Yes, I think there is little art in *Deronda*, but I think there is a vast amount of life. In life without art you can find your account; but art without life is a poor affair." This last statement by Constantius is close to James's own language in the Preface to *The Portrait*: To resolve the "inane dispute" over the "immoral" subject in fiction, he offered the axiom of "the perfect dependence of the 'moral' sense of a work of art on the amount of felt life concerned in producing it." But Pulcheria's preference for the French realists because of their "sense of form" can be attributed to James also.

This is the very point on which his final estimate of George Eliot turns. Reviewing a biography of her in 1885, he notes a statement in her journal, after reading *Père Goriot*, that she considered it "a hateful book." This reaction to Balzac calls forth a strong criticism: "It illuminates the author's general attitude with regard to the novel, which, for her, was not primarily a picture of life, capable of deriving a high value from its form, but a moralized fable.... It is striking that from the first her conception of the novelist's task is never in the least as the game of art." For a writer whose imagination was so rich there were surprising limitations to her artistic sense. Then with specific reference to *Deronda* and *Middlemarch* he declares that her characters and situations are "evolved from her moral consciousness" and are only indirectly the products of observation: "they are not *seen*, in the irresponsible plastic way." To clarify his point he concludes by citing a leading exponent of the opposite school, Daudet: "To *his* mind, the personal impression, the effort of direct observation, was the most precious source of information for the novelist.... [George Eliot] would have had no desire to pass for an impressionist."

James's affinity for the mode of Alphonse Daudet, cited here in an essay written four years after publication of *The Portrait*, finds its fullest expression in *The Ambassadors* at the end of his career. Yet it must have been apparent even in his early masterpiece since it was noted by W. D. Howells, who was only tangentially concerned with fictional techniques. In his review of *The Portrait*, he makes an initial comparison: "with George Eliot an ethical purpose is dominant, and with Mr. James an artistic purpose." Then he classes the latter with the new school, the realism of Daudet: "This school, which is so largely of the future as well as the present, finds its chief exemplar in Mr. James." All available evidence points to this period as a turning point

[88]

in James's career. But in 1880–81, during the gestation of *The Portrait*, his chief problem was how to achieve moral significance in his fiction without compromising his art. The choice between Eliot and the French realists brought it to a head.

The most striking new directions pioneered by *The Portrait of a Lady* are concerned with the use of symbol and scene. Both show a marked breaking away from traditional novelistic techniques. Using George Eliot again as a touchstone: though she employs a fair amount of imagery, it is largely provided by the narrator and so belongs to authorial commentary rather than to the scene. This is very different from the method of James, beginning with *The Portrait*. His characters, in their consciousnesses more than in their comments, convert directly into images the people-places-things that they see, and by sustained elaboration certain of these images become symbols. This elevation of the role of symbolism from a subordinate to a principal function is part of the process by which the realistic novel is transformed into what we think of as characteristic of the twentieth century from Joyce onward. So with scene, in which George Eliot follows the Victorian convention of using it to advance the plot or as a climax for releasing emotions, with an omniscient narrator to help convey the scene's significance. As for James, the revolutionary mode he had been experimenting with here and there in earlier novels becomes dominant in his first masterpiece. The scene is now used almost exclusively as a means of aligning the characters and defining their relationships, and its presentation is closer than ever to drama, depending more on dialogue and "stage directions," with the commenting author virtually absent.

The Portrait of a Lady goes even further in its experimental techniques. Many of its external scenes are analogues for internal states, such as Flaubert had used in *Madame Bovary*, depending on the suggestive power of style rather than on detailed correspondences. Others are really "pictures," taking place entirely in a character's consciousness, in which outward action and dialogue are replaced by an inner drama of images. By such means James gradually achieves the fusion of scene and symbol. The enlarged concept of picture-as-scene reaches its full development in the novels of his major phase, after 1900, but it is also used with great effect in *The Portrait*, notably in the climactic scene of Isabel's midnight vigil. A combination of the two methods of scenic presentation is made possible by the extended architectural imagery applied to five important houses: the family home back in America, her cousins' English country house, Lord Warburton's moated castle, Osmond's Tuscan villa, Isabel's Roman palace. In each setting there are scenes that exist simultaneously on the realistic level of the enacted drama and on the symbolic level as perceived in the heroine's consciousness. All these houses are described in great detail, and two of them undergo considerable change in the developing perspective through which she and the reader see them. They come to symbolize not only the people who live in them and the events that take place there but the several stages of Isabel's education, thus forming the thematic structure of the novel.

Narrative structure is another matter entirely. Whether the span of time to be covered in a fiction is long or short—the entire life of the protagonist, or the events of a single day—there is always a temporal problem for the novelist. He must decide which parts of his story to elaborate and which parts to skimp, or to skip altogether. That is, he must proportion the time scheme he has chosen to the space at his command. In *The Portrait* James limited himself to a six-year period in the life of his heroine and allowed himself the maximum spaciousness of the Victorian three-volume novel, but still he ran into trouble. As he warned himself in *The Notebooks*, during the process of composition, he had used up so much space in the earlier part (for elaborating Isabel Archer's initial experience of Europe) that he would have to foreshorten dramatically at the end. But in solving this strictly technical problem he created the climactic scene of the novel, Isabel's midnight vigil. Put in specific terms of proportioning, this means that almost two-thirds of the book (thirty-five chapters out of fifty-five) are given over to her European "education" during the first two years abroad. Then, skipping the first four years of her married life, the next few chapters take up the story with a series of incidents culminating in a recognition scene, which reveals the sinister relation between her husband and Madame Merle. This leads swiftly to the midnight vigil in chapter forty-two, three-fourths the way through the book, in which Isabel reviews the high hopes and tragic outcome of her life.

For the author this was a brilliant device for evoking in a symbolic vision the long years of Isabel's ordeal by marriage, instead of having to spell them out in discursive narrative. For the reader, who follows the heroine sympathetically in her exploration, it opens a door into the novel's full significance. And for the critic, faced with the impossible task of explicating a novel of nearly eight hundred pages, it offers a single compact chapter for close reading.

I have suggested previously that, beginning with *The Portrait of a Lady*, the characters in James's fictions arrive at meaningful relations only when they come to understand the objects—places or things—which they think of as symbolizing each other. It is in keeping with the basic techniques of this novel that now at last understanding comes to Isabel also through imagery, much of it being inversions of the same images she had failed to grasp the meaning of earlier. Remarkable as it may be for so much significance to be contained in one brief chapter, it is even more remarkable that the key revelation comes from a single image. This is achieved by an elaborate play on the ambivalent meaning of *vista*—from the Latin *videre*, "to see," the controlling word in the novel. At strategic points throughout the story of Isabel's education a *vista*, in the Italian sense of a panorama, has been used as symbolic of the opportunities her European experiences were spreading out before her for art and knowledge, for love and marriage. But in English the word *vista* is normally used in the very different sense of a long *allée* whose lines seem, by perspective, to converge on some object—happily on some object of beauty. Now in chapter forty-two, four years after marriage, the image is used in both opposed meanings simultaneously, with startling effect. As she takes stock of her life in this midnight meditation, aware at last of her husband's subtle villainy, she suddenly finds "the infinite vista of a multiplied life to be a dark, narrow alley, with a dead wall at the end"—no statue or fountain there to take the eye with beauty. To follow the transformations of this image throughout the novel is to discover much of its meaning.

Panoramas of Opportunity

The first European vista that opened up for Isabel Archer can be found at the beginning of chapter one. At Gardencourt, the fine old country house of her aunt and uncle, she literally walked onto the "high and lighted stage of Europe." The scene was at tea time on the lawn, as the "flood of summer light had begun to ebb." Since Isabel had just arrived from America she was still indoors. It was from this vantage point she got her initial glimpse of the park outside:

> Her uncle's house seemed a picture made real; no refinement of the agree-able was lost upon Isabel; the rich perfection of Gardencourt at once re-vealed a world and gratified a need. The large, low rooms, with brown ceilings and dusky corners, the deep embrasures and curious casements, the quiet light on dark, polished panels, the deep greenness outside, that seemed always peeping in, the sense of a well-ordered privacy, in the cen-tre of a "property"—these things were much to the taste of our young lady. (I, 66)

As she emerged, the doorway of Gardencourt framed the world that awaited her: guests assembled on the lawn for tea, great oaks making a shade like velvet curtains, tables and cushioned seats furnishing the place as if it were an outdoor living room. This was her first English vista: "Privacy here reigned supreme, and the wide carpet of turf that covered the level hill-top seemed but the extension of a luxurious interior" (I, 3). Later on she explored the grounds with her cousin Ralph all the way to their boundary at the river, "where the opposite shore seemed still a part of the foreground of the land-scape" (I, 78). But on this first afternoon it was the figures in the middle distance that caught her eye, especially the handsome Lord Warburton, booted and spurred, who had just ridden over from his neighboring estate. "Oh, I hoped there would be a lord," Isabel exclaimed characteristically as her cousin led her forward to be introduced: "It's just like a novel!" (I, 17).

Looking back from the lawn, after tea, Isabel's wondering gaze took in the whole impressive vision of the Touchetts' stately home:

> It stood upon a low hill, above the river—the river being the Thames, at some forty miles from London. A long gabled front of red brick ... presented itself to the lawn with its patches of ivy, its clustered chimneys, its windows smothered in creepers. The house had a name and a history; ... it had been built under Edward the Sixth, had offered a night's hospitality to the great Elizabeth; ... had been a good deal bruised and defaced in Cromwell's wars, and then, under the Restoration, repaired and much enlarged; finally, after having been remodelled and disfigured in the eighteenth century, it had passed into the careful keeping of a shrewd American banker. (I, 2, 3)

Old Mr. Touchett was only too happy to call his niece's attention to all the picturesque points of his early Tudor house "at just the hour when the shadows of its various protuberances—which fell so softly upon the warm, weary brickwork—were of the right measure." Beauty and history, exactly what Isabel's preconceptions of Europe had led her to expect. As she furthered her education by pressing questions on her uncle—about England, the national character, the manners and customs of the aristocracy—she always asked "whether they corresponded with the descriptions in the books" (I, 68). (Novels, histories, illustrated books—the traditional travel-guides for Americans in Europe!) On later occasions Isabel pursued the English vista far beyond Gardencourt, driving with her cousin Ralph over the surrounding country "through winding lanes and byways full of the rural incidents she had confidently expected to find; past cottages thatched and timbered, past ale-houses latticed and sanded, past patches of ancient common and glimpses of empty parks, between hedgerows made thick by midsummer" (I, 79). So the picture book of England, as American visitors preconceive it, was turned page by page before her eyes.

Did James have a real-life model for fictional Gardencourt and its owners? His biographer identifies an elderly friend, the retired American banker Russell Sturgis, as "a type of expatriate he incorporated in the Touchetts." In the summer of 1880, while working on *The Portrait*, James was visiting him at Grove Farm, Leatherhead, and wrote from there on 26 July to a young friend back home: "I wish you might have a glimpse of the peculiar loveliness of this place, which is in the midst of the sweetest scenery of one of the sweetest parts of England—the charming, richly rural, yet most convenient-to-London Surrey." So much for the setting, but he does not describe the country home other than to call it "This supremely luxurious house." Sturgis's son Julian has left an account of their family life from about 1860 to 1882, the year his father retired from Baring Brothers, London, but he says their home was "Mount Felix" at Walton-on-Thames. (This was an eighteenth-century country house about fifteen miles from Leatherhead, Italianized in Victorian times, and demolished in 1967.) There are a few descriptive phrases that seem pertinent: "Our house at Walton was large, and it never pleased my father so well as when it was full of relations and friends.... The group beneath the trees, where, as the shadows on the shaven green grew long, the tea-table was brought,... the tranquil beauty of the great lawn, which stretched away so velvet-smooth behind the house, and the sweet influence of the passing Thames." That is all. A few tantalizing phrases and no reference to Henry James, though a dozen American and English literary friends are mentioned among the guests. And did the Sturgises have two country homes, the fictional one of the Touchetts being a composite of these with ingredients added from others? Such was often the starting point for James's compositional process, but the finished creations always transcended their factual origins.

What Isabel saw at Gardencourt was just the opposite of what she had left behind. By contrast the American landscape seemed bare of the picturesque, without history or art to relieve its monotony. The Archer home in Albany was particularly bleak, as pictured in a flashback (chapter 3) to that cold rainy afternoon in spring when Mrs. Touchett had arrived and found her niece reading a dull book in a shabbily furnished room behind a permanently bolted front door: "[Isabel] knew that this silent, motionless portal opened into the street; if the sidelights had not been filled with green paper, she might have looked out upon the little brown stoop and the well-worn brick pavement. But she had no wish to look out" (I, 27). (Several other details in the description—but not the ones given above—indicate that this is a diminished picture of James's grandmother's house in Albany, seen as provincial and bleak in the perspective of a dozen years living abroad—similar enough to suggest a kinship between author and heroine.) Life in America seemed to offer her little more prospect than was afforded by this house; marriage to her fellow countryman Caspar Goodwood, most persistent of her suitors, would have meant only a more expensive version of the same bareness. It was to rescue Isabel from this that her aunt (Lydia *Touchett*) tapped her with a magic wand and brought her to Europe, where the opportunities were infinitely richer.

In a figurative sense this is the story of Isabel's leaving an American house for a European one, one way of life for another. But the first possibility offered by England failed to materialize for her, though not through any fault of its own. Within weeks of her arrival the dashing Lord Warburton proposed marriage, but she turned him down. Knowing her devotion to "romantic effects" he had invited her to lunch at Lockleigh, his family's "curious old place," as he referred to it:

> As they saw it from the gardens, a stout, grey pile, of the softest, deepest, most weather-fretted hue, rising from a broad, still moat, it seemed to Isabel a castle in a fairy-tale.... the watery sunshine rested on the walls in blurred and desultory gleams, washing them, as it were, in places tenderly chosen, where the ache of antiquity was keenest. (I, 97–98)

On a return visit to Gardencourt, shortly afterwards, Lord Warburton made his proposal. He had everything to offer: wealth, position, and power in fabulous degree; extraordinary good looks and a character that even the cynical Ralph pronounced faultless. What prompted a presumptuous American girl to reject such a veritable Prince Charming?

The ambivalence of Isabel's response to this offer is symbolic of her own paradoxical nature: romantic, yet calculating and even a bit cold; idealistic, yet detached and self-engrossed. "What she felt was that a territorial, a political, a social magnate had conceived the design of drawing her into the system in which he rather invidiously lived and moved. A certain instinct told her to resist—... she had a system and an orbit of her own" (I, 130–131). Yet she had been told by her uncle that Warburton was "a nobleman of the newest pattern, a reformer, a radical, a contemner of ancient ways," and she had chided him for not taking the stance proper for a member of the House of Lords (I, 86). As for the medieval family seat of this scion of the landed aristocracy, when he offered her the choice of several other houses in case she thought Lockleigh too old and damp—"some people don't like a moat, you know"—Isabel replied with fine irrelevance, "I delight in a moat." Perhaps it was not as a political or territorial magnate but as a social one that Lord Warburton seemed a threat to her freedom; to be the wife of the greatest nobleman in the county "failed to correspond to any vision of happiness that she had hitherto entertained" (I, 140, 141). The full tragic irony of this does not come out until the end, when the husband of her choice, Gilbert Osmond, imprisons her in a house of darkness.

Warburton is the only person in this novel continuously associated with light, with what is easy and natural rather than formal. All the imagery applied to him is drawn from nature. On the occasion when he offered his hand and title to Isabel, in the lovely green park at Gardencourt, it seemed to her

that a "radiance surrounded him like a zone of fine June weather"—though
it was a day in late autumn. (June is the month of bridegrooms as well as
brides; a year and a half later June was the month of marriage for Isabel—to
Osmond.) When Warburton spoke to her of marriage, "These words were
uttered with a tender eagerness,... like the fragrance of she knew not what
strange gardens" (I, 129, 138). Yet Isabel failed to respond to this rare trait,
so in harmony with her own temperament:

> Her nature had, for her own imagination, a certain garden-like quality,
> a suggestion of perfume and murmuring boughs, of shady bowers and
> lengthening vistas, which made her feel that... a visit to the recesses of
> one's mind was harmless when one returned from it with a lapful of
> roses. But she was often reminded that there were other gardens in the
> world than those of her virginal soul. (I, 65)

One, of course, was the actual garden she was in at the time of these musings,
which was not only an extension of Gardencourt but the setting for more
action than the house itself was, at least until the end of the novel. It provides
an external vista corresponding to the internal one mentioned above. And
in view of Isabel's Eve-like innocence, it suggests a kind of twilight Eden.

That James had the Miltonic archetype in mind seems evident from his
echoing the language of *Paradise Lost* when describing Isabel as she sets out
on her adventures: "The world lay before her—she could do whatever she
chose" (II, 151). These were the words applied to Eve on leaving Eden. So
with Isabel, who had concluded her musings: "[There were] a great many
places which were not gardens at all—only dusky, pestiferous tracts, planted
thick with ugliness and misery." This clearly looks forward to her fall, which
occurred not at Gardencourt but in her dark Roman palace several years later.
The piercing memory of it is fixed in one of images for her satanic husband
Osmond, during the midnight vigil: "Under all his culture, his cleverness,
his amenity, under his good-nature, his facility, his knowledge of life, his
egotism lay hidden like a serpent in a bank of flowers" (III, 38). She had
turned away from the radiant Lord only to fall under the spell of the Prince
of Darkness.

On the more practical level, Warburton's proposal was rejected because it
came too soon and because it was too much like a romance to be acceptable
as reality. It will be remembered that when Ralph first led Isabel across the
lawn at Gardencourt to present her to Warburton she had exclaimed: "Oh,
I hoped there would be a lord; it's just like a novel!" Some weeks later when
he proposed, in this same garden, he invoked the language of a true romantic
hero in recalling their first meeting: "I fell in love with you then. It was at
first sight, as the novels say" (I, 133). James was well aware that one of the

popular themes in current fiction was the international marriage: the American heiress seeking a titled husband, the European nobleman seeking a fortune. He had been one of the first to make use of the theme, though he always gave it a new turn. In *The Portrait*, where he only flirts with it, he has the wealthy English lord proposing when the American girl is still virtually penniless. Even so, James did not want his novel to seem like a novel. By having his heroine decline Warburton's offer he opened up the prospect of more subtly interesting adventures than those afforded by conventional romance. Further, acceptance of his offer might have brought Isabel's European experience to an end just as it was beginning. This was what she had in mind when she replied to Ralph's inquiry as to her motives: "I don't wish to marry until I have seen Europe!" (I, 193). She was determined to see the broader vistas promised by the Continent before considering her education complete.

Meanwhile, Isabel's cousin had arranged for a large part of the Touchett fortune to be settled on her. Ralph's elderly father had died in early December and the son, disabled from an active role, took his pleasure as an appreciator in watching her "soar," as he put it. (Isabel *Archer*—the name conjures up the archetypal archer, Diana, the virginal goddess of the chase.) Her first flight was across France to Italy, where the next great panorama was to open out for her. (chap. 21) Pausing just over the border at San Remo, "on the edge of this larger adventure," she looked with yearning eyes along the eastward curve of the Italian Riviera: "The charm of the Mediterranean coast only deepened for our heroine on acquaintance, for it was the threshold of Italy—the gate of admirations. Italy, as yet imperfectly seen and felt, stretched before her as a land of promise, a land in which a love of the beautiful might be comforted by endless knowledge" (II, 23).

This generalized prospect came to focus almost immediately in the view from Gilbert Osmond's villa on the outskirts of Florence, as elaborated in the next five chapters. The meanings of the two vistas for Isabel are given in identical terms, but the preliminary description of the latter differs in a curiously interesting detail. As one wound up the narrow road to the top of Bellosguardo and approached Osmond's villa from its little grassy piazza, its imposing front had a somewhat incommunicative character. "It was the mask of the house; it was not its face. It had heavy lids, but no eyes; the house in reality looked another way—looked off behind, into splendid openness and the range of the afternoon light" (II, 27). When Isabel is taken there by Madame Merle, to meet her future husband, she walks straight through this façade (the blank-looking brown wall with its small doorway) to the terrace at the rear with its expansive view of Tuscan hills and valleys. The sequence here is exactly the reverse of the key image used in her midnight vigil: "she had suddenly found the infinite vista of a multiplied life to be a dark, narrow alley, with a dead wall at the end" (III, 32).

Once inside, Isabel discovered that Osmond's villa was a kind of miniature museum of the art and history of Italy—presumably a symbol of its owner, who had devoted his life to high connoisseurship. As he showed her through the numerous apartments filled with his treasures, she felt almost "oppressed at last with the accumulation of beauty and knowledge to which she found herself introduced" (II, 74). But this had been her avowed purpose in coming to Italy, to pursue her education in such matters. And when she was led to the terrace at the rear, where his twelve-year-old daughter was making tea, the panorama opened out to her eyes there complemented what she had seen inside:

> The sun had got low, the golden light took a deeper tone, and on the mountains and the plain that stretched beneath them the masses of purple shadow seemed to glow.... The scene had an extraordinary charm. The air was almost solemnly still, and the large expanse of the landscape, with its gardenlike culture and nobleness of outline, its teeming valley and delicately-fretted hills, its peculiarly human-looking touches of habitation, lay there in splendid harmony and classic grace. (II, 75)

As Isabel returned to Florence at the end of the day, landscape and villa, owner and his convent-bred *jeune fille*, tended to fuse into one picture:

> She had carried away an image from her visit to his hill-top ... : the image of a quiet, clever, sensitive, distinguished man, strolling on a moss-grown terrace above the sweet Val d'Arno and holding by the hand a little girl whose sympathetic docility gave a new aspect to childhood. The picture was not brilliant, but she liked its lowness of tone, and the atmosphere of summer twilight that pervaded it. It seemed to tell a story ... of a lonely, studious life in a lovely land; ... of a care for beauty and perfection so natural and so cultivated together, that it had been the main occupation of a lifetime. (II, 92)

This romantic vista was evoked by James from a real one he had long been familiar with, now touched by the artist's brush. During a stay of some weeks in Florence, October 1877, he had made daily visits to Villa Castellani on Bellosguardo, where his old friend Frank Boott, an expatriated American, lived with his young daughter. The charm of the situation and of the uniquely civilized pair who lived in this "villa on a hill-top" overlooking the Arno is recorded in a travel sketch James wrote at the time, though he was too discrete to name either the place or the people:

What a tranquil, contented life it seemed, with exquisite beauty as a part of its daily texture!—the sunny terrace, with its tangled *podere* beneath it; ... and beyond the most beautiful of views, changing color, shifting shadows, and through all its changes remaining grandly familiar. Within the villa was a great love of art ..., so that if human life there seemed very tranquil, the tranquility meant simply contentment and devoted occupation. A beautiful occupation in that beautiful position, what could possibly be better? ... When, however, the people who live [such a life] move as figures in an ancient, noble landscape, and their walks and contemplations are like a turning of the leaves of history, we seem to be witnessing an admirable case of virtue made easy; meaning here by virtue ... the love of privacy and of study.

The essay was probably before him as he wrote the account in his novel, but he also refreshed his vision of Villa Castellani by calling on the Bootts in March 1880 as he settled down at last, in Florence again, to the actual composition of *The Portrait*.

The poetic skills James had been developing in the last two or three years are manifest in his transformation from the conventional language of the travel sketch to the evocative phrasing that describes Isabel's visit to Osmond's hilltop. Other changes were made to fit the intricate patterns of imagery in the novel. For example, the blank wall of the façade through which the heroine walked to the terrace at the rear with its splendid vista is entirely absent from the original description. Again, the shift of time-setting from a bright sunny morning in early October to a waning afternoon in late spring makes this episode part of a subtle sequence of light-dark images that pervade the book.

However transformed, Villa Castellani served as the model from which Osmond's villa was drawn, both house and setting. But James's autobiography, where the identification is explicit, makes an important distinction. Though the general situation and relationship of Frank and Lizzie Boott, he admits, were part of "the vision of things" that triggered the novelist's imagination— "a lonely and bereft American, addicted to the arts and endowed for them, housed ... in a massive old Tuscan residence with a treasured and tended little daughter by his side"—they were in no sense models for his fictional pair. Lizzie was a grown young lady, though she retained some of the *jeune fille* traits that accounted for the whole personality of twelve-year-old Pansy Osmond. More significant is James's express statement that Frank Boott "had no single note of character or temper ... in common with my Gilbert Osmond." This is germane to the whole question of "putting people into books, ... the relation of 'people' to art," James goes on to say; the Bootts-picture had to have "its connections above ground successively cut" and to become something "thoroughly other" before it could be made into the Osmond-picture.

It seems clear that Gilbert Osmond, the most complex and the most interesting character in *The Portrait of a Lady*, was a product of the creative imagination. The critic, moreover, is less concerned with his possible antecedents than with his paradoxical and provocative presence. What makes him interesting is the basic ambiguity of his character and the subtlety with which he disguises his true nature. There are two conflicting views of him: the limited and idealistic one that Isabel clings to in spite of the evidence before her, the broader and more realistic one that James offers to the reader by going outside her range of vision and seeing him through other eyes. As the story proceeds these two views tend to become superimposed, finally revealing Gilbert Osmond in three-dimensional perspective as he really is—or at any rate as he appears to be for heroine and reader in the end. Since he is a consummate poseur, he is a constant subject for analysis by the others who are trying to find the man behind the mask.

Much discussion revolves around the question of his being an expatriate and a dilettante, both attributes having more than one meaning. In one of her earliest talks with Isabel, Madame Merle herself warned of the dangers of living abroad: "If we are not good Americans we are certainly poor Europeans; we have no natural place here. We are mere parasites." So, even of the clever friend Gilbert Osmond, whom she wanted Isabel to meet ("a man made to be distinguished"), one could hardly say more than of Ralph Touchett, he's "an American who lives in Europe" (I, 280). Osmond likewise admits as much to Isabel on one of their first meetings: "I sometimes think we have got into a rather bad way, living off here among things and people not our own, without responsibilities or attachments, forming artificial tastes" (II, 71). But of course most of the Americans in this novel are expatriates—the whole Touchett family, Merle and Osmond, the author himself and his heroine—all but Henrietta Stackpole and Caspar Goodwood, the comic and pathetic minor characters. In James's fictions Europe is where all good Americans go to live, more or less permanently, for the sake of culture, in spite of the dangers of uprooting.

Madame Merle had also much to say on the favorable side when recommending Osmond to Isabel: one should not attempt to live in Italy, she urged, without becoming a friend of the man who knew more about that country than almost any one (II, 51). Indeed when they met at his villa on Bellosguardo he talked much about Florence, about Italy, and the advantages of living in a country which contained "the greatest sum of beauty." But he added that Italy tended to spoil many people because it had no discipline for the character: "It made people idle and dilettantish and second-rate" (II, 68). This self-depreciation was part of Osmond's calculated manner, and its effect on Isabel was just what he wanted. She took it as a sign of charming modesty in a man so distinguished for his knowledge of art and history: "Ralph had something of this same quality, this appearance of thinking that life was a matter of connoisseurship; but in Ralph it was an anomaly, a kind of humorous excrescence, whereas in Mr. Osmond it was the keynote, and everything was in harmony with it" (II, 73). Such was the view of him she took away from her first visit to his Tuscan villa. But there is a significant ambiguity here. A *dilettante* originally meant one who "delights in the fine arts," similar to an *amateur* or "lover," but in the nineteenth century it had acquired the same kind of ambivalence, signifying a lack of professional discipline. Even if Osmond was a *connoisseur*, he was only interested in art as a pastime or for some other purpose ulterior to serious study. It was when Isabel announced her intention of marrying him that Ralph added the clarifying adjective, calling him "a sterile dilettante" (II, 182).

More revealing than this commentary, all of which took place in Isabel's presence, are the images applied to Osmond. One of them comes early in the story, before her acceptance of his proposal, on the occasion of his initial call at Mrs. Touchett's Florentine palace. As the heroine sat somewhat apart, listening to him while he talked with Madame Merle, she made a mental note: "His talk was like the tinkling of glass, and if she had put out her finger she might have changed the pitch and spoiled the concert" (II, 54–55). The second image comes at the end of the novel, where Osmond is likened to the antique coin he is making a watercolor copy of (III, 171). It is notable that both these images (and others in between) are drawn from artifacts, whereas those applied to Warburton are always drawn from nature. It is ironical that Osmond had sounded what should have been a warning for Isabel when classing himself with the dilettantish expatriates who tended to form "artificial tastes." She had actually thought in similar terms of Madame Merle: "If for Isabel she had a fault it was that she was not natural" (I, 247). But these portents failed to alert the innocent heroine to any potential inhumanity in her new friends. She had had no experience that would lead her to suspect that such a polished surface masked the exploiter. And the sophisticated Osmond kept entirely to himself his conception of Isabel as the splendid new item he would add to his collection.

What goes on entirely behind Isabel's back is the plan conceived by Madame Merle for her former lover to carry out, but the reader is privy to it from the start, of course. When old Mr. Touchett agreed to leave a part of his fortune to the young American niece, he had warned his son that she "may fall a victim to the fortune-hunters." Ralph admitted that this was a risk, but one he was prepared to take (I, 240). When Merle heard from Mrs. Touchett about the legacy, her casually mentioned plan of introducing Isabel to an old friend in Italy was transformed in her own mind into a sinister scheme of exploitation. On arriving at Florence early in May, she went at once to Osmond's villa. This momentous visit is recounted in a long chapter, from which Isabel is conspicuously absent. In response to Merle's opening gambit, that she had a charming American friend she wanted to introduce to him, Osmond pleaded his boredom with people, with society in general. When she urged that he might at least show her his art treasures—"As a cicerone in your own museum you appear to particular advantage"—he pleaded his indolence, and asked why he should make a special effort for this unknown young lady. "I want you of course to marry her," was the prompt reply. The nature of Osmond's possible interest in Isabel is put in straightforward terms: "Is she beautiful, clever, rich, splendid, universally intelligent and unprecedentedly virtuous?" Merle's answer underscores the real point: "She fills all your requirements, quite literally, . . . and she has a handsome fortune" (II, 44–49).

This is in striking contrast to what Osmond had to offer as a suitor for Isabel's hand according to her aunt, who took a "political view" of matrimony: "An obscure American dilettante, a middle-aged widower with an overgrown daughter and an ambiguous income, this answered to nothing in Mrs. Touchett's conception of success," especially for a girl who had refused an English peer. "I trust she won't have the folly to listen to him," she said to her son. Ralph took a more relaxed view of the danger, saying that his young cousin would certainly not yield to the present "besieger," and that he looked forward to a third, a fourth, a tenth: "She would keep the gate ajar and open a parley." To this his mother replied impatiently: "You use too many metaphors; I could never understand allegories" (II, 88–89).

So much behind Isabel's back. To her face Ralph was much more enigmatic. After several riddling guesses about the real "identity" of Gilbert Osmond he concluded: "For all I do know he may be a prince in disguise" (II, 56). Why in disguise? and what kind of prince? Perhaps the author gives his reader a clue to this "allegory," out of earshot for his heroine, in the first detailed portrait of Osmond. He had a "thin, delicate, sharply-cut face" whose only fault was that "it looked too pointed; an appearance to which the shape of his beard contributed not a little, . . . a beard, cut in the manner of the portraits of the sixteenth century"—that is, the pointed ones later made famous by Vandyke—"surmounted by a fair moustache, of which the ends had a picturesque upward flourish"; and to complete the picture a "luminous intelligent eye, an eye which expressed both softness and keenness." In sum, he had "a foreign, traditional look" suggesting that he was "a gentleman who studied effect" (II, 30). A more worldly observer than Isabel would easily have recognized the Prince of Darkness, this time in his metamorphosis as a man instead of his traditionary guise as the "serpent in a bank of flowers." But she had been completely taken in by the performance Osmond had "staged" at his hilltop villa on the occasion of her visit, the first move in his cunning suit for her hand and fortune. He would have been gratified to know how perfectly he had achieved his "studied effect." But he was a long time finding out his success, because she was determined to continue her education before making any decision about marriage.

Images of Light

To observe the great capitals of Europe and absorb the art and history they had to offer was an important part of Isabel's plan. Her brief weeks in London had served as a prologue; her winter in Paris had introduced her to the opportunities open to the American living abroad; but it was Italy that revealed a whole new world. In Florence, with Ralph as her guide,

> She went to the galleries and palaces; she looked at the pictures and statues...; she felt her heart beat in the presence of immortal genius. ...At first [her aunt's palace] had struck her as a sort of prison; but very soon its prison-like quality became a merit.... The spirit of the past was shut up there.... Isabel found that to live in such a place might be a source of happiness. (II, 52–53)

Then near the end of May her cousin offered to be her cicerone on a sightseeing trip to Rome; and Osmond, whose courtship was reaching a climax, expressed a desire to join her there. In the Eternal City Isabel's education in history and art moves onto the postgraduate level. Her first reactions seem on the surface like those of the traditional pilgrim, derived as they were from visits to two standard tourist spots, the Forum and Saint Peter's. But a closer reading shows them to be very personal, even prophetic. The ambivalence of her perceptions is echoed in the light-dark imagery that pervades both scenes.

It was a foregone conclusion that Isabel would become a "Rome-lover," and this is borne out in the opening paragraph of the chapter devoted to that episode:

> She had always been fond of history, and here was history in the stones of the street and the atoms of the sunshine.... The sense of the mighty human past was heavy upon her, but...she went about in a kind of repressed ecstasy of contemplation, seeing often in the things she looked at a great deal more than was there, and yet not seeing many of the items enumerated in "Murray." (II, 104–105)

As a foil for the sentimental pilgrim James offers the brashness of Isabel's American newspaper friend, for whom the past, in spite of all the richness of its art and history, merely symbolized a despised feudalism. As for the Forum, "Henrietta Stackpole was struck with the fact that ancient Rome had been paved a good deal like New York" (II, 105). The past is redeemable for her only if it can be related to the present. For Isabel, on the other hand, the past produced an "ecstasy of contemplation," as indicated in the above account of her excursion one afternoon to look at the latest excavations in the Forum. This is one of the very rare scenes in the novel that is set in bright light, at least to start with; but when Ralph went off with an archeological guide and she remained behind, the hour and the place were exactly suited to her mood of the moment: "The sun had begun to sink, the air was filled with a golden haze, and the long shadows of broken column and formless pedestal were thrown across the field of ruin" (II, 105). So the twilight of day is added to the twilight of classical history.

The sense of a dark and bloody past inspired in American pilgrims by the relics of ancient Rome is well known. James had chided Hawthorne for brooding over it in *The Marble Faun,* but he fell into a similar vein in a travel essay of 1873. As he looked out over the "field of ruin" disinterred by recent excavations in the Roman Forum, it increased his sense of the sublime: "It gives one the oddest feeling to see the past, the ancient world, as one stands there, bodily turned up with the spade.... The pleasure is the same as what you enjoy at Pompeii, and the pain is the same." This attitude toward history is given a special turn in *The Portrait of a Lady.* Near the end Isabel, in the depth of her misery, had come to identify herself with old Rome, the place where so many countless generations had suffered: "for in a world of ruins the ruin of her own happiness seemed a less unnatural catastrophe" (II, 327). This connection between her first and last impressions of the Eternal City may well occur to the critic, but in the spring of 1872 the young heroine was afflicted by nothing more serious than a touch of romantic melancholy, in the best literary tradition.

"From the Roman past to Isabel Archer's future was a long stride, but her imagination had taken it in a single flight," we are told, as the heroine sits down on a prostrate column near the foundations of the Capitol and meditates. The burden of so much history bearing down on the present threatens her sunny afternoon with a dark cloud, though she clings to her basic conviction that knowledge of any sort is a bringer of light. When after the lapse of some time "a shadow was thrown across the line of her vision," it was not from the terrible human past of ancient Rome but from her own recent past (II, 106). It was the sudden apparition of Lord Warburton, whose offer of marriage she had declined because the values she sought were not ancestral but of the here and now. There was nothing dark about this fair nobleman, to be sure, except for the cloud that passed over Isabel's mind when she feared he would renew his suit for her hand. On this occasion he was the incarnation of light. He had been travelling in the Near East for the past six months, and now loomed before her "splendidly sunburnt," his handsome face and beard "burnished by the fire of Asia" (II, 108). Though she permitted him to renew relations with her, it was on a strict basis of friendship.

On the Sunday following, Lord Warburton and Ralph accompanied Isabel on her first visit to Saint Peter's, adopting the custom of the foreign colony in Rome of going to vespers there, as much for social as for religious reasons. Wanting to give her reactions to the famous basilica just the right touch of "repressed ecstasy," James recalled his own youthful enthusiasm of nearly a decade before, as recorded in "A Roman Holiday":

> I go there often on rainy days, with prosaic intentions of "exercise." . . . As a mere promenade, St. Peter's is unequalled. . . . You think you have taken its measure; but it expands again, and leaves your vision shrunken. I never let the ponderous leather curtain bang down behind me, without feeling as if all former visits were but a vague prevision. . . . Tourists will never cease to be asked, I suppose, if they have not been disappointed in the size of St. Peter's. . . . It seemed to me from the first the hugest thing conceivable—a real exaltation of one's idea of space, . . . the far-spreading tessellated plain of the pavement, when the light has a quality which lets things look their largest, and the scattered figures mark happily the scale of certain details. Then you have only to stroll and stroll, and gaze and gaze, . . . and feel yourself, at the bottom of the abysmal shaft of the dome, dwindle to a crawling dot. . . . There are no shadows, to speak of, no marked effects of shade; but effects of light innumerable—points at which the light seems to mass itself in airy density, and scatter itself in enchanting gradations and cadences. It hangs like a rolling mist along the gilded vault of the nave, melts into bright interfusion the mosaic scintillations of the dome, clings and clusters and lingers . . . [on] the universal incrustation of marble.

The phrasing he uses to describe Isabel's impressions is strikingly similar. But the revisions and reorderings show how far the novelist of 1881 has come from the youthful writer of travel essays:

> In the church, as she strolled over its tesselated acres, . . . [she was not] one of the superior tourists who are "disappointed," in St. Peter's and find it smaller than its fame; the first time she passed beneath the huge leathern curtain that strains and bangs at the entrance—the first time she

found herself beneath the far-arching dome and saw the light drizzle down through the air thickened with incense and with the reflections of marble and gilt, of mosaic and bronze, her conception of greatness received an extension. After this it never lacked space to soar. She gazed and wondered, like a child or a peasant, and paid her silent tribute to visible grandeur. There is something almost profane in the vastness of the place, which seems meant as much for physical as for spiritual exercise, the different figures and groups, the mingled worshippers and spectators, may follow their various intentions without mutual scandal. (II, 114)

Young James as the romantic seeker of the picturesque is transformed into the innocent Isabel, wondering "like a child or a peasant" in presence of the sublime. The travel-writer's slightly ironic treatment of Saint Peter's as a secular promenade is used in the novel as a means of turning the setting into a scene.

As the heroine strolls with Warburton down the vast nave toward the choir, they meet Gilbert Osmond, and in accord with the social graces of the day she is allowed to change escorts. We are given only one sample of their conversation, but it is extremely interesting. When Isabel is asked her opinion of Saint Peter's by her new suitor,

"It's very large and very bright," said the girl.
"It's too large: it makes one feel like an atom." (II, 116)

Osmond's rejoinder is taken right out of James's early travel essay—"[You] feel yourself, at the bottom of the abysmal shaft of the dome, dwindle to a crawling dot"—which thus provides the clue to villain as well as heroine. The scene concludes with a significant exchange:

"You ought indeed to be a Pope!" Isabel exclaimed, remembering something he had said to her in Florence.
"Ah, I should have enjoyed that!" said Gilbert Osmond.

At the beginning of their courtship some weeks before, he had confessed that there were only two or three people in the world he envied—including the Pope of Rome and the Sultan of Turkey. This confession of identification with absolute rulers links Osmond not only with the spiritual Father who demands unhesitating obedience but with the despot who tyrannizes over women. And the image of being dwindled to an atom by being looked down on from a height prefigures one in Isabel's climactic vision: "Osmond's beautiful mind seemed to peep down from a small high window and mock at her." The combination of these suggestions is what brings an ominous shadow into the radiant light-filled cathedral.

All these omens alert the perceptive reader, who finds more of the novel's meaning in its structure of images than in its narrative structure. And since to read them rightly calls for a certain critical objectivity, Isabel's lack of this trait helps to make plausible one aspect of the plot: her seeming perversity in walking straight into what others suspect is a cunning trap. With her willful and idealizing temperament she saw only what she wanted to see, until at long last her eyes were opened on the occasion of that fateful midnight meditation four years after marriage. However, it should be mentioned also that, while this strangely assorted group continued their sight-seeing during the days in Rome leading up to Osmond's proposal, he conducted himself with such tact and geniality, with so much knowledge of the right fact and skill in producing the right word, that even Ralph was obliged to admit he was at present a delightful associate. This sense of success prompted Osmond to make his declaration, somewhat precipitately since Isabel had just announced her plan to set off on a European tour that might last for months.

Though this proposal is a momentous episode in Isabel's life, the language in which it is rendered is strangely flat. "What I wish to say to you," Osmond declared in the sitting room of her Roman hotel, whose sham splendor he thought vulgar, "is that I find I am in love with you." Then he repeated the announcement "in a tone of almost impersonal discretion" (II, 135). The reader can scarcely help remembering the contrast of Warburton's proposal; when he told her he had fallen in love with her at first sight, his eyes "shone with the light of a passion . . . which burned as steadily as a lamp in a windless place" (I, 134). But Isabel, who was unmoved by the declaration of her first suitor, was curiously moved to tears by her second. That James intended his reader to compare the two proposals, though they come six months and nearly three hundred pages apart, is indicated by the fact that not only is Warburton actually in Rome at the time of Osmond's declaration but also his noble presence and his long ago offer of marriage are in the air again for both Isabel and her new suitor. "How detestably fortunate!—to be a great English magnate, to be clever and handsome into the bargain, and, by way of finishing off, to enjoy your high favor!" Osmond confessed to her: "That's a man I could envy" (II, 121). After he learned a few days later that she had refused his lordship, he indulged in a bit of self-congratulation to which only the reader is made privy: "He perceived a new attraction in the idea of taking to himself a young lady who had qualified herself to figure in his *collection of choice objects* by rejecting the splendid offer of a British aristocrat" (II, 125; italics added).

Gilbert Osmond's proposal of marriage followed quickly, but Isabel delayed her answer for nearly a year, meanwhile restlessly seeking out everything romantic in travels all over Europe. Returning to Florence, she put her experiences under review in order to reach a decision:

Isabel had [been] seeing the world.... She was now, to her own sense, a very different person from the frivolous young woman from Albany who had begun to see Europe on the lawn at Gardencourt a couple of years before.... If her thoughts just now had inclined themselves to retrospect, instead of fluttering their wings nervously about the present, they would have evoked a multitude of interesting pictures. These pictures would have been both landscapes and figure-pieces. (II, 148)

Having finally made up her mind, Isabel could now put the right figures in the right landscape. After the engagement was made public, the affianced pair spent their mornings in the "suburban wilderness" of the Cascine, strolling through "the grey Italian shade" and listening "to the nightingales" (II, 174). The setting is an appropriately romantic one for lovers, but the "grey shade" is in striking contrast to the sunny streets of Florence through which she had strolled with her cousin Ralph on "clear May mornings" a year before, in the youthful enthusiasm of a first visit to Italy.

That Isabel's acceptance of Osmond was opposed by family and friends— by everyone close to her except Madame Merle—only made this headstrong young lady all the more confident that her choice was right: she was marrying to please herself. It was only Ralph's displeasure that concerned her and made her willing to listen to him. She had believed in him and she returned his great affection, especially now that he was clearly a doomed man: "He was a bright, free, generous spirit, he had all the illumination of wisdom and none of its pedantry, and yet he was dying" (II, 171). (In the revised edition James added a splendid image of light for the invalid Ralph.) Her poor cousin was thinking hard how to express Gilbert Osmond's "sinister attributes" without seeming invidious. After beating about the bush he came to the point: "I think he's narrow, selfish, ... well, small." Isabel's defense leaped like a flame: "There may be nobler natures, but.... Mr. Osmond is the best I know" (II, 180, 182).

Ralph's disappointment is most poignantly revealed in the imagery he uses. First, he would have urged her to "Wait ... for a little more light," saying that he could have struck a spark or two. Then, reminding her that just a year ago she had valued her freedom beyond everything, he recurred to the metaphor he had applied to the Miss "Archer" he had just endowed with a fortune: "You seemed to me to be soaring ... in the bright light, over the heads of men. Suddenly someone tosses up a faded rosebud ... and down you drop to the ground. It hurts me," he finished, "as if I had fallen myself!" (II, 177, 181). But Isabel had her own versions of these images. From the time of her arrival in England she had envisioned her life as moving "in a realm of light"; and though there was "something pure and proud" in her that made her hold aloof from the idea of marrying, she knew that "if a certain light should dawn, she could give herself completely" (I, 62, 65). Now, after two years of European experience, the opportunities opening out for her there had brought the fulfillment she wanted:

> The desire for unlimited expansion had been succeeded in her mind by the sense that life was vacant without some private duty which gathered one's energies to a point.... It simplified the future at a stroke, it came down from above, like the light of the stars, ... that [Gilbert Osmond] was her lover, her own, and that she should be able to be of use to him. She could marry him with a kind of pride; she was not only taking, she was giving. (II, 82)

Isabel had had enough of vistas, but there was one more spread before her now by her husband-to-be, who clinched his courtship by a dramatic appeal to the scene of their first meeting at his Tuscan villa that had so impressed her. He did this by making a new metaphor out of the vista from his terrace and applying it to their future married years:

> My dear girl, I can't tell you how life seems to stretch there before us— what a long summer afternoon awaits us. It's the latter half of an Italian day—with a golden haze, and the shadows just lengthening, and that divine delicacy in the light, the air, the landscape, which I have loved all my life and which you love today.... It's all soft and mellow—it has the Italian colouring. (II, 190–191)

The House of Darkness

The one striking point all these vistas have in common is that they are set in a waning afternoon or in actual twilight, and in the autumn of the year or something that is likened to it. This is strange indeed since, as images, their function is to suggest the possibilities unfolding for a beautiful young lady on the verge of maturity and on the threshold of marriage. Morning in spring or noon in early summer would seem more appropriate. Their twilight aspect is clearly prophetic. First seen by the romantic Isabel as "a golden haze," in the end it is recognized by the disillusioned Isabel as an omen of the wintry night that is closing about her life. Though this recognition does not come until nearly four years have passed, it follows in the novel rather closely on the courtship episode in Florence, referred to above. For James at this point makes the most dramatic foreshortening in the book: from late spring of 1873, just before the June wedding, he skips to the winter of 1876–

77 in Rome, by which time the marriage has foundered. (The other fore-shortening was the omission of Isabel's year of European travels, between Osmond's proposal and her acceptance.)

Now during her midnight vigil at Palazzo Roccanera, on that climactic day in the middle of January, the imagery of light is replaced by imagery of dark-ness, and the expansive panorama that had been opening out horizontally for Isabel is replaced by a vertical shaft looking down into a kind of dungeon. The key passage quoted near the beginning of this chapter—about the "infinite vista of a multiplied life" which is first changed to a "dark, narrow alley"—continues, with increasingly portentous overtones:

> Instead of leading to the high places of happiness, from which the world would seem to lie below one, so that one could look down with a sense of exaltation and advantage, and judge and choose and pity, it led rather downward and earthward, into realms of restriction and depression, where the sound of other lives, easier and freer, was heard as from above, and served to deepen the feeling of failure. It was her deep distrust of her husband—this was what darkened the world.... Then the shadows began to gather; it was as if Osmond deliberately, almost malignantly, had put the lights out one by one. The dusk at first was vague and thin, and she could still see her way in it. But it steadily increased,... [until] there were certain corners of her life that were impenetrably black. (III, 32)

Several chapters and two months earlier, when the reader was first intro-duced to the Osmonds' married life in Rome, similar imagery of dark-light and dungeon-palace should have prepared him for what was to come, but it was so phrased as to be immediately discounted. Little Mr. Rosier, formerly a hanger-on of Isabel's and now a hopeless suitor of her stepdaughter Pansy, was on his way to one of the Osmonds' celebrated Thursday evening *salons*. As he approached Palazzo Roccanera it struck him as living up to its name (black rock, or less literally black castle-keep):

> A high house in the very heart of Rome, a dark and massive structure ... —a palace in Roman parlance, but a dungeon to poor Rosier's appre-hensive mind. It seemed to him of evil omen that the young lady he wished to marry...should be immured in a kind of domestic fortress, which bore a stern old Roman name, which smelt of historic deeds, of crime and craft and violence. (II, 206–207)

Foreboding as this fictional palace may seem, James had some justification in fact for such a description. He himself implies that Roccanera was modelled on a real palace, saying that it was "mentioned in 'Murray' and visited by tourists" who though conceding that the architectural scale of the exterior gave it "quite the grand air," were disappoined and depressed when they went through the outer gate and found a number of "mutilated statues and dusty urns" built into the walls of the "loggia overhanging the damp court where a fountain gushed out of a mossy niche" (II, 207). James's original was beyond question Palazzo Antici-Mattei (which *is* described in Murray's *Handbook for Rome*). It was built at the turn of the seventeenth century for that rich and powerful family who in those troublous times had the right of occupying militarily with their own men-at-arms the whole area between Piazza Mattei and the Tiber. The façade of this actual palace constitutes an unusually austere example of early Roman baroque, but this is in contrast to what most visitors today feel is the charm of the inner courtyard, where the architect made unique use of the family's famous collection of antique statuary and bas-reliefs from classical sarcophagi, displaying them in the garden and the loggias as in an open air museum.

Although Isabel's Roman palace bore some resemblance both in appearance and in its history to a "domestic fortress," there was no warrant for thinking of it as "a dungeon ... which smelt of crime and craft and violence."

> But Rosier was haunted by the conviction that at picturesque periods young girls had been shut up there to keep them from their true loves, and, under the threat of being thrown into convents, had been forced into unholy marriages. (II, 207)

This is too melodramatic, to be sure, for anyone to take stock in other than the immature Ned Rosier. Even he dismissed it as soon as he entered Mrs. Osmond's "warm, rich-looking reception rooms" and saw her, dressed in black velvet, looking "brilliant and noble." He was sure the years had touched her only to enhance her "lustre." "Now, at all events, framed in the gilded doorway, she struck our young man as the picture of a gracious lady" (II, 210–211). This is the scene that gives the novel its title. But it was ironically a false portrait of Isabel behind which she hid her suffering, her true portrait being turned to the wall. Her devoted cousin Ralph, also in Rome on a visit at this time, was not taken in by appearances. "She lived with a certain magnificence," he admitted, and seemed even "lovelier than before," but he knew that what he saw was not her real self:

> She wore a mask [and] it completely covered her face. There was something fixed and mechanical in the serenity painted upon it.... What he saw was the fine lady who was supposed to represent something. "What did Isabel represent?" Ralph asked himself; and he could only answer by saying that she represented Gilbert Osmond. "Good heavens, what a function!" he exclaimed. He was lost in wonder at the mystery of things. (II, 243–245)

Indeed Rosier's foreboding as he approached Palazzo Roccanera, romantic and unfounded though it seemed, turned out to be a truer picture of the actual situation inside Isabel's Roman palace than the portrait of a "brilliant and noble" lady presented to him by his hostess. At first her new home had promised to combine all that had impressed her at Gardencourt and Osmond's villa, with the added note of grandeur. She was to be the great lady, surrounded by beauty and knowledge, mistress of a house with a storied past that yet offered the present opportunity of elegant privacy or a richly patterned social life, as one chose. Instead, during her midnight vigil, it is revealed as a house of darkness with no light of love or even of humanity:

> She could live it over again, the incredulous terror with which she had taken the measure of her dwelling. Between those four walls she had lived ever since; they were to surround her for the rest of her life. It was the house of darkness, the house of dumbness, the house of suffocation. Osmond's beautiful mind gave it neither light nor air; Osmond's beautiful mind, indeed, seemed to peep down from a small high window and mock at her. (III, 37)

The ambiguous meaning of this phrase—"Osmond's beautiful mind"—has ironic repercussions back through the novel. It will be remembered that she had first thought of Italy as the land of promise, where "a love of the beautiful might be comforted by endless knowledge." And when she first met Osmond he seemed the very embodiment of this concept of Italy: "There was an indefinable beauty about him—in his situation, in his mind, in his face." At last, during her lonely meditation, the paradox is made clear:

> She had not been mistaken about the beauty of his mind; she knew that organ perfectly now. She had lived with it, she had lived *in* it almost—it appeared to have become her habitation.... A mind more ingenious, more subtle, more cultivated, more trained to admirable exercises, she had not encountered; and it was this exquisite instrument she had now to reckon with. (III, 35–36)

"Osmond's beautiful mind" has become both her prison and her torture chamber. At this point one remembers that when Isabel first approached the rather forbidding façade of his Tuscan villa, "it looked somehow as if, once you were in, it would not be easy to get out" (II, 62). Then one also recalls the ominous word she had inadvertently used when shown through his miniature museum; she felt "oppressed," she said to herself, "with the accumulation of beauty and knowledge" she found there, though she may have meant by this only "overwhelmed." Because of her ignorance and lack of disciplined taste, her admiration for his art collections was always touched by some curiously suggestive phrasing: "faded hangings of damask and tapestry," "primitive specimens of pictorial art," "perverse-looking relics of medieval brass," "empty, dusky rooms" with just an occasional gleam of "tarnished gilt in the rich-looking gloom" (II, 28, 143). If his taste for the beautiful thus had its dark side, the knowledge he offered had its severe limitations. Before marriage he had told her "he loved the conventional" but, thinking he meant "the love of harmony and order and decency," she had been pleased. Then gradually she discovered what he really meant: "There were certain things they must do, a certain posture they must take, certain people they must know and not know." The collection of social conventions they must adhere to was as large as the collection of art objects he had assembled. On the night of her vigil they are fused in one image: "When Isabel saw this rigid system close about her, draped though it was in pictured tapestries, that sense of darkness and suffocation of which I have spoken took possession of her; she seemed to be shut up with an odour of mould and decay" (III, 40).

So much for the dungeon image that had replaced the bright prospect of art and knowledge. Now for the torture chamber that Osmond's beautiful mind turned out to be. Such an "exquisite instrument" did not deal in physical violence, of course, but inflicted the subtlest kind of mental and spiritual pain. "She had a certain way of looking at life which he took as a personal offence," James confides to his reader; then to Isabel: "[Osmond] said to her one day that she had too many ideas and that she must get rid of them" (III, 36, 37). Even before marriage he had implied something of the sort, but she had paid no attention, thinking he meant it only superficially, and half agreeing that she did give utterance to more opinions than she had understanding to back up. But in the deepening experience of their lives together these words came back to her as "portentous"; they meant that he literally wanted her to have nothing of her own but her pretty appearance:

> The real offence, as she ultimately perceived, was her having a mind of her own at all. Her mind was to be his—attached to his own like a small garden-plot to a deer-park. He would rake the soil gently and water the flowers; he would weed the beds and gather an occasional nosegay. It would be a pretty piece of property for a proprietor already far-reaching. (III, 40–41)

There is tragic irony in this image of being "owned" by Osmond that comes to Isabel during her midnight meditation; even though drawn from nature, for once, it still pictures him as an exploiter, suggesting exactly the opposite of what marriage to Lord Warburton had offered early in the novel. His love and admiration for her were such that he would have respected her right to an independent and happy life. Engrossed in service to his country, he would have had neither time nor inclination to exploit other people. If she had accepted his proposal, instead of being "a small garden-plot" attached to his extensive deer park, she would have been the mistress of Lockleigh, which had struck her as "a castle in a fairy-tale." Far more important than the romance of being Lady Warburton would have been her proud function as the wife of a liberal peer in the forefront of reform.

Another aspect of Osmond's cruelty comes out in his attempt to force Isabel into line with his narrow estheticism. It finds its way into the vigil scene only indirectly, as she turns over in her mind her recent meetings with Ralph, whose final visit to Rome had proved to be "a lamp in the darkness." Now she remembers his warning on a spring morning, years before, in the garden at Florence: "She had only to close her eyes to see the place, to hear his voice" (III, 44). One can follow her act of remembrance by simply turning back to chapter thirty-four, where her cousin was trying to dissuade her from marrying Osmond. "He is the incarnation of taste," Ralph had admitted of her suitor; but he quickly added: "He judges and measures, approves and condemns, altogether by that.... You were not meant to be measured in that way—you were meant for something better than to keep guard over the sensibilities of a sterile dilettante!" (II, 182). Aware of the element of truth in this accusation, Isabel had winced even as she defended her fiancé. Yet from the beginning she had realized there were things about Osmond that gave her pause: "He was certainly fastidious and critical; he was probably irritable. His sensibility governed him—possibly governed him too much; it had made him impatient of vulgar troubles and led him to live by himself." This does not sound like the ideal description of a lover and husband. But at that time she marked it all up to his credit, to "his taste in everything—... art and beauty and history" (II, 73).

As long as Isabel remained under the spell of Osmond's calculated charm she misunderstood both him and Ralph. Seeing each one for what he truly is comprises the resolution of the novel, and it is achieved largely through imagery. But she is a long time in arriving at this understanding, and her constant comparison of them forms a major pattern of the story's development. A significant contrast may be found in the "imaginary houses" projected as the habitations of these two men. Very early in the novel Ralph had said jokingly to Isabel of his own quarters at Gardencourt:

> "I keep a band of music in my ante-room.... It has orders to play without stopping; it renders me two excellent services. It keeps the sounds of the world from reaching the private apartments, and it makes the world think

that dancing's going on within."... Isabel often found herself irritated by this perpetual fiddling; she would have liked to pass through the ante-room, as her cousin called it, and enter the private apartments. (I, 74)

The reader takes this as a whimsical fabrication by the plucky invalid to spare others the distress of knowing his actual situation. But Isabel does not understand until the very end of the novel, when she penetrates at last to the "private apartments" of the dying Ralph. His valiant wit had been used for concealing not only his suffering and defeat but his hopeless love for her. In sharp contrast is Osmond's metaphorical house as imaged for the reader by Ralph during his final visit to Palazzo Roccanera:

> His ambition was not to please the world, but to please himself by ex-citing the world's curiosity and then declining to satisfy it.... To sur-round his interior with a sort of invidious sanctity, to tantalize society with a sense of exclusion, to make people believe his house was different from every other, to impart to the face that he presented to the world a cold originality—.... Under the guise of caring only for intrinsic values Osmond lived exclusively for the world. (II, 245–246)

So Ralph pictured the polished shell of an egotist, designed to deceive people into believing that the Osmonds lived in a house made brilliant by beautiful things and rare accomplishments. Though he kept this image to himself, it is confirmed and supplemented by the images that came to Isabel several weeks later during her midnight vigil, symbolizing for herself what it was like to be shut up in such a house.

Ralph and Osmond are natural foils since they stand for opposite values in James's moral code. One is the "appreciator," one the "exploiter," of other people. It is true that many aspects of their lives are parallel: both are Ameri-cans who have lived so long in Europe as to become cosmopolites; both are highly cultivated men of leisure whose interests have centered on art and history, beauty and knowledge; both are bachelors who find themselves in mid-career drawn into Isabel's orbit. Yet it is in these apparent similarities that their differences are revealed, most dramatically in relation to their theory that "life was a matter of connoisseurship." It is not until Isabel understands the images applied to them, and applied by them to her, that she understands the two men who mean most in her life, for good and for ill. (Isabel herself falls somewhere between the "exploiter" and "appreciator," in her self-center-edness "using" all of her suitors, yet not an egotist in any real sense as proved by her unselfish devotion to her stepdaughter.)

Osmond's subtlest cruelty is rendered in terms of his ownership of her not as a piece of property but as an *objet d'art*. The image first setting up this pattern brands him unmistakably as an exploiter. When his suit for her hand and fortune had proved successful, he phrased his elation to himself in an elaborate metaphor: she was to be "a silver plate" that reflected his thoughts on its "scintillating surface"; further, she was to be "a plate that he might heap up with ripe fruits...so that conversation might become for him a sort of perpetual dessert." Thus she would be useful as well as ornamental. His final extension of the image seems to encompass the use he intended to make of her fortune of seventy thousand pounds sterling: "He found the silvery quality in perfection in Isabel; he could tap her imagination with his knuckle and make it ring" (II, 189). Though the reader overhears these egotistical musings they never reach Isabel's ears, of course. Yet she was not without ample forewarning.

One example will suffice. Early in their courtship Osmond had said: "Don't you remember my telling you that one ought to make one's life a work of art?" (II, 132–133). The high sounding tone of this aphorism collapses as soon as one stops to remember the obvious distinction between life and art, between the animate and the inanimate. It should have occurred to her immediately, because the previous occasion when he used such a dehumanizing formula was in reference to his having intentionally formed Pansy into a perfect *jeune fille*, rather than into a beloved and loving daughter. Indeed, Osmond's exploitative attitude towards Isabel is mirrored in miniature in his treatment of Pansy. Though he had fashioned her into a work of art, when she reached marriageable age he realized this was one piece in his collection he might not be able to keep permanently. But if she must be disposed of he insisted on getting the top market price. Hence little Mr. Rosier (a collector on a lesser scale, who thought of Pansy "in amorous meditation" as he might have thought of "a dresden-china shepherdess") was unacceptable as a suitor. Told that Pansy loved him, Osmond replied: "I don't think that matters at all." Rosier's flaw went too deep: his income was inadequate, barely sufficient to support her in "genteel misery." When the poor young man made the supreme sacrifice and auctioned his entire collection in order to make himself rich enough to be acceptable, Osmond merely thought him a fool. Without his bibelots, to which he had devoted a lifetime, he was nothing; he had sold his identity (II, 198, 219; III, 164–165).

The many images over the years that provided Isabel with clues to Gilbert Osmond's cold egotism reach their culmination in the scene of his final appearance in the novel—thus showing that the climactic vigil (chap. 42) is prospective as well as retrospective. In chapter fifty-one she receives a telegram that Ralph is dying and wants her to come to him in England. When she goes to her husband's study to ask his "permission," she finds him seated at a table with an old folio propped in front of him: "This volume was open at a page of small coloured plates, and Isabel presently saw that he had been copying from it the drawing of an antique coin. A box of water-colours and fine brushes lay before him, and he had already transferred to a sheet of immaculate paper the delicate, finely-tinted disk" (III, 171). Osmond not only refuses his assent, he even refuses to divert his attention from his work, talking to her with his back turned. But many things have combined to clarify Isabel's understanding and restore her independence: the recognition scene when she had discovered him in strangely intimate converse with Madame Merle—"an image, lasting only a moment, like a sudden flicker of light" (III, 20); the stock-taking during her own midnight meditation; and now the combination of love and duty that draws her to her cousin.

In the dialogue that follows she makes an open break, uttering aloud for the first time "her worst thought" about her husband, declaring that his opposition to her desires is "malignant." His only reply to this is that appearances must be kept up, the form of their marriage preserved even though love has long gone out of it. "I really can't argue with you on the hypothesis of your defying me," he announces, breaking off the discussion abruptly and turning back to his study table: "I prefer my drawing" (III, 172-179). What makes this scene memorable is not the argument but the characterizing image of Osmond copying the antique coin. It symbolizes his concern with the formal aspects of art, the faultless imitation rather than the inspired creation; his treatment of marriage as a mere social convention rather than a private affair of the heart; his cold metallic nature, calculating values either in terms of the rarity of an old coin or the current purchasing power of Isabel's fortune.

The characterizing image for Ralph Touchett paints him as just the opposite type of man. It occurred early in the novel (chap. 10) when he was showing the art gallery at Gardencourt to a guest. Most of the pictures were of his own choosing and he singled out one, a small painting by Lancret, as especially symbolic of his tastes: "[It] represented a gentleman in a pink doublet and hose and a ruff, leaning against the pedestal of the statue of a nymph in a garden, and playing the guitar to two ladies seated on the grass. 'That's my ideal of a regular occupation,' he said" (I, 112). (Lancret's *Conversation Galante* in the Wallace Collection, London, answers his description perfectly, and even has a title appropriate to Ralph Touchett.) Ralph's boast about his idleness should not mislead; it was part of the ironic mode adopted by an invalid to avoid self-pity. The real meaning of this image should be clear enough: he wanted art to be a joyous thing, he wanted to express his own life as a service to beauty. Similarly it was in terms of painting that he saw Isabel. When he was showing his gallery to her somewhat earlier, he found himself concentrating on his beautiful cousin more than on the pictures, and thinking that "she was better worth looking at than most works of art" (I, 55). At the end of the novel, after he knows the tragedy of her life, he reflects: "She was meant to be original, to be natural, to be the full portrait of confident zestful life." This was the ideal portrait of a lady Ralph would have liked to paint.

Although Isabel was not privy to these inner thoughts, everything about Ralph's behavior to her from the beginning had bespoken the same dedication to beauty—to appreciating and serving her—the same selfless love. But she had remained blind to all this, treating his attitude to art as that of a dilettanete and taking his devotion to her for granted as merely that of a cousin. When his reserve broke and he excused himself for opposing her marriage with Osmond by confessing, "I love you but I love without hope," even then she persisted in misunderstanding him: "Ralph apparently wished her not to marry at all—that was what it really meant—because he was amused with the spectacle of her adventures as a single woman" (II, 183, 188). By the time of the midnight vigil, however, her vision of the true nature of her husband brings with it a much clearer view of Ralph, as she comes back once again to a comparison of the two men. "He was after all as intelligent as Osmond—quite apart from his being better," she now decides. Indeed, his penetration of Osmond's evil nature from the start strikes her as being "a wonder of wisdom," making him decidedly the more intelligent of the two. But Isabel is becoming aware of something far more important than her cousin's superiority of mind: "It was simply that Ralph was generous and that her husband was not. There was something in Ralph's talk, in his smile, ...that made the blasted circle round which she walked more spacious. He made her feel the good of the world; he made her feel *what might have been*" (III, 54; italics added). The rest of the novel is given over to a resolution of this last phrase.

When at the end of April 1877 Isabel leaves Rome and goes to her dying cousin's bedside, in defiance of her husband, she knows far more about both of them. She has learned all the details about Osmond's relations with Madame Merle and their connivance to snatch her fortune, even at the expense of wrecking her life. She has learned that Ralph was the one who had been responsible for her Touchett inheritance, his generosity being thus ironically the proximate cause of her tragedy. All this fills her mind as she makes the long journey by train across Europe. The countries through which she passed were decked out in "the richest freshness of spring," but her thoughts wandered "through other countries—strange-looking, dimly-lighted, pathless lands, in which there was no change of seasons, but only, as it seemed, a perpetual dreariness of winter" (III, 207). There was "something terrible" about her arrival in London:

> The dusky, smoky, far-arching vault of the station, the strange, livid light, the dense, dark, pushing crowd, filled her with a nervous fear.... She remembered that she had once liked these things; they seemed part of a mighty spectacle in which there was something that touched her. She remembered how she had walked away from Euston [Station], in the winter dusk, in the crowded streets, five years before. (III, 210)

Her flashback is to the occasion, near the beginning of her European tour, when her feeling of freedom was at its peak: "The world lay before her—she could do whatever she chose." Today she knew she could do nothing of the sort, and she felt like an entirely different person.

In such a mood Isabel returns to the scene of her European launching. It is now full spring but the "season" for her is still controlled by the occasion:

> Gardencourt had been her starting-point, and to those muffled chambers it was at least a temporary solution to return.... The day was dark and cold; the dusk was thick in the corners of the wide brown rooms. The house was perfectly still—a stillness that Isabel remembered; it had filled all the place for days before the death of her uncle. (III, 208, 219)

If it seems once again like a house of death it had actually been one when she first arrived, in a prophetic sense, a kind of twilight Eden presided over by a dying uncle and his doomed son. Now she wanders alone through the great drawing room and library, then on to the deserted gallery of pictures, pausing to admire all the fine objects and works of art, which only grow more beautiful and valuable with time. "Things change but little," she reflects, "while people change so much" (III, 219). In the six long years that have passed nothing has changed but Isabel. Yet once more she meditates on her tragic career: "She might have had another life, and today she might have been a happier woman" (III, 219, 220). One version of what her life "might have been" is brought to mind by the announcement that Ralph's noble neighbor had driven over to Gardencourt the day before. But she had not come to England to struggle again with Lord Warburton, and she is relieved to hear that he is engaged to be married.

Far more important is the revelation at Ralph's bedside of another way in which she might have been a happier woman. With his death imminent, they are determined now to be open and frank with each other, looking at the truth together. Isabel confesses the tragic failure of her marriage—Osmond's villainy, her own suffering—and her blindness to Ralph's love. He at last drops the pretense of cousinly devotion, so long maintained because he felt that an invalid should not aspire to be her husband. At the very beginning of the novel James had confided to the reader that "though the liberty of falling in love had a place in Ralph Touchett's programme," it was a liberty to be "very temperately used." In the revised edition this reads "[Ralph had] the imagination of loving—as distinguished from that of being loved" (I, 48). Now it is confided to her in his last words, which are just barely audible: "Remember this, . . . that if you have been hated you have also been loved" (III, 231). Though nothing more is stated, what is evoked by the whole scene is a vision of the life they might have had together, at least for a few years. As mistress of Gardencourt she would have enjoyed a freedom quite as untrammeled as at Lockleigh; and if her position would have been higher as Lady Warburton, her situation would have been happier as the wife of Ralph Touchett. Gardencourt could have been transformed from a house of death into a house of sweetness and light. The glow of Ralph's love and the lambent play of his wit would have made it the opposite of Palazzo Roccanera, "the house of darkness and suffocation." ("To be as happy as possible," Isabel had said to Ralph at the beginning of the novel, "that's what I came to Europe for.")

The final possibility of "another life" she might have had comes over Isabel as she pauses in the art gallery that first day of her return to Gardencourt. She seems to be looking at a picture, but acually she is wondering "whether if her aunt had not come that day in Albany she would have married Caspar Goodwood" (III, 220). Some days later, at Ralph's funeral, this earliest and most persistent of her suitors materializes in the flesh. He has come to press his case again, for the last time, as a very corporeal lover. The field seems clear before him. Warburton is engaged to another, Ralph is dead, and Goodwood has learned the truth about her marriage. Now, looming before her at Gardencourt, he seems like a modern version of the knight-errant, come to rescue a damsel in distress—but one who does not want to be rescued. He opens with a challenge she cannot refute: "You are the most unhappy of women, and your husband's a devil" (III, 244). Then as he gives up argument and lets passion take over, she feels "that she has never been loved before." Though she admits to herself he is justified, her resistance suggests she is still afraid of sexual love, still essentially virginal in spite of years of marriage. (The reader can find sufficient evidence scattered through the novel to support this view.) Of all her suitors, indeed, Goodwood is the most masculine one: "He glared at her a moment through the dusk, and the next instant she felt his arms about her, and his lips on her own lips. His kiss was a flash of lightning; when it was dark again she was free. She never looked about her; she only darted away from the spot" (III, 247). She flees from him back to Rome and duty, back to the house of darkness. (At this point, Isabel's self-diagnosis just before her marriage should be recalled; a life of "unlimited expansion," her desire up until then, would prove unsatisfying without "some private duty" that would bring her energies to focus; by marrying Osmond "she was not only taking, she was giving." Would Pansy serve now?)

Goodwood's first preparation for his bold attempt at a rescue act came from what he learned at first hand during a visit to Isabel in Rome a few months earlier. There Osmond, in a perverse kind of humor, put on a genial show of friendliness with him, pretending to be very confidential about "the conjugal harmony" prevailing at Palazzo Roccanera. The curiously paradoxical image he used was only vaguely understood by Goodwood at the time: "We are as united, you know, as the candlestick and the snuffers" (III, 135). The real fiendishness of the double meaning here becomes apparent only when one follows out the dictionary definitions. "Snuffers" normally refers to an instrument for extinguishing candles. But "to snuff" can also mean to trim the carbon from a candlewick, hence "to make clearer or brighter, to purge." This is the perfect image for an exploiter. Osmond's idea of marriage was that it gave him the right to trim Isabel's flame in order to make it burn for his pleasure, then when he tired of her to put it out. Ralph had known this about him intuitively from the beginning and so tried to dissuade her from marrying him. Goodwood found it out late and tried to dissuade her from going back to him.

The revelation had come to Isabel herself during the midnight vigil in an image that foreshadows the candlestick and snuffers: "It was as if Osmond deliberately, almost malignantly, had put out the lights one by one" (III, 32). The key chapter itself, in keeping with the fine artistry that controls the whole of *The Portrait*, is framed by similar imagery. It begins as the heroine leans back in her chair, closes her eyes, and for a long time ("far into the night, and still further") sits in the deserted drawing room given up to her meditation: "A servant came in to attend to the fire, and she bade him bring fresh candles and then go to bed" (III, 24). Then, after she has explored the meaning of her life through the intricate system of images and counter-images analyzed earlier in this chapter, the episode concludes: "When the clock struck four she got up; she was going to bed at last, for the lamp had long since gone out and the candles had burned down to their sockets" (III, 45). Isabel remains in the house of darkness, but she has seen the light.

When James brought *The Portrait* to a close by having Isabel return to an obscure and uncertain future at Palazzo Roccanera after all the illumination that had come to her during the final visit at Gardencourt, he realized that this ending would not satisfy some of his readers. His commentary in the *Notebooks,* prior to the novel's publication, anticipates them: "The obvious criticism of course will be that it is not finished—that I have not seen the heroine to the end of her situation—that I have left her *en l'air*.—This is both true and false. The *whole* of anything is never told; you can only take what groups together. What I have done has that unity—it groups together. It is complete in itself." Like many of James's novels the story ends not in a re-solving action but in a clarifying awareness, a new understanding that comes from self-knowledge. What gives *The Portrait of a Lady* its special distinction is the brilliant new technique by which this is rendered in the midnight vigil.

The Vigil as Technique

It would be absurd to claim that the "retrospective meditation" was invented by Henry James. Novelists for a long time had made use of this convenient device, either to speed up the narration by using the faster pace of exposition, or to comment on the story through the voice of a character and so avoid author-intrusion. Two examples will illustrate, drawn from Jane Austen and Nathaniel Hawthorne, predecessors he knew and admired. At one of the numerous minor crises in *Pride and Prejudice* Elizabeth Bennet abruptly terminated a conversation with Mr. Darcy's cousin and withdrew to the Par-sonage, where "shut into her own room she could think without interrup-tion of all she had heard" and then try to apply it to understanding the conduct and character of the man she was eventually to marry; but her brief review of recent events (less than two pages) only "brought on a headache" and one more true-false estimate of Darcy. In *The Scarlet Letter*, for the other exam-ple, there is Dimmesdale's meditation as he returned alone from his rendez-vous in the forest with Hester Prynne; in an effort to bring back some sense of reality after this dreamlike experience, "he recalled and more thoroughly defined the plans which [they] had sketched for their departure," and so in a brief expository flashback (again less than two pages) we are given an episode that would have filled a chapter or more if rendered in dramatic dialogue between the conspiring lovers.

Examples could be multiplied, but these are probably representative of the retrospective meditation as used by novelists before James. It tends to be brief in itself, and it has reference to only a short past episode in the story. Further-more, the expository manner in which it is presented seems more suited to the rational and analytical powers of the author than to the emotionally tense state of the character sunk in the reverie. As a consequence the reader accepts it as a useful plot summary rather than as a convincing part of the fiction. The midnight vigil in *The Portrait of a Lady* is something different altogether. In the first place it is a full-scale meditation, elaborated through a twenty-page chapter, and it refers to the entire novel—retrospectively to what has gone before, prospectively to what follows. More important than the scope of reference, however, is the mode of presentation. By having Isabel explore the meaning of her entire European experience through a labyrinth of images, James is as psychologically right as he is poetically effective. In the reverie-under-stress, as in dreams, the mind understands in pictures rather than by logically ordered recapitulation. Finally, a dramatic dimension is added by making the disillusioned heroine use for her self-exploration a cluster of images that are the reverse of those by which, as a romantically impressionable young lady, she had trapped herself in a tragic marriage.

James had been fully conscious from the start that he was striking out in a new direction with *The Portrait of a Lady*. Early in 1880, when his friend T. S. Perry wanted to write an article on his works to date—some ten volumes of fiction, including *Roderick Hudson*, *The American*, and his one popular success *Daisy Miller*—he was told to wait until the novel-in-progress (*The Portrait*) came out: "It is from that I myself shall pretend to date—on that I shall take my stand." A quarter century later, summing up his life work in one of the famous Prefaces, he placed his early masterpiece second only to *The Ambassadors* in its "architectural competence." Its success, he concluded, was due to the technical rigor with which the fictional materials had been given their formal structure. And he singled out as "obviously the best thing in the book" Isabel's "extraordinary meditative vigil." Having chosen to write a drama of the "inward life" rather than "of the moving accident, of battle and murder and sudden death," he was convinced that this searching self-analysis furthered the plot better than twenty incidents would have done:

> It was designed to have all the vivacity of incident and all the economy of picture.... It is a representation simply of her motionlessly *seeing*, and an attempt withal to make the mere still lucidity of her act as "interesting" as the surprise of a caravan or the identification of a pirate.... But it all goes on without her being approached by another person and without her leaving her chair.

The very extravagance of James's figurative language here indicates the importance he assigns to the vigil scene. What Isabel sees and *how* she sees—through colored or distorting glasses at first, with the clarity of a sharply focussed lens at the end—these are essential to any understanding of her story. In the present chapter I have tried to demonstrate how the intricate system of imagery comprised in this vigil provides the best clues for interpreting Isabel's character and its relation to her fate—the central thematic concerns for critics of this novel.

In conclusion, as examples of the possibilities for fiction opened up by such techniques, one may point to Conrad's *Heart of Darkness* and Joyce's *Ulysses*, among the works of acknowledged followers. Then there is the particularly interesting parallel between James's vigil scene and the last third of *Absalom, Absalom!*, written half a century later. In this novel Faulkner also uses a midnight meditation to explore for meaning. Having failed to understand Thomas Sutpen's story by rational analysis and factual research, Quentin Compson and his Canadian roommate one cold January night at Harvard allow themselves to sink into a reverie. Gradually they fix their attention on the image of two half-brothers riding away from Sutpen's Hundred on that Christmas Day long ago, project themselves backward in time, then identify imaginatively with Charles Bon and Henry Sutpen. By the end of their long and intricate vigil they have found the human love that was buried under a saga of inhumanity. This is not to suggest that Faulkner was directly influenced by *The Portrait of a Lady*, a novel utterly different in subject matter and theme, but that Henry James was one of the masters who showed him what miracles could be performed by experimenting with fictional techniques.

At any rate, it is such devices as the midnight vigil that mark *The Portrait* as a new departure, a break with the conventions of Victorian fiction. Indeed, the boldness with which James staked all on technique is what makes him one of the founders of the modern novel. For example in *The Turn of the Screw* he fused the modes of symbol, allegory, and fable so closely as to raise an unending storm of controversy over its meaning. In *The Golden Bowl* he extended a single metaphysical conceit into an outsized novel. What he did with dramatic scene and symbolic picture in *The Wings of the Dove* and *The Ambassadors* will be shown in my last two chapters. These are some of the brilliant experiments that enabled fiction to break away from the conventional realism of Trollope and Howells, that paved the way for the even bolder new departures of Joyce and Faulkner. But James's first triumph as a technical innovator came as early as 1881 with *The Portrait of a Lady*.

Lost Between Two Worlds

The Princess Casamassima

London is the scene of Henry James's most sociological novel. In *The Princess Casamassima* (1886), more than anywhere else, he is concerned with social problems—specifically, the first rumblings of the class war that has become a major issue in the twentieth century. But this impending clash between the "haves" and the "have-nots" is confined to the outer plot. Its sole function is to symbolize the inner conflict of James's tragic hero, who wanders between the two worlds unable to find a footing in either. Hyacinth Robinson, from early youth, spent most of his free hours taking "interminable, restless, melancholy, moody, yet all-observant strolls" through the great city, equally fascinated by the sights of Soho and Mayfair. Because of the haphazard layout of London (as compared, for example with Paris), his rambles invariably took him across a hodgepodge of the "high" and the "low." These walks form the structural plan of the book. They lead him, through the maze of London's streets, to those places toward which the two halves of his divided self are ineluctably drawn: the slums he was born to and the haunts of the aristocracy he yearns for. In one sense this novel may be taken as a variation on the international theme, the contrast of two cultures here being hierarchical rather than geographical (no longer America versus Europe).

The Streets of London

As a young man of twenty Hyacinth's long-ingrained habit still clings to him, but now he has a companion in his wanderings. When Millicent Henning returns to Lomax Place for a visit to her childhood playmate, he sees at once that she has come a long way from the disreputable little neighborhood girl he remembered. She has a job modelling fashionable clothes, some of which on the present occasion set off to advantage her handsome face and figure, so that he eagerly offers to see her home:

> It was a long walk from Lomax Place to [Pimlico, but Hyacinth]
> liked the streets at all times, especially at nightfall in the autumn, of a

Saturday, when in the vulgar districts the smaller shops and open-air industries were doubly active, and big clumsy torches flared and smoked over handcarts and costermongers' barrows drawn up in the gutters. Hyacinth's imagination had never ceased to be stirred by the preparations for Sunday that went on in the evening among the toilers and spinners, his brothers and sisters.... He liked the reflexion of the lamps on the wet pavements, the feeling and smell of the carboniferous London damp; the way the winter fog blurred and suffused the whole place, made it seem bigger and more crowded, produced halos and dim radiations, trickles and evaporations on the plates of glass. (71–72)

The renewal of friendship between them plays only a small part in developing the plot, but their rambles through London's streets together, across "low" and "high," symbolize the novel's theme. Milly's view of things, opposite from Hyacinth's in every way, throws his own view into high relief, and this odd companionship gives new zest to his interminable walks. Her tastes are grossly materialistic; they could have been easily satisfied if she had her pick, in unlimited quantity, of the luxury articles in such establishments as the haberdasher's where she works or the gaudy ones in a certain "jeweler's gas-lighted display in Great Portland Street" before which she lingers enviously—all of which her companion laughs to scorn. Hyacinth also longs for material things, but chiefly for the way of life symbolized by the "refinements of civilization." Exactly what this means to him is one of the major themes explored in the novel. His understanding is at first both superficial and vague. Yet, like Milly, when his sense of deprivation finds any definition at all it is in pictorial terms:

In such hours the great roaring indifferent world of London seemed to him a huge organisation for mocking at his poverty; the young man in a white tie and a crush-hat who dandled by on his way to a dinner-party in a hansom that nearly ran over one ... became symbolic, insolent, defiant.... Sometimes of a Saturday in the long evenings of June and July he made his way into Hyde Park at the hour when the throng of carriages, of riders, of brilliant pedestrians was thickest; and a tremendous little drama had taken place privately on the stage of his inner consciousness. He wanted to drive in every carriage, to mount on every horse, to feel on his arm the hand of every pretty woman in the place. (125–126)

Scenes like these made him "smart with the sense that *he* was above all out of it."

What differentiates Hyacinth from Milly—and it puts them poles apart—is his sensibility. She sees what is obvious and expensive, unable to tell the

fine from the vulgar. He discriminates with the eye of an artist. His perceptive talent is actively at work throughout this novel which, even for James,
is notable for the profusion of its visual imagery. It is rendered in concentrated form in these passages quoted from Hyacinth's "all-observant" strolls.
He not only sees the parade of equestrian elegance in Hyde Park so vividly
that he identifies with it in his "inner consciousness," but also finds beauty
in the impressionistic effects of fog and the reflection of lamps on the wet
pavements in slum areas.

In a word, the central concern of *The Princess Casamassima* is not with the
coming revolution but with the familiar Jamesian theme of awareness. It is
the story of a "sentient youth on whom nothing is lost," and his response to
the rich possibilities of life—whether realized or only yearned for. The "impressions and reflections" that come to him through the visual sense are his
only methods of knowing the world and understanding himself. The author
had a formidable artistic problem on his hands. How could he present the
awareness of a protagonist who had little capacity for thought or expression?
He found his solution in a kaleidoscopic portrayal of the London scene: as a
stage; as a powerful agent influencing Hyacinth; as a chorus to bring out the
meaning of other characters and their actions, in their relation to the sensitive
young hero's life.

The portrait of Hyacinth Robinson sketched above shows a remarkable
resemblance (except in one important respect) to Henry James as embryonic
artist. The two youths, real and imagined, could hardly have been more different in outward circumstances: in the situations, events, and personal relations that constituted their lives. The author is model for his hero not in
substantive biography but in the projection of a potentiality. This is the most
interesting, and possibly the most valid, kind of autobiographical fiction.
Novelists frequently give their protagonists a strong artistic bent—the temperament they know most intimately—but make them painters or composers
or architects, instead of writers, to achieve objectivity. Better still to make
the hero only a potential artist, as here. A number of James's stories are about
actual painters and writers, but none of these fictional characters are as convincing as the potential artists: Touchett and Osmond in *The Portrait of a
Lady*, Strether in *The Ambassadors*, and here Hyacinth Robinson. (A comparison of Hyacinth's success as a fictional character with that of the sculptor
in *Roderick Hudson* will prove the point.)

Hyacinth is a bookbinder by trade, responds passionately to the fine arts as
well as the decorative, but merely dreams of becoming a creative writer. In
this novel by dealing with the esthetic response to life as merely the essential
quality of his hero, James avoids entangling him in the facts of his own career
or his theories as a creator. But the parallel between them as artistic sensibilities

is close, as a few comparisons with the first volume of James's autobiography will demonstrate. When Henry was a very small boy he felt strangely isolated and wanted desperately to establish relations with people in the world outside himself:

> They were so *other*—that was what I felt; and to *be* other, other almost anyhow, seemed as good as the probable taste of the bright compound wistfully watched in the confectioner's window; unattainable, impossible, of course, but as to which just this impossibility and just that privation ... [were] the question.

The privations suffered by young Hyacinth differ widely in many ways, but their impact on his consciousness is rendered by the same image. When he was about ten years of age, we are told, his Aunt Pinnie knew where to find him if she wanted to call him in for his tea:

> At this time of day the boy was often planted in front of the little sweet-shop on the other side of the street, an establishment where periodical literature, as well as tough toffy and hard lollipops, was dispensed and where song-books and pictorial sheets were attractively exhibited in the small-paned dirty window. He used to stand there for half an hour at a time and spell out the first page of the romances in the *Family Herald* and the *London Journal* [whose heroes were always noblemen]. (24)

At the very climax of the novel the Princess applies the same image to the mature Hyacinth: "Fancy the strange, bitter fate: to be constituted as you're constituted, to be conscious of the capacity you must feel, and yet to look at the good things of life only through the pastry-cook's window!" (283).

The "hero" of *A Small Boy and Others*, like Hyacinth Robinson, gets his real education through his five senses. The account of James's formal schooling serves largely as a contrast to what he learns by "dawdling and gaping," by soaking up "impressions" like a sponge, by continuously "reflecting" on all he perceives. It is only so that he comes to know the world of others and to discover himself in relation to it. The mode of young Henry's sensibility differs from that of Hyacinth chiefly in the emphasis on taste and smell, appropriate to a very "small boy" whose story ends at the age of fourteen. In the next volume, *Notes of a Son and Brother*, dealing with his young manhood, the emphasis shifts to his visual sense—as in *The Princess*, which is mostly concerned with Hyacinth in his twenties.

As a matter of fact, in his Preface to *The Princess Casamassima* (written like the autobiography in his old age) Henry James commented on the link between himself and Hyacinth, not as boys but as young men, in a passage that also confirms my argument as to the structure and meaning of this novel.

Here we learn that the author's own perambulations in London, like those of his hero, constituted his chief mode of knowing it:

> The simplest account of the origin of "The Princess Casamassima" is, I think, that this fiction proceeded quite directly, during the first year of a long residence in London, from the habit and the interest of walking the streets. I walked a great deal—for exercise, for amusement, for acquisition...; and as to do this was to receive many impressions, so the impressions worked and sought an issue, so the book after a time was born.

Since James, unlike Hyacinth, was a creative writer, these early exploratory walks in the British capital served the imagination as well as the understanding. If we are to believe the testimony of his Preface, *The Princess Casamassima* sprang full born from the London streets:

> There was a moment [James declares] when they offered me no image more vivid than that of some individual sensitive nature or fine mind, some small obscure intelligent creature whose education should have been almost wholly derived from them, capable of profiting by all the civilisation, all the accumulations to which they testify, yet condemned to see these things only from outside.... I arrived so at the history of little Hyacinth Robinson—he sprang up for me out of the London pavement.

At this point the identity between creator and created is made explicit:

> To find his possible adventure interesting I had only to conceive his watching the same public show, the same innumerable appearances, I had watched myself, and of his watching very much as I had watched; save indeed for one little difference. This difference would be that so far as all the swarming facts should speak of freedom and ease, knowledge and power, money, opportunity, satiety, he should be able to revolve round them but at the most respectful of distances and with every door of approach shut in his face. For one's self, all conveniently, there had been doors that opened.

This "one little difference" constitutes understatement of the most extreme kind. The similarity between them is confined to their sensibilities; in all else they differed radically.

Two passages from James's essay "London" (1886), a record of his own rambles of the past decade, when compared with Hyacinth's vision of the metropolis (see p. 125, above, on fog and Hyde Park), will point up the likenesses and differences between hero and creator. One notable feature of London is its sheer immensity, James said:

Another is the atmosphere, with its magnificent mystifications, which flatters and superfuses, makes everything brown, rich, dim, vague, magnifies distances and minimises details, confirms the inference of vastness by suggesting that, as the great city makes everything, it makes its own system of weather and its own optical laws.

The third notable feature of London is its "congregation of parks,...delightfully romantic, like parks in novels." In Hyde Park he prefers to follow the Serpentine or to watch the "scattered early riders" in Rotten Row:

> The salient figures of English society during the present century ... have bobbed in the saddle between Apsley House and Queen's Gate.... [But] I am free to admit that in the Season, at the conventional hours, the Row becomes a weariness (save perhaps just for a glimpse once a year, to remind one's self how much it is like Du Maurier); the preoccupied citizen eschews it and leaves it for the most part to the gaping barbarian.

James endowed the little bookbinder with his esthetic sensibility, but not with his social sophistication. Though the essay touches on the slums, the poverty and misery of the masses, much of it concerns the London beyond Hyacinth's reach: Mayfair and Belgravia, the clubs of Pall Mall, theater-going and dining out.

Henry James had all the opportunities that Hyacinth Robinson felt so deprived of: access to the repositories of art and the sources of culture, the society of the fortunate few, freedom to follow his talent from potential artist to full achievement. The inestimable value James placed on all these opportunities enabled him to sympathize to the full with Hyacinth's sense of deprivation, and to imagine his tragic end. But for all the outward circumstances of his hero's life—milieu, characters, actions—there was nothing from the author's personal experiences to transcribe. All these novelistic features of the book had to be invented, and it is to these we must now turn. But, as James intended, they come to us through the consciousness of the hero.

Millbank Prison

Some of Hyacinth's London walks were quite literally *perambulations*, the point of departure and arrival barely mentioned, with all the emphasis on rambling through the great city to immerse himself in the endless variety of its life. These "all-observant strolls" establish the hero's character, or rather his sensibility, and so are a clue to the novel's meaning, the theme of wandering between two worlds. They come mostly in the first and the last quarter of the novel, setting the pattern of his life and mocking the pathos of his death. Many of his walks were of a very different sort. Their purpose was strictly *transportation*, appropriately enough for the story of a young man too poor to afford rides in cabs or buses, except on rare occasions. Knowing Hyacinth, one can assume that even on such pedestrian journeys he absorbed what the London streets offered him en route. But all the emphasis is on the destinations reached: the scenes of his work and recreation, homes of friends and acquaintances, public places and private rendezvous. These walks involve the hero in the novel's plot and plunge him deep into relations with the other characters.

The most dramatic situation Hyacinth was precipitated into by one of his early journeys across London was the confrontation, at the age of ten, with his dying mother in Millbank Prison. Of the lurid circumstances surrounding his origin he was totally unaware: that his mother, a French courtesan, had murdered his putative father, Lord Frederick Purvis, for refusing to make her child legitimate. Now Miss Pynsent, the timorous little dressmaker who had adopted Hyacinth, responds to the deathbed plea of Florentine Vivier to see her son, even at the risk of his discovering the truth. It is this visit to Millbank Prison that launches the action of the novel. And since it leads to the discovery of his mixed plebeian and aristocratic heritage it becomes a symbolic episode, prefiguring the theme that echoes through all the succeeding pages: Hyacinth's unanswerable cry, Who am I?

By way of preparation "Aunt" Pinnie embroidered the reality with fibs, concealing as much as revealing her long guarded secret. Then she set out with Hyacinth on the long journey from lowly Lomax Place in north London (Pentonville) through the fashionable West End to Millbank Prison on the Thames, near Vauxhall Bridge (where the Tate Gallery is today). Because of the distance and the tender years of Hyacinth, she took as much of the trip as possible on a succession of omnibuses:

> They made the last part of their approach on foot, . . . till they came to a big dark-towered building . . . [lifting] its dusky mass from the bank of the Thames, lying there and sprawling over the whole neighborhood with brown, bare, windowless walls, ugly truncated pinnacles and a character unspeakably sad and stern. It looked very sinister and wicked, to Miss Pynsent's eyes, and she wondered why a prison should have such an evil air if it was erected in the interest of justice and order—a builded protest, precisely, against vice and villainy. This particular penitentiary struck her as about as bad and wrong as those who were in it; it threw a blight on the face of day, making the river seem foul and poisonous and the opposite bank, with a protrusion of long-necked chimneys, unsightly

gasometers and deposits of rubbish, wear the aspect of a region at whose expense the jail had been populated. (47)

Referring to the architectural ugliness of this penitentiary, Henry James said of it in his previously quoted essay on London: "Millbank Prison is a worse act of violence than any it was erected to punish"—using words similar to those he put in the mouth of Miss Pynsent. Even more interesting is his comment in a letter to an American friend, written in December 1884 while *The Princess Casamassima* was under way: "I have been all the morning at Millbank Prison (horrible place) collecting notes for a fiction scene. You see, I am quite the Naturalist." James was well-versed in the novels of Zola and the other French Naturalists, knew several of them personally, and as a matter of fact had just renewed his acquaintance with them, after the lapse of several years, during a holiday trip to Paris in mid-winter 1884. But he never subscribed to their mode of writing, as is made clear in his several essays on them and in his own manifesto, "The Art of Fiction."

It would be a mistake, specifically with reference to *The Princess*, to take literally James's casual remark, "You see, I am quite the Naturalist." The Preface to that novel is lucid on the matter:

My notes then, on the much-mixed world of my hero's both overt and covert consciousness, were exactly my gathered impressions and stirred perceptions, the deposit in my working imagination of all my visual and all my constructive sense of London.... I recall pulling no wires, knocking at no closed doors, applying for no "authentic" information.... To haunt the great city and by this habit to penetrate it, imaginatively, in as many places as possible—*that* was to be informed, *that* was to pull wires, *that* was to open doors, *that* was positively to groan at times under the weight of one's accumulations.

This does not sound like the compositional method of Zola and the French Naturalists. Whatever Henry James learned about Millbank Prison by "scientific" investigation (according to the slice-of-life school), all that has come down to us in his own voice are the two sentences given above, from essay and letter. The rest comes through the narrator of *The Princess*, transformed into fiction.

To return now to Miss Pynsent and Hyacinth, who have been left standing dismayed outside the huge and forbidding gates. He has resisted her entreaties, but Pinnie finally persuades him to let her ring the great bell:

A moment later they found themselves in a vast interior dimness, while a grinding of keys and bolts went on behind them.... She had

...a confused impression of being surrounded with high black walls, whose inner face was more dreadful than the other, the one that overlooked the river; of passing through grey stony courts, in some of which dreadful figures, scarcely female, in hideous brown misfitting uniforms and perfect frights of hoods, were marching round in a circle.... She never had felt so immured; there were walls within walls and galleries on top of galleries; even the daylight lost its colour and you couldn't imagine what o'clock it was. (49–50)

In its profusion of detail the description of Millbank goes beyond James's normal use of realism, and in this sense it shows some influence of the French school, probably Balzac. But the elaboration of setting, inside and outside, serves only one purpose: to make the prison the scene of a brief melodramatic action, more like Dickens than Zola.

In the "naked and grated chambers of the infirmary," Miss Pynsent scarcely recognizes her former friend, so transformed is she by a decade in prison. She looks terribly old—"a speechless, motionless creature, dazed and stupid,... disfigured and ugly"—whereas the Florentine Vivier in the long ago "obliterated past" had been pretty and vivacious. If Pinnie is dismayed by this spectacle Hyacinth is appalled, quite naturally. But, true to his temperament, he holds back more from distaste than from fright. What makes the situation more difficult is that Mlle Vivier, having apparently forgotten all her English, speaks to them only in French and so fails to communicate.

Finally, when the dying woman utters an anguished cry, Pinnie drops to her knees and literally pushes the little boy into his mother's arms: " 'Kiss her, kiss her well, and we'll go home!' she whispered.... It was a terrible, irresistible embrace, to which Hyacinth submitted with instant patience" (54–56). All that keeps this tearful scene from dissolving into pure melodrama is the aloofness of Hyacinth—a basic trait that holds him back from any real human involvement throughout his life. James may allow other characters in *The Princess Casamassima* to "let themselves go," but in most situations that verge on the melodramatic he maintains control of his materials through the cool detachment of his hero, whose perspective is also that of both author and reader. Even so this is not a scene in James's new mode, for the purpose of establishing relations among the characters, but a conventional scene of the old-fashioned sort, for the release of emotions and the advancement of his plot—possibly because Dickens was lurking in the back of his mind.

James was too much the artist to risk anticlimax by a "revelation scene," with Pinnie spelling out to Hyacinth the meaning of their visit to Millbank. There is a skip of ten years between the prison scene and the one that takes place in the following chapter, at their home in Lomax Place. Then in a flashback—Hyacinth is now aged twenty (84)—we are given a condensed version of the episode when he had discovered the truth, at about the age of sixteen. "Who was that awful woman ... in the prison years ago," he had suddenly demanded, "who was dying and who kissed me so, as I've never been kissed, as I never shall be again! Who *was* she, was WAS she?" (64).

To supplement Pinnie's confession, which was at once "too much and too little," Hyacinth had mustered the courage to go to the British Museum and dig out of the *Times* the full account of his mother's trial for the murder of her lover. He read every syllable of the ghastly record, and though the evidence was only circumstantial "he regarded himself immutably as the son of the recreant and sacrificed Lord Frederick." As all these facts fell into place they were formulated into Hyacinth's chief article of faith: "the reflexion that he was a bastard involved in a remarkable manner the reflexion that he was a gentleman" (128–129). But gradually he adjusted himself to his fate and came to forgive the little dressmaker for the fabric of legend she had created and thrown around him from his earliest years, "that there was a grandeur in his past" if the truth could only be known. It struck him as just another feature of the poor woman's professional life—"so much cutting and trimming and shaping and embroidering, so much turning and altering and doing up" (28, 129). The grace of wit, here attributed to Hyacinth, was another means by which James enabled the hero to detach himself from what seemed the inescapable melodrama of his life. At the same time Pinnie's activities as a dressmaker have been given a symbolic turn of great importance to his story.

The effect on Miss Pynsent was quite different. By temperament she was drawn into every emotional excess, whether of romantic fantasy or nightmarish despair. From the day she made her "hideous mistake," making her boy conscious of his stigma and sowing the seeds of rancor in his mind, she entered upon a slow but steady decline. Except for Hyacinth's ghostly mother, whom he had only seen for one terrible moment, Amanda Pynsent was the only woman who played a role in his life up to the age of twenty. She had dedicated her life to the child she had adopted. But she was limited in taste, intelligence, and knowledge of the world. To live with her was to have a severely restricted life.

Miss Pynsent's house on Lomax Place, "a scarce-dissimulated slum" (62), was the center of Hyacinth's life during these same dreary circumscribed years. It was also, in its shabbiness and forlorn simplicity, symbolic of its owner, so that a description of the house gives a better picture of Pinnie than can be had from the few sketchy phrases used by James to describe her directly. The first full account of it is given by Milly Henning when she comes back to Lomax Place for a visit to her childhood playmate, now the twenty-year-old Hyacinth—the episode with which this chapter began. When the dressmaker ushered her into the tiny parlor, calling it in her professional manner "the showroom," Milly took a seat on the sofa which she recognized was still covered in the same "tight shrunken shroud of strange yellow stuff," faded from years of washing:

> The old implements were there on the table: the pincushions and needle-books, and the same collection of fashion-plates (she could see in a min-ute) crumpled, sallow and fly-blown.... [Millicent] noticed that though it was already November there was no fire in the neatly-kept grate be-neath the chimney-piece, on which a design, partly architectural, partly botanical, executed in the hair of Miss Pynsent's parents, was flanked by a pair of vases, under glass, containing muslin flowers. (57, 60)

To Millicent, who was, comparatively speaking, prosperous, the whole place seemed to smell of poverty and failure. And as with the house so with its owner. Her childhood image of the dressmaker had shown her as "neat, fine, superior," with "associations of brilliancy" arising from her constant work-ing with precious satins and brocades. All was quite different now: "The little woman before her was bald and white and pinched; she looked sickly and insufficiently nourished;...drudging over needlework year after year in that undiscoverable street, in a dismal little room where nothing had changed for ages" (59).

The impression made on Miss Pynsent by Milly was exactly the opposite. From a smutty-faced little brat, she had "improved" beyond recognition, being dressed in the height of fashion:

> She was certainly handsome, with a shining, bold, good-natured eye, ...and her robust young figure was rich in feminine curves. [Miss Pyn-sent made the observation] that she was common, despite her magnif-icence; but there was something about her indescribably fresh, successful, and satisfying. She was to her blunt, expanded finger-tips a daughter of London, of the crowded streets and bustling traffic of the great city. (59)

Such is the vision through Pinnie's eyes of Millicent Henning. If the little old dressmaker is symbolized by her shabby parlor and her shrunken trade, the young haberdasher's model is epitomized by the ambitious materialism of the London cockney. Milly is the third woman in Hyacinth's life. She has several thematic functions in the novel—to anchor him to the "real" London, among others. And though her role is a minor one, her meetings with Hy-acinth frequently form narrative links to episodes of the highest significance. An early one of these leads to his meeting with the last and most important woman in his life, the one from whom the novel takes its title.

The Strand Theater

Much as Milly enjoyed the companionship of Hyacinth, she was not one to let him off with mere window-shopping strolls. After some months of growing intimacy she demanded of her new beau what she called "a high-class treat"; she wanted to be taken to a theater in the Strand, to see *The Pearl of Paraguay*, and made it clear that on such an occasion she expected something better than the pit. "Should you want the royal box or a couple of stalls at ten bob apiece?" he asked with the tone of irony that was one of his customary defenses. She settled amicably for seats in the first row of the balcony. But since even these were beyond his purse he sought two complimentary tickets from his old friend and neighbor Anastasius Vetch, who played in the orchestra of a run-down Bloomsbury theater. "Do you want a box?" was the old fiddler's ironic query. "Oh no; something more modest," Hyacinth replies: "Because I haven't the clothes people wear in that sort of place" (132). This second use of irony as to a "box," involving the ambiguity of his social status, is a preparation for what follows, during the entr'acte, when the two young people have their evening at the theater some days later.

The route they took in getting there is not given, but the reader can assume they went on foot, out of habit as well as necessity. This would mean that Hyacinth walked from the squalid neighborhood of Lomax Place, past Buckingham Palace, to the scrubby purlieus of Pimlico where Milly occupied "a modest back room"; thence, with her, along the grand boulevard of the Mall (first laid out by Charles II) with its mansions and palaces on one side and St. James's Park on the other, to the glittering theater district on the edge of Soho. Like most of Hyacinth's London walks, it led him across disparate areas of the low and the high, the two worlds he wanders between.

The scene at the Strand presents a dramatic counterpart to the theatrical horror of Hyacinth's visit to his dying mother, ten years before. Just as the prison episode occupies two chapters at the beginning of Book First, one as preparation and one for the scene itself, so the theater episode occupies the two opening chapters of Book Second, one for the play on stage and one for the play-within-the-play that takes place at the interval in a box. As the curtain goes up Hyacinth surrenders to the "sweet deception" of the theater: "His imagination projected itself lovingly across the footlights, gilded and coloured the shabby canvas and battered accessories, losing itself effectually in the fictive world." Milly finds the audience more exciting than the play being acted before them. From the principal box on the left of the stage a gentleman has been watching him for the last half hour, she whispers to Hyacinth. From where he is placed he sees just enough of the occupants to focus his attention: "One of them was a lady concealed by the curtain; her arm, bare

[135]

save for its bracelets, was visible at moments on the cushioned ledge" (137).

This indirect and partial glimpse of the woman who soon comes to dominate his life strikes just the right note of romance and mystery. Then, to heighten the suspense, all the delaying tactics of a skilled craftsman are made use of. Hyacinth recognizes the gentleman in the box as Captain Sholto, whom he had met casually at the Sun and Moon in Bloomsbury where the Underground assembled, but it is not until the entr'acte that he is able to make his way up to their high perch. When he announces that the Princess Casamassima wishes to make Hyacinth's acquaintance, the proposal "makes things dance, appear fictive and phantasmagoric" for him. "Being whistled for by a princess presented itself to Hyacinth as an indignity endured gracefully enough by the heroes of several French novels in which he had found a thrilling interest"—so the chapter ends by transferring the sense of fiction from stage to audience. The real gentleman, whose evening dress and courtly manners are appropriate to a theater box, resigns his seat beside the Princess Casamassima to an obscure little bookbinder, then takes his place beside the vulgar cockney beauty in the balcony. As in a fairy tale, the roles of high and low are reversed. Preparation for the climactic scene is now complete.

The next chapter opens with Hyacinth's entry into the box, just as the curtain goes up and the play resumes, so that he can barely see two ladies seated at the front, who turn their heads to look at him. One he makes out to be the companion and the other, partly overshadowed by the curtain which she has drawn forward to shield her from the audience, to be clearly the Princess herself: "The simplest way to express the instant effect upon Hyacinth of her fair face of welcome is to say that she dazzled him." Silently but graciously she beckons him to move his chair forward, then turns her attention back to the stage: "He looked at the play, but was far from seeing it."

Little by little he recovers himself and at length dares to look at the Princess again. She responds at once, returning his glance with a bright benevolence:

> She might well be a princess—it was impossible to conform more to the finest evocations of that romantic word. She was fair, shining, slender, with an effortless majesty. Her beauty had an air of perfection; it . . . suggested to Hyacinth something antique and celebrated, something he had admired of old—the memory was vague—in a statue, in a picture, in a museum. . . . He was content, he would like it to go on; so pleasant was it to be enthroned with fine ladies in a dusky, spacious receptacle which framed the bright picture of the stage and made one's own situation seem a play within the play. (147–148)

Although James lavishes a considerable amount of conventional description on his heroine, the overall effect on his hero derives from the symbolic setting in which he first sees her—a box at the theater. Is she real, or just a dazzling illusion? And throughout the book her conduct constantly raises the question (for reader as well as hero): Is she sincere, or merely playacting?

The contrast between this scene and the one at Millbank Prison is extreme in every way, most importantly because of a difference in technique. For Hyacinth's meeting with his mother, James follows the conventional mode of using scene for releasing emotions and advancing the plot; for his meeting with the Princess, the new mode of using scene for the realignment of characters. Also, they differ substantively in several ways. The present setting, in a theater, creates the height of romantic illusion; the former, in a penitentiary, the depth of sordid reality. On both occasions Hyacinth had been sent for, out of the blue, by women he had never heard of—women who are antithetical in every conceivable way. At the prison he was confronted by ugliness, poverty, age, death, and infamy (the murderess in "*a cause célèbre*"). In the theater box he finds himself face to face with beauty, wealth, radiant life, and fame (the "most remarkable woman in Europe"). His mother manages to communicate to him, without benefit of words, the outrageous behaviour of an aristocrat who left him a homeless bastard and her a condemned criminal. The Princess wants to talk to him, as one of the People, about the Underground and the coming revolution. The rest of the chapter is taken up with just such talk—though of a general and rather histrionic sort (153–154).

Hyacinth's meeting with his mother was the key episode in the first part of his life. His meeting with the Princess Casamassima, who adopts him as a protégé, is one of two factors that control the last part.

The Two Worlds: High and Low

In order to emphasize the contrast between these two great scenes—prison and theater—they have been brought closer together here than they are in the novel. In the intervening pages there occur several small incidents which lead to an important result—Hyacinth's commitment to the "Cause," the revolutionary Underground. This is the second major factor in the last part of his life. It is characteristic of the novel's mode that these "incidents," and the people involved in them, are rendered almost exclusively in visual images, of places and things. The critic's concern is with the mode, not the narrative.

In his late teens Hyacinth had been apprenticed to a bookbinder, a "career" that would launch him into the world beyond Lomax Place. This connection was arranged by Mr. Vetch, his adoptive father, who introduced him to Eustache Poupin (a Republican exile in England since the fall of the Commune in 1871), who was the finest craftsman in London. The first meeting was at supper in the Poupins' apartment:

> Hyacinth naturally had never been to Paris, but he always supposed that the *intérieur* of his friends in Lisson Grove gave rather a vivid idea of that city. The two small rooms constituting their establishment contained a great many mirrors as well as little portraits (old-fashioned prints) of revolutionary heroes. The chimney-piece in the bedroom was muffled in some red drapery which appeared to Hyacinth extraordinarily magnificent; the principal ornament of the saloon was a group of small and highly decorated cups, on a tray, accompanied by gilt bottles and glasses, the latter still more diminutive—the whole intended for black coffee and liqueurs.

For Hyacinth the apartment, that is to say the things in it, symbolized the exotic world opened up to him by the Poupins—their Frenchness, which should properly be a part of his own heritage too. M. Poupin showed him his bindings, the finest products of his skill, and "it seemed to Hyacinth that on the spot he was initiated into a fascinating mystery" (81).

The actual initiation took place shortly after this when Hyacinth entered Mr. Crookenden's workshop, "situated in a small superannuated square in Soho," to learn the art of bookbinding under the tutelage of Eustache Poupin. The Frenchman not only found Hyacinth a vocation but, with his wife, provided him with a second pair of surrogate parents (Pinnie and Vetch being the first). The shop itself was the opposite of the Poupins' apartment, which to Hyacinth's inexperienced eyes seemed charmingly foreign, even a little elegant.

The difference between these two places—the scenes of his work and his recreation—is reflected in the routes to them from Hyacinth's home in Lomax Place. His walks westward out to Lisson Grove, though they began in "a scarce dissimulated slum" and ended in a "cockney suburb" near Paddington, took him for a good part of the way through Regent's Park and along the fashionable terraces of Beau Nash. His daily course eastward to "the old familiar shabby shop," on the other hand, lay without relief through Pentonville to Islington to Soho along "the shabby sinuous ways that unite these regions of labour." Old Crook's establishment is a symbol of all that is sordid:

> In this busy, pasty, sticky, leathery little world ... the hand of practice endeavoured to disengage a little beauty—the ugliness of a dingy belittered interior, of battered dispapered walls, of work tables stained and hacked, of windows opening into a foul drizzling street, of the bared

arms, the sordid waistcoat-backs, the smeared aprons, the personal odour
of his fellow-labourers. (221–222)

But eventually he developed such skill with his tools that he flattered himself
unsurpassed unless by the "supreme Eustache." So the bookbindery stands
ambiguously for the two worlds of Hyacinth Robinson: a place of foulness
and brutality out of which come objects of art for the elite.

However much of his time Hyacinth had to spend in Crook's gloomy shop
earning a living, he lived out of it still more, qualitatively, and so "had in a
manner a double identity"—in fact, a fourfold one. For inside the bindery
there were two selves, the yearning artist and the toiling underpaid worker;
outside, two more, the young esthete touched into life by a fairy princess and
the young revolutionary fired by a French idealist into sacrificing that life for
the People.

It was at Poupin's apartment, several years later, that Hyacinth met the
"leader" who initiated him into the Underground. While waiting to be introduced, he had an opportunity to study closely this stranger whom he
found in animated conversation with Eustache:

> He was tall and fair and good-natured looking, but you couldn't tell if
> he were handsome or ugly, with his large head and square forehead,
> his thick, straight hair, his heavy mouth and rather vulgar nose. [Yet]
> his face had a marked expression of intelligence and resolution.... He
> was dressed as a workman in his Sunday toggery,...wearing in par-
> ticular a necktie which was both cheap and pretentious and of which
> Hyacinth, who noticed everything of that kind, observed the crude false
> blue. He had very big shoes—the shoes almost of a country labourer—
> and spoke with a provincial accent. (91)

He was Paul Muniment, the dominant spirit in a revolutionary group of
workers, who from this point on became one of the two most important influences in Hyacinth's life.

This being the case, it is notable that the description of him here is almost
a reverse image of Hyacinth, as seen through the eyes of Millicent Henning
and reported just a few pages earlier in the novel.

> His bones were small, his chest was narrow, his complexion pale, his
> whole figure almost childishly slight; and...he had a very delicate hand
> —the hand, as she said to herself, of a gentleman. What she liked was
> his face and something jaunty and romantic, almost theatrical, in his
> whole little person.... Hyacinth's features were perfect.... The waves

[139]

of his dense fine hair clustered round a forehead which was high enough
to suggest remarkable things.... He was dressed in an old brown vel-
veteen jacket and wore exactly the bright-coloured necktie which Miss
Pynsent's quick fingers used of old to shape out of hoarded remnants of
silk and muslin. He was shabby and work-stained, but...there was
something exotic about him. (69–70)

The two opposing portraits are prophetic of the careers of these strangely
paired friends. For in a short time they become "brothers" in the familial as
well as the socialist sense, or so it seems for a while; but as the plot moves
toward its climax they more nearly serve as foils to each other.

On the occasion of their first meeting, when their visit to the Poupins came
to an end, Hyacinth asked permission to accompany Mr. Muniment to his
home, even though it was "in the far south of London." It was a long walk
from Lisson Grove to Audley Court. We are not told which way they went,
but the most direct route would have been across Hyde Park, or skirting it
along Park Lane, then through the edges of Pimlico and Belgravia, finally
over Vauxhall Bridge to the tenements of Camberwell (directly across the
river from Millbank Prison). So, as with many of his journeys across London,
Hyacinth presumably once more cut across alternate regions of high and low.
(On many later occasions, when he went directly from his home to Paul's
—from one semi-slum to another—he made a shortcut through aristocratic
Mayfair; 223.)

Audley Court proved to be "a still dingier nook" than Lomax Place. It
could only be reached through a narrow, black alley and by climbing a steep,
dark staircase. At the top, Muniment opened a door into an unlit room and
struck a match to a tallow candle:

This enabled Hyacinth to perceive a narrow bed in a corner and a small
object stretched upon it—an object revealed to him mainly by the bright
fixedness of a pair of large eyes, ... which gazed at him across a counterpane of gaudy patchwork. The brown room seemed crowded with heterogeneous objects and ... small prints, both plain and coloured.... The
little person in the corner had the air of having gone to bed in a picture
gallery, and as soon as Hyacinth became aware of this his impression
deepened that Paul Muniment and his sister were very wonderful people.
(96, 95)

The concluding sentence explicitly makes the apartment a key to Hyacinth's
understanding of its owners.

Audley Court becomes the setting for a scene of Dickensian color and pitch,
one evening at midsummer, when Hyacinth takes Aunt Pinnie there for tea

to meet his new friends. Rosy Muniment clutches at the little dressmaker's arm, fixes her with shining eyes, and lays her needle under contribution for "a sweet pink dressing-gown." At the same time Hyacinth falls into conversation with Lady Aurora Langrish, an old friend who often comes to sit with the little cripple while her brother is away. The grotesqueness of both characters as individuals is heightened by the incongruity of such an odd friendship and by their reversal of roles in the projected class war. Rosy, daughter of a drunken coal miner and sister of the revolutionary leader, perversely takes the aristocratic stand; Lady Aurora, who sides with the People, fascinates and baffles Hyacinth even more. The first member of the nobility he has ever met socially, she seems to have few of the qualities of her caste. About thirty years old, tall and tremulous, with a retreating chin and protruding teeth and myopic eyes, wearing clothes that looked worn and in disrepair, she was clearly "one of the caprices" of the aristocracy. This impression is confirmed when she delivers herself of an autobiography that runs on breathlessly for two pages. She had escaped from society and gained her own liberty by cultivating the reputation of being queer, she declares: "I'm quite a proper lunatic and I might as well keep up the character" (166–176). (It was a neat stroke on James's part to put the statement of her eccentricity in her own mouth.) The talk between both pairs exemplifies the topsy-turvy character of the gathering at Audley Court.

At this point their conversation is interrupted by the appearance at the door of Paul Muniment, accompanied by another guest, whom he has brought up for Rosy's amusement. Hyacinth immediately recognizes the gentleman who had recently introduced him to the Princess Casamassima. But on the present occasion the Captain has assumed yet another guise: "Sholto had not the same grand air that hovered about him at the theatre; he was dressed with ingenious cheapness, to an effect coinciding, however different the cause, with poor Hyacinth's own; but his disguise prompted our young man to wonder what made him so unmistakably a gentleman in spite of it" (177–178). This time it is notable that a second character who is to serve as a foil to Hyacinth should, on the occasion of being first fully described, present a mirror image of him (a direct rather than a reverse one), at least in one small respect.

The camera eye now focusses on Rosy's bed, where the Captain is exerting himself to entertain her. It next shifts to a tête-à-tête between Lady Aurora and Miss Pynsent, the latter ecstatic at having just been invited to her ladyship's home in Belgravia to get some materials for Rosy's dressing gown. Finally the focus comes to rest in a still shot at the window, where Hyacinth has drawn Paul aside to ask what he thinks of Sholto. "He's a tout. . . . Well, a cat's paw," was the answer, and as the innocent disciple was still puzzled, the master expatiated: "He throws nets and hauls in the little fishes—the pretty little shining, wriggling fishes. They are all for *her* [the Princess]; she swallows 'em down.... Take care, my tadpole!" (177–180).

Lady Aurora "writhed in her pain" at the vulgarity of this new acquaintance, who was clearly "slumming" to collect local color. Then at the first opportunity after tea was served she begged to be excused, taking Miss Pynsent home with her, and so brought the bizarre party to an end. This scene at the Muniments' is in James's new mode, its function being solely for the purpose of aligning a half-dozen characters in a complex of relationships drawn from the two worlds of the novel (178–183). Hyacinth, having been invited to accompany the Captain home, "saw no reason why he on his side shouldn't embrace an occasion of ascertaining how ... a man of fashion would live." Sholto's chambers in the West End, which he took to symbolize their owner, both excited and depressed Hyacinth, "so poignant was the thought that it took thousands of things he then should never possess to make a civilized being" (183–184).

Hyacinth's circle had now extended beyond the world of workers to the world of leisure. Through Captain Sholto he had met the Princess Casamassima in a theater box. Through the same auspices he now received an invitation to her house in South Street, Mayfair. Ushered into her salon Hyacinth sank into a seat covered with rose-colored brocade, "of which the legs and frame appeared of pure gold," and looked around him:

> The splendours and suggestions of Captain Sholto's apartment were thrown completely into the shade by the scene before him, and as the Princess didn't scruple to keep him waiting twenty minutes (during which the butler came in and set out on a small table a glittering tea-service) Hyacinth had time to count over the innumerable *bibelots* (most of which he had never dreamed of) involved in the character of a woman of high fashion and to feel that their beauty and oddity revealed not only whole provinces of art, but refinements of choice on the part of their owner, complications of mind and—almost—terrible depths of temperament. (197)

This is the fifth in a sequence of Balzacian interiors, described in such a way as to be symbolic of the principal characters in Hyacinth's world: Pinnie's parlor, the Poupins' apartment, the Muniments' attic room, Sholto's chambers, and the drawing room of the Princess Casamassima. In the final sentence of the above description James once again is explicit: the *bibelots* with which the Princess has surrounded herself reveal the complex character of the owner.

Hyacinth had been warned by Paul, by Mr. Vetch, and by Mme Grandoni (companion to the Princess) as to what a brilliant woman might do with a young innocent like him. But all to no avail. Waiting for her now: "Hyacinth's suspense became very acute; it was much the same feeling with which, at the theatre, he had sometimes awaited the entrance of a celebrated actress. In this case the actress was to perform for him alone" (197). When she finally entered she was so simply dressed she seemed a different person from before, but with "a beauty even more radiant." They talked for an hour or so, during which he learned that she was not a princess of the blood at all, but a young American woman forced by her parents into a mercenary marriage with an Italian prince that had proved disastrous. It is her disgust with the aristocracy that has attracted her to the impending revolt of the masses. Despite their apparently increasing intimacy, the occasion remained for him more a dream than a reality. Now she must go to the country for some months, but perhaps he will pay her a visit. During her absence he devoted his spare time to binding a volume of Tennyson as a gift for her. (Was it Tennyson's *The Princess*, 1847, dealing with the emancipation of women?)

The gallery of characters is now complete, all presented in habitats symbolizing their owners, thus extending their meanings. The cast is larger and more varied than in the usual novel by James—a full dozen playing principal roles, plus a number of supernumeraries—so that one wonders how the author became acquainted with such a wide spectrum of society. In the normal course of his European experience he would have known the several levels of the high world exemplified by Captain Sholto, the Princess, Lady Aurora, and would have been familiar with their surroundings. But how would the London clubman, literary lion of country houses, intimate of the great and near-great—how would a novelist living in this exclusive world have been able to penetrate the lower side of London life? Those endless prowlings in the great city, emphasized in his Preface, could have provided him with character-types, street scenes, the exterior of shabby tenements, even the interior of such public places as Millbank Prison. But how did James get inside the world of Hyacinth and Miss Pynsent, the Poupins, the Muniments, and the rest?

For answer one needs to make a new definition of what "observation" and "experience" can mean to an imaginative artist. Fortunately James has provided one, in the form of an anecdote used to illustrate a central point in one of his most important commentaries, "The Art of Fiction," an essay written in the summer of 1884 at the very period when *The Princess* was germinating. In rebutting a pronouncement by a conventional Victorian writer, that the novelist must write from his own experience and stick to the social class he belongs to, James quotes a notable English novelist who had been praised for her account of the way of life of French Protestant youth, in one of her tales, and asked about her peculiar opportunities for learning so much about this "recondite being." This was her answer:

> These opportunities consisted in her having once, in Paris, as she ascended a staircase, passed an open door where, in the household of a *pasteur*, some of the young Protestants were seated at table round a finished meal. The glimpse made a picture; it lasted only a moment, but that moment was experience. She had got her direct personal impression, and she turned out her type. She knew what youth was, and what Protestantism; she also had the advantage of having seen what it was to be French, so that she converted these ideas into a concrete image and produced a reality.

This anecdote is evidence, so much more persuasive than argument, of how little observation of the "real thing" is needed by an imaginative artist to create a substantial fiction.

A novelist draws his raw materials not only from his personal experience and from what he observes in the world around him, both greatly transformed by the imagination, but also from his reading, especially in history, biography, and fiction. What James learned from one of his favorite English novelists, Dickens, is highly pertinent at this point. It can be set forth under two headings: first, a sense of the immensity of London and the teeming variety of its life; second, a belief that these qualities can be rendered best by heightening, by using techniques other than those of strict realism. Certainly *The Princess Casamassima*, unique among his novels, is Dickensian in the wide panorama it offers of the great capital, such as one finds in *Oliver Twist* and *David Copperfield*. As for the second point, though James also desired to lift character and action above the realistic level, he was only indirectly indebted to the techniques used by Dickens: farce and melodrama, caricature and the grotesque-picturesque. It is true that some of the action in *The Princess* has elements of the farcical, as in the tea at Audley Court, or of the melodramatic, as at Millbank Prison and in Hyacinth's revolutionary oath at the Sun and Moon (soon to be recounted). But the great difference is that the mode by which this novel's meaning is rendered is a sequence of pictures and scenes, whereas the novels of Dickens unfold in a series of rapidly moving events, such as one finds in *Bleak House* and *Our Mutual Friend*. For the heightening of character and scene James uses paradox and symbolism—only faintly reminiscent of the techniques used by Dickens—in his effort to create a new genre that he came increasingly to refer to as "fable."

One aspect of the fabulous as developed in *The Princess* is the choice of names with a kind of allegorical suggestiveness, which enables James to extend his meanings without becoming trapped in the rigidities of formal allegory. (His use of picturesque and comic names—even more thoroughgoing here than in *The American*—may have been another indirect influence from Dickens: Scrooge, Pecksniff, Oliver Twist.) The reader gets his cue from the tendency of several characters to comment overtly on their symbolic naming. On first meeting Hyacinth, Paul's sister Rose pipes up brightly: "Your name, like mine, represents a flower." Then she continues with her chatter about names: "Her ladyship's is Aurora Langrish.... Isn't it right she should be called the dawn when she brings light where she goes?" This accounts for her given name, but her surname is suggestive too. With her blushing, tremulous manner she seems to Hyacinth like "a personage in a comedy"; and her creator adds, "She sounded the letter *r* as *w*" (97–99). The lisping, and the submerged literary allusion, are picked up two hundred pages later when the Princess, by a slip of the tongue, actually refers to her as "Lady Lydia Languish"—the comic-romantic heroine of Sheridan's *The Rivals*.

The most deliberate pun in the novel is the name of the heroine, Princess Casamassima, though it is made unobtrusive by being in a foreign language. Her husband is the heir of one of the oldest noble families in Europe, the "greatest house" not only in a palatial but more importantly in a dynastic sense. It is from such a height that this fabulous beauty married to a fabulously wealthy prince wants to come down and mingle with the People. Readers of *Roderick Hudson* will remember her as Christina Light, the leading lady of that early novel. Her maiden name is thus also suggestive. There is undoubtedly less Christian charity in her wish to help the oppressed than in Lady Aurora, and though she is constantly associated with images of radiance there is more ambiguity in the figure of her as a bringer of light. All of her names reflect the enigma that she is: princess or revolutionary, genuine or fake. To the hero she is successively a fairy princess, an angel, an actress, though in the end even his infatuation yields to bewilderment. A shining, baffling figure.

With the lesser characters James continues his name-game, though not so insistently. The nickname for Hyacinth's adoptive mother, "Pinnie," suggests the vocation of this characterless little dressmaker, bristling "with needles and pins stuck all over her front." His cockney friend Miss Henning is anonymous in a different way. "A daughter of London," Millicent is one-in-a-hundred-thousand of the crowded streets of this great city; yet Hyacinth finds her magnificent as well as common. One can be less certain that James intended any suggestiveness in the name of Hyacinth's first mentor in radical socialism. But what more appropriate for this histrionic character than Poupin, bringing to mind the French word *poupette*, a "doll" or "puppet"? (Everyone but the hero pronounces his name Puppin.) What is he but an animated French doll? Pull the string marked Revolution and he begins to perform at once, gesticulating wildly and delivering eloquent tirades against the aristocracy.

The second key figure in the last part of the young hero's life is Paul Muniment. The Princess, before meeting him, speaks of his "odd name," adding, "If he resembles it I think I should like him." Milly, who scorns Hyacinth's radical friends, refers to him as "that Mr. Monument (what do you call him?)" (139, 270). James clearly expected us to find his name something to conjure with. There is indeed a monumental quality about him, as he towers in size and in dominance of character over the others. He is also the strong point of the Underground in London, Muniment being the anglicized form of *munimentum*, meaning "rampart" or "fortification." Even his commonplace first name adds to the symbolic characterization, Paul suggesting the militant and masculine, if only because it was the name of that great Apostle who finally put Christianity across. (It is noteworthy that Muniment points out St. Paul's dome as the single object that redeems the view from his attic window.) Yet Paul Muniment also is an enigma, first and last, to those who know him well. James was truly prophetic in creating such a character: a socialistic leader deeply concerned about the plight of the downtrodden, but equally concerned about using the revolution itself as an opportunity for seizing power.

Most ambiguous of all is Hyacinth Robinson, whose name quite literally signifies the central dilemma of his life. In giving his hero a flower name James took a considerable risk. Hyacinth is alternately embarrassed and sarcastic about it. He is only reconciled to his given name when Poupin calls him *Hyacinthe*, after his French grandfather. This forms a satisfying link between the revolutionary ancestor who gave his life for the proletariat in 1848 and the little bookbinder who has pledged to give his life for a similar cause many years later. At the same time he feels increasingly drawn to the world of the aristocracy, where his name-link is by the left hand, in the heraldic sense; for he was not entitled to the surname of his father, Lord Purvis, and had to be content with the name adopted by him for the purposes of his *affaire*, simple "Mr. Robinson." The two together spell out the paradox of the hero's life: a fancy name that came from a heroic commoner, a common one taken from a noble *flâneur*.

James's elaborate play on names tends to make his principal characters comic (Lady Aurora, Pinnie, Poupin), or fabulous (the Princess and Hyacinth), or ambiguous (Milly and Muniment). As a consequence, the only really convincing members of the working class and of the aristocracy are a few vaguely sketched supernumeraries hovering in the wings. By this technique, and all the others at his command, James prevents the impending struggle between the classes from becoming his subject and reduces it to a symbol of the hero's inner conflict—his real theme. Yet he keeps the outward plot before us in sufficiently detailed scenes to provide a realistic contrast to his fable of the little bastard bookbinder, wandering lost between two worlds. The scenes lying at the center of the novel, one dealing with each world, call for consideration since they are crucial to theme as well as plot.

The Sun and Moon

The only fully developed episode devoted to the Underground is the one that occurred at the dingy public house in Bloomsbury on the night when Hyacinth took an oath that turned his young life in the direction of death. Though this is the first meeting of the revolutionaries' "club" to be described, it is clear from references here and there that the hero had been attending them for about a year.

> They came oftener this second winter, for the season was terribly hard; ...the deep perpetual groan of London misery seemed to swell and swell and form the whole undertone of life. The filthy air reached the place in the damp coats of silent men and hung there till it was brewed to a nauseous warmth, and ugly serious faces squared themselves through it, and strong-smelling pipes contributed their element in a fierce dogged manner. (233)

When the talk was running high at the Sun and Moon it seemed to Hyacinth an earnest that the People was only "a sleeping lion." He did not know what part he would play when the awakening came, but his ambition was to offer a brilliant example "of pure youthful, almost juvenile, consecration." There was "a quick pulse of high fever tonight" in the back parlor of the Sun and Moon and he caught the contagion:

> He felt hot and nervous; he got up suddenly and, through the dark tortuous greasy passage communicating with the outer world, went forth into the street. The air was foul and sleety but refreshed him, and he stood in front of the public-house and smoked another pipe. Bedraggled figures passed in and out...in the brutal blaze of the row of lamps. The puddles glittered roundabout and the silent vista of the street, bordered with low black houses, stretched away in the wintry drizzle to right

and left, losing itself in the huge tragic city where unmeasured misery lurked beneath the dirty night, ominously, monstrously still, only howling, for its pain, in the heated human cockpit behind him. (242–243)

This sounds like something right out of Dickens, yet when one leafs through his novels he does not find a really convincing model for James's scene. Of all the fictions Dickens laid in the London slums, *Oliver Twist* offers the nearest parallel to the Sun and Moon. There is even a slight similarity between the two young heroes. Oliver also is an abandoned orphan, and for a brief period early in his career he is cared for by a kind gentleman who lives near Pentonville—the district of London where Miss Pynsent lives, in Lomax Place. Then when he is kidnapped by thieves and forced to live in their underworld, his manners and dress and taste make him seem out of place. This is as far as the parallel to Hyacinth goes. But many of Dickens's descriptions of streets and street scenes in *Oliver Twist* must have been recalled by James as he wrote *The Princess*. For example, one of the favorite hangouts of Bill Sikes: "In the obscure parlour of a low public-house, in the filthiest part of Little Saffron Hill; a dark and gloomy den, where a flaring gaslight burnt all day in the winter-time; and where no ray of sun ever shone in the summer."

Here James could have found a clue for his pub, named ironically the Sun and Moon, both these luminaries being obscured by the wintry weather, so that darkness is the characterizing word for the particular public house where the light of a new day is to dawn. A hundred pages later Dickens's pub is identified by name, when the villain Fagin slips into "a narrow and dismal alley leading to Saffron Hill," enters the Three Cripples, and makes his way to an upstairs chamber:

> The room was illuminated by two gas-lights, the glare of which was prevented by the barred shutters, and closely-drawn curtains of faded red, from being visible outside. The ceiling was blackened, to prevent its color from being injured by the flaring of the lamps; and the place was so full of dense tobacco smoke, that at first it was scarcely possible to discern anything more. By degrees, however, as some of it cleared away through the open door, an assemblage of heads, as confused as the noises that greeted the ear, might be made out; and as the eye grew more accustomed to the scene, the spectator gradually became aware of the presence of a numerous company . . . crowded round a long table: at the upper end of which sat a chairman with a hammer of office in his hand.

This is hardly a model for the Sun and Moon, but it is a suggestive parallel that may have hovered in the back of James's mind as he composed his climactic scene. What he took from Dickens as from other "masters," was not borrowed but stolen—as Eliot says the true artist should do—assimilated to his observations of the real world, then recast by his own creative imagination. One great difference here is that the Cripples is a den of thieves, of the physically and morally deformed, finding brief respite from their criminal life in a drunken revel; the Sun and Moon is the rendezvous of revolutionaries, motivated by a vague idealism, soberly though confusedly planning to share the wealth but in a very different way. The naming of both accords with the picturesque tradition of English public houses. At the same time both names symbolize the particular functions of the pubs in the two novels and so emphasize one of many differences between them. The most important influence of Dickens on the Sun and Moon episode may well have been to throw James back again, as in the Millbank Prison episode, to the old-fashioned mode of using scene for releasing emotions and advancing the plot, as will appear. (It is an interesting point that the "low" scenes in this novel—the ones that seem to owe a debt to Dickens—are the ones that use the conventional mode; whereas in the "high" scenes—at the theater and later with the Princess at Medley—James ventures to use his new experimental mode, a scene for clarifying the relations among characters. The one with a Dickensian touch that does use the new mode, the tea party at Audley Court, is a mixture of high and low.)

When Hyacinth finally returned to his noisy clubroom he saw that the group was breaking up in disorder, or at all events in confusion, a confusion that resulted from the same cause that had sent him outside "hot and nervous" to get a breath of air. What had happened was that Muniment had dropped a bombshell in the meeting by announcing, "Hoffendahl's in London." Though the news of a clandestine visit from this "purest martyr of their cause" had set them all by the ears, it evoked nothing more than revolutionary platitudes from the rank and file of workers, those anonymous members of the Underground who served James as a chorus: the shoemaker, the fat man who fancied dogs, the hairdresser, and so on. Even the few who had some idea of what was going on—Muniment, Poupin, and Schinkel the German cabinetmaker—were unable to come up with any plan of action. As for Hyacinth: "He was in a state of inward exaltation, possessed by an intense desire to stand face to face with the sublime Hoffendahl, to hear his voice and touch his mutilated hand" (241). Quite unexpectedly, at the far end of the room, the barber jumped on a chair and shrieked out an accusation that made every one stare: "Well, I want you all to know what strikes me before we part company. There isn't a man in the blessed lot of you that isn't afraid of his bloody skin" (243).

This challenge was like a quick blow in the face to Hyacinth. Before he knew it he found he had sprung up himself on an opposite chair and was making a speech: "I'm not afraid; I'm very sure I'm not. I'm ready to do anything that will do any good; anything, anything—I don't care a damned rap. In such a case I should like the idea of danger. I don't consider my bones precious in the least, compared with some other things" (244). The leaders were going to meet Hoffendahl, it was announced, and Hyacinth was asked to come along. "He wants a perfect little gentleman. Yes, you're the lamb of sacrifice he wants"—such was Muniment's epithet for the hero of the hour: "It's at the other end of London. We must have a growler" (245). The drive seemed interminable, as the cab jogged along the murky miles; by the time it stopped "our young man had wholly lost, in the drizzling gloom, a sense of their whereabouts" (246).

It is three months and three chapters later before we learn exactly what happened that winter night. The revelation is made one spring morning in the park at Medley, the country house where Hyacinth is paying an extended visit to the Princess. She is the first person to learn his secret. He has taken a solemn vow to be ready at any time during the next five years to carry out a command that will probably cost him his life: "Very likely it would be to shoot some one—some blatant humbug in a high place" (279). The settings for these two events, Hyacinth's secret oath and his revelation of it, are opposite in the extreme: a dark night in winter and a bright day in spring, the slums of the oppressed masses and the great house of an aristocrat, the grim faces of fellow revolutionaries and the radiant presence of the Princess.

These contrasts are heightened by the ambiguity of what seems at first like a shift in roles of the two principal characters. Though Hyacinth cannot help being pleased to see that in telling his story he is thrilling to the Princess, like the hero in some famous novel, he blurts out in the end: "Isn't it enough now to give my life to the beastly cause . . . without giving my sympathy?" The new world of beauty and wealth that has been opened up to him at Medley makes him declare, in reply to her surprised query ("the *beastly* cause?"), that the only people he finds himself pitying now are "the rich, the happy," those whose way of life will be destroyed by the revolution (280, 282). The Princess, on the other hand, in the first of several speeches that led him to believe she could be trusted with his confession, has just declared:

I determined to see [English society] . . . , to learn for myself what it really is before we blow it up. I've been here now a year and a half and, as I tell you, I feel I've seen. It's the old regime again, the rottenness and extravagance, bristling with every iniquity and every abuse, over which the French Revolution passed like a whirlwind; or perhaps even more a reproduction of the Roman world in its decadence, gouty, apoplectic, depraved, gorged and clogged with wealth and spoils, selfishness and scepticism, and waiting for the onset of the barbarians. You and I are the barbarians, you know. (260)

These apparent reversals are not the result of confusion in James's conception of his characters but of an ambivalence he deliberately built into their temperaments, plus their tendency to be histrionic. On Hyacinth's first day at Medley the Princess had struck him as an incarnation of the heroine in a French romance she had given him to read (255). Later, on the same day when she made her revolutionary speech, he said to himself: "Her performance of the part she had undertaken to play was certainly complete, and everything lay before him but the reason she might have for playing it" (257). Because they both had conflicting attitudes toward a world in which they occupied ambiguous situations, they both tended to take on whatever role seemed suited to a particular occasion.

It is surprising to find that Henry James, whose sympathies seem to be all on the side of wealth and art, was capable of a similarly ambivalent vision. In December 1886, just a few weeks after *The Princess* was published, he wrote to one of his closest American friends:

The condition of [the English upper class] ... seems to me to be in many ways very much the same rotten and *collapsible* one as that of the French aristocracy before the revolution—minus cleverness and conversation; or perhaps it's more like the heavy, congested and depraved Roman world upon which the barbarians came down. In England the Huns and Vandals will have to come up—from the black depths of the (in the people) enormous misery.... At all events, much of English life is grossly materialistic and wants blood-letting.

Did James seriously hold this opinion? The fact that his speech takes its words right out of the mouth of the Princess Casamassima, his own fictional creation, makes one ask if he also was playing a role, in this letter, for the benefit of his American correspondent. More likely it was because of his own double vision that he could create both of these ambivalent characters, Hyacinth and Christina. Though James lived in the world of privilege and his interests were centered there, he became increasingly convinced, as the nineteenth century drew to a close, how precarious the future of that world was; and on several occasions he gave expression to what he called the "imagination of disaster." But he needed something more substantial to work on if he wanted to embody that threat in a convincing fiction.

As a matter of fact during the early 1880s, the period covered by James's novel, he could have found all he needed for the general pattern of his outer plot in current English books, magazines, and newspapers. He was a careful reader of the London *Times,* and in that journal alone the accounts of assassinations and other violent acts in England as well as on the Continent—by "an international conspiracy for the overthrow of Governments," whose members "are willing to lay down their lives in the execution of its commands" —would have furnished not only the model for his Underground Movement but proof for his readers of its entire credibility. Though the *Times* was vague as to the backgrounds of this revolutionary activity, nothing could have suited the novelist better than to be thus unhampered by too much specific knowledge. As James put it in his Preface a quarter-century later, by way of justification for the sketchiness of his "picture": "The value I wished most to render and the effect I wished most to produce were precisely those of our not knowing, of society's not knowing, but only guessing and suspecting and trying to ignore what 'goes on' irreconcilably, subversively, beneath the vast smug surface." The readers of his novel, of course, would not be members of any "knowing" Underground but members of an established society, only faintly aware of the first rumblings coming from some mysterious subterranean forces that threatened the foundations of their world.

Neither the London *Times* nor any of the other contemporary accounts had anything to offer about the revolutionists themselves, their characters and motivations. For these matters James had to depend on his own creative imagination, triggered quite possibly by suggestions from a fellow novelist who was very much in his thoughts at this time. Deeply moved by the death of Ivan Turgenev, one of his acknowledged masters, he published a long memorial essay on him in December 1884, just as he began writing *The Princess.* One of the novels he reread in preparation for this essay was *Virgin Soil,* dealing with some idealistic revolutionaries of the Populist Movement in Russia. James's review of this book, on its appearance several years before, holds considerable interest for readers of *The Princess:*

[Turgenev's] central figure is usually a person in a false position, generally not of his own making, which, according to the peculiar perversity of fate, is only aggravated by his own effort to right himself. Such eminently is the case with young Nezhdanov, who is the natural son of a nobleman, not recognized by his father's family, and who, drifting through irritation and smothered rage and vague aspiration into the stream of occult radicalism, finds himself fatally fastidious and skeptical and "aesthetic"—more essentially an aristocrat, in a word, than any of the aristocrats he has agreed to conspire against. He has not the gift of faith, and he is most uncomfortably at odds with his companions who have it in a high degree.

This account seems on the surface to fit Hyacinth as well as Turgenev's hero, and source hunters have exhausted every possible parallel between *Virgin Soil* (1876) and *The Princess* (1886) in an attempt to prove that this is James's most derivative novel—in plot, events, and characters. But a comparison of the novels themselves, instead of such skeletal outlines, will show the futility of such source studies. The only real parallels are the ones suggested by James's review, and even these differ widely in the way they are worked out by the two authors. Hyacinth's illegitimacy and his esthetic bent are central to his story; Nezhdanov's are tangential. The motives that lead the heroes to join their respective conspiracies, and the reasons for their disillusionment, have little if anything in common. There is a final apparent parallel in the endings of these books. But Hyacinth's suicide, when he loses faith in his companions and his cause, is the inevitable end of a tragic career; Nezhdanov's seems contrived. In all other ways the two novels are poles apart. *Virgin Soil* is concerned with the plight of Russian society and the impact of this on a wide range of young revolutionaries and older conservatives. *The Princess* is concerned with the plight of a sensitive but deprived protagonist who is lost between two worlds, and whose inner turmoil is symbolized by the threat of a class war.

What James learned from Turgenev was far more important than the faint resemblances pointed out above. His earliest essay on the Russian (1874) compares him with Dickens, to the disadvantage of the English novelist, whose passion for an exciting story led him into the habit of "specializing people by their vivid oddities" instead of by characterization in depth. His memorial essay, ten years later, points out that the germ of a story with Turgenev "was never an affair of plot," but came to him "as the figure of an individual whom he wished to see in action." The influence of this on *The Portrait* has already been discussed. It is equally marked in the case of *The Princess*. Finally, his review of *Virgin Soil* in 1877 was prophetic of his own method in both these novels, when he observed that the Russian's heroes are usually "conspicuous as failures, interesting but impotent persons who are losers at the game of life."

Whatever its debt to other novels and to contemporary newspaper stories, the Underground Movement in *The Princess* takes up surprisingly little space. James's skill in assimilating what he borrowed, for a subject he had limited knowledge of, is matched by his skill in creating the illusion that a conspiracy is everywhere present just under the surface, achieved by suggestion and a minimum of scenes. To summarize: there is discussion of the coming revolution at the Poupins' flat and at the Muniments', also briefly with the Princess at Medley. But except for the closing chapters, after receipt of Hoffendahl's letter commanding Hyacinth to assassinate a duke, the only detailed episode in the book dealing with the Underground is the climactic scene at the Sun and Moon. This occupies but a single chapter (chap. 21), the one that brings Book Second to a close. On the next page begins the brilliantly contrasting scene at Medley, though Hyacinth's visit to the Princess's country house did not occur until months after the night of his oath—the juxtaposition being a stroke of consummate art. For the hero this shift of scene represents a translation from London's slums to a rural paradise. For his creator it is a transition from the theatrical world of Dickens to the poetic world of Keats, at least as far as setting goes. The Medley episode occupies the first five chapters of Book Third—five-to-one being just about typical of the proportionate space allotted to inner theme and to outer plot throughout the novel. This scene calls for extended treatment now.

Medley

Since Hyacinth arrived late at night, it was not until the next morning that he had his first view of the great house and its romantic park: "What he saw from his window made him dress quickly.... He had never in his life been in the country—the real country, as he called it, the country which was not the mere ravelled fringe of London—and there entered through his open casement the breath of a world enchantingly new, ... musical [with] the voices of many birds" (247). The literary reader finds echoing in his mind at this point two lines from near the end of the "Ode to a Nightingale," that poetic bird whose song had often

> Charmed magic casements, opening on the foam
> Of perilous seas, in faery lands forlorn.

Even as the phrasing in general fits the present enchantment of Hyacinth at Medley, so Keats's modifiers "perilous" and "forlorn" recall the background of anxiety the hero has brought with him because of his recent pledge to sacrifice his life. That foreboding is echoed with ironic inversion in the cry that opens this same penultimate stanza:

> Thou wast not born for death, immortal Bird!
> No hungry generations tread thee down.

[154]

What is denied as to the nightingale is tragically prophetic for Hyacinth.

Indeed, the theme of Keats's great ode—a dream of magical beauty shot through with the pained awareness of transience as man's ineluctable destiny —permeates the whole interlude at Medley. Lest one should think that the critic here is reading into the novel's text literary allusions that exist only in his own mind, James himself can be cited in support. On the second page of chapter twenty-two there is a flashback to Hyacinth's arrival the night before. As it was quite late, the Princess had retired and he was served his supper alone in a vast high hall: "The repast was delicate—though his other senses were so awake that hunger dropped out and he ate, as it were, without eating—and the grave automatic servant filled his glass wih a liquor that reminded him of some lines of Keats in the "Ode to a Nightingale." He wondered if he should hear a nightingale at Medley" (248). The author's intention of making a Keatsian parallel is dramatized by having his hero do the recollecting. Hearing a poetic nightingale will enrich his experiences at Medley even more than hearing an actual one. The lines Hyacinth is reminded of are beyond question those of the second stanza, with its sensuous evocation of beauty in nature and in poetry:

> O, for a draught of vintage! that hath been
> Cool'd a long age in the deep-delved earth,
> Tasting of Flora and the country green,
> Dance, and Provençal song, and sunburnt mirth!
> O, for a beaker full of the warm South,
> Full of the true, the blushful Hippocrene,
> With beaded bubbles winking at the brim,
> And purple-stained mouth ....

These lines are echoed in Hyacinth's own words at the end of his first twenty-four hours at Medley: "The cup of an exquisite experience ... was at his lips; it was purple with the wine of romance, of reality, of civilization, and he couldn't push it aside without drinking" (271).

The glories that the great house has in store for him—the world of nature as "improved" by the aristocracy, the world of art as an international heritage —all these are symbolized by the ritual draught from the fountain of the Muses offered him in Keats's Ode. But the lines that follow must have taken him back to the night at the Sun and Moon:

> That I might drink, and leave the world unseen,
>
> · · · · · · · · · · · · ·
> The weariness, the fever, and the fret
> Here, where men sit and hear each other groan.

[155]

Once again the "Ode to a Nightingale" answers to both aspects of the hero: the despairing and disillusioned revolutionary, the young esthete ecstatic before the unfolding glories of Medley

If Keats's poem is in Hyacinth's mind during these experiences, it may also quite properly be in the mind of the reader, extending the meaning of this central episode. James's allusion is limited to a single phrase, but this is enough to bring into play an external reference system of richness and complexity. There has always been a suggestion of the poet about Hyacinth in James's descriptions: large eyes set in a pale complexion, sensitive features, golden brown hair clustered in curls around a high forehead. Of all the Romantic poets who may have served as something of a model, surely Keats is the most likely—a cockney, an apostle of beauty who died at the age of twenty-five, a poet whose face in the Severn portrait is at least suggestive of James's hero (sensuous but delicate features and a high forehead framed by the kind of curling hair the Greeks called "hyacinthine").

In his long conversation with the Princess about the Underground Hyacinth reverts once to the dark winter night of his oath, but most of the Medley interlude is set in spring sunshine. He had arrived at the end of April and remained for three weeks (249, 301)—precisely the "seasonable month" chosen by Keats as a setting for his ode, the period of the "coming musk-rose, . . . mid-May's eldest child." On the morning after his arrival Hyacinth took a long walk through the park before breakfast:

> He rambled an hour in breathless ecstasy, brushing the dew from the deep fern and bracken and the rich borders of the garden, tasting the fragrant air and stopping everywhere, in murmuring rapture, at the touch of some exquisite impression. His whole walk was peopled with recognitions; he had been dreaming all his life of just such a place and such objects, such a morning and such a chance. (249)

For an innocent like Hyacinth what could his "recognitions" come from other than his reading? ("I cannot see what flowers are at my feet, / Nor what soft incense hangs upon the boughs.")

When the Princess took him for a long drive one afternoon, carrying out her promise to show him the whole of this exquisitely beautiful countryside, "he was by this time quite at sea and could recognize no shores." The last occasion when Hyacinth had "wholly lost a sense of his whereabouts" was during the drive to Hoffendahl's through the murky miles of drizzling gloom. As totally different as these two occasions were, they had one thing in common: both were so far removed from the real world of the little bookbinder that he felt quite lost each time, though in very different ways. As for his present drive in the Princess's old-fashioned barouche, the author concludes:

"If Hyacinth was uplifted during these delightful hours he at least measured his vertiginous eminence, and it kept him quite solemnly still, as with the fear that a wrong movement of any sort would break the charm, cause the curtain to fall on the play" (262–263). The Cinderella role, in this version of the story, is assigned not to the Princess but to Hyacinth.

Medley Hall itself was equally enchanting—like a fairy-tale palace, complete with "ramparts" and a "moat"—opening up for him the splendors of the aristocracy's privileged world. Of all the great houses in James's novels it is the most fully described, inside and outside—probably to emphasize the contrast between the richness of its beauty and the poverty of experience of Hyacinth, the viewing consciousness. The Princess took a personal pleasure in showing him through the interior. At the end of the tour she made a curious kind of apology as to why she, who wanted to associate herself with the uprising of the poor, should be living in a house with forty or fifty rooms. She needed a rest (such was her plea) and only rented this place for the season because it was so "cheap." Hyacinth was aware of this anomaly all day: "it added much to his sense of the tragicomical to think of the Princess's having retired to a private paradise to think out the problems of the slums" (256). The other anomaly, that all this grandeur was only borrowed, so to speak, merely made that lady more of an enigma than ever to the little bookbinder.

Two particularized descriptions of the interior of Medley are symbolic of the hero's evolving notion of himself and of his most important relationship in the novel, namely with the Princess. On his first night at Medley he had lain down on a bed in "a large high room where long dressing-glasses emitted ghostly glances even after the light was extinguished." Getting up several times to peer by candlelight at the fine prints and rare old engravings on the walls: "He looked at himself in one of the long glasses, and in a place where everything was on such a scale it seemed to him more than ever that Mademoiselle Vivier's son, lacking all the social dimensions, was scarce a perceptible person at all" (249). Hyacinth's mirror image of himself as almost invisible at Medley is suggestive of several things. Coming from such an obscure background he doesn't even make a reflection in these splendid glasses, amid such grandeur he doesn't even exist. This may have been the hero's self-deprecating image of himself on arrival. In an opposite sense, the self that he brought with him may have already begun to fade out, so as to make way for a new self to appear.

At all events, under the spell of his hostess and her great house, a magical transformation takes place in the hero during the next twenty-four hours. Before lunch, and before his first confrontation with the Princess, he was conducted by a butler to the library, a great room lined with row upon row of finely-bound books:

> A fire of logs crackled in a great chimney, and there were alcoves with deep window-seats, and armchairs such as he had never seen, luxurious, leather-covered, with an adjustment for holding one's volume.... In the course of an hour he had ravaged the collection, taken down almost every book, wishing he could keep it a week, and then put it back as quickly as his eye caught the next, which glowed with a sharper challenge. He came upon rare bindings and extracted precious hints—hints by which he felt himself perfectly capable of profiting. Altogether his vision of true happiness at this moment was that for a month or two he should be locked into the treasure-house of Medley. He forgot the outer world and the morning waned. (250–251)

With this scene begins the emergence of a new self. "He forgot the outer world"—that is, old Crook's shop where binding books was simply working for wages, the Sun and the Moon where he had pledged to sacrifice his life for the People, the whole shabby milieu to which he had been born. He was aware now only of "the treasure-house of Medley," where he yearned to browse endlessly. The bindings showed him that his trade could be turned into an art. And as he took down book after book, he was even more entranced with their contents. James does not specify which authors drew him, but the reader can guess from previous references to Hyacinth's reading: Bulwer and Balzac, Tennyson and Keats. Though it is some months yet before his "transition into literature," from binding books to writing them (340–341), he has already begun to feel at home in an entirely different milieu, a gentleman's library. When this aspect of Hyacinth's new self fully materializes it gives him confidence that he has a visible identity, even in the presence of the mistress of Medley.

Hyacinth had determined that he would only spend a weekend at the great house; he must return to London where he earned his living. But he could not resist her pleading, "Let me then give you wages. You'll work for me," she said persuasively, "You'll bind all my books" (268). Even in the act of submitting to her desire he asserted a true craftsman's pride in his skill. But this was only half of the influence that pressed on him to stay for a prolonged visit. The rest was the desire of the incipient artist for more of what had only just now wakened him to life (271).

By the third day of his visit the new image of Hyacinth as a gentleman connoisseur is fully established. At the end of a long talk with him, on a rainy afternoon, the Princess said quite forthrightly: "You come out of the poor cramped hole you've described to me, and yet you might have stayed in country-houses all your life." There are Italians with that sort of "natural tact," she concluded, but she had never found it in any Anglo-Saxon except the most cultivated (283). "Do you mean I'm a gentleman?" Hyacinth asked, highly conscious of the meaning of "natural" as applied to himself. At this point he revealed to her that he was, indeed, the natural son of a nobleman. Convinced of her sense of delicacy and of her sympathy for him, he told her that which had never before passed his lips, the whole secret of his sordid origin. (What he does not know, of course, is that the Princess also was born a bastard and that one of the mainsprings of her behavior is her awareness of this fact. Even though the point is quite properly passed over without mention in the present novel, readers of the earlier *Roderick Hudson* are aware of the ironic situation, as James knew they would be.)

These references back to his dismal London life, inevitable for a temperament like Hyacinth's, only serve to heighten the fabulous quality of the Medley interlude. And James gives a final fairy-tale touch to this experience by framing it with poetic allusions, submerged though they may be. Months before he visited the Princess in her country house he had a prophetic vision of it—from the window of an attic tenement, of all places, during the Muniments' tea party. Looking out over this slum area, he saw with an inward as well as an outward eye: "High above, in a clearer smokeless zone, a sky still fair and luminous, a faint silver star looked down. The sky was the same that bent far away in the country over golden fields and purple hills and gardens where nightingales sang" (170–171). Surely there must have come to the mind of this wishful-thinking young man, as it does to the reader's, the well-known nursery-rhyme:

> Starlight, star bright,
> First star I've seen tonight,
> I wish I may, I wish I might....

All of the astrological implications of this scene are fulfilled for our star-crossed hero the following April. His first view of Medley, on the night of his arrival, was that of "a range of vague grand effects [lifted] into the starlight" (248); it was only minutes later that he heard his first nightingale, a poetic one as previously noted. And as at the beginning of this interlude so at the end. Less than a month after he had left the Princess and her country house he looked back over his recent experience, savoring its rarest strangest moments: "His last week at Medley in especial had already become a far-off fable, the echo of a song; he could read it over as a romance bound in vellum and gold" (322). Here the little poetic bookbinder is certainly echoing the closing lines of Keats's great ode:

Was it a vision, or a waking dream?
Fled is that music:—Do I wake or sleep?

At Medley Hyacinth had momentarily stepped through a storied window
into the world of his lost paternity. Pinnie's illness called him back to the
prison of his maternity, her death reenacting that of his mother. When he
returned to Lomax Place, that "scarce-dissimulated slum," he found it more
depressing than ever. Though spring was far advanced, the day outside was
"a dark drizzle" and the little parlor seemed dismal and clammy. What was
most vivid to him was his own changed vision. "He had known the scene for
hideous and sordid, but its aspect today was pitiful to the verge of the sick-
ening; he couldn't believe that for years he had accepted and even a little
revered it. He was frightened at the sort of service his experience of grandeur
had rendered him" (302). At this juncture—the final contrast between the
two places that symbolize the two worlds Hyacinth is lost between—it seems
appropriate to point out that James's play on names extends to them too, as
part of his fable-making. The proper name Lomax is connected by Webster
with *lummox* ("a clumsy or stupid person"), and its etymology suggests the
"corner or recess of a pool." This gives a final touch of unpleasantness to the
only place he was ever to know as home. As for Medley, the implied meanings
are more complex. It is a convincing name for an English country house, to
be sure, but it also suggests music though of an impure kind, because "medley"
in that art means a mixture of "incongruous passages from heterogeneous
compositions." To the hero, in memory, it was "the echo of a song"—like that
of Keats's nightingale, "In some melodious plot / Singing of summer in full-
throated ease." But to readers, Medley is a strange mixture of high and low,
an aristocratic seat where theatrical talk of the revolution went on.

"While *he* was masquerading in high life," so Hyacinth accused himself,
"his wretched little foster-mother [had] struggled alone with her death-stroke"
(300–301). Some such ending was necessary to the proper working out of
James's fable, since it was impossible that the young man who had been
transformed by Medley should come back to Lomax Place and resume his old
life there. Out of her pinching and scraping Pinnie had left him a legacy of
thirty-seven pounds, hoping he would "go abroad and see the world." In a
matter of weeks the little bookbinder, like any proper young gentleman, had
launched himself on the Grand Tour.

Dream and Nightmare

The opening page of Book Fourth finds Hyacinth seated at a sidewalk café
in the French capital, taking stock of the myriad impressions of the past

week. The whole of his Parisian experience is rendered by picture and scene during this evening revery, which occupies the next two chapters. (The device, a minor version of Isabel's midnight vigil in *The Portrait of a Lady*, solved the technical problem of how the author could report on what happened when his hero was entirely alone.) Quite naturally Hyacinth's understanding of the new civilization across the Channel came through contrasting it with the one he had known in England:

All Paris struck him as tremendously artistic and decorative; he felt as if hitherto he had lived in a dusky, frowsy, Philistine world, a world in which the taste was the taste of Little Peddlington and the idea of beautiful arrangement had never had an influence. In his ancestral city it had been active from the first, and that was why his quick sensibility responded and why he murmured his constant refrain whenever the fairness of the great monuments arrested him in the pearly silvery light or he saw them take grey-blue, delicate tones at the end of stately vistas. It seemed to him the place expressed herself, and did it in the grand style, while London remained vague and blurred, inarticulate, blunt and dim. Splendid Paris, charming Paris indeed! (320, 321)

Once again James has transferred to Hyacinth his own education by visual contrasts. In an essay of 1877, "Paris Revisited," James had used the same phrase ("Splendid Paris, charming Paris") for his own response on returning after a year in London, "looking at the most brilliant city in the world with eyes attuned to a different pitch." Actually, the novelist's deepest experiences of the two cities came in reverse order. His essay entitled "London" describes the English capital as he saw it during the decade following directly on his climactic year, 1875-76, in the French capital. For him also a comparison was unavoidable:

The absence of style, or rather of the intention of style, is certainly the most general characteristic of the face of London. To cross to Paris under this impression is to find one's self surrounded with far other standards. There everything reminds you that the idea of beautiful and stately arrangement has never been out of fashion, that the art of composition has always been at work or at play. Avenues and squares, gardens and quays, have been distributed for effect, and to-day the splendid city reaps the accumulation of all this ingenuity; ... the whole air of the place is architectural. On the banks of the Thames it is a tremendous chapter of accidents—the London-lover has to confess to the existence of miles upon miles of the dreariest, stodgiest commoness.

The similarity of phrasing is sufficient proof of the link between author and hero here, at least in esthetic response.

On arrival in the French capital Hyacinth had resumed his old habit of taking interminable strolls, his one sure mode of knowing the world outside himself. Because of the haphazard development of London, as previously pointed out, every walk he took there led him across a hodge-podge of "high" and "low." In Paris, because of architectural planning he could walk for miles without straying from "the grand style." So, paradoxically, his ancestral city freed him, at least visually, from the sense of being lost between the two worlds of his mismatched parents.

Another dimension was added to his new freedom by a trick of the imagination. Being alone, what more natural than that he should resurrect the grandfather for whom he was named, Hyacinthe Vivier, to be the companion of his walks in Paris. Fantastic as this apparition may seem, the hero of 1848 is closer to young Hyacinth's psychological "realities" at the moment than any of his friends, so that it is quite convincing for such a double or alter ego to materialize for him. In this way it may be said that the hero's two selves merge, as he roams the streets of the most beautiful city in the world with this harmless wraith of a departed revolutionary.

After Paris a postscript is all that Venice calls for. This time James solved the technical problem of reporting on his solitary traveller by falling back on one of the oldest novelistic modes, the epistolary. What Hyacinth chose to record in his letter to the Princess was the picture he saw through the window of his *pensione*, framed like a stage set: lovely young Venetian girls gliding across a little *campo* to fill their copper water jugs at the fountain in front of a shabby church (332–333). Venice offered this important lesson in Hyacinth's *education sentimentale*: beauty is not necessarily dependent on wealth and privilege. In Paris he had been overwhelmed by the art and architecture made possible by Church and Monarchy. But in Italy, more than anywhere in Europe, beauty permeates all levels of life and can be found everywhere—in the commonest street scenes, in the poorest quarters, in the costume and posture and *bel camino* of the working classes. It can be shared by all without need of the violence of revolution.

The half-dozen essays on Venice written over several decades by James provided him with all the details he needed for Hyacinth's visual experience of this enchanted city. In addition to the obscure little square, the hero surrendered himself as a matter of course to all the glory of cathedral and gallery and palace surrounding the most famous square in the world. The single shining sentence describing Saint Mark's as "an immense open-air drawing-room" prepares for the momentous conclusion to Hyacinth's letter. His language echoes that of the Princess at Medley, in her attack on the unfairness of the social order, but he turns her argument the other way round:

> The monuments and treasures of art, the great palaces and properties, the conquests of learning and taste, the general fabric of civilization as we know it, based if you will upon all the despotisms, the cruelties, the exclusions, the monopolies and rapacities of the past, but thanks to which, all the same, the world is less of a "bloody sell" and life more of a lark. (334-335)

Hoffendahl is specifically named as one of the "barbarians" who want to redistribute all this wealth and beauty, and by implication the Princess is another. As for himself, he has outgrown the narrow view of the revolutionist, has "lost sight of the sacred cause almost altogether" as the result of his recent adventures.

The Grand Tour was Hyacinth's finishing school. It had educated him out of the world he was born to—which he had pledged to sacrifice his life for—and into a world he could never take part in except as an observer. His transformation was now complete, symbolized by his description of two great continental capitals of art, Paris and Venice.

During the few months that remained for Hyacinth to live, after his return to England, he escaped whenever he could into dreams of that beauty he had come to know at Medley, then on the Continent. But for the most part he was bound down to his daily life in London, with the nightmare of his oath and its fulfillment always hovering over him. One of the most disturbing aspects of all bad dreams is that even the most familiar places and the most stable relationships tend to shift and slide away from under one's feet. So it was with Hyacinth now. The first change was voluntary, to be sure. With Pinnie dead he could not go home again to Lomax Place. Instead of looking for a new lodging in the same old quarter, he found one in the slums of Westminster. It was nearer to the bookbindery, he told himself. It was also in a neighborhood where he was totally unknown, one may add, and anonymity was congenial to his present mood.

The second change was disconcerting. Going to Mayfair for a visit with the Princess, Hyacinth was startled to find an auctioneer's advertisement in the window of her house and no word as to where she had moved. The circumstances under which they came together again, shortly afterwards, added to the shock. When Hyacinth went to call on his other best friend, at Audley Court, he found four people crowded into the tiny attic room. But he only had eyes for the newcomer to that familiar circle. Though dressed in a simple bonnet and mantle, the Princess looked "like a radiant angel...ministering charity" (343–344). Her conquest of Rosy Muniment and Lady Aurora had been immediate, and apparently she had made quite an impression on Paul also: "In short she held the trio in her hand,...and she performed admirably and artistically for their benefit" (345). She signalled Hyacinth not to notice her too much, not to "make any kind of scene." But in compensation he gained a perspective that enabled him to see, as if for the first time, what a consummate actress she was.

Whenever human behavior approaches the theatrical, it raises the question of sincerity. Hyacinth was always fascinated by Christina's ability to play many roles, and in this he showed his kinship once again with the author. For Henry James found the mirror relationship of theater and reality much to his purpose as an artist. Just as characters on stage seek to create the illusion of real life, so people in their actual lives go in for a good deal of acting—as do many characters in his fictions: Roderick Hudson, Isabel Archer, the Bellegarde family, Lambert Strether, Kate Croy, and Hyacinth Robinson as well as the Princess Casamassima. James learned about this relationship between appearance and reality quite early, according to the evidence of *A Small Boy and Others*. He was very young indeed when he witnessed a little domestic "drama" at Linwood, the home of an uncle dying of tuberculosis. His small cousin Marie, not wanting to obey her father and go to bed, rushed into the arms of her mother, who said with quiet discipline: "Come now, don't make a scene!" Suddenly the young James realized that at crises life becomes "scenes" and we can *make* them or not, as we choose—a valuable lesson for the future novelist.

On the summer afternoon at Audley Court it was the Princess who made a scene. Or rather it was James who created a scene in his new mode, using her as a catalyst. The new relations between Paul, Lady Aurora, and Christina—brought about through the latter's manifold talent as an actress—had left Hyacinth feeling excluded from this intimate though complex triangle, an outsider in the little flat where he had previously felt most at home. Even when he escorted the Princess home, the experience was as strange as it was delightful, for she was still acting. He was curiously reminded of previous rambles: "She stopped as Millicent had done to look into the windows of vulgar establishments and amused herself with picking out the abominable objects she should like to possess" (354). The characters closest to Hyacinth now tend to shift and merge with their polar opposites, like figures in a disturbing dream. (When he went to see Milly on the last day of his life he found that she, in her desire to rise in the world, had slipped into a discarded pair of the Princess's shoes—that is, she had begun an affaire with Captain Sholto.)

The walk itself repeated the familiar pattern of wandering between two worlds, the low and the high. The route is not specified, but it can be conjectured: from the slums of Camberwell across Westminster Bridge, through Hyde Park, then past Kensington Palace into the lower-middle-class regions of Paddington. The Princess had given up all her beautiful things and was living in an ugly little house on Madeira Crescent, almost as shabby as Lomax Place: "The street was not squalid, but it was mean and meagre and fourth-rate and had in the highest degree that petty parochial air, that absence of style and elevation, which is the stamp of whole districts of London and which Hyacinth had already more than once mentally compared with the high-piled, important look of the Parisian perspective" (353). Surveying the street scene from a window in one of the houses in this "paltry Philistine row" was "a gentleman in a dirty dressing-gown, smoking a pipe, who made Hyacinth think of Mr. Micawber." From Keatsian magic casements to a cockney villa suggestive of Dickens! "The abruptness of the transformation took away his breath."

Yearning for a long fraternizing talk with Paul Muniment such as had marked their earlier relations, Hyacinth returned to Audley Court one Sunday in September and the two friends decided to make a day of it by embarking on a penny steamer for Greenwich. Squeezed into the crowd "amid the fumes of vile tobacco, beneath a shower of soot" they watched the shore-line, "the big black fringe of the yellow stream," as the little boat moved slowly down the Thames from Westminster Bridge:

> The river had always for Hyacinth a deep beguilement. The ambiguous appeal he had felt as a child in all the aspects of London came back to him from the dark detail of its banks and the sordid agitation of its bosom; the great arches and pillars of the bridges, where the water rushed and the funnels tipped and sounds made an echo and there seemed an overhanging of interminable processions; the miles of ugly wharves and warehouses; the lean protrusion of chimney, mast and crane; the painted signs of grimy industries staring from shore to shore; the strange, flat, obstructive barges, straining and bumping on some business as to which everything was vague but that it was remarkably dirty; the clumsy coasters and colliers which thickened as one went down; ... in short all the grinding, puffing, smoking, splashing activity of the turbid flood. (373)

This description of London-on-the-Thames is reminiscent of the prison scene at the beginning of the novel. When the reader turns back to chapter three, he finds spelled out there the ambiguous appeal Hyacinth had felt as a child:

the city like a great factory, Millbank Prison the epitome of all that is sinister, the river foul but powerful with energy (47).

James had made a similar excursion himself on a "little grimy sixpenny steamer," during the first year of his English residence, and it is clearly his own vision that is assigned to Hyacinth during his trip down the Thames with Paul. In his essay "London at Midsummer" James recorded:

> I scarce know how to speak of the little voyage from Westminster Bridge to Greenwich.... It initiates you into the duskiness, the blackness, the crowdedness, the intensely commercial character of London. For miles and miles you see nothing but the sooty backs of warehouses, a sordid river-front.... They stand massed together on the banks of the wide turbid stream.... A damp-looking, dirty blackness is the universal tone. The river is almost black, and is covered with black barges; above the black housetops, from among the far-stretching docks and basins, rises a dusky wilderness of masts. The little puffing steamer is dingy and gritty— it belches a sable cloud that keeps you company as you go.

There are several more details of James's essay that found their way into his novel; one of these must be saved for the end, another fits into the picture here. When his steamer reached its destination, James wandered over the slopes of Greenwich Park, "a charming place, rather shabby and footworn," and admired the "views of the widening Thames...and the great pompous buildings of the old Hospital." Similarly in the novel:

> [Hyacinth and his friend] lay in the brown, crushed grass on one of the slopes of Greenwich Park and saw the river stretch away and shine beyond the pompous colonades of the Hospital.... The companions had [already] wandered through the great halls and courts of the Hospital; had gazed up at the glories of the famous painted chamber and admired the long and lurid series of the naval victories of England—Muniment remarking to his friend that he supposed he had seen the match to all that in foreign parts, offensive little travelled beggar that he was (374).

As James draws upon his travel sketch it is interesting to watch him sharpen his picture by eliminating superfluous details and recomposing the whole. But what is most interesting is the way he transforms these simple descriptions to illuminate his theme.

Hyacinth's river-trip to Greenwich, like his rambles through London, represented once again the low and high worlds of his dilemma, but this time ambiguously. The dirty Thames with those dark buildings lining its banks could only seem to him ugly and depressing, yet it symbolized the commercial wealth and power of the great city in contrast to the sordid crowd of fellow toilers taking a holiday on the little steamer. On the other hand, the "pompous" hospital at Greenwich with its grand scale wall paintings, as he undoubtedly knew, was founded by a king as a home for seamen pensioners. Again, the grassy slope of the "shabby, charming park," which James had merely strolled over as a casual tourist, now became the setting for a serious but confusing conversation between the two young men, haunted by Hyacinth's dream of past beauty as well the nightmare of his present situation.

What muddled everything was Paul's equivocal attitude toward his predicament. The challenge, quite out of the blue, that Hyacinth no longer believed in the cause brought forth the following exchange:

> "I don't know what I believe, God help me! ... I don't want you to think I've ceased to care for the people. What am I but one of the poorest and meanest of them?"
>
> "You, my boy? You're a duke in disguise." (379)

This taunt, plus the earlier twitting that he had seen finer art on the Continent than the great hospital at Greenwich could boast, reminded Hyacinth once again of his frustrating double vision: "He saw the immeasurable misery of the people, ... and yet he saw all the treasures, the felicities, the splendours, the successes of the world." Sometimes, to his imagination, these took the form of a "dazzling irradiation of light from objects undefined, mixed with the atmosphere of Paris and of Venice" (379). Never had his vision of beauty for the lucky few been more dramatically juxtaposed with his awareness of the people's hideous reality, and his own. Thinking of this made him burst out with a cry: "I don't want to *make a scene*, ... but how will you like it when I am strung upon the gallows " (375; italics added). In his reply Paul was simply evasive. So the holiday ended with a final ambiguity. For some months Hyacinth had been aware of a "strange conversion taking place in his mental image of the man whose hardness—of course he was obliged to be hard—he had never expected to see turned upon a passionate admirer" (370). Muniment's behavior on this Sunday excursion was such as to confirm his worst apprehensions.

Similarly Hyacinth's renewed intimacy with the Princess, which Book Fifth begins with, was ambiguous in many ways. Since she had given him a standing invitation to come to tea, he spent many evenings at Madeira Crescent. He yearned for someone with whom to share his glorious experience of the world of art on the Continent, and the Princess was the only one of his acquaintances who was equal to that. But in the new role she had decided to play she wanted only to talk of the revolution and to make pilgrimages to the wretched poor with him as guide. The reversal of their deepest concerns was now almost complete.

As autumn drifted into winter this conflict was resolved. Hyacinth's services as guide to the slums and as companion in revolutionary plotting were gradually taken over by the Princess's new friends, Lady Aurora and Paul Muniment. Hyacinth himself was glad enough to be freed from concern with the "everlasting nightmare" (415). He and the Princess developed an entirely new kind of relationship, settling for those matters on which they could not possibly differ. She would relate episodes from her past life in a variety of foreign courts. He would read poetry aloud to her, Browning's *Men and Women* for example, or talk to her about his passion for the arts. "Hyacinth, on the opposite side of the fire, felt at times almost as if he were married to his hostess, so many things were taken for granted between them" (410).

Under the spell of these pleasant evenings, there were moments when he allowed himself to believe that a meaningful life might open up for him again, moments when he substituted for his haunting vision of Europe's past art a seemingly more attainable present dream of beauty:

> There were nights of November and December, as he trod the greasy pavements that lay between Westminster and Paddington, groping his way through the baffled lamplight and tasting the smoke-seasoned fog, when there was more happiness in his heart than he had ever known. The influence of his permeating London had closed over him again; Paris and Milan and Venice had shimmered away into reminiscence and picture; and as the great city which was most his own lay round him under her pall like an immeasurable breathing monster he felt a vague excitement, as he had felt before, only now with more knowledge, that it was the richest expression of man.... He suspended, so to say, his small sensibility in the midst of it, to quiver there with joy and hope and ambition as well as with the effort of renunciation. (409)

Though the passage does not specify the "ambition" the mere thought of which fills Hyacinth with happiness, readers will remember his recent resolution. He had no intention of remaining a bookbinder to the end of his days. He had proposed to himself, instead, to write something: "That was to be his transition—into literature: to bind the book, charming as the process might be, was after all much less fundamental than to write it" (341). And the context above suggests the kind of writer he might hope to be, the poet of London's streets and people.

A similar ambition had motivated Henry James in his choice of London as his permanent residence. It was the ideal post of observation for a novelist, he recorded in a Notebook entry of 1881, some five years after coming there from Paris, in spite of its obvious unpleasantness:

> The fogs, the smoke, the dirt, the darkness, the wet, the distances, the ugliness, the brutal size of the place.... But these are occasional moods; and for one who takes it as I take it, London is on the whole the most possible form of life. I take it as an artist... whose business is the study of human life. It is the biggest aggregation of human life—the most complete compendium of the world.... I was in a state of deep delight.... I used to take long walks in the rain. I took possession of London; I felt it to be the right place.

It is clear that the great city lying around Hyacinth was the source of his unnamed ambition in the above meditation. One may even hazard a guess that he was hoping to write an English counterpart of the book he had just been reading aloud to the Princess, *Men and Women*. Browning's masterpiece, inspired by the rich pageant of Italian life, is filled with those portraits for which he is chiefly remembered: "Andrea del Sarto," "A Light Woman," "Up at a Villa—Down in the City," and a dozen more. Hyacinth's London could offer him an equally varied gallery of characters to sketch. Also, one of the dominant themes of *Men and Women* is the range of subtle relationships possible between those in love. Some of these poems are strongly suggestive of Hyacinth's recent experiences and his present situation: "Any Wife to Any Husband," "Love Among the Ruins," love perfectly realized in "By the Fireside," love defeated by the very nature of life in "Two in the Campagna."

Is James offering the literary reader a clue to his hero's development during this crucial period in the sequence of poets referred to as his favorites? First Tennyson, a volume of whose poems Hyacinth had chosen to bind as a gift for the Princess at the beginning of their friendship. Then, after the magic weeks at Medley, Keats seems clearly the poet he would emulate: "It had occurred to Hyacinth more than once that it would be a fine thing to produce a rare death-song" (341). And now Browning, though of course it is only a conjecture that *Men and Women* was in his mind as a model this winter. To be a poet was merely part of his dream of beauty, cut short by suicide, but necessary to his survival during the interval that remained.

It may seem unduly pessimistic for Hyacinth to add "renunciation" as an alternative to ambition at the very moment when "joy and hope" had reached a new high for him. But he had had enough shocks since his return from Europe to make him realize how precarious his hold on happiness was. Then came the belated discovery of something that had been going on quite literally behind his back. Exigencies of plot and of his hero's character had forced James to "go behind" in two chapters preceding and in two following the chapter setting forth his illusory happiness. (These are the first episodes not seen through Hyacinth's eyes since the beginning of the novel.) At last Prince Casamassima told him, what readers had suspected for some time, that Muniment was his wife's lover. It is ironical in the extreme that Hyacinth should learn about the defection of his two best friends through the surreptitious peeping of the Prince, who has been an outsider to everything throughout the novel. Renunciation was all that remained for the excluded little bookbinder. The joy and hope that had flickered in his breast for a little while went out, and without them the ambition to be a creative artist could only fade away.

After this Hyacinth's visits to Audley Court as well as to Madeira Crescent came to an end. Where could he turn now? Determined not to be alone, one Sunday night at the end of winter, he made a call on Lady Aurora. (Darkness had become a "haunted element" for him, and he feared the evenings in advance.) Since she always treated him quite naturally as a gentleman, he felt comfortable in her presence. On this occasion, "A tacit confession passed and repassed" between them, and each understood the situation of the other (464). She was in love with Paul just as he was with the Princess, and the burgeoning affair between those two left Lady Aurora and Hyacinth equally deprived. They, like the Prince, were now outsiders.

As the evening was only half spent, he made the familiar pilgrimage to Lisson Grove, in a final search for companionship, looking forward to his usual warm reception. But the Poupins greeted him with embarrassment and confusion instead, because another visitor had preceded him bearing a sealed letter. Hyacinth's visit came to an abrupt end when he walked out of the apartment, exasperated with his friends for evading the truth. Schinkel, the messenger, followed and accompanied him on the long walk home—from the cockney suburb of Paddington, through the Park, then Mayfair, to his lodging in the slums of Westminster—but did not give him the letter until they parted. Without looking at it, Hyacinth transferred it to his own pocket, where it "pressed against his heart ... as the very penetration of a fatal knife" (482).

It was not until he was alone in his own room that he opened the letter and read it. (It is not until two days later, and indirectly, that the reader learns its contents: Hoffendahl's command to Hyacinth to assassinate a duke.) He did not close his eyes that night. And on Monday he walked about in his torment all day, unable to go to work. Hyacinth was in desperate need of help, or advice, or at least comfort. But none of his old friends availed him in his hour of crisis. Now he was facing another day, with the grim realization that he had nothing to do save that which he could not bring himself to do. When he tried to forget his change of heart and commit himself to one brave act in the name of the revolution, it came over him with horror that by assassinating a lord he would simply be repeating his mother's bloody crime.

Hyacinth's contradictory loyalties to two entirely different worlds had brought him to an impasse that could have only one resolution. His basic emotional and mental state, balanced precariously throughout the novel between perceptiveness and bewilderment (the predicament on which everything depends, according to James's Preface), had foundered in that sea of uncertainty essential to tragedy. He was alone and mocked and misunderstood. He had nothing to do and quite literally nowhere to go. Visits to all his friends had failed.

The alternative, to fall back on his old habit of roaming through London, was the last resort of loneliness and despair:

> Anyhow he went forth again into the streets, into the squares, into the parks, solicited by an aimless desire to steep himself yet once again in the great, indifferent city he so knew and so loved and which had had so many of his smiles and tears and confidences. The day was grey and damp, though no rain fell, and London had never appeared to him to wear more proudly and publicly the stamp of her imperial history. He passed slowly to and fro over Westminster bridge and watched the black barges drift on the great brown river; looked up at the huge fretted palace [of Parliament] that rose there as a fortress of the social order which he, like the young David, had been commissioned to attack with a sling and pebble. (504)

Henry James's sketch of London-on-the-Thames, in the essay recording his excursion down to Greenwich, concludes with a similar suggestion that this scene symbolizes British imperial power. After dilating on the glutinous London fog and the dirty blackness that characterizes the whole picture, James adds:

> But it is very impressive in spite of its want of lightness and brightness, and though it is ugly it is anything but trivial.... It sounds rather absurd, but all this smudgy detail may remind you of nothing less than the wealth and power of the British Empire at large.... I know that when I look off to the left at the East India Docks, or pass under the dark hugely piled bridges, where the railway trains and the human processions are forever moving, I feel a kind of imaginative thrill. The tremendous piers of the bridges, in especial, seem the very pillars of the Empire.

The "imaginative thrill" felt by the author when confronting the symbols of British imperial power is transmuted into a feeling of helplessness in the breast of his tragic hero. It is not in the destiny of young Hyacinth to become a victorious David, nor even a sufficiently noble traitor to merit being condemned to death by the House of Lords. The vision of London on the river trip with Paul Muniment last summer had represented the vast economic forces beyond his comprehension; the same scene now symbolizes the huge indifference and power of the city that will crush him. This is his last view of London. It is also the last day of his life. His suicide follows immediately.

The final scene of the novel is a mere vignette, a post-mortem of the suicide itself, which could not be presented through the consciousness of the hero. Here, one last time, James had to "go behind" his chosen method. The Princess, having heard from Paul that the fatal letter had been delivered to Hyacinth, drove alone in a hansom to his lodgings in Westminster. Waiting outside his locked room was Schinkel, who broke in the door at her request, while she waited "with her hand against her heart." "Hyacinth lay there as if asleep, but there was a horrible thing, a mess of blood, on the counterpane, in his side, in his heart. . . . So much Schinkel saw, but only for an instant; a convulsive movement of the Princess, bending over the body while a strange low cry came from her lips, covered it up" (510). The pistol bought to bring sudden death to a duke Hyacinth had turned against himself. A person committing suicide with a pistol would normally shoot himself through the head. But the vulnerable organ of the hero of *The Princess Cassamassima* was located elsewhere.

For Love or Money

THE WINGS OF THE DOVE

The situation of some young creature ... who, at 20, on the threshold of a life that has seemed boundless, is suddenly condemned to death (by consumption, heart-disease, or whatever) .... She learns that she has but a short time to live, and she rebels, she is terrified, she cries out in her anguish, her tragic young despair. She is in love with life, her dreams of it have been immense, and she clings to it with passion.

So in the *Notebooks* for 3 November 1894 James made his first entry for *The Wings of the Dove*. Just ten days previously, in one of those self-communings that mark the crucial decisions of his career, he had committed himself to the kind of subject that eventually flowered in the three great novels of his major phase. "It comes home to me that solidity of subject, importance, emotional capacity of subject, is the only thing on which, henceforth, it is of the slightest use for me to expend myself," he confided to his *Notebooks*: "Only the fine, the large, the human, the natural, the fundamental, the passionate things."

The notation for *The Wings of the Dove* suggests such a subject, one of universal appeal and also of a deeply personal appeal to James, being based on a primary emotional experience of his youth, the death in 1870 from tuberculosis of his beloved cousin Minny Temple at the age of twenty-four. It is not until the final page of *Notes of a Son and Brother* (1914), that he identifies Minny with Milly Theale, saying that in the novel he sought "to lay the ghost by wrapping it in the beauty and dignity of art." In the last chapter of that autobiographical volume we learn of his cousin's slim fairness and extraordinary pallor, her "dancing flame of thought," her sensibility and her lightly ironic touch, her moral spontaneity and all-embracing humanity. She was "the supreme case of a taste for life as life," James sums up, believing she could conquer her illness if only her will to live were strong enough: "Death, at the last, was dreadful to her; she would have given anything to live." Readers of *The Wings of the Dove* will recognize here many of the fictional heroine's traits. But the parallels to Minny Temple, which are limited to these

[173]

and to Milly Theale's initial situation, are matters for the biographer rather than the literary critic.

During the disastrous years of James's attempt to write plays, 1891–95, there are constant exhortations in the *Notebooks* to "dip my pen [again] into the *other* ink—the sacred fluid of fiction," as compensation for the delays and disappointments of "the horrid theatric trade." He could come back to literature now, he told himself in the winter of 1891–92, with "augmented capacity," with a wealth of newly acquired experience. Then on 30 August 1893 he resolved to get away from the brief fictions he had been experimenting with between stints of writing for the stage: "I want to do something that brings into play character and sincerity and passion; something that marches like a drama." The starting point for such a "large and confident action" was suggested to James by Minny Temple, whose death in the prime of life struck him as being "so of the essence of tragedy."

The actual Minny is left behind, however, as soon as the novelist begins to develop his *donnée* in the three-thousand-word Notebook sketch. There James unfolds the main outline of the plot by which the fictional Milly reaches out for her "taste of happiness," which can only be "the chance to love and be loved," her little snatched experience of life. This is to occur "somewhere" in the social world of Europe, among people who are attracted to her less as appreciators of what she is than as potential exploiters of her fabulous wealth. The characters who lay the "trap" for her are specified, and the point is fully worked out that it will be her discovery of all this, quite as much as her fatal disease, that brings on her tragic death. None of these matters fit the experience of James's cousin. Also shadowed forth in the *Notebooks* is the great theme of *The Wings of the Dove*: the power of love in mortal conflict with the power of money. This theme, the plot (later considerably altered), and especially the method by which all is rendered—these comprise the "splendid and supreme creation" James envisioned. And they are the critic's sole concern.

Picture and Scene

James's new mode, derived from his recent experiences in writing for the stage, was already being hinted at in the Notebook entry of August 1893, more than a year before the conception of *The Wings*, when he resolved to do something "that marches like a drama." Then on 5 January 1895, just two months after the first enthusiastic sketch for his ambitious new novel, came the dismal failure of *Guy Domville* (his first play to reach the stage) and the collapse of all his hopes of writing for the theater. James was over fifty and his career seemed finished. Yet only a few days passed before he recorded in his *Notebooks* a resolution to begin all over again as a novelist, a rededication to literature that was nothing short of heroic: "I take up my *own* old pen again—the pen of all my old unforgettable efforts and sacred struggles. To myself—today—I need say no more. Large and full and high the future still opens. It is now indeed that I may do the work of my life." Finally, in the *Notebooks* for 14 February 1895, as he speculated a second time on the potentialities of his project for *The Wings of the Dove*, he wondered if he should not set down a "scenario" at once, concluding that the one lesson he had learned from the cruel experience of the last five years was "*the singular value for a narrative plan too* of the ... divine principle of the Scenario." This standard term for the outline or synopsis of a drama meant a great deal more to James. For him, as applied to fiction, it was a far more conscious and artful technique for constructing a novel than the older discursive method, which merely let the plot develop gradually from the needs of characters and situations as the writing progressed. By "scenario" he meant a principle of planning that would enable him to work out in advance, as carefully and exactly as possible, details of characters, actions, and specific scenes.

Another and even more important technique that he salvaged from his disaster was the method of scenic construction. This includes, but goes far beyond, the extensive use he had made in earlier fictions of dramatic scenes, largely in dialogue, for moments of crisis. Now he realized that the same method could be made the whole basis of representation in the novel, a technique for rendering rather than telling. His experiments during the next decade developed it into a thoroughgoing principle of conception and execution. By 1895 James had discovered these two closely related techniques that could be translated from the dramatic to the fictional mode, full of promise for that "high future" he felt opening before him. But with the foresight of genius he knew that his projected themes for three major novels should wait until he had tried all kinds of experiments with his new techniques. And they did wait for five to ten years. So with the humility of a confident master he took up his fictional pen again as cautiously as if he were an apprentice.

First he experimented with dramatic possibilities in the short story and the nouvelle. Then came three remarkable novels, appearing between 1896 and 1899. *The Spoils of Poynton* is a short novel about the intrigues and questionable conduct of people desiring to gain possession of valuable old treasures; though he departed from the clear-cut divisions that would have been necessary for "acts" on the stage, he achieved a technical triumph by giving it the compactness of a drama. *What Maisie Knew* explores the theme of evil in the adult world as it is gradually discovered by a highly perceptive child; when, during composition, it threatened to spread itself out at too great length, he warned himself "to stick to the march of an action...—the *scenic* method is my absolute, my imperative, my *only* salvation." *The Awkward Age*, a novel of standard length, is a study of decadence in modern society as revealed by the devious manners and morals of a highly sophisticated coterie; it consists of a series of scenes like concentric circles drawn round its central theme, composed almost exclusively in dialogue—"straight as a play" the author said in summary.

For *Maisie* and *The Spoils* James wrote down in the *Notebooks* fuller initial plans and discussions than for any other works recorded there, some six thousand and ten thousand words respectively, what might be called developing scenarios that could be altered as need arose. For *The Awkward Age* he seems to have written out a full-scale scenario, although it has been lost. This practice was continued for the three great novels of his final period, when he felt himself ready at last to write them, 1900–1904. By a lucky accident the twenty-thousand-word preliminary statement for *The Ambassadors* has survived, of inestimable value to the critic in tracing the evolution of that novel, as will be seen in the next chapter. James states explicitly that he also wrote one for *The Wings of the Dove*, though "only half as long and proportionately less developed," but he destroyed it. (The plan to write one for *The Golden Bowl* was apparently abandoned when that novel failed of serialization.) The careful preparation provided by his use of scenarios enabled James not only to apply his newly learned dramatic techniques but to work out those other formal and structural features that enrich his later novels: elaboration of a central situation; refinements on the device of using as his point of view a single consciousness (or the shifting perspectives of two or three); the method of "balance" or paralleling halves; a new extravagance of imagery that turned his prose into poetry; a new kind of symbolism such as Ibsen had used for the stage; a more subtle use of art objects (especially paintings) as reflectors of character.

If James had not delayed for some years the composition of the three great novels of his major phase, they might have lacked this richness. And for these grand-scale works he found it necessary to create a freer form than the strict scenic method he had used so effectively for the much shorter novels such as *Maisie*. In his Preface to *The Wings of the Dove* he describes the principal structural technique used in this masterpiece as an alternation of "picture" and "scene." He begins his new definition of these terms by speaking of "the odd inveteracy with which picture ... is jealous of drama, and drama ... suspicious of picture." The conflict, by implication, is between the need of space for "picture" and the need of compression for "scene." It is not until his Preface to the next novel that James finally clarifies his definition of picture-and-scene:

The material of "The Ambassadors," conforming in this respect exactly to that of "The Wings of the Dove," published just before it, is taken absolutely for the stuff of drama; so that, availing myself of the opportunity ... for some prefatory remarks on the latter work, I had mainly to make on its behalf the point of its scenic consistency. It disguises that virtue, in the oddest way in the world, by just *looking*, as we turn its pages, as little scenic as possible; but it sharply divides itself into the parts that prepare, that tend in fact to over-prepare, for scenes, and ... the scenes that justify and crown the preparation. It may definitely be said, I think, that everything in it that is not scene ... is discriminated preparation, is the fusion and synthesis of picture.

For readers of *The Wings of the Dove* (as opposed to those who merely "turn its pages"), the scenes provide an understanding of the characters, both in themselves and in their relations to each other; the picture elements either carry the narrative forward or are themselves to a certain extent dramatized and become "scene-settings," scenes without dialogue, taking place in the mind of a character.

The Wings takes its form from this alternation of "picture" and "scene," and most importantly from a combination of the two, as James concludes his definition in the Preface to that novel:

> The secret of the discriminated occasion—that aspect of the subject which we have our noted choice of treating either as picture or scenically, but which is apt, I think, to show its fullest worth in the Scene. Beautiful exceedingly, for that matter, those occasions or parts of an occasion when the boundary line between picture and scene bears a little the weight of the double pressure.

James then goes on to point out two such occasions when picture and scene are blended. The first is the dinner party at Lancaster Gate in Book Fourth, when Mrs. Lowder introduces the heroine to the whole brilliant circle of London society (as far as she can muster it), "where all the offered life centres, in intensity, in the disclosure of Milly's single throbbing consciousness." The second, which is a kind of "mate" or answering parallel to that scene, takes place in Venice much later on in the novel (Book Eighth); this time it is in Kate Croy's consciousness that the drama is brought to a head, "the occasion on which, in the splendid saloon of poor Milly's hired palace, she takes the measure of her friend's festal evening."

This pair of picture-scenes—one-fourth and three-fourths the way through the book respectively—offers a way into the structure and meaning of a novel of nearly eight hundred pages. Grateful to the author for providing such a clue, the critic proceeds at once to an analysis of these chapters, with a slight modification of James's choice of scenes. The dinner party at Lancaster Gate is really a preparation for the even more important picture-scene at Matcham, a great English country house, in Book Fifth. Similarly, the reception at the Venetian palace is preceded and followed by supplementary scenes, set in the frame of resplendent Saint Mark's Square, in which Kate and her fiancé Densher "take the measure" of their own love relation, which is so fatally involved with their relation to Milly. Finally, there is a special added value in focussing on these two occasions: in both the full significance is revealed by a famous painting which serves as a reflecting mirror. At Matcham a very real Bronzino raises the specter of impending death in the midst of a scene that is vibrant with the possibilities of life for Milly. At Palazzo Leporelli an imaginary (or rather a composite) Veronese provides a picture of the high Renaissance style of living, ironically, in the very presence of the dying heroine. A close reading of these two clusters will take us deep into *The Wings of the Dove*, clarifying that strangely ambiguous remark Milly made to her confidante one evening between the two occasions: "Since I've lived all these years as if I were dead, I shall die, no doubt, as if I were alive" (I, 220).

The Bronzino Portrait

They were already dining, she and her friend, at Lancaster Gate, and surrounded, as it seemed to her, with every English accessory.... The smallest things, the faces, the hands, the jewels of the women, the sound of words, especially of names, across the table, the shape of the forks, the arrangement of the flowers, the attitude of the servants, the walls of the room, were all touches in a picture and denotements in a play, and they marked for her, moreover, her alertness of vision. (161, 165)

Such is Milly Theale's launching into the social world of London, at the beginning of Book Fourth. Like so many of James's Americans this fabulous heiress had come to Europe on an extended visit to enrich her experience of life. She had settled for a while in London, where her companion and confidante, Susan Shepherd, got in touch with an old schoolmate, Maud Lowder, now a prominent figure in society. Mrs. Lowder promptly called, with her remarkable niece Kate Croy, and just three days later here the American ladies were "dining at Lancaster Gate."

Milly told herself that she had not wished to do anything so inane as "get into society." She was motivated only by "a desire to see the places she had read about." But now, seated at Mrs. Lowder's end of the great table, with her American companion at the other end near the handsome niece and "twenty persons between them," she began to realize how "her poor prevision had been rebuked by the majesty ... of the event" (165, 166). She had been brought in to dinner by Lord Mark, an enigmatic English nobleman, who was placed between her and their hostess. "Mrs. Lowder's other neighbour was the Bishop of Murrum—a real bishop, such as Milly had never seen, with a complicated costume, a voice like an old-fashioned wind instrument, and a face all the portrait of a prelate; while the gentleman on our young lady's left, a gentleman thick-necked, large and literal, ... clearly counted as an offset to the possession of Lord Mark" (163–164). The table partners had been carefully arranged.

This is the extent of the "picture" or scene-setting. Out of all the numerous company gathered at dinner, James, with the economy of a dramatist, specifies only a half-dozen. Yet all the rest are palpably there, both for the reader and for Milly, who, though she concentrated her attention even more narrowly, felt "justified of her plea for people and her love of life." The whole meaning of the occasion is rendered in her dialogue with Lord Mark, which continues like a running fire throughout, "while plates were changed and dishes presented and periods in the banquet marked" (177)—even the reality of the dinner being skimped, as it would be on stage, to avoid distraction from the main line of interest. James has come a long way from the richly detailed Balzacian settings used in his earlier novels.

The dialogue itself is ambiguous in the extreme, and the meanings that emerge from it keep readers as well as Milly on the alert. Her initial reaction to this great occasion was that it was "really romantic," like a fairy tale, "positively rich and strange" (161, 164). Milly did her best to keep her head, but it had all gone so fast that she merely uttered the truth nearest to hand when she said in her opening gambit to Lord Mark "that she scarce even then knew where she was." When he replied, he gave this an entirely new turn: "He explained ... that there was no such thing, today in London, as saying where any one was. Every one was everywhere—nobody was anywhere" (166–167). When he added that he would be put to it to give a name of any sort to their hostess's "set," even wondered if there were really any such things as "sets" in London any more, Milly was baffled. She had thought she was already "in society," without even wishing to be, and it was disconcerting to have such doubts thrown out by the one person above all at Mrs. Lowder's dinner party who struck her as the prime representative of "an historic patriciate, a class that ... she had never heard otherwise described than as 'fashion'" (169).

Everything about Lord Mark was puzzling to her. She could not tell whether he was a young man who looked old or an old man who looked young, whether he was the most intellectual person present or the most frivolous, and "why did he hover before her as a potentially insolent noble?" He made such ambiguous remarks about Americans in general, and about herself as a representative one, that she could not tell whether he was being complimentary or condescending. She joined in the badinage, understanding as best she could, and James even lets her score an occasional point so as to avoid the triteness of American innocence contrasted with European experience. "You're *blasé*, but you're not enlightened," she said in response to his claim of having run about all over the world so as to leave nothing unlearned: "You're familiar with everything, but conscious really of nothing. What I mean is that you've no imagination" (179–180). With this he was at last amused.

Lord Mark was equally baffling when he pretended to be ignorant. Milly asked for help in understanding her new friends, Mrs. Lowder and the niece, but he only replied that the former was "an extraordinary woman" and the latter "tremendously, yes, quite tremendously, good-looking" (167). What finally came out was something unexpected and, by implication, portentous. When Milly pursued the question by wondering why such a personage as their hostess had taken up two stray American ladies in such a grand way, he explained that it was because Susan Shepherd had given her old schoolmate a most valuable possession in the form of her young protégé. Milly, protesting that she made rather a poor present, asked what in the world Mrs. Lowder could do with her. " 'She'll get back,' he pleasantly said, 'her money.' He could say it too—which was singular—without affecting her as either vulgar or as 'nasty'; and he had soon explained himself by adding: 'Nobody here, you know, does anything for nothing' " (178).

This pronouncement completes his previous hint about the breakdown of a traditional society by implying that it has been replaced by a materialistic one. Then he had said that, today in London, "Every one was everywhere"; now his meaning was clear: any one can get into society if they have money, Mrs. Lowder and even more so Milly herself. When she applied the same question to Kate Croy, "What has she to gain by *her* lovely welcome?" his answer came promptly: "To gain? Why, your acquaintance" (181–182). The motivation of the handsome girl is merely suggested, to be sure, since James did not want to be explicit at this point about the "money-temptation" which is the secret basis of his plot. Milly's understanding of Lord Mark's intricate web of implications was only vague, but it is hinted at in one sentence: "She had, on the spot, with her first plunge into the obscure depths of a society constituted from far back, encountered the interesting phenomenon of complicated, of possibly sinister motive" (171).

Nor was Milly comforted when her dinner companion assured her that she was a *success*. "To be seen you must recognise, *is*, for you, to be jumped at. ... Look round the table and you'll make out, I think, that you're being, from top to bottom, jumped at." She quipped in reply that she preferred that to being made fun of. To which he presently added: "You haven't had time yet ... ; this is nothing. But you'll see. You'll see everything. You can, you know —everything you dream of." (She will *see*, the reader says to himself, but will she distinguish appearance from reality?) She felt almost as if he were "showing her visions," and it had the effect for an instant of making her wonder "if she were after all going to be afraid" (172, 175). At this juncture, for reasons known only to herself, there recurred to her the very question she had put to Susan Shepherd on the eve of their arrival in London, in response to the latter's vision of the rich possibilities for life that might open out for her in that great capital. "Should she have it, whatever she did have, ... for long?" Now, what she had half-learned half-surmised at Mrs. Lowder's dinner party, from her conversation with Lord Mark, "almost terribly suggested to her that her doom was to live fast" (176, 177). Before this portentous occasion comes to an end the theme as well as the plot of *The Wings of the Dove* has been prefigured, however dimly.

It is in keeping with James's indirect method of presentation in this novel that the two ladies at the Lancaster Gate dinner pary who are to play principal roles in Milly's life are perceived only out of the side of her eye or reflected in her dialogue with a subsidiary figure, Lord Mark, as he fills her in on the ambiguities of the London social world. The heroine's developing intimacy with Kate Croy and that of her companion with Aunt Maud are the subject of the two following chapters, told as past narrative rather than rendered dramatically. They are all *picture*, in preparation for the great companion *scene* at Matcham, and only need to be highlighted here. Milly's clearest perception of what Kate is like is revealed in a twofold metaphor, drawn from the arts James felt to be so closely associated, painting and fiction:

> The handsome English girl from the heavy English house had been as a figure in a picture stepping by magic out of its frame.... Kate Croy really presented herself to Milly ... as the wondrous London girl in person, by what she had conceived, from far back, of the London girl; conceived from the tales of travellers and the anecdotes of New York, from old porings over *Punch* and a liberal acquaintance with the fiction of the day.... She placed this striking young person from the first in a story, saw her, by a necessity of the imagination, for a heroine of English, of eccentric, of Thackerayan character. (189–191)

The figure that leaps out of the page here, for the literary reader at least, is the antiheroine of *Vanity Fair*. Surely Becky Sharp is the prototype of Kate Croy in several ways—handsome, charming, clever, and unscrupulous, an exploiter who uses everyone to help her rise from a deprived situation to wealth and social position—unlike as they may be in other ways. In the passage just quoted James is making use of one of the favorite strategies in his fiction (something also well established in fact) : that the experience of Americans in Europe, especially in England, is strongly influenced by preconceptions from their reading. They know what they expect to find and convince themselves they have found it, though often the discrepancy between their "myth" of Europe and the reality they eventually come to understand is one of the complicating factors in his plots. Whether Milly herself had in mind such a parallel between Becky and Kate we are not told, but much of what takes place in these two chapters suggests that such a premonition was dawning on her.

In the week or so following the dinner party the two young ladies were constantly together. As they exchanged confidences about their backgrounds, what all this chiefly signified for Kate was that her new friend is "the mistress of millions" whereas she is "a mere middle-class nobody from Bayswater" (193). The money theme was sounded even more insistently as they moved from backgrounds to the present situation. When Milly asked to be enlightened about Lord Mark, Kate replied that what she and her aunt knew of him was difficult to explain, other than that "he was working Lancaster Gate for all it was worth: just as it was, no doubt, working *him*, and just as the working and the worked were, in London, . . . the parties in every relation." Her own Aunt Maud was proof enough that "everyone who had anything to give . . . made the sharpest possible bargain for it." If she had taken up her niece, snatched her from near poverty, she could be trusted to get in return whatever Kate had to give. As for Milly's own "paying power," this was not even discussable: "that Milly would pay a hundred per cent—and even to the end, doubtless, through the nose—was just the beautiful basis on which they found themselves" (197–99). These accounts of the exploitative nature of London society they treated as mere pleasantries, ironies, the luxuries of sophisticated gossip. Yet Milly could not help realizing that "the handsome girl was, with twenty other splendid qualities, the least bit brutal too."

What Susan Shepherd learned from Maud Lowder was equally important, the first little trickle of evidence that opened up the other half of the book's theme, that of love and marriage. Kate and her aunt were very well acquainted, it transpired, with the young English journalist Milly had come to know quite well in New York. All the bits and pieces of this new complication that "come out" for the reader are reported in retrospective talks at bed-time between the heroine and her companion. Nothing has passed between Milly and Kate about Mr. Densher so far, and Aunt Maud seems precautionary, "afraid of something":

> "She's afraid, you mean," Milly asked, "of their—a—liking each other?"
> "My dear child, we move in a labyrinth." (205)

When Susan went on to report that Mrs. Lowder would like her niece to marry Lord Mark, it now came over Milly in a clear, cold way that her new friend, who had not mentioned this either, was concealing far more than she was revealing. But the heroine had made some discoveries on her own. Mr. Densher is in love with Kate, so her widowed and deprived sister confided to Milly during a visit to Mrs. Condrip's grim little flat in Chelsea. But "Aunt Maud herself won't hear of any such person," she added, explaining that it was not because he was dreadful: "It's the state of his fortunes.... He had no 'private means,' and no prospect of any" (213-215). With this the money theme and the love theme are ominously linked.

It is now clear how the aunt feels about Merton Densher, but not how the niece herself feels: "Kate came and went, kissed her for greeting and for parting, talked, as usual, of everything but...*the* thing" (210). Milly also concealed how she felt, not only by volunteering nothing to Kate but by her vague and tenuous responses to Susan's probings. (It is not until Densher's return to London, delayed for seven more chapters, that clarification begins.) But on the theme of money everyone was outspoken. As the heroine remarked to her companion, "they all appeared—every one they saw—to think tremendously about money." Susan qualified this by saying that Mrs. Lowder, who was apparently keeping her wealth for purposes and ambitions of her own, was at least not ostentatious about it: "Aunt Maud sat somehow in the midst of her money, founded on it and surrounded by it, even if with a clever high manner about it, her manner of looking, hard and bright, as if it weren't there" (215-216).

One of Mrs. Lowder's ambitions, to launch Kate, now seemed clear to Milly. But the clarity of her perception is immediately overlaid by another preconception from her reading. Her glimpse of Mrs. Condrip's dismal life, the world from which Kate had been rescued by her aunt, made her ponder the gap between the situation of the two sisters, "the skipped leaves of the social atlas," which she could not conceive of as possible except in "an hierarchical, aristocratic order." She could only understand it in terms of her knowledge of the "literary legend—a mixed, wandering echo of Trollope, of Thackeray, perhaps mostly of Dickens"—on second thought "the adored author of *The Newcomes*...had been on the whole the note" (211–212). Was Mrs. Condrip another Mrs. Nickleby or a widowed and aggravated Mrs. Micawber, Aunt Maud a younger Countess of Kew, and Kate even more a Becky Sharp? How much do the fictions help Milly to understand the facts?

In a large-scale novel like *The Wings of the Dove* the narrative method is unavoidable for certain parts of the subject, if only to get on with the story. So James admitted in his Preface, though he added: "the discriminated occasion...is apt, I think, to show its fullest worth in the Scene." This is brilliantly demonstrated in the great scene at Matcham, for which these two prosy preceding chapters have made all needful preparation:

> The great historic house had, for Milly, beyond terrace and garden, as the centre of an almost extravagantly grand Watteau-composition, a tone as of old gold kept "down" by the quality of the air, summer full-flushed, but attuned to the general perfect taste. Much, for the previous hour, appeared...to have happened to her—a quantity expressed in introductions of charming new people, in walks through halls of armour, of pictures, of cabinets, of tapestry, of tea-tables, in an assault of reminders that this largeness of style was the sign of *appointed* felicity. The largeness of style was the great containing vessel, while everything else, the pleasant personal affluence, the easy, murmurous welcome, the honoured age of illustrious host and hostess, all at once so distinguished and so plain, so public and so shy, became but this or that element of the infusion. (228–229)

The difference between Matcham and Lancaster Gate is a measure of the progress Milly had made in the social world in just three weeks. The only full picture we have of Mrs. Lowder's house is the one drawn by Merton Densher, early in the book, but everything he saw was still there for Milly to see, though she may not have had such a sensitive esthetic eye:

> Lancaster Gate looked rich—that was all the effect.... It was the language of the house itself that spoke to him, writing out for him...the ideals and possibilities of the mistress. Never, he flattered himself, had he ever seen anything so gregariously ugly—operatively, ominously so cruel. ...He couldn't describe and dismiss [its heavy horrors] collectively, call them either Mid-Victorian or Early.... It was only manifest that they were splendid and were furthermore conclusively British. They constituted an order and they abounded in rare material—precious woods, metals, stuffs, stones.... He had never dreamed of so much gilt and glass, so much satin and plush, so much rosewood and marble and mal-

achite. But it was above all the solid forms, the wasted finish, the mis-
guided cost, the general attestation of morality and money, a good conscience and a big balance. (87–88)

Lancaster Gate is a symbol of wealth, Matcham a symbol of taste.

That the two occasions—the former dinner party and the present reception—are to be taken as complementary halves of one triumphant whole is
underscored by James's odd metaphor. On the lawn of the great country house
Aunt Maud had just said to Milly: "You must stay among us—you must
stay; ... you can stay in *any* position." This struck the girl as a kind of consecration, a high-water mark in her career: "It was to be the end of the short
parenthesis which had begun but the other day at Lancaster Gate with Lord
Mark's informing her that she was a 'success'—the key thus again struck"
(230).

A large number of people were standing together near a marquee that had
been erected on a stretch of sward "as a temple of refreshment," making Milly
think of a "durbar." She was mindful that Susan had often referred to her as
an Oriental princess (at least a Byzantine one) and "the heiress of all the
ages," because of her fabulous wealth, her great freedom, her striking presence. Milly was now thinking not of herself but of the assemblage of guests,
certain of whom might have represented the contingent of "native princes"
at an official reception in India, a "durbar." (231–232) The place itself and
the brilliant life spread out before the heroine's eyes began to impart some of
its magic even to the people she knew. Kate, she discovered with wonder-
ment, was a person whose essence was "to be peculiarly what the occasion,
whatever it might be, demanded when its demand was highest"; she seemed
to have at such a given moment the extraordinary property of showing "as
a beautiful *stranger*" (italics added). Aunt Maud rose to the occasion herself
and partook of its brilliancy. "They were all swimming together in the blue.
... Lord Mark seemed slowly to pass and repass and conveniently to linger
before them; he was personally the note of the blue" (232–233). It was he
who had launched them at Matcham.

" 'Have you seen the picture in the house, the beautiful one that's so like
you?'—he was asking that as he stood before her.... She was the image of
the wonderful Bronzino, which she must have a look at on every ground. He
had thus called her off and led her away" (238). Milly's progress through the
house with Lord Mark was one with many pauses, as ladies and gentlemen,
singly, in couples, in groups, brought them to a stand with, " I say, Mark."
Every one seemed to know him, and he them. Milly had "a sense of pleasant
voices, pleasanter than those of actors, of friendly, empty words and kind,
lingering eyes. The lingering eyes looked her over, the lingering eyes were

what went, in almost confessed simplicity, with the pointless 'I say, Mark.' "
Something had clearly gone round about her—"that of the awfully rich young
American who was so queer to behold, but nice, by all accounts, to know"—
though it was the easiest thing in the world "to run the gauntlet with *him*."

Milly's apprehensions were gradually allayed—"kind eyes were always kind
eyes, if it were never to be worse than that!"—and everything now melted together again. She could simply give back "the particular bland stare that appeared in such cases to mark civilisation at its highest" (239–240). But the
Bronzino was deep within the house, and they went on and on through nooks
and opening vistas: "Once more things melted together—the beauty and the
history and the facility and the splendid midsummer glow: it was a sort of
magnificent maximum, the pink dawn of an apotheosis, coming so curiously
soon." At last they came within sight of the picture:

> She found herself, for the first moment, looking at the mysterious por-
> trait through tears. Perhaps it was her tears that made it just then so
> strange and fair—as wonderful as he had said: the face of a young woman,
> all magnificently drawn, down to the hands, and magnificently dressed;
> a face almost livid in hue, yet handsome in sadness and crowned with a
> mass of hair rolled back and high, that must, before fading with time,
> have had a family resemblance to her own. The lady in question, at all
> events, with her slightly Michaelangelesque squareness, her eyes of other
> days, her full lips, her long neck, her recorded jewels, her brocaded and
> wasted reds, was a very great personage—only unaccompanied by a joy.
> And she was dead, dead, dead. (241–242)

"I shall never be better than this," said Milly, turning to Lord Mark. But
he failed to understand. So she said the same thing with an entirely different
meaning: "I mean that everything this afternoon has been too beautiful, and
that perhaps everything together will never be so right again" (243). As he
was commenting on details of the likeness another party came up, Miss Croy
bringing a lady and gentleman to see the same thing. Kate looked straight
at Milly ("again it was, all round indeed, kind, kind eyes") and said: "Yes,
there you are, my dear, if you want to know. And you're superb." Lord Al-
dershaw commented with a laugh, "*Les grands esprits se rencontrent!*" His
wife, without saying a word, made explicit James's use of the portrait as a
reflecting mirror: "[She] looked at Milly quite as if Milly had been the
Bronzino and the Bronzino only Milly" (244–245).

For the reader, there is yet another check on the resemblance between Milly
and the Bronzino portrait, in the sketch of her made by Susan Shepherd in
the early part of the book, at the time of their first meeting back in New York:

The slim, constantly pale, delicately haggard, anomalously, agreeably angular young person, of not more than two-and-twenty . . . , whose hair was somehow exceptionally red even for the real thing, which it innocently confessed to being. . . . A face that, thanks, doubtless, to rather too much forehead, too much nose and too much mouth, together with too little mere conventional colour and conventional line, was expressive, irregular, exquisite. (118, 132)

Happily, for further comparison, the particular painting James had in mind has been identified as Bronzino's portrait of Lucrezia Panciatichi. The critic who made this identification, from a Medici Society print, commented on the characteristic aloofness of Bronzino's aristocratic subjects and the expressive stillness of the pose in this one, suggesting self-control allied to a capacity for intense feeling. It was also pointed out that James could not have missed seeing the original in the Uffizi Gallery on one of his many trips to Florence (the first being in 1869, as his cousin Minny Temple lay dying) and that he must have looked long and hard at this portrait, as proved by his phrase "her recorded jewels." On the green beads of a necklace worn by Lucrezia, Bronzino has "recorded" the carved legend: *Amour dure sans fin.* No motto could be more exact for the love bestowed on all by Milly, whose wings-of-a-dove even from the grave "cover us," Densher says to Kate at the end. So far the previous critic.

The present critic, on a pilgrimage to the Sala Baroccio in the Uffizi, spotted one more interesting detail that shows up in the larger-than-life original. Lucrezia is holding a book in her hand, and though only part of a page is visible James could have made out (by bending over to read it upside down) the Latin text of a hymn to the Virgin! What more poignant symbol for Milly? Both the missal and the motto on the beads relate to the novel's conclusion, and consequently neither of them is mentioned by the author. But James knew that many of his readers shared his interest in the arts, and it seems clear that he left clues like this (and the submerged reference to Keats in *The Princess*) as added meanings to be discovered by the persevering.

To return now to Matcham, where the Bronzino portrait was "on loan" from the Uffizi for James's private "exhibition." As Milly confronted what everyone declared was her mirror image, she saw only that the great Italian lady, her double, was "dead, dead, dead." At the beginning of the reception, one may recall, she had pictured this occasion as being like "an extravagantly grand Watteau-composition"—the favorite subject of this painter being an idealized version of the gay and elegant life of aristocratic society, as James had noted in an early essay. Before the party is over this picture has been replaced by another, symbolizing mutability and mortality, at least to the heroine. (At the end of the novel the Bronzino portrait acquires yet another meaning: that Milly's ultimate beauty only emerges at her death.) "Thus it was that, aloft there in the great gilded historic chamber and the presence of the pale personage on the wall, whose eyes all the while seemed engaged with her own, she found herself suddenly sunk in something quite intimate and humble and to which these grandeurs were strange enough witnesses" (246–247). At the same time there was something else present in her mind because of the way Kate had appeared to her just a few minutes before—"perversely *there*" because of her remembrance that her friend was somehow intimately involved with Merton Densher: "Is it the way she looks to him?" But being generous and tender she had a horror even of imputing any fault to either of them.

To compensate for having such a thought, she acted on an impulse and asked Kate to do her a great service tomorrow:

> "But it's a secret one—nobody must know. I must be wicked and false about it."
> "Then I'm your woman," Kate smiled, "for that's the kind of thing I love. *Do* let us do something bad. You're impossibly without sin, you know." (247–248)

It was presently settled that Milly would have the aid and comfort of her presence for a visit in the morning to Sir Luke Strett, "the greatest of medical lights." Kate was startled, particularly to hear her talking of *such* things at *such* a time, and demanded to know if she was ill. " 'Well, if I am, it must of course finally come out. But I can go for a long time.' Milly spoke with her eyes again on her painted sister's.... 'I think I could die without its being noticed' " (249–250). From this point on the story moves steadily from the rich promise of life to the threat of death.

Abyss and Labyrinth

James was sharply aware, from the first Notebook entry through the composition of the book and on to the later Preface, just what a difficulty was posed by having a heroine who was mortally ill. "The poet essentially *can't* be concerned with the act of dying," he confessed, looking back on his problem; "it is still by the act of living that [his fictional characters] appeal to him." Then he had found his solution. "The soul of drama," he reminded himself, "is the portrayal...of a catastrophe determined in spite of oppositions"—he needed only to think of Medea and Agamemnon, of Lady Macbeth and

Hamlet; "to be menaced with death or danger [has been] from time immemorial, for heroine or hero, the very shortest of all cuts to the interesting state." With Milly his emphasis was not to be on her illness, much less her dying, but on her contesting every inch of the way. As he summed it up in the Preface:

> The idea, reduced to its essence, is that of a young person conscious of a great capacity for life, but early stricken and doomed, condemned to die under short respite, while also enamoured of the world; ... and passionately desiring ... to achieve, however briefly and brokenly, the sense of having lived.... If her impulse to wrest from her shrinking hour still as much of the fruit of life as possible, if this longing can take effect only by the aid of others, their participation... becomes their drama.

(A comparison of this with the statement of his project in the *Notebooks*, quoted on the first page of the present chapter, will show how the idea for *The Wings of the Dove* had evolved during the eight years between its inception and its completion.) Just as the dying could be made to take place offstage, so the illness should be treated only indirectly.

This decision solved the problem for the novelist, but it raised another for some of his readers. Milly's unnamed disease, and the consistent sidestepping of any direct treatment of it, is a striking example of one of the devices frequently used in the novels of James's major phase: what might be called the "mystery convention," the deliberate withholding of information that does not affect either his dramatic intention or his form. To a certain class of readers, those who demand specific answers as to what is going on at every point in the story line and how it all comes out in the end, such withholding seems mannered or even coy. But James had his own opinion of those who merely "turn the page," and in his last great period he was writing for that special audience whose attention he wanted to concentrate on the drama of relations—of persons, places, and things—by which the essential meaning of his protagonist is revealed. And this new technique is neither mannered nor coy. It is integrally related to his fundamental esthetic: to the "open ending" of novels like *The Wings* and *The Ambassadors*, to his famous ambiguity, and especially to his vision of human reality as something that we understand only in an indirect and fragmentary way. How much do we know of anyone else's life, especially as concerns love and fortune, health and the threat of death?

We are prepared now for the morning after Matcham and Milly's visit to Sir Luke, the distinguished physician of Harley Street. Of his diagnosis Kate learns nothing, the reader next to nothing. The first visit was very brief, lasting only ten minutes. When the heroine came back to the waiting room, her young friend asked eagerly what the great man had said. Milly was almost gay: "That I'm not to worry about anything in the world, and that if I'll be a good girl and do exactly as he tells me, he'll take care of me for ever and ever" (254). For the next time, she added, she would be brave enough to come alone. That disposed of Kate, though it left her completely in the dark. On the second visit, which was a long one, the reader is allowed into the consulting room. What took place there seemed to Milly like confessing to a priest, to the modern reader like a consultation with a psychiatrist.

Milly gave Sir Luke her whole past history. What he gave her was more like absolution than medical advice. Other than asking her to obey "a small prescription or two," he merely urged that, after he had called on her at her hotel in a few days, she should get out of London. She could go where she liked, in England or on the Continent, "anywhere that's pleasant, convenient, decent, will be all right" (268). If it were tuberculosis (the fatal disease of cousin Minny Temple) wouldn't he have ordered her to some dry and sunny climate on the Mediterranean? And why get out of London, except to escape the tensions of her involvement in the social world? But nothing is specified, medically or otherwise, as to her condition. What little we learn comes from Milly's private meditation at the beginning of the interview and from her final exchange with Sir Luke. "It would be strange," she said to herself, that what comfort she might gain by this visit to an eminent doctor should come "from her learning in these agreeable conditions that she was in some way doomed; ... and it was ridiculously true that her thus sitting there to see her life put into the scales represented her first approach to the taste of orderly living" (258–259). At the end of an hour or so, during which perfect understanding was established between physician and patient, Milly wound up with a question:

"Shall I, at any rate, suffer?"
"Not a bit."
"And yet then live?"
"My dear young lady," said her distinguished friend, "isn't to 'live' exactly what I'm trying to persuade you to take the trouble to do?" (269)

By withholding and ambiguity James has achieved exactly what he intended: to emphasize her living rather than her dying.

This intention is clarified and extended by a kind of *scene-without-dialogue* that took place in the heroine's mind, touched off by a *picture* of "the grey immensity of London" into which she wandered alone after leaving Harley Street, feeling that her only company must be "the human race at large," now present all round her but inspiringly impersonal:

Grey immensity had somehow of a sudden become her element; grey immensity was what her distinguished friend had, for the moment, furnished her world with and what the question of 'living', as he put it to her, living by option, by volition, inevitably took on for its immediate face.... She had been treated—hadn't she?—as if it were in her power to live; and yet one wasn't treated so unless it came up, quite as much, that one might die.... But the beauty of a great adventure, a big dim experiment or struggle in which she might, more responsibly than ever before, take a hand, had been offered her instead. (270–271)

Such were the thoughts preparatory to her vision, as she wandered through slum-like side streets, into the great square, then on through the entrance to Regent's Park, round the great pompous crescent of which she had driven in her chariot with Kate. But she went further into it now, on to the stretches of shabby grass near the center:

Here were benches and smutty sheep; here were idle lads at games of ball, with their cries mild in the thick air; here were wanderers, anxious and tired like herself; here doubtless were hundreds of others just in the same box. Their box, their great common anxiety, what was it, in this grim breathing-space, but the practical question of life? They could live if they would; that is, like herself, they had been told so; she saw them all about her, on seats, digesting the information, feeling it altered, assimilated, recognizing it again as something, in a slightly different shape, familiar enough, the blessed old truth that they would live if they could. All she thus shared with them made her wish to sit in their company. (273)

When Milly entered Regent's Park she entered the human condition, man's ineluctable awareness that one day he too will die. Though she selected an empty bench to sit on, her compassion related her to the general emptiness. Since death is nameless, a kind of nothingness, it is rendered in the novel by an absence of specificity as to the illness that would eventually cause it. Milly is simply dying of human mortality, as are all her fellows in the park, and elsewhere. This is the fundamental existential situation. As she left the park she was turning over in her mind once again the paradox: "It was perhaps superficially more striking that one could live if one would; but it was more appealing, insinuating, irresistible, in short, that one would live if one could" (278). Such was the abyss into which Milly had sunk after only one month of her promising new life in England.

It brings to mind the picture of Milly sitting on the edge of a very different abyss in Switzerland, shortly after her first consultation with a doctor in

New York. Though all is seen through the eyes of her companion, who is undeniably romantic, James clearly intended this as a prophetic picture. Milly had gone for a walk alone, up into the higher Alpine meadows, and when after an hour she had not returned, Susan followed her with some anxiety. The path led up and up, then over a crest, and finally dropped down again alarmingly, "apparently quite into space, for the great side of the mountain [seemed] to fall away altogether." There, on the dizzy edge of an abyss, she found her protégé seated:

> The whole place... appeared to fall precipitously and to become a "view" pure and simple, a view of great extent and beauty, but thrown forward and vertiginous.... What had first been offered her was the possibility of a latent intention—however wild the idea.... [Her second thought was that] if the girl was deeply and recklessly meditating there, she was not meditating a jump.... She was looking down on the kingdoms of earth, and it wouldn't be with a view of renouncing them. Was she choosing among them, or did she want them all? (137-139)

She chose England, when the two friends talked over their travel plans that evening; and they went there straight from the Brünig.

From some of the metaphorical language used in connection with her immersion in the social world of that "kingdom," it is as if Milly had literally leaped off the Alpine precipice to get there. As she became involved in the ambiguous table talk with Lord Mark at the Lancaster Gate dinner party, she feared that this, "her first plunge into the obscure depths" of a traditional society, might have something dangerous about it (171). When a week or so later the heroine and her companion were piecing together the bits of evidence they had picked up suggesting a love-relationship between Kate and Merton Densher (concealed by both of them from Milly and opposed by Aunt Maud, who favored Lord Mark for her niece), Milly said to Susan Shepherd with a strange gaiety: "Don't tell me that—in this for instance—there are no abysses. I want abysses" (206). Returning for a moment to the abyss in Switzerland, there is one more aspect of that prophetic picture that must be followed out. As Susan's first fears were allayed, she became convinced that "the future was not to exist for her princess in the form of any sharp or simple release from the human predicament." Then she foresaw what that future probably would be: "[Milly] wouldn't have committed suicide; she knew herself unmistakably reserved for some more complicated passage.... It wouldn't be for her a question of a flying leap and thereby a quick escape. It would be a question of taking full in the face the whole assault of life" (140). This prophecy seems fulfilled in the vision that came to the heroine in Regent's Park, following her last consultation with the great London doctor.

The first volume of this novel comes to a close with one more important scene, a very brief one but lifted up again by the mirror imagery of painting. On the day that Sir Luke Strett was to call on her at the hotel, Milly skipped out and went alone to the National Gallery, leaving her companion to receive him and learn his final report. During her busy London weeks she had never had enough time for "pictures and things," the usual cultural "musts" of Americans touring Europe. Now though she felt some positive desire to see the Titians and the Turners, her motive was more particularly one of escape: "If I could lose myself *here*!" Unable to concentrate seriously on the pictures, she found herself watching the lady copyists, who "seemed to show her for the time the right way to live." She should have been a lady copyist herself—"it met so the case"—that is, she seemed only able to copy a "copy" of life, unable really to live or even to create an illusion of life (314). Then her attention wandered to the great stream of her compatriots flowing through the gallery, this being August.

One group particularly caught her eye, a mother and two daughters, who were standing in front of Milly and looking past her at some object on the other side of the room, apparently. "Handsome? Well if you choose to say so," the mother was replying to one of her girls. Then she qualified by adding, "In the English style" (318). When they had passed on, Milly, who took the reference as being to a picture, turned round to have a look herself, assuming the "English style" would be the English School, which she liked. Quickly she realized that she was in a room given over to small Dutch paintings and that it was presumably not a picture at all that had arrested the three ladies. Of the new visitors coming through the entrance which she now faced, a handsome couple focussed her gaze. It was indeed "the English style" of the gentleman, in contrast to the American style, that had been the arresting power. She recognized him instantly as Merton Densher and the lady with him as Kate Croy. Just as the painting at Matcham had resembled Milly, so now this striking couple resembled a painting. Then Kate's stare, as blank at first as Milly's own, broke into "a far smile." They stepped out of the frame and the picture came to life (319–320).

"Whatever were the facts, their perfect manners, all round, saw them through" (322). The line that Milly took, as soon as they all three accepted the fact that they had come together, however unexpectedly, was to invite them to lunch at her hotel. "Kate was a prodigious person; [she] had somehow made her provisionally take everything as natural," and the way they all avoided putting their predicament into words struck the American girl as "a characteristic triumph of the civilised state" (320–321). Since Susan Shepherd took care of the handsome girl, Milly had Densher all to herself during the postluncheon period. At first she could not tell whether her impression of him would be different from the one she had received in New York. Then she realized that she did not know or care: "She liked him, as she put it to herself, as much as ever" (326). But the most important decision Milly arrived at was the one furthest from the truth: "Merton Densher was in love, and Kate couldn't help it—could only be sorry and kind" (325). When one sees reality reflected as a painting, even an imaginary one, does one see what one fears or what one wants to see? The handsome couple, in the English style, presented the heroine with a problem in the relation of appearance to reality. She was now deeper in the labyrinth.

If the reception given to Milly at Matcham is the center of the first volume of *The Wings of the Dove*, the reception given by her at Palazzo Leporelli is the center of the second. But a novel with two centers is one that calls for some commentary on its form. James himself was the first to raise the problem. Writing to a friend shortly after publication of *The Wings* he described it as "too inordinately drawn out," too long-winded for so small a subject: "The centre, moreover, isn't in the middle, or the middle, rather, isn't in the centre, but ever so much too near the end, so that what was to come after is truncated." The center here referred to is presumably the party at Milly's Venetian palace in the last chapter of Book Eighth, about three-fourths the way through the novel. In the later Preface James says: "The actual centre of the work, resting on a misplaced pivot, [is] lodged in Book Fifth"—the first two chapters of which record the party at Matcham, about one-fourth the way through. He goes on to lament that *The Wings* is "the most striking example...of my regular failure to keep the appointed halves of my whole equal." The first half, he finds in retrospect, shows the "felicitous application of method," that of alternating *picture* and *scene*. The second is "the false and deformed half," that bristles with "dodges...for disguising the reduced scale of the exhibition, for foreshortening at any cost."

The "centers" that James designates for the two halves of his novel clearly refer to their dramatic centers. They are united by another kind of center, his subject, his stricken heroine, since they comprise the two great climaxes in the working out of her destiny. Her stricken state—"possessed of all things, ...freedom and money and a mobile mind and personal charm, the power to interest and attach," he spelled out, "all but the single most precious assurance"—is only part of James's subject. The other part is the state of those who are affected by her and who act upon her. In the Preface he described the final technique by which he hoped to solve the complicated problem of form in *The Wings of the Dove*. "Though my regenerate young New Yorker ...should form my centre, my circumference was every whit as treatable," he said: "one began, in the event, with the outer ring, approaching the centre thus by narrowing circumvallations."

There was still a danger that James's subject would split into two parts and that the story of the others, Kate and Merton, would steal the show from the heroine. Theirs is more active, more a matter of passion; hers is passive, a story of compassion. And theirs takes up the largest amount of space in the novel. Milly does not appear until after the first hundred pages, and she is off-stage completely during the last hundred. In the long middle part of the book, the three hundred pages that lie between the great scenes at Matcham and Palazzo Leporelli, she is largely in the background while they occupy the foreground, working out their exploitative scheme. Even in the few chapters at the beginning of this middle section where she is dominant—at the doctor's office, in Regent's Park, at the National Gallery—she is being prepared as a potential victim for exploiters. "A young person so devoted and exposed, a creature with her security hanging so by a hair, couldn't but fall somehow into some abysmal trap," James said retrospectively.

One may add, as a previous critic has pointed out, that he kept the emphasis equal on victim and exploiters by a complete revision of his old theory of "relations." In *The Portrait of a Lady*, as a prime example of his early method at its best, he had used character relations as means rather than ends, all the others existing solely to reveal the heroine. In *The Wings of the Dove* relations among characters, and the requisite technique of multiple points of view, actually constitute the subject. (In the first two books we see everything through Kate's consciousness; in the next three through Milly's; in four of the last five through Densher's.) This novel, the critic concludes, is not a "portrait" but "a pure instance of the novel of relations." It is by making his real subject neither Milly nor Kate and Merton, but the intricate relations among them, that James keeps *The Wings* from splitting into two parts. Their relations are, as the author himself said, those of a circumference to a center, the heroine becoming gradually enclosed in the "circumvallations" of their plot; and it is to this aspect of the novel's form that we must now turn our attention.

It will be remembered that when the first suspicion of a love relation between Kate and Merton began to dawn on the two American ladies, Milly said that an "abyss" might be opening out before them, Susan that they were moving in a "labyrinth." Both terms are fittingly portentous, suggesting either the depths and obscurities one might fall into as a newcomer in a complex society or the maze one might wander in until lost. The metaphor of a labyrinth will help the critic to extract all he needs from the long sprawling middle of the novel, and to relate it briefly to the two centers. From the first hundred pages as well, since long before meeting Milly, Kate Croy and Merton Densher, "all unconsciously and with the best faith in the world, all by force of the terms of their superior passion combined with their superior diplomacy.... are laying a trap for the great innocence to come"—to borrow a final commentary from James's Preface. Such was their great need that it is as if their "exasperated patience," months later, recognized "the possibilities shining out of Milly Theale." Just as the American heroine has everything but health, the young English pair have everything but wealth. To keep them from seeming too villainous in their scheme to use her, James filled in the background of their great need in considerable detail. Their story is an absorbing one in its own right, but the reader can follow that without guidance. For the critic a few highlights will serve to relate it to Milly's, the circumference to the center.

Exploiters and Appreciators

On the death of her mother, Kate had gone to live at Lancaster Gate with Aunt Maud Lowder. But as the winter drew to an end her father sent for her and she went, moved by one of her better impulses, resolved to give up all and go back to take care of him. What ensues is less a scene than a picture that flickers into desultory scene and back to picture again, all that could be expected of a meeting with such a vacuous character as Lionel Croy, "so particularly the English gentleman" but also a symbol of "the failure of fortune and of honour" (3–4). The picture alone supplies part of the backdrop needed for judging Kate's later behavior fairly: the dismal world of near-poverty and familial hopelessness from which Aunt Maud had offered to rescue her. When it comes into action briefly as a scene, something more portentous looms. In the devious exchanges between them, her father insists she must break off relations with him and with her presumed lover ("some blackguard without a penny") and go back to her aunt, who will provide for her handsomely. When Kate has been properly married to a rich man, he will resume relations. Her function in life will be to serve as a channel through which Aunt Maud's money could flow to him, to all of them. The fade-out picture includes the first view we have of Kate's beauty, which we get by looking over her shoulder in the dismal flat on Chirk Street as she "stared into the tarnished glass, too hard indeed to be staring at her beauty alone" (5). It was her glory. Was it to be also her fate? Both her father and her aunt planned to make use of it. She herself was learning the first lesson in exploitation.

In the "tall, rich, heavy house at Lancaster Gate," during the whole of a dark winter afternoon, Kate Croy moved endlessly between her seat before the upstairs fire, in the charming quarters her aunt had assigned to her, and the high south window with its view over Kensington Park. "She saw as she had never seen before how material things spoke to her.... She had a dire accessibility to pleasure from such sources" (29, 31). Her situation now was in the sharpest contrast with what she had just left behind: "the loss of her mother, the submersion of her father, the discomfort of her sister, the confirmation of their shrunken prospects" (33). The picture offered by this second episode exists entirely inside Kate's mind. Though encompassing past and future, it is focussed on the present and rendered in a highly metaphorical vision. Mrs. Lowder, who furnished the contrast, was a "prodigious" personality, the great mass of which loomed for Kate "in the thick foglike air of her arranged existence." As she meditated in her high refuge, the niece likened herself to "a trembling kid" waiting her turn to be introduced into "the cage of the lioness."

> The cage was Aunt Maud's own room, her office, her counting-house, her battlefield, her especial scene, in fine, of action, situated on the ground-floor, opening from the main hall and figuring rather to our young woman on exit and entrance as a guard-house or a toll-gate.... Her niece had a quiet name for her—... Britannia of the Market Place—Britannia unmistakable, but with a pen in her ear, and [Kate] felt she should not be happy till she might on some occasion add to the rest of the panoply a helmet, a shield, a trident, and a ledger.... There was a whole side of Britannia, the side of her florid philistinism, her plumes and her train, her fantastic furniture and heaving bosom, the false gods of her taste and false notes of her talk, the sole contemplation of which would be dangerously misleading. She was a complex and subtle Britannia, as passionate as she was practical, with a reticule for her prejudices as deep as that other pocket, the pocket full of coins stamped in her image, that the world best knew her by.... So, at all events, in silent sessions, Kate conveniently pictured her. (33–35)

One of the plans being worked out in Mrs. Lowder's counting-house was the best bargain she could strike in disposing of her niece.

Kate's "menacing and uncompromising aunt" serves as the complement to her nagging and importuning family, as shown during the visit to Mrs. Condrip that forms a sequel to this vigil. The sister echoes the father in lecturing Kate as to her duty: "She desired her to 'work' Lancaster Gate as she believed that scene of abundance could be worked" (48). The sister is equally explicit in how that is to be done, and more outspoken in that she names names. Merton Densher is the man she hates and fears, and regardless of the fact that Kate loves him she must give him up; Lord Mark is the one she approves because he is "Aunt Maud's man," and Kate must marry him. With sister and father unabashed in their determination to use her as a way of getting Aunt Maud's money, and Aunt Maud more subtly scheming to use her for catching a coronet, Kate can only conclude that exploitation is the keynote of the world she lives in.

An understanding of Kate's relation to Merton Densher will complete her background, as preparation for the exploitative relation she was to establish toward Milly the following summer. This can be arrived at from a single scene involving the young English pair, a meeting in Kensington Gardens at the beginning of spring, the climax of a series of rendezvous throughout the fall and winter during which their initial attraction to each other had grown into a joyously acknowledged but necessarily secret love affair. The present meeting was given a special significance by a recent event, his call on Mrs. Lowder, at Kate's insistence, to see if he might in some way win her over and make it possible for them to be together other than surreptitiously. It produced a most ambivalent result. Aunt Maud acquainted him with her plans for her niece in such a way as to let him know that he was not a part of them:

"I want to see her high, high up—high up and in the light."
"Ah, you naturally want to marry her to a duke, and are eager to smoothe away any hitch." (92–93)

Kate put a better meaning on it. Perhaps he was so unimportant that Aunt Maud, who liked to have "intellect and culture adorn her board," would consent to his coming to her house. This would give them time "to play a waiting game with success." Their great need for each other was linked with their great need of money, which must come from some other source than themselves. Kate was determined to have both her love and the kind of life symbolized by Lancaster Gate: "That's just my situation, that I want and that I shall try for everything" (82). The way to achieve this double goal was not clear to them now, but they felt they could win to it if they had wisdom and patience.

The vagueness of any possible solution to their problem did not keep them from then lapsing happily into lovers' talk, filling each other in more and more on their lives before meeting. That he was complicated and brilliant was one of the chief reasons why Kate loved him, just as it was her talent for life that drew him most. When he had told Mrs. Lowder about his background, his youth and education mostly spent abroad, this "foreignness" added to his deplorable lack of means was the finishing touch for her. But he noticed that Kate was not listening:

Suddenly she said to him with extraordinary beauty: "I engage myself to you for ever."
The beauty was in everything.... They were in the open air, in an alley of the Gardens.... They moved by a common instinct to a spot,

within sight, that struck them as fairly sequestered, and there, before their time together was spent, ... they had exchanged vows and tokens, sealed their rich compact, solemnized, so far as breathed words and murmured sounds and lighted eyes and clasped hands could do it, their agreement to belong only, and to belong tremendously, to each other. They were to leave the place accordingly an affianced couple. (106–107)

Merton Densher was now sure of Kate's love. But how would she act if that came in conflict with her other great desire, for the kind of luxurious life that Lancaster Gate could provide? When he put it to her that the question of their actual relation might be brought up any day by Aunt Maud, Kate responded:

"If she asks if there's anything definite between us, I know perfectly what I shall say."
"That I *am*, of course, 'gone' for you?"
"That I love you as I shall never in my life love any one else, and that she can make what she likes of that." (110)

Her declaration of what she would do was gallant. It "drew him again as close to her, and held him as long, as their conditions permitted" (111). This love scene is as near as Henry James ever came to treating physical passion; and readers at the turn of the century would have accepted it as such, however restrained it might seem today.

The actual inception and working out of Kate's scheme belongs to the middle section of the book, after Milly's swift triumph in London society and after Merton's return from America, though some unconscious preparation had been taking place before he came back. An exploiter is instinctively drawn to great wealth, wherever and whenever accessible, knowing it is wise to be nearby and ready to avail oneself of any opportunity that may present itself. Kate's cultivation of Milly had been partly so motivated from the first. As the size of the heroine's fortune and the precarious state of her health gradually became known, vague possibilities suggested themselves of a way to use her; and when the extent of Milly's liking for Merton also came out, the definite outline of a plan began to take shape in her mind. At the same time Aunt Maud was concocting a plan of her own, identical on the surface but with a purpose quite opposite to that of Kate. Mrs. Lowder wanted to marry Densher to the American heiress in order to get rid of him as a menacing suitor of her niece (74–76). The latter, aware of Milly's presumably mortal illness, planned to use the match as a means to a very different end, as will be seen. But the scheming of aunt and niece is so subtle and their talk about their plans so devious that even Merton, the pawn of both schemes, has only the vaguest and most tenuous understanding of what is going on. And the poor reader would have to fumble his way through these obfuscations were it not for an extraordinary sequence of animal imagery by which the author provides clues through the labyrinth of exploiters and victims.

The image first introduced is a dual one: Kate in her upper chamber at Lancaster Gate, thinking of Aunt Maud in her "counting-house" on the ground floor, has likened herself to "a trembling kid" about to be introduced into "the cage of the lioness." But there is nothing here or elsewhere to suggest that anyone shares the niece's notion, only temporary even with her, that she is to be a sacrificial animal. That image more nearly applies to Merton Densher. It is hinted at when, meditating on his want of means and his conviction that he will never be rich, he thinks of these two handicaps to marrying as "the pair of smudges from the thumb of fortune, the brand on the passive fleece" (72). This image of him as a lamb is given substance during one of their meetings in Kensington Gardens, when Kate had been insisting that he go to call on Mrs. Lowder, since she sees her own danger "of doing something base" unless the aunt could be won over. To which Merton demurred:

> "Then what can be so base as sacrificing me?"
> "I *shan't* sacrifice you; don't cry out till you're hurt." (82)

(One wonders in the end of he *was* sacrificed, if he was an innocent victim?) When he made his call at Lancaster Gate he did indeed feel very much like a lamb in "the cage of the lioness," even imagining Mrs. Lowder as saying, "I can bite your head off any day, any day I really open my mouth" (86, 94). But she turned out to be a very reasonable lioness, like the one on Britannia's shield, and if the lamb were amenable he could sit down to some kind of harmonious understanding with her, in terms of the biblical paradox.

The animal imagery takes a new turn the next summer as Kate shifts from the role of potential victim to that of predator. Her own scheming and that of her aunt had gone so far that, in a momentary revulsion against their exploitativeness, she broke out suddenly to Milly during one of their late night confidences: "We're of no use to you—it's decent to tell you. You'd be of use to us, but that's a different matter. My honest advice to you would be . . . to drop us while you can." The heroine tried to be amused to keep from being frightened: "She felt herself alone with a creature who paced like a panther. That was a violent image, but it made her a little less ashamed of having been scared." When she asked Kate why she said such things, the reply came unexpectedly, "Because you're a dove." As Milly meditated on this afterwards, she said of herself: "*That* was what was the matter with her. She was a dove"

(307–309). The image for the heroine, which is far more complicated than that of an innocent victim, must be saved for later comment. The one for the antiheroine leads into another cluster and must be examined now. It is richly suggestive in its own right, *panther* being a kind of generic name for the large family of wild cats—mountain lion, cougar, jaguar, tiger, and leopard.

The last of these is especially to James's purpose. Leopard (lion + pard) is the name given to the Asian panther, noted for its lithe beauty and cunning as well as its predatory habits. Webster extends the meaning: "**leopard** ... 3. in *heraldry*, a lion represented in side view, with one foreleg raised and the head facing to the front." This is the same symbol of Great Britain previously applied to Mrs. Lowder, suggesting the kinship between niece and aunt. A final dimension is supplied by the book of English silver: both the leopard's head and the lion *passant* have been the traditional hallmarks of sterling. Kate, as well as Aunt Maud, symbolizes her country, especially in its materialistic aspects. These paired images of lion and panther appear in the sequel, a second dinner given by Mrs. Lowder, this time for the purpose of bringing together the American ladies and the English couple, along with some young noblemen, except that Milly at the last minute had to decline because of illness. The table talk about the social success of the rich American girl, in her absence, was such as to be embarrassing to Merton Densher: "What touched him most nearly was that the occasion took on somehow the air of a commemorative banquet, a feast to celebrate a brilliant if brief career" (II, 41). Milly's anxious companion, Susan Shepherd, was affected more sharply; she sat and looked on, "Very much as some spectator in an old-time circus might have watched the oddity of a Christian maiden, in the arena, mildly, caressingly being martyred. It was the nosing and fumbling not of lions and tigers but of domestic animals let loose for the joke" (46). Heraldic animals, or beasts of prey tamed and civilized? This sequence of animal imagery helps readers to see through the smooth surface of manners to the world of exploiters and victims beneath.

It must be pointed out, of course, that these images, scattered over several hundred pages, are almost imperceptible on a first reading. Their full significance only comes out when they are drawn together for analysis, another example of the method of indirection used throughout this novel. Similarly, it should be remembered, the allusions on several social occasions to money and to people "working" each other are so submerged in a mesh of sophisticated talk as to be almost inaudible. In a formal society, which is both effete and potentially evil, faces are used to mask rather than to reveal feelings, words to muffle the truth as well as speak it. The texture of manners is dense and it takes the keenest of perceptive powers to discern the morals beneath. In *The Wings of the Dove* James matches his techniques of rendering to the special world he has chosen. And the system he provides for arriving at his code of moral values is just what the reader needs to find his way in this labyrinth. Since in the Jamesian world there are no criminal acts—murder, rape, arson, burglary—evil consists of sins against the spirit rather than against the flesh. The "bad" characters are those who exploit others, using them exclusively for selfish ends. The "good" characters are those who appreciate others and only want to help them realize their essential selves. This system he had first employed full-scale in *The Portrait*; it is brought to its finest development in *The Wings*.

Mrs. Lowder and Kate Croy are the prime exploiters, as already pointed out. The aunt uses her niece, and everyone else who comes her way, especially those who will aid her plan to do what she wants with Kate; the niece, exploited by her aunt and the Croy family, is determined in return to use one and all in furthering her own plan—Aunt Maud, her fiancé Merton, her godsent American heiress. Milly Theale, clearly from all that has been presented about her, is the appreciator beyond compare in this novel. She has been referred to up until now as the (potential) victim of those who would exploit her, but this is a negative view of the heroine. Besides, in Jamesian terms, the exploiter is frequently the one who is a victim, victim of his own egotism, having narrowed his world to the horizon of self; the appreciator on the other hand, though vulnerable to exploitation, broadens his or her horizon by the very act of living for the enjoyment of others. Milly's compassionate love goes out not only to those who are good, or want to be good, but also to the domestic lions and tigers even at the very moment she is being martyred by them. Knowing how difficult it is to make a practicing Christian complex enough to be interesting, James chose the dodge of sainthood. This is the chief reason for the tendency of reader interest to shift to Kate, who is no simple villainess. For one thing, she had more provocation to self-centeredness than any of the exploiters. For another, when her very real capacity for appreciating others comes to the fore, she has momentary misgivings about her evil plan—to marry her fiancé to a dying heiress so as to gain a fortune and still get back again her much used and abused lover. Most interesting of all, in the moral sense, is the enigmatic position of Merton Densher. Is he exploiter? or appreciator?

He is indeed the chief instrument used by Kate to work her will, and if their case were thought of in terms applicable to criminal law he too would be judged guilty, but as accomplice rather than principal he would draw a lighter sentence. Tried by Jamesian moral law, Merton cannot be disposed of in such a facile legalistic way, especially since Milly serves in the capacity of judge as as well as victim. Of course one may discount her opinion by pointing out that she is a very partial judge, because of her close relations with both defendants. She was first an appreciator of Kate, second of Merton. The former led to intense admiration, the latter to overwhelming love. It was because of this that she knew instinctively, when she discovered they had been engaged all along, that Merton was at heart an appreciator like herself, only caught up in the scheme of another to whom he was already dedicated before she came along. It was the impossibility of having his love that killed Milly. The sentence she passed on him was to make him heir to her fortune as a token of her love, covering him even from the grave. The critic as reader, determined to make his own judgment on the moral enigma of Merton Densher, demands more evidence. The critic as analyst is more concerned with how James worked out his own theme by completing the relation of his circumference to his center, the story of the English couple in its fatal involvement with the American heroine. Happily these are two aspects of the same thing.

Since the labyrinth in which Milly lost her way was created by Kate, one would expect that her confederate had been given the key to it. But Merton Densher is so ill-informed as to its twistings and turnings that he is all but trapped in it himself. The metaphor James applies to him is a variant of labyrinth—"He was in a wonderous silken web" (II, 70)—but with similar connotations as to weaver and victim. Shortly after the confrontation in the National Gallery, and the subsequent luncheon at Milly's hotel, Kate gave him the first inkling of her plan: "I want to make things pleasant for her.... I use, for the purpose, what I have. You're what I have of most precious, and you're therefore what I use most" (58). This vague suggestion followed her revelation to Merton of two facts: that Milly's fortune was "absolutely huge" so that it was open to her to make "the very greatest marriage"; and a conjecture she considered as good as a fact, that Milly was fatally ill. When he asked how he could in these circumstances be of any use Kate replied, "You can console her"—for if she really is stricken, all her possibilities will be swept away (57). As the light began to dawn he said, "What you want of me then is to make up to a sick girl." When she explained that Milly would never strike anyone as being ill, and that besides there would be plenty of others making up to her, "all the young dukes," he protested that "the others are free." To which she replied, "But so are you, my dear!" (62).

It was then that the metaphor of being in "a web" occurred to him, though for the present he was less aware that this might prove to be a trap or snare than that the web being woven around him had qualities that struck him as "wondrous" and "silken." For he still had only the faintest notion of why he was to make up to Milly: at the most to comfort her, at the least because intimacy with her might provide protection and a place for future meetings of the English pair. And what cast the spell on him was his love for Kate, his admiration for her brilliance and subtlety:

[203]

Something suddenly . . . welled up in him and overflowed—the sense of his good fortune and her variety, of the future she promised, the interest she supplied. "All women but you are stupid. How can I look at another? You're different and different—and then you're different again. No marvel Aunt Maud builds on you—except that you're so much too good for what she builds *for*. Even 'society' won't know how good for it you are; it's too stupid, and you're beyond it. . . . You're a whole library of the unknown, the uncut." He almost moaned, he ached, from the depth of his content. (68)

An appreciator is slow to suspect exploitation as motive to human relationships, especially in a loved one, but quick to recognize a kinship with those who instinctively appreciate others for what they are and want to serve them. So it was when Mr. Densher went to call on Miss Theale, ostensibly in grateful recognition of her kindness to him on several occasions in New York. His impression from the start was that American girls, "when they were as charming as Milly," were clearly the easiest people in the world to get along with. Gradually he realized that though his purpose in coming had been to console her for what she seemed doomed to miss, she on her part was moved by a feeling of tenderness toward him for what he had already missed. In a word it became clear that Kate had lied to her, had declared herself "indifferent, inexorable, . . . and if he was unhappy, it was because his passion for Kate had spent itself in vain." He knew now that his relation with Milly was false, that "her beautiful delusion and her wasted charity" were things he would have to reckon with soon, in all common decency and honesty (83).

At the same time Densher had to accept the fact that Milly really liked him and that in telling her the truth he would be striking "at the root, in her soul, of a pure pleasure." Furthermore such an exposure would constitute a kind of betrayal of his fiancée:

Kate's design was something so extraordinarily special to Kate that he felt himself shrink from the complications involved in judging it. Not to give away the woman one loved, but to back her up in her mistakes—once they had gone a certain length—that was perhaps chief among the inevitabilities of the abjection of love. Loyalty was, of course, sovereignty, prescribed in presence of any design on her part, however roundabout, to do one nothing but good. (84–85)

If he spoke the truth he would be doing serious injury to the two people he most appreciated, each one of whom he wanted to help realize her essential self. If on the other hand he did not speak soon, his silence would make him a party to the deception.

Such was the web he found himself caught up in. But is he an altogether innocent victim? Kate had warned that she was going to "use" him, though she did not specify how. Even when he discovered she had lied, his love made him decide to "back her up in her mistake." Since he became part of her "design," however unwillingly and even unconsciously, he does not come to Milly as a pure appreciator. The final sequence with Kate, before the scene shifts from London to Venice, adds the merest postscript. "If you'll swear again you love me—!" Merton said. "For it's only for that, you know, that I'm letting you do—well, God knows what with me" (102, 104). Then, promising that he would do only what he was told to do, he asked for instructions:

> "You must simply be kind to her."
> "And leave the rest to you?"
> "Leave the rest to her," said Kate. (105)

One remembers the same ambiguous usage in the "kind eyes" that lingered on Milly as she ran the gauntlet of guests at Matcham—bidding her welcome? or assessing her worth?

The Veronese Feast

> The warmth of the southern summer was still in the high, florid rooms, palatial chambers where hard, cool pavements took reflections in their lifelong polish, and where the sun on the stirred sea-water, flickered up through open windows, played over the painted "subjects" in the splendid ceilings—medallions of purple and brown, of brave old melancholy colour, medals as of old reddened gold, embossed and beribboned, all toned with time and all flourished and scalloped and gilded about, set in their great moulded and figured concavity (a nest of white cherubs, friendly creatures of the air), and appreciated by the aid of that second tier of smaller lights, straight openings to the front, which did everything . . . to make the place an apartment of state. (145)

Milly and her companion had gone to Venice in late September, for a change and to get out of London as her doctor advised. She had told her courier Eugenio to find her a place for several months, "a palace, historic and picturesque, . . . with servants, frescoes, tapestries, antiquities, the thorough make-believe of a settlement" (149). The result of his search was Palazzo Leporelli, epitome of the rich Venetian past. One entered by a water gate from the Grand Canal, which led through a high-ceilinged gallery to a sunny court.

From there a massive outer staircase led up and up to the *piano nobile*, just described; and above that was another storey, with a *sala* corresponding to the *sala* below, and fronting the great canal with its gothic arches and casements opening onto a broad balcony overhanging the water (163, 280–281).

Milly's Venetian palace was modelled on Palazzo Barbaro, home of the Daniel Curtises, Henry James's friends with whom he had spent many months. (The identification is certain, and the fictional palace corresponds closely to the factual one, located on the Grand Canal at the Accademia Bridge.) He described it briefly in a travel sketch written at the time of a long visit in 1899, when *The Wings of the Dove* was taking shape in his mind. One sentence in particular seems suggestive of that novel: "It was a high historic house, with such a quantity of recorded past twinkling in the multitudinous candles that one grasped at the idea of something waning..., and might even fondly and secretly nurse the conceit that what one was having was just the very last." James was well aware that Venetian life, in the proper sense of the princely life led by natives of that city during its heyday, had long since come to an end. Throughout the nineteenth century it had become a place where tourists came to stare at its wonders, but where other outsiders, more enchanted by its beauty, had come to stay for longer periods: painters and poets, royal exiles, rich Americans who took up residence in its old palaces on a more or less permanent basis.

Such a one was Milly Theale. It was the "great" Eugenio, recommended by grand-dukes and Americans, who had first brought home to her the idea of some complete use of her wealth, "some use of it as a counter-move to fate." It was "preposterous," he suggested, that with her great fortune she should "any more want a life, a career, a consciousness, than want a house, a carriage, or a cook" (156). Of course this was a scheme, at the same time, to enrich himself. She had judged him from the first as probably a swindler, "for he was forever carrying one well-kept Italian hand to his heart and plunging the other straight into her pocket" (146). But he was very dear to her and very useful, promoted now from courier to majordomo. As the relatively innocuous professional exploiter, Eugenio offers a contrast to the others who would exploit her person as well as her purse. And it was his romantic imagination that had launched her high plan for a new life in Palazzo Leporelli.

A series of images that symbolize her inner state at the beginning of this final period are applied by Milly to this great house. All her English friends had followed her abroad and these were joined by others from America, forming a kind of entourage. The weeks of socializing in Venice had left her physically exhausted and weary in spirit. Now on an October morning she had told Eugenio to take the others off, anywhere, and give her an hour to herself in Palazzo Leporelli.

She made now, alone, the full circuit of the place, noble and peaceful while the summer sea, stirring here and there a curtain or an outer blind, breathed into its veiled spaces.... She was *in* it, as in the ark of her deluge.... She would never, never leave it—she would engage to that; would ask nothing more than to sit tight in it and float on and on. (157)

The objective part of this image needs no explaining for anyone who has visited this city-in-the-sea, where every house seems like a ship afloat. But what of the feeling symbolized by "ark of her deluge"? In an essay written ten years before, "The Grand Canal," when describing the great middle stretch of water which is visible from the windows of Palazzo Barbaro, James had spoken of "the oddity of its general Deluge air,...its resemblance to a flooded city"; this is the only part of Venice, he said, "in which the houses look as if the water had overtaken them." Palazzo Leporelli would be Milly's refuge from whatever flood might threaten to drown her.

Her morning of solitude and peace there was rudely interrupted by a call from Lord Mark, who had unexpectedly arrived in Venice. Everything about his visit made it clear to her that he had come to make her a proposal, or rather a proposition: to bargain his title for her fortune. This was the great era of the international marriage, and everyone expected her to marry a lord. Milly, in her high historic house, turned it over:

"Oh, the impossible romance—!" The romance for her, yet once more, would be to sit there forever, through all her time, as in a fortress; and the idea became an image of never going down, of remaining aloft in the divine, dustless air, where she would hear but the plash of the water against stone.... "Ah, not to go down—never, never to go down!" she strangely sighed to her friend. (162)

Palazzo Leporelli was also to be her stronghold against the siege of exploiters, according to this second image. (Lord Mark, as usual, had misunderstood her, taking her "never, never to go down" literally instead of figuratively.) She declined his offer before he had a chance to make it. Then, as if to bring his mercenary motive into bold relief, she suddenly blurted out the secret she had told to no one before: that she was very badly ill. "With that there came to her a light; wouldn't her value, for the man who should marry her, be precisely in the ravage of her disease? *She* mightn't last, but her money would" (164, 170).

Her rueful thought, though applied in her mind to Lord Mark, was also prescient of that other suitor, unwilling though he was and still unconscious of just how deeply involved he was in a scheme of exploitation. For Merton Densher had come to Venice too and had been at Palazzo Leporelli almost

continuously since his arrival, though not alone with Milly until one afternoon when Aunt Maud, Kate, and Susan Shepherd conspired to arrange it.
He found it perfectly easy to be with her so, as simple as sitting with his
sister, and not much more thrilling. And since she had been "kind" to him
in New York, "he was perfectly willing to be kind in return," though without
making too much of it for either of them. The one thing he asked her to
explain was why she found it best to remain indoors:

> She wouldn't let him call it keeping quiet, for she insisted that her palace—
> with all its romance and art and history—had set up round her a whirl-
> wind of suggestion that never dropped for an hour. It wasn't, therefore,
> within such walls, confinement, it was the freedom of all the centuries:
> in respect to which Densher granted good-humoredly that they were then
> blown together, she and he, as much as she liked, through space. (190–191)

Palazzo Leporelli was an ark and a fortress; not a prison, but a magic carpet.
Such is the "picture" or scene-setting for the great Veronese-like feast to come.

"There's to be a little party," Susan Shepherd Stringham said to Merton
Densher one evening about a week after his arrival in Venice. He had come
to the palace for dinner, as usual, and this was said by way of explanation as to
why Milly would not come down until later. She was saving herself for the
gala occasion being staged for a few friends—the principal one being Sir Luke
Strett, just arrived from London—who were to come around from their hotels
after dinner. In reply Merton chaffed her about the "aggravated grandeur" of
the unusually large number of candles that lighted up the great salon this
evening, clearly betokening the "style" she intended for her party:

> "Well, it *is* lovely, isn't it? I want the whole thing. She's lodged for the
> first time as she ought, from her type, to be; and doing it—I mean bring-
> ing out all the glory of the place—makes her really happy. It's a Veronese
> picture, as near as can be—with me as the inevitable dwarf, the small
> blackamoor, put into a corner of the foreground for effect. If I only had
> a hawk or a hound or something of that sort I should do the scene more
> honour. The old housekeeper, the woman in charge here, has a big red
> cockatoo that I might borrow and perch on my thumb for the evening."
> These explanations and sundry others Mrs. Stringham gave, though not
> all with the result of making him feel that the picture closed him in. What
> part was there for *him*, with his attitude that lacked the highest style, in a
> composition in which everything else would have it?
> [His misgivings were allayed by her urging that he should stay on.]
> "Why we're to have music—beautiful instruments and songs; and not

Tasso declaimed as in the guide-books either. She has arranged it—or at least I have. That is Eugenio has. Besides, you're in the picture.... You'll be the grand young man who surpasses the others and holds up his head and the wine cup." (225–226)

Responsibility for this extravagant conceit James is careful to shoulder off on the romanticizing companion who always thinks of Milly as a "princess," and who amplifies on this occasion by telling Densher that her protégé presides over "such a court as never was: one of the courts of heaven, the court of an angel" (230). But the picture she conjures up is a recognizable Veronese, or rather a composite of several of his great paintings, all well known to James.

The Feast in the House of Levi (Accademia, Venice) has a dwarf in the foreground at the left, with a bird perched on his wrist which a small black boy is reaching for. The scene is the *sala* of a Venetian palace; standing on one side are two young men with wine cups, seated in the background at center is the figure of Christ. *The Marriage at Cana* (Louvre, Paris) also shows a dwarf with a bird, placed inconspicuously in the left foreground. When asked by the Inquisition why he used such figures in religious paintings, Veronese replied for "ornament" only, the custom in Venetian life as well as art. The scene again is that of a sumptuous banquet; on the right, holding up a cup, stands the host's wine steward, in the center foreground is a group of musicians, and behind them at the head of a great U-shaped table are Christ and the Virgin Mary. A third painting, *The Supper in the House of Simon the Pharisee* (Pinacoteca Sabauda, Torino), also represents a feast, but with a smaller number of guests, closer to the size of Milly's party. The focal point this time is Mary Magdalene washing the feet of Christ, who is seated in the center foreground of a palatial loggia. Splendid up above, bathed in light, is a group of figures on a balcony that gives perspective to the mass of figures on the *piano nobile*. Most striking among the upper group is a lady in white with a rope of pearls around her neck, and on the coping below her a cockatoo, the bright colored parrot of the East Indies.

The biblical occasion presented in the first painting is that of Christ being entertained in a rich man's house through the invitation of his disciple Matthew, a collector of taxes; when asked why he associated with the worldly and the wealthy, Christ replied: "I come not to call the righteous, but sinners to repentance" (Luke 5:27–35). The biblical occasion that makes the subject of the second painting is that of a wedding feast at which Christ and his mother were guests; when the host ran out of wine He performed what one of the Gospels refers to as his first miracle, turning the jugs of water into a superior wine. (John 2:1–11) The biblical occasion recorded in the third painting is the equally famous one of the scarlet woman who broke an alabaster box and annointed the feet of Christ; and when his host Simon murmured to himself that a prophet should allow such a woman to touch him, "for she is a sinner," He answered by declaring that her sins had been forgiven "for she loved much" (Luke 7:36–50).

Certainly the figures in the composite Veronese that symbolize Densher and Mrs. Stringham are clear enough. As for the others, the festive guests at Cana seem to represent one aspect of those at Palazzo Leporelli; the publicans and sinners at Levi's house, and the pharisaical guests at Simon's, another aspect. Further, the compassionate but doomed figure of Christ tempts one to find an analogy with Milly, who is also surrounded by potential betrayers as well as by those who would serve her. Indeed, these paintings and their biblical sources so bristle with possibilities for interpreting the finale of James's novel that the temptation is strong to read the whole scene-setting at Palazzo Leporelli as an allegory—the very mode that he had rejected early in his career. But such a reading would produce more confusion than illumination. As Milly's wealth was far more fabulous than that of Levi and his friends, though she was far from being a sinner herself, how could she be the messiah who came to save the worldly? Again, is she not better symbolized by the Magdalene who "loved much" than by Christ who forgave her sins? Finally, can she be thought of, except in the most ironic sense, as giving her blessing to the marriage of the affianced English pair by turning their water into wine through the magic of her fortune? Since the novelist himself says that "the Veronese picture was not quite constituted" in the scene following Mrs. Stringham's fancy sketch, it seems best to take the pictorial analogy of James's scene-setting as merely suggestive.

The way in which James intended his readers to use this imaginary painting as a mirror image for the climax of his novel can best be arrived at by referring to his comments on Veronese over the years. The first time it occurred to him to turn a picture into prose, as a matter of fact, he had another painter in mind. On his first visit to Venice, 1869, he wrote back to John LaFarge, the American artist he had studied under desultorily for a while, that Veronese is "great" but Tintoretto "well-nigh omnipotent." Then, in his earliest essay on Venice (based on visits in 1869 and 1872), he explained why: "[Tintoretto] *felt*, pictorially, the great, beautiful, terrible spectacle of human life very much as Shakespeare felt it poetically.... I'd give a great deal to be able to fling down a dozen of his pictures into prose of corresponding force and colour."

James's prognostication about the uses of Tintoretto, at the beginning of his career, foreshadows the actual use he was to make of Veronese in *The Wings* many years later. Why the shift? It was not because he changed his opinion about the relative merits of the two painters; simply that one was more suitable to his fictional purpose than the other. Tintoretto remained for him the greatest of the Venetian painters, for his are works of the imagination rather than of observation, reverent when on religious subjects and grave even for the worldly ones. Veronese, on the other hand, is typical of those painters who found life in Venice "so pictorial that [their] art couldn't help becoming so"; never was there a city where "art and life seem so interfused." These comments by James in his principal essay on "Venice" in 1882 fit perfectly his fictional mode in the party scene at Palazzo Leporelli twenty years later, especially when supplemented by his final word on Veronese: "Never was a painter more nobly joyous, never did an artist take a greater delight in life, seeing it all as a kind of breezy festival."

The Veronese picture composed by Mrs. Stringham is completed when Milly comes down after dinner to greet her guests. (Like the lady on the balcony in the third painting, she is wearing a white dress and a string of pearls.) Densher felt her as diffusing "in wide warm waves, the spell of a ... beatific mildness":

> The effect of the place, the beauty of the scene, had probably much to do with it; the golden grace of the high rooms, chambers of art in themselves, took care, as an influence, of the general manner, and made people bland without making them solemn.... Milly, let loose among them in a wonderful white dress, brought them somehow into relation with something that made them more finely genial. She was different, younger, fairer, with the colour of her braided hair more than ever a challenge to attention. (233–234)

James's imaginary painting—feasting and music, wine and song, grandeur and ornament for its own sake—has the momentary effect of a reenactment of Venetian life in the High Renaissance style, symbolizing the romantic hope of the heroine as she tried to make her countermove to fate. As such it is the answering opposite to the Bronzino portrait at Matcham, symbolizing the fear of death that unaccountably loomed before the heroine at the height of her possibilities for triumphant living. The events at Matcham had been sharply brought back to her mind just a few days before by Lord Mark's visit, "the moments that had exactly made the high-water-mark of her security, the moments during which her tears themselves, those she had been ashamed of, were the sign of her consciously rounding her protective promontory, quitting the blue gulf of comparative ignorance and reaching her view of the troubled sea" (158–159). These contrasting occasions of Milly's fears and Milly's hopes invoke once again her strangely ambiguous comment to her companion, early in the novel: "Since I've lived all these years as if I were dead, I shall die, no doubt, as if I were alive" (I, 220).

The ambiguity is reinforced now by her appearing in "a wonderful white dress" at her Venetian party. White is the most ambiguous of colors: the dress of a bride, the burial garment of the dead; a symbol of innocence, purity, holiness, and at the same time a symbol of nothingness. Whatever emblematic meanings one may guess that James had in mind, there is one concrete meaning that he spells out. Milly's dress as hostess on her festal evening is the opposite of "her almost monastic, her hitherto inveterate black" (234). Mourning had become habitual with her because of the death one after the other of all her family. Now she has cast it off for the first time in years and put on white to suit the show of life she is staging, chiefly for the eyes of Sir Luke Strett. Yet, with his "strong face and type," he is "less assimilated by the scene perhaps than any others." This is presumably because his very presence strikes the note of ambiguity again: as her good physician, to be sure, he is the one who urged her to live, but she would never have consulted him as an eminent specialist in the first place except for her fear that she was going to die.

Now also the dual meanings of Milly's images for Palazzo Leporelli recur with more clarity. "Ah, not to go down," she had said to Lord Mark: "I stay up. That's how you happily found me" (163). To stay up high in the romantic world created for her by Eugenio's imagination, a kind of protective fortress, never to descend to the sordid world of arranged marriages to which her exploitative suitor invited her—that was one formulation of her hope. To fly with Merton Densher on a magic carpet, defying space and time—the two limits of mortality—that was another image of escape into freedom offered by her palace. Finally, as the ark floated on over subsiding flood-waters, one remembers, it was a dove that was sent out and returned with an olive branch in its beak, signifying the possibility of new life on this earth. Three paradoxes.

Such is the elaborate scene-setting for the evening party at Palazzo Leporelli. But this is one of those "discriminated occasions," according to James's Preface, that bear the weight of the "double pressure," when picture merges into scene. The action is brief and scarcely rises out of tableau into motion. At one end of the great *sala* Milly is receiving; James's painterly eye told him that by putting her in white, in such a highly colored setting, he was putting her in the spotlight so that she was truly the cynosure, drawing all to her without need of moving herself. On the other side of the canvas two of the painted figures, Merton and Kate, slowly stir into life. But he is no longer "the grand young man who surpasses all the others and holds up his head and the wine cup." And Kate is somehow wanting in lustre: "As a striking young presence she was practically superseded; ... she might fairly have been dressed tonight in the little black frock that Milly had laid aside" (236). For they are engaged in dark exchanges that refer to quite other matters than the gala event before them, the hall being spacious enough and the company large enough to give them privacy. Their tête-à-tête comprises all the action afforded by this great "Veronese" scene, but it is climactic.

Kate began their talk by drawing Merton's attention to Milly far across the gilded saloon of Palazzo Leporelli:

> "Everything suits her so—especially her pearls. They go so with her old lace. I'll trouble you really to look at them." ... The long, priceless chain, wound twice round the neck, hung heavy and pure, down the front of the wearer's breast—.... "She's a dove," Kate went on, "and one somehow doesn't think of doves as bejewelled. Yet they suit her down to the ground." (237–238)

He agreed, feeling that both the dove image and the soft iridescence of pearls were apt descriptions of Milly's spirit. But he realized it was the combination of the two—the dove-like color of pearls suggesting innocence as well as wealth —that dominated Kate's impression of the heroine this evening. The power of wealth was "dove-like," he reflected, "only so far as one remembered that doves have wings and wondrous flights, have them as well as tender tints and soft sounds" (238).

A similar metaphor for wealth as a power was applied to Mrs. Lowder early in the novel. Merton had accused Kate of speaking of her as if she were a vulture. The reply: "Call it an eagle—with a gilded beak as well, and with wings for great flights" (I, 83). One is a bird of prey; the other is generally thought of as quarry. Yet, at the same time, the dove is traditionally associated with love, both sacred and profane—being equally a symbol of the pagan Venus and the Christian Sanctus Spiritus. Two kinds of power, two uses of wealth. Kate, as surrogate of Aunt Maud, takes on the likeness of an eagle in this the last of James's animal images. And the pearl colors of the dove merge with the dove-like color of pearls. A final suggestion that occurred to Merton, dimly, was that "such wings could ... spread themselves for protection. Hadn't they, for that matter, lately taken an inordinate reach, and weren't Kate and Mrs. Lowder, weren't Susan Shepherd and he, wasn't *he* in particular, nestling under them to a great increase of immediate ease?" (238–239). Do the wings of the dove here symbolize encompassing love or supporting wealth?

This question is answered with startling frankness in the ensuing dialogue. As Kate continued to emphasize the bejewelled aspect of the dove, her fiancé realized with a pang that "pearls were exactly what Merton Densher would never be able to give her. ... Milly's royal ornament had—under pressure now not wholly occult—taken on the character of a symbol of differences" (239). Merton knew that Kate's plan envisaged overcoming this difference somehow, but she had concealed all along even from him the final range of her intention. As she continued to spar with him this evening—though coming closer with hints about how really ill Milly was and how Milly considered her "situation" with Merton as "too precious to be spoiled" by Lord Mark's proposal of marriage—he decided to force Kate's secret into the open, between them:

> "Since she's to die I'm to marry her?"
> Her lips bravely moved. "To marry her."
> "So that when her death has taken place I shall in the natural course have money?"
> It was before him enough now, ... that all along—to his stupidity, his timidity—it had been, it had been only what she meant. [Now the words she had never pronounced before] broke through her controlled and colourless voice as if she should be ashamed, to the very end, to have flinched: "You'll in the natural course have money. We shall in the natural course be free."
> "Oh, oh, oh!" Densher softly murmured. (246–247)

When Kate announced the rest of her plan, that she and Aunt Maud were returning to London in a few days, leaving him in Venice to carry out his assignment, he balked: "I might stay, you know, without trying. ... One has to try a little hard to propose to a dying girl" (250–251). She replied that it would be quite enough, for Milly, if he only stayed behind to be alone with her. "You think it then possible she may *offer* marriage?" Densher asked: "In the manner of princesses, who do such things?" Then he answered his own query: "It will be for me then to accept. But that's the way it must come" (251). This was his last desperate effort to escape from a feeling of complicity in Kate's exploitative scheme.

After such guilty confidences, their eyes instinctively sought out again their dove-like hostess at the far end of the *sala*. "Milly, from the other side, happened at the moment to notice them, and she sent across toward them in response all the candour of her smile, the lustre of her pearls, the value of her life, the essence of her wealth" (250–251). That is what *they* saw. Since we are not told what *she* saw, in this exchange of stares, it was presumably nothing. With this, Milly's last appearance, the lights go down on the stage at Palazzo Leporelli, leaving the other possible meanings of "whiteness" to flicker in the reader's mind—marriage or death, saintliness or nothingness? The great scene has been illuminated by a backdrop painted in Veronese's atelier by his pupil Susan Shepherd. Now it is lit indirectly from the wings, so to speak, by two slighter scenes set in another and even grander drawing room.

The first scene had already occurred on the morning of Milly's party, when her indisposition had sent her friends out on the town to entertain themselves. As Mrs. Lowder and Mrs. Stringham wanted to do some shopping, Kate and

Merton seized the chance for an hour to themselves on the excuse that they had had no opportunity till now for even a look-in at the basilica of St. Mark. Their rendezvous in the spring garden at Kensington, as lovers seeking refuge from Aunt Maud's disapproving eyes, was quite a different thing from their present skulking about the great piazza, full of their unspoken scheme to exploit the American heiress. James's choice of place for this occasion was a bold stroke—the most famous square in the world because it offers the most dazzling display that can be achieved by fabulous wealth. The grand sweep of palatial buildings on three sides, with their classical façades rising above one continuous loggia, forms an incomparable setting for the ornate Byzantine cathedral, flanked by the sumptuous ducal residence, at the eastern end.

The Piazza San Marco beggars description, as James was well aware. Besides, it had been raved over so countless many times that he felt it would be banal for a professional writer to describe it in his own voice. Accordingly, though he devoted half-a-dozen essays to the glories of Venice, spanning his career, he consistently bypassed the celebrated square, saving it instead for his fictions. It would be perfectly natural for his characters, as mere visitors in Venice, to try to find words to express their wonder. The response of the little bookbinder in *The Princess* was chiefly to its beauty, recorded by James in a single shining sentence: "I shall spend the evening in that enchanted square of St. Mark's which resembles an immense open-air drawing room, listening to music and feeling the sea-breeze" (see chap. 4).

The more sophisticated English pair in *The Wings* responded instead to its grandeur and to its aura of high social uses.

> [Their colloquy took place] in the middle of Piazza San Marco, always, as a great social saloon, a smooth-floored, blue-roofed chamber of amenity, favourable to talk; or rather, to be exact, not in the middle, but at the point where our pair had paused by a common impulse after leaving the great mosque-like church. It rose now, domed and pinnacled, but a little way behind them, and they had in front the vast empty space, enclosed by its arcades.... The splendid Square, which had so notoriously, in all the years, witnessed more of the joy of life than any equal area in Europe, furnished them, in their remoteness from earshot, with solitude and security. (208, 211)

Kate had still not made it clear to Densher what she meant by his "being kind to Milly," but the fact that she had paved the way for him by a deliberate lie (telling Milly that she, Kate, did not return Merton's love) made him constantly apprehensive that he was getting in too deep, though into what he didn't quite know. And several times recently he had felt a kind of exasperation, "a resentment...that he was perpetually bent to her will" (192). It came back to him on this morning in St. Mark's square, and he suddenly flared up: "Why not have done with all and face the music as we are?" Though Kate felt his rebellion as more sweet than bitter, she countered: "We've gone too far.... Do you want to kill her?... We've told too many lies." At this his head went up: "I, my dear, have told none!" (217, 218).

As she continued to apply the pressure, he decided to assert his will, declaring that so far it had been a matter of what she expected of him, not at all what he might expect of her:

> "What I wish is to be loved. How can I feel at this rate that I *am*?... I'll tell any lie you want, any your idea requires, if you'll only come to me."...
>
> "How? Where?"
>
> She spoke low, but there was somehow, for his uncertainty, a wonder in her being so equal to him. "To my rooms, which are perfectly possible.... We can arrange it—with two grains of courage. People in our case always arrange it." (217, 219)

At this crucial point their talk was interrupted by the reappearance of Mrs. Lowder and Mrs. Stringham. He picked it up again at the end of the evening party in Palazzo Leporelli, after Kate had made clear exactly what lie she expected him to tell—rather, to live out, by proposing to Milly, or letting himself be proposed to—and had demanded a pledge that he would stay on in Venice for that purpose. "Well," he said, "I'll stay, on my honour, if you'll come to me. On *your* honour." When she answered, "I'll come," he knew that in all their relation he had never known "anything so sharp—too sharp for mere sweetness—as the vividness with which he saw himself master in the conflict" (252–253). The word honor has a hollow ring here, being reduced to a kind of honor among thieves; both of them were now committed, each in a different sense, to "stealing" a fortune.

The sequel is rendered not as a scene but in a retrospective narrative: "Kate had come to him; it was only once—...yet she had come, that once, to stay, as people called it" (257–258). The earliest Notebook sketch for *The Wings of the Dove* shows Henry James toying with the possibility of a very different assignation, with the tempting young man having persuaded the heroine herself to a love-surrender. But on second thought he decided to cancel such an episode: "this idea of the physical possession, the brief physical, passional rapture which at first appeared essential to it, bothered me on account of the ugliness, the incongruity, the nastiness, *en somme*, of the man's 'having' a sick girl:...something vulgar in the presentation of such a remedy for her despair." For once James's prudery was esthetically and dramatically right. Everything that the novel reveals about the three principal characters and their interrelations squares with this decision. It is unthinkable that Milly's love should be treated otherwise than as ideal, and virginal—as prophesied in her likeness to the Bronzino portrait of Lucrezia Panciatichi, who was reading a book of hymns to the Virgin Mary!

As for Merton and Kate, it was inevitable that their great love should achieve physical consummation. Even the handling of this as an event occurring offstage is appropriate to James's concern, his sole interest being in the effect on Merton of Kate's surrender. The lingering memory of their tryst is at once a torment and an ecstasy for him. It was, first of all, the fulfillment of that passionate attachment smouldering within them during the long months since their declaration in Kensington Gardens of "belonging tremendously" to each other. Now, since she had come to him, Kate's presence "lingered there as an obsession importunate to all his senses"; lingered there "in his faded old rooms," so sadly in contrast with the grandeur of their other Venetian settings, reminding the reader of Merton's rueful thought during the party that "pearls were exactly what Merton Densher would never be able to give her" (257, 239).

In the weeks after Kate's departure, whenever he thought of her he was reminded also of his pledge, and that conjured up a vision of Milly and of his strange situation between the two of them: "The actual grand queerness was that to be faithful to Kate he had positively to take his eyes, his arms, his lips straight off her—he had to let her alone. He had to remember it was time to go to the palace" (260). There, in Milly's presence each day, he found himself ever more deeply drawn in by "her welcome, her frankness, sweetness, sadness, brightness, her disconcerting poetry, as he made shift at moments to call it, helped as it was by the beauty of her whole setting" (202); so that he seemed to have left Kate behind, shut up in his "poor rooms." Merton's plight was that no matter what he did or said he was disloyal and lying either to Kate or to Milly. The role Kate had assigned him, by implication, was that "he should lie with his lips ... straight in the white face of his young hostess, divine in her trust, or at any rate inscrutable in her mercy" (265). What he actually did, when he discovered how much Milly cared for him and depended on him for happiness—even for a reason to want to live—was to do nothing. "To be kind" to her was "the same as being still," he decided. "He felt himself ... shut up in a room, on the wall of which something precious was too precariously hung. A false step would bring it down, and it must hang as long as possible" (276). (The Matcham portrait?)

Merton continued drifting like this for a month, weaving his own threads of unreality into the silken web of Kate's scheme until, cocoon-like, he had wrapped himself away from the world of moral responsibility. Then one day, on going to the palace at teatime as usual, he was met by the information that the signorina padrona was not "receiving." Something had happened, but Eugenio would give no inkling of what it was. Merton had "a sudden sharp sense that everything had turned to the dismal" (279, 282). He felt as if he had seen "the obliteration, at a stroke, of the margin of a faith in which they were all living." He made his way in shock and despair to the Piazza San Marco where he could have the shelter of the galleries, the first sea-storm of autumn having broken upon the city. Here the second of the paired scenes occurs, a scene-without-dialogue, taking place entirely in the mind of Merton Densher:

> It was a Venice all of evil that had broken out for them alike...; a Venice of cold, lashing rain from a low black sky, of wicked wind raging through narrow passes.... Here, in the high arcade, half Venice was crowded close, while, on the Molo, at the limit of the expanse, the old columns of St. Mark and of the Lion were like the lintels of a door wide open to the storm.... There were stretches of the gallery paved with squares of red marble, greasy now with the salt spray; and the whole place, in its huge elegance, the grace of its conception and the beauty of its detail, was more than ever like a great drawing-room, the drawing-room of Europe, profaned and bewildered by some reverse of fortune. (283–285)

For the alert reader James has left a clue here in his concluding phrase, "the drawing-room of Europe," which echoes the celebrated *mot* of Napoleon, the archetypal exploiter in the modern world.

Merton had made the whole circuit of the galleries around the square three times before he stopped short, in front of Florian's, where his eye caught a familiar face behind the plate glass window of the café. Another character has entered the scene, Lord Mark. But though they exchanged a glance of recognition they did not exchange a word. (A perverse mirror image of Merton as he might-have-been?) Everything that happens continues to do so only in Merton's mind. "The weather had changed, the rain was ugly, the wind wicked, the sea impossible, *because* of Lord Mark," he ruminated, as he continued his restless prowling: "It was because of him, *a fortiori*, that the palace was closed" (287). Merton had only a hunch as to what Mark had done or said, being certain only that he had come back as a kind of sequel to his earlier visit, to take revenge somehow for having been rejected. The hunch was confirmed three days later when Mrs. Stringham came to his lodgings to report her distress about Milly's state: "She has turned her face to the wall" (294). When Merton asked, "Is she dying?" and then, inconsequently, "Does she utterly hate me?" her reply turned the blame, at least as to the cruel blow that was the immediate cause, away from him and onto

Lord Mark: "What I mean is that he told her you've been all the while engaged to Miss Croy" (296, 300, 309–310).

As a novel of relations *The Wings of the Dove* is all but brought to a conclusion with the great Veronese scene at Palazzo Leporelli and the two slighter flanking scenes set in Piazza San Marco. The dénouement, absorbing though it may be as a piece of subtle storytelling, seems a bit long-drawn-out to the critic because its mode of presentation is discursive rather than scenic. But it serves two valid purposes. For one thing it is James's concession to that class of readers who want to know how it all came out: what became of the fortune? since the hero did not marry the blond, did he get the brunette? Even while unwinding his plot to the satisfaction of everyone, short of the most literal-minded, James manages to keep his novel open-ended and to keep his emphasis where he wants it. For the second and most important use of these hundred pages is a final clarification of Merton Densher's relations to the heroine and the antiheroine, the two most important relations in the book. Milly died in far-off Venice, though not before she had opened the palace doors once again to Merton for a last meeting. Since the reader is not present on either occasion, the little that he learns about them comes later, in London. This is fitting, because they are both really aspects of that far more complex relation with Kate Croy. At the same time it must be emphasized that the resolution of Milly's story is exactly what determines the outcome of the other story, that of the affianced English couple.

Many things about Merton Densher after his return to England suggest how much he has come under the spell of Milly's spirit, for example, his being in London for a fortnight before giving Kate any sign he was back. Even in Venice there had been pointers indicating a shift in his relations with his fiancée. His insistence that she come to him in his lodgings was proof enough that only his love for her made him willing to be a party to her terrible scheme of deception; but Kate's motivation was not so simply a matter of the heart. Then his scruple, that he will not propose to Milly though he will accept if she proposes, though it may seem like splitting hairs in a tenuously Jamesian kind of distinction, underlines a real difference between him and Kate—the difference between a passive and an aggressive exploiter. Even the heroine's death did not release Merton from his dilemma; by bequeathing all her wealth to him, she was still vividly present in his life. With his awakened conscience, he could not have both Milly's fortune and Kate's hand in marriage; to be true to either of them still meant being false to the other. On the other hand, Kate insisted on having both Merton's love and Milly's money. The resolution of James's plot, it would seem, makes the dissolution of their engagement inevitable. All of this is suggested rather than spelled out in the dénouement.

Through the Picture Frame

THE AMBASSADORS

In the final summing up of his life's work as an author, Henry James declared that this novel was "quite the best, 'all round,'" of his productions. Some readers have agreed with this judgment, some have preferred *The Wings of the Dove*, and others, feeling that the later novels are too mannered, are convinced that *The Portrait of a Lady* is the high point of his achievement. Personal preferences aside, all Jamesians would agree that *The Ambassadors* is one of his half-dozen masterpieces. Certainly it shows a culminating mastery of all the artistic techniques he had been developing over a period of three or four decades.

For the first time in more than twenty years James returned, in a major work, to the international theme that had won him his early successes. In *The American* (1877) his treatment of the contrast had been sociological; in *The Portrait* (1881) it was humanistic, a marked improvement. Now in *The Ambassadors* (1903) there is a further refinement: the mode of presenting the contrast is strictly poetic, with respect to the hero; further, it is tangential to the main argument except for the comic interlude of the substitute "Ambassador," as will be seen. (Though *The Wings of the Dove*, 1902, is the story of an American girl's experiences in Europe, the contrast of two national cultures is not its theme.)

James's great new discovery was the "method of myth" for catching the total impact of Europe on American character, by weaving a fictional fabric of three strands. First, the observed reality, presented in this novel through that consummate Parisian Madame de Vionnet, the thoroughly Gallicized Miss Gostrey, young Chad Newsome and his expatriate friends. Second, the various American preconceptions of Europe, assigned to minor characters: Waymarsh the foil, the awesomely absent Mrs. Newsome, and the blatantly present Pococks. Finally, Henry James's own deliberately invented myth or fable of "Europe," which includes the other two strands and adds to the novel's representational powers the suggestiveness of poetry. The full effect of this multiple way of seeing is achieved by looking at everything through the eyes of the hero, who fits to a certain extent in all three categories. When

Strether first comes out he shares some of the prejudices of Woollett, Massachusetts, or at least thinks he does. But his desire to *know* Europe is so genuine that he makes an apt pupil in learning to distinguish between false and true notions about it. As the enchantment of Paris grows on him he becomes as much of a mythmaker as his creator, with whom he has several traits in common.

Development of the technique of point of view—filtering the story entirely through the central consciousness of a single character—is generally regarded as one of James's major contributions to the modern novel. It avoids the tendency to "saturation" and looseness of structure that results from the use of an omniscient author. It brings into focus the chaotic stream of real-life experience. And if it means some sacrifice by the author of the quantity and range of material at his disposal, it also means a great gain in intensity of what he does use. James had been experimenting with the possibilities of this method for many years. In his first extensive use of it, *The Portrait of a Lady*, he had the advantage of a heroine whose responsiveness to Europe and to her adventures there made it possible for the reader to see a great deal through her consciousness alone; but since there were many things she did not understand, the author found it necessary to "go behind" right and left. In *The Princess Casamassima* he sticks even closer to the point of view of a single character, because the hero's esthetic sensibility is such that he understands almost everything through his eyes, and the reader is able to see with him; but there are a few matters that need to be understood through the mind, and his limitation there makes it necessary for the reader to learn about things that are denied to the hero.

In *The Ambassadors* James is able to carry his new technique to its fulfillment; for, in addition to the traits possessed by Isabel Archer and Hyacinth Robinson, Lambert Strether has imagination and intelligence. As a character both involved in the action and detached from it, he is capable of special insights. By being endowed with a detective's passion for exploring, he can circle round the character-situations and grope for all possible clues. And since he is a character rather than the creator, he can even confess in the end quite convincingly that this is all of the truth he has been able to discover, leaving much still unknown or ambiguous, just as in real life—though this is something a reader might well resent in an author, who ought to *know*! In his Preface to this novel James boasted that he had made use of "the splendid particular economy ... of employing but one centre and keeping it all within my hero's compass." Numerous other persons were "to people the scene," he added, each with his own situation or relation calling for treatment, but "only Strether's sense of these things" should avail for presenting them. He chose to use this technical device, he said, because it gave his novel "a large unity, ... and the grace of intensity." The author's claim has been accepted by the critical consensus ever since.

As a story that takes place almost entirely within the consciousness of one character, *The Ambassadors* would seem to be the most nondramatic of subjects. What then does James mean by saying, in this same Preface, that the material of this novel is taken by the author "absolutely for the stuff of drama"? For one thing, throughout the story he treats Strether's consciousness as a play: even when he is picturing the hero's mind as it is brushed by each new experience, he makes a little interior scene of it, the cumulative effect being similar to that of a drama enacted on the stage. Again, though the point of view in *The Ambassadors* is primarily Strether's, and though it is made to appear as his throughout, there are scenic episodes with dialogue in which the author creates the illusion that we are outside Strether's mind and watching him quite as much as we are watching the other characters. This "easy sleight of hand" is explained by one of James's most perceptive critics: "Simply it consists in treating the scene as dramatically as possible—keeping it framed in Strether's vision, certainly, but keeping his consciousness out of sight, his thought unexplored." Finally, in addition to two scenes that actually take place in a theater, using that setting for symbolic purposes, there is a constant employment of theatrical terms—stage, performance, role—used figuratively.

In these different ways James succeeds in dramatizing the picture of his hero's experiences. As a matter of fact, he declares that the mode for *The Ambassadors* is exactly the same as that used in *The Wings of the Dove*, an alternation of "picture" and "scene." To summarize here what I set forth in some detail in my preceding chapter: the scenes are keys to an understanding of the characters, both in themselves and in their relations to each other; the picture elements either carry the narrative forward or are themselves to a certain extent dramatized and become scene-settings, scenes without dialogue, taking place in the mind of a character. In his Preface to *The Wings* James declares: "These alternations [also make up] ... the very form and figure of *The Ambassadors*."

By such techniques the kind of discursive novel likely to have been written under the convention of an omniscient author—by Balzac, Dickens, George Eliot, to mention only a few of James's acknowledged masters—was transformed in *The Ambassadors* into a marvel of dramatic structure. And the control of fictional materials made possible by a Lambert Strether (whose impressions, and expressions, virtually create the world of that novel) was carried still further by Conrad with his ubiquitous Marlowe and by the compact first person narrations of Hemingway and Fitzgerald—to name only acknowledged disciples of James. With them, as occasionally with the master himself, this center of consciousness becomes a narrator whose voice alone tells us the story. (His desire to free his novels from authorial intrusion had first been prompted by the example of Flaubert, whose dictum James quoted with approval. "The artist must be present in his work [only] like God in Creation, invisible and almighty, everywhere felt but nowhere seen.")

Although James's two late masterpieces are similar in that both are structured by the dual mode of picture-and-scene, they differ in emphasis. In *The Wings* "scene" is dominant; in *The Ambassadors*, "scene" and "picture" are kept in balance. The latter term not only means pictures in the sense of scene-settings, as described above, but verbal pictures that are analogous to paintings. Two climactic episodes in *The Wings* are made memorable by explicit references to Mannerist paintings by Bronzino and Veronese, as already discussed at length. In *The Ambassadors* the use of pictures is even more important. Though the similarities are only implicit, a strong case can be made that most of the series of small climaxes by which the novel's inner theme is revealed were inspired by contemporary paintings of the French Impressionists. To the extent that these analogues are convincing, as presented in the following pages, they constitute a brilliant new technique by James for illuminating the subtlest nuances of his meanings. There is plenty of supporting evidence that *is* direct, in the form of references throughout *The Ambassadors* to the terminology of painting—picture, pastel, portrait, miniature, frame—especially in the key episodes. Then there is the explicit comment in the epilogue, following the final revelation of meaning to Lambert Strether: "He was moving in these days, as in a gallery, from clever canvas to clever canvas." The hero here brings to mind a portrait of the author himself, that striking photograph by Alice Boughton of James-the-Observer looking at paintings.

Even a summary glance at the techniques employed in *The Ambassadors* makes it clear that this novel offers the fullest validation of my own method for analyzing the fictions of Henry James, the thesis expressed in my title: "Person, Place, and Thing." My purpose is to show that his characters arrive at relations only indirectly through the places and things that symbolize what they are and hence reveal their true meanings to each other, as set forth in my introductory chapter. Lambert Strether has practically no relations with any of the other characters in *The Ambassadors* in a direct way, in the normal sense of relations in human society. But with his sensitive powers of observation, as he gradually comes to realize the meanings of the places and things associated with them, he establishes symbolic relationships that enable him to understand Chad, Madame de Vionnet, and the others. Once he has accomplished this he is really done with them, because through this process he has come to understand himself—self-knowledge being the whole point of the novel.

[223]

Birth of a Masterpiece

"Never can a composition of this sort have sprung straighter from a dropped grain of suggestion," James says in his Preface to *The Ambassadors*. He then points us to the second chapter of Book Five, almost halfway through his novel, where the hero makes his celebrated declaration that one should live all he can before it is too late. The germ of *The Ambassadors* is recorded succinctly in James's Notebooks under date of 31 October 1895 after a visit from Jonathan Sturges, a young American friend. They had been talking of William Dean Howells and of Sturges's glimpse of him the year before in Paris during an abortive stay, Howells having been suddenly called back to America because his father was dying. The first version of this incident follows:

> [Howells] had scarcely been in Paris, ever, in former days.... Virtually in the evening, as it were, of life, it was all new to him: all, all, all. Sturges said he seemed sad—rather brooding; and I asked him what gave him (Sturges) that impression. "Oh—somewhere—I forget, when I was with him—he laid his hand on my shoulder and said *a propos* of some remark of mine: 'Oh, you are young, you are young—be glad of it and *live*. Live all you can: it's a mistake not to. It doesn't so much matter what you do —but live. This place makes it all come over me. I see it now. I haven't done so—and now I'm old. It's too late. It has gone past me—I've lost it. You have time. You are young. Live!' " I amplify and improve a little— but that was the tone. It touches me—I can see him—I can hear him.

James adds: "I seem to see something, of a tiny kind, springing out of it." But the seed lay dormant for four or five years, and when it did at last germinate it produced the full flower of his masterpiece.

There were two principal reasons for this delay in developing his *donnée* into a novel. One of them has already been explained in the preceding chapter. At this point in his career, James felt the need to try all kinds of experiments with several new techniques before venturing on the composition of three major novels he had projected in Notebook entries of great promise: *The Golden Bowl* (28 November 1892), *The Wings* (3 November 1894), and now *The Ambassadors* (31 October 1895). The second reason can only be conjectured, but I think the evidence is as convincing as its application to an understanding of *The Ambassadors* is crucially important. On 1 September 1900 James submitted a "Project" for his new novel to Harpers with a view to serial publication in their monthly magazine. The fortunate survival of this document provides the critic with a unique opportunity for tracing the evolution of this particular novel. (Similar preliminary statements were written for several others but they were either lost or destroyed.) For *The*

Ambassadors the analyst thus has four stages instead of the usual three: the initial *donnée* and discussion in the Notebooks, running to a little over a thousand words; the much longer "Project," twenty thousand words, written five years later; the text of the novel itself, composed immediately following and running to more than one hundred and fifty thousand words; and the twenty-page Preface, looking back after the lapse of six or seven years on the whole process of inception and composition. Of these four, what concerns us now is the unique "Project," or "Scenario" as James also called it. (See p. 175, above.)

The "Project" sent to Harpers has something especially significant to say about the climactic scene of *The Ambassadors*. By way of introduction James remarks: "It occurs to me that it may conduce to interest to begin with a mention of the comparatively small matter that gave me the germ of my subject." There follows the second version of the *donnée* for his novel, with the principals unnamed but with the scene at last specified:

> He [Sturges] had found himself, one Sunday afternoon, with various other people, in the charming old garden attached to the house of a friend (also a friend of mine) in a particularly old-fashioned and pleasantly quiet part of the town [Paris]; a garden that ... I myself knew, so that I could easily focus the setting. The old houses of the Faubourg St. Germain close round their gardens and shut them in.

James then continues with an account of Sunday afternoon visits he used to pay many years ago to "an ancient lady" who owned the house next door to the garden just described, concluding: "But I mention these slightly irrelevant things only to show that I *saw* the scene of my young friend's anecdote."

This specification of the setting seems highly significant. The first version of the anecdote, in the Notebook entry of 1895, is explicit about *not* locating it, other than merely "in Paris"; Sturges is reported as saying: "Oh—somewhere—I forget." (And this was recorded on the morning after his visit.) By the time James began writing the novel some five years later, as indicated in the "Project" sent to Harpers, the particular setting had become so vivid and so important to his theme that he attributed it to Sturges, the original teller of the anecdote. This emphasis on the setting is continued in the second version of the declaration-for-living by Howells (here referred to anonymously as "an American distinguished and mature") which is now extended by two extremely interesting sentences: "I'm too old for what I *see*. Oh, I *do* see, at least—I see a lot." Just what he *does see* James underscores for the editor at Harpers:

> But think of the place again first—the charming June afternoon in Paris, the tea under the trees, the 'intimate' nook, consecrated to 'artistic and

[225]

literary' talk, types, freedoms of (for the *désorienté* elderly American) an unprecedented sort; think above all of the so-possible presence of a charming woman or two, of peculiarly 'European' tradition, such as it had never yet been given him to encounter. Well, this is what the whole thing, as with a slow rush the sense of it came over him, made him say, "Oh, *you're* young."

The Howells anecdote simply did not kindle the novelist's imagination until he could place it in this picturesque garden, where he could visualize it and then endow his fictional hero with his own talent for seeing. James was indeed quite familiar with the locale. During his Paris year, 1875–76, he had paid several visits to a lady in her eighties, Mme Jules Mohl, who lived at 120, rue du Bac (the house in the Faubourg St. Germain where Chateaubriand had died with his mistress, Mme Recamier, at his bedside); and from the windows of her apartment he could look down into the garden in question. Many years later, in 1893, he had paid a visit to the painter Whistler, who had rented the house that went with this very garden. Just when James discovered that Howells actually made his declaration to Sturges in this same setting is not known. What is important is that there is no mention of it in the Notebook entry of 1895, whereas the "Project" of 1900 locates it specifically, and the composition of *The Ambassadors* proceeded at once, the great two-volume novel being completed in about eight months thereafter.

The "gift" of the old Paris garden, as he referred to it in his late Preface, "the place and the time and the scene they sketched," enabled him to expand the few sentences quoted above from the "Project" into what is probably the most brilliant scene in all of James's fictions, occupying three chapters in the middle of his masterpiece and giving the "note absolute" to the whole of it. The Preface is explicit about this latter point too. When he had conceived of his hero, Lambert Strether, as asking himself if it really was too late or if there might yet be time to repair his mistake, James added: "The answer to which is that he now at all events *sees*; so that the business of my tale and the march of my action, not to say the precious moral of everything, is just my demonstration of this process of vision."

Essential to the working out of such a story was the conception of his hero as a man of such imagination, intelligence, and sensitivity that his awareness of what it means *to live*, of what he himself has missed, could be revealed exclusively by "picture" and "scene." James's initial discussion in the Notebooks shows him exploring the possibilities. A clergyman is too obvious, he decided; a journalist or a lawyer "WOULD in a manner have 'lived' . . . a doctor—an artist too." A business man would not be of the right "intellectual grain," and though a college professor might be, he would have too much knowledge of the lives of the young. "I want him 'intellectual,' I want him *fine*, clever, literary almost," he concluded, but "I can't make him a novelist—too like W.D.H." Later, in his retrospective Preface James amplified this: for maximum development of his story he realized the necessity "at the earliest stage [to nip] the thread of connection with . . . the actual reported speaker. *He* remains but the happiest of accidents; his actualities, all too definite, precluded any range of possibilities."

For some of the essential traits of Lambert Strether the author could draw on himself, as his casual aside in a letter of a decade later makes clear. Sending a copy of *The Ambassadors* to a friend, he wrote: "Try to like the poor old hero, in whom you will perhaps find a vague resemblance (though not facial!) to your always / Henry James." This is not to suggest that James's hero is autobiographical in any substantive way, only in the projection of a potentiality, as was true of his hero in *The Princess Casamassima*. (See pages 124 ff. above.) What the creator of Strether drew on especially was memories of his earlier self, his own responsiveness to visual impressions during his first experiences of Europe. Demonstrations of this will form an integral part of my analyses of the pictures-and-scenes through which the theme of *The Ambassadors* is unfolded.

> My subject may be most simply described, then, as the picture of a certain momentous and interesting period, of some six months or so, in the history of a man no longer in the prime of life, yet still able to live with sufficient intensity to be a source of what may be called excitement to himself, not less than to the reader of his record.

These are the opening words of James's "Project" or "Scenario" for *The Ambassadors*, following the brief introductory paragraphs containing the amplified version of the *donnée* which has proved so helpful in understanding his whole conception. Before turning to the novel itself, we may also throw a little light on his method of composition by calling attention to two important ways in which the "Project" differs from the finished work. Surprisingly enough for a novel that was to be one of his greatest triumphs in the mode of revelation by scenes, the climactic scene in the Paris garden is the only one out of ten major scenes, or scene-settings, that is really presented in this long preliminary outline. The opening one at Chester and the final one at the riverside inn outside Paris are vaguely sketched in, but none of the others are even mentioned, much less put before us as potential scenes. This does not mean that James only invented his new techniques of rendering when he was in the throes of composing *The Ambassadors*, during the months immediately following—he had actually been experimenting with them for a number of years—merely that the necessities of space in presenting his "Project" to Harpers restricted him to exposition and plot summary.

The second difference is that the "Project" contains much more of past narrative and background than the novel does—more on Woollett, Massachusetts, and Mrs. Newsome (even the late Mr. Newsome), more on Strether's past (including the early loss of his wife and his son), and so on. It is essential for the novelist to work out in advance full dossiers so that he can present his characters as "round" rather than "flat," in the apt terminology of E. M. Forster, making use of only the necessary minimum in the actual fictions. James also knew how to condense the American background of his international novels in a "flashback" so as to achieve unity by an all-European setting; his structural mistake in *Roderick Hudson* (1875) had been rectified in his treatment of the same problem in *The Portrait of a Lady* (1881). These differences between the "Project" for *The Ambassadors* and the novel itself have been mentioned here only for the purpose of emphasizing the prime importance of the techniques of rendering in James's masterpiece. In many ways the two versions are quite similar, especially in laying down the story line. But in their impact on the reader they are worlds apart. Nothing could have transformed this discursive outline into *The Ambassadors* but the superb art of Henry James.

Chester

For sounding the "first 'note' of Europe" Lambert Strether chose the medieval walled town of Chester. He went there directly from Liverpool, his port of arrival from America. To have a look at this remembered old town would be to treat himself to "a qualified draught of Europe":

> All sorts of other pleasant small things—small things that were yet large for him—flowered in the air of the occasion.... The tortuous wall—girdle, long since snapped, of the little swollen city, half held in place by careful civic hands—wanders in narrow file between parapets smoothed by peaceful generations, pausing here and there for a dismantled gate or a bridged gap, with rises and drops, steps up and steps down, queer twists, queer contacts, peeps into homely streets and under the brows of gables, views of cathedral tower and waterside fields, of huddled English town and ordered English country. Too deep almost for words was the delight of these things to Strether; yet as deeply mixed with it were certain images of his inward picture. He had trod this walk in the far-off time, at twenty-five; but that, instead of spoiling it, only enriched it for present feeling.

Strether's previous trip abroad—his all-too-brief wedding journey of thirty years before, had begun at Chester; then a stop at London before going on to Paris. Of particular interest to the analyst is the fact that his first visit to Chester must have occurred in the late 1860s, which is reasonably close to James's first visit. A second factual parallel between author and hero is that they are approximately the same age, in their middle fifties, at the time of the novel's setting. In order to launch Strether on "the wave of Europe," accordingly, all James needed to do was to call back to mind his own response to the charms of Chester as a young man, then imagine a man fifty-five years old capable of having the same response because of the "deprived" life he has led. Fortunately he did not have to rely on memory, for he had published a travel essay recording his impressions of Chester at the time of his first visit.

After the Atlantic voyage, James had written in 1872, "the American traveller arriving at this venerable town finds himself transported, without a sensible gradation, from the edge of the New World to the very heart of the Old." Chester is a rare and complete specimen of the antique:

The wall enfolds the place in a continuous ring, which, passing through innumerable picturesque vicissitudes, often threatens to snap, but never fairly breaks the link; ... now sloping, now bending, now broadening into a terrace, now narrowing into an alley, now swelling into an arch, now dipping into steps, now passing some thorn-screened garden, and now ... the extrusion of a rugged ivy-smothered tower.... The civic consciousness, sunning itself thus on the city's rim and glancing at the little swarming towered and gabled town within, and then at the blue undulations of the near Welsh border, may easily deepen to delicious complacency.... It is full of that delightful element of the crooked, the accidental, the unforeseen, which, to American eyes, accustomed to our eternal straight lines and right angles, is the striking feature of European street scenery. An American strolling in the Chester streets finds a perfect feast of crookedness—of those random corners, projections and recesses, odd domestic interspaces charmingly saved or lost, those innumerable architectural surprises and caprices and fantasies which lead to such refreshing exercise a vision benumbed by brown-stone fronts. An American is born to the idea that on his walks [in his own country] it is perpetual level wall ahead of him, and such a revelation as he finds here of infinite accident and infinite effect gives a wholly novel zest to the use of his eyes.

All the descriptive details of Chester seen through Strether's eyes in the fiction can be found in James's early essay, sharpened now by the novelist's pencil. Much more interesting is the difference between the two, contained in the last half of the essay passage and in its introductory sentence, where the travel writer is plucking at the American reader's sleeve to tell him what to look for: the striking contrast between the Old World and the New. All of this expository matter is omitted in the novel where statement gives way to rendering. James's rebuke to a younger novelist, Hugh Walpole, for his misconception of the method of *The Ambassadors* is apropos. "How can you say that I do anything so foul and abject as to 'state'? You deserve that I should condemn you to read the book over once again," he wrote: "All of it that is my subject seems to me given by dramatic projection."

The way in which Chester sounds for Strether the note of Europe—old, complex, devious—is brought out by turning the setting into a scene. He had companions on his walks around the old walled town, and it is in his dialogue with them that all is revealed. "The whole thing is, ... to intensity, a picture of relations," James had concluded in his letter to Walpole—that is, scenes in his new mode. On the first evening he took his walk with a new acquaintance, Maria Gostrey; the next morning they were joined by his old friend Waymarsh (an American lawyer who had been abroad for several months recovering from nervous prostration). Since the latter plays only a minor part in the novel, he will be dealt with first.

James may have taken a cue for Waymarsh from a little aside in his early travel essay. To give a lift to his descriptive passages there, he had introduced two fictional characters, casting himself in the role of "the sentimental tourist" and pitting his own first impressions of England against those of "a cynical adversary." This "certain friend," during their strolls around the ancient town, has been treating the narrator to "a bitter lament on the decay of his relish for the picturesque." "'I have turned the corner of youth,' is his ceaseless plaint; ... 'I find nothing but the hard heavy prose of British civilization.' But little by little I have grown used to my friend's sad monody, and indeed feel half indebted to it as a warning against cheap infatuations." With a little embroidery this "friend" could easily be remade into Waymarsh, whose sole function in the novel is to serve as a foil for the hero, an embodiment of the old self that he is sloughing off with every new experience of Europe. "Europe," Strether's friend complained when they met late the first night, had up to now "failed of its message to him; he hadn't got into tune with it." Even England was not his kind of country: "There ain't a country I've seen over here that *does* seem my kind. ... Look here—I want to go back" (29, 32). This declaration was made just as Strether was becoming aware of a desire to let himself go, to enjoy a personal adventure in Europe in addition to carrying out the "mission" he had come on.

[230]

The catalyst of the hero's transformation is Maria Gostrey, described by one of James's higher flights in his Preface as "the most unmitigated and abandoned of *ficelles*." Having denied himself the "romantic privilege" of a first person narrator, he allowed himself a confidante to set his drama going, "so that such an agent as Miss Gostrey, pre-engaged at a high salary, but waits in the draughty wing with her shawl and her smelling-salts." Maria Gostrey's description of herself fixes her role: "I'm a general guide—to 'Europe,' don't you know? I wait for people—I put them through.... I bear on my back the huge load of our national consciousness" (26). By placing "Europe" in quotation marks James is making one of his significant distinctions: the American preconceptions of that world rather than the reality itself. As an expatriate American who has dedicated herself to being "a sort of superior courier-maid," she is the perfect confidante for Lambert Strether —to release him from the bonds of his past, to launch him on his present experience of Europe, and later to serve as a sounding-board for the problems that arise from his "mission."

Quick to size people up, especially Americans travelling abroad, Miss Gostrey begins by drawing him out skilfully along the lines of two of his characteristic traits: the extraordinary visual talent that makes him so responsive to the very real differences presented by the English scene, also his tendency to give a romantic coloring to what he is seeing by recognizing its similarity to pictures and books he has known. For example, when Strether met her in the hotel dining room, seated at a table by the window with the morning papers beside her, "she reminded him, as he let her know, of Major Pendennis breakfasting at his club.... She must teach him to order breakfast as breakfast was ordered in Europe." Waymarsh was insistent on having his "matutinal beefsteak and oranges," American style (34–35).

On her side, learning that his full name is Lewis Lambert Strether, she remarked that this was the name of a novel by Balzac, but "an awfully bad one." He agreed, with a smile, and it was obvious that they enjoyed these little literary games. But when Strether added, "I come from Woollett Massachusetts," she laughed at the apparent irrelevance, then realized that it was only apparent: "Balzac had described many cities, but hadn't described Woollett Massachusetts" (24). James was not going to describe it himself, either directly or through his hero's report. (He remembered his mistake in *Roderick Hudson* where he tried to emulate the French master in his description of Northampton, Mass.) Woollett comes into *The Ambassadors* only by symbolic or dramatic projection, not by expository statement, as will be seen. And Balzac's influence comes in not through using the novel *Louis Lambert* as a model but through his technique of using material objects, places and things, as extensions of the minds and personalities of his fictional characters. A sentence in the early travel essay on Chester seems to prefigure this. Referring to an especially picturesque part of the town, James had said: "The Rows are 'scenic' as one could wish, and it is a pity that ... there was no English Balzac to introduce them into a realistic romance with a psychological commentary." Since *The Ambassadors* is in one sense just such a book, the sentence was not repeated there.

The famous "Rows" of Chester, as described by James the traveller, are "a sort of Gothic edition of the arcades of Italy" and consist of a running public passage tunnelled through the houses: "The shop-fronts face along the arcade and admit you to little caverns of traffic.... If the picturesque be measured by its hostility to our modern notions of convenience, Chester is probably the most romantic city in the world." In the novel, on the second day of their strolls through the medieval town, the three Americans turned from the Ramparts to the Rows. As Strether looked into the windows of shops "that were not as the shops of Woollett" he felt that they were in some odd way "demoralizing" him, making him want more things than he should know what to do with: "These first walks in Europe were in fact a kind of finely lurid intimation of what one might find at the end of that process." Maria Gostrey was there to remind him that there were more important things for him to acquire than smart neckties and a pair of gloves.

In the travel essay on Chester James had said: "As you pass with the bustling current from shop to shop, you feel custom and tradition—another tone of things—pressing on you from every side, ... the fine differences in national manners." So as Strether and Miss Gostrey paused in places "where the low-browed galleries were darkest, the opposite gables queerest, the solicitations of every kind densest," exchanging remarks about "passers, figures, faces, personal types," they felt that Waymarsh was drawing apart because they seemed to him too sophisticated. It was then that Strether realized what was happening to himself: "a woman of fashion was floating him into society" and an old friend deserted on the brink was watching, baffled and outraged. The "enemy" for Waymarsh was "exactly society, ... exactly the discrimination of types and tones, exactly the wicked old Rows of Chester, rank with feudalism; exactly in short Europe" (37–39). Woollett, undescribed though it remains, is made vividly present by being personified in his attitudes. Even the hero has not entirely shaken off its influence yet, he admits, when his confidante accuses him of not enjoying himself as he should. "Woollett isn't sure it ought to enjoy," he continues. "But it hasn't, poor thing, any one to show it how. It's not like me. I have somebody" (25). Gostrey, having spent a lifetime in Paris, is a prime example of the American who has become an insider in Europe. Waymarsh is "out" and belligerently determined to stay that way. Strether is still on the fringes but desirous of getting in, and he has found his guide. In their relations to each other and to the very English scene at Chester all three are defined for what they are.

The sequel takes place in London. There, by the time the hero has taken Miss Gostrey to dinner and the theater, her role as a *ficelle* has been expertly justified, James boasts in his Preface: "Thanks to it we have treated scenically, and scenically alone, the whole lumpish question of Strether's 'past.'" It is rendered by dialogue, and a comparison with the discursive outline of this sequence in the "Project" will confirm the author's boast. Still, the London episode is a scene only in the conventional mode, for the purpose of advancing the plot. The reader learns, as Miss Gostrey with infinite tact elicits the story from poor Strether, that he has come abroad as an "ambassador" for a wealthy widow, Mrs. Newsome, to bring back her son Chad, an obstinate young man of twenty-eight who has been living in Paris for five or six years, refusing to come home and take his proper place in the family business, so that Woollett is convinced he is in the clutches of some "bad" woman. The family business is a great industry, built up into a virtual monopoly by the late Mr. Newsome, a tycoon who also laid it down in his will that the son must take up his post by a certain time or else forfeit it. The time has now come, and since Chad will not respond to his mother's urgings she has sent out Strether to fetch him home.

In the community of Woollett, Massachusetts, Mrs. Newsome is the dominant figure, empowered as she is by the large family fortune, and also moved to a life of "large beneficence" in order to atone for the ruthlessness by which it was amassed. One of her good works has been to subsidize a "Review," highly idealistic in content and low in circulation, of which Strether is the editor, his name on the cover being his "one presentable little scrap of identity." In compensation for the "grey middle desert" of his life (between the early death of his wife and that of his son ten years later) he now has a sort of career for himself as Mrs. Newsome's right-hand man, in almost everything except the business itself. His current function is in the role of her ambassador extraordinary to France. (All of this story line, the necessary background for the plot, had to be put down on the page so that the author—and the critic —could get on with his real concern, "the story of the story," which is the novel's inner theme.)

What Strether says to Maria Gostrey is less revealing than what is implied by her probings. When he confesses that he subscribes to the Woollett view —that Chad is leading a degenerate life, or at the best a loosely Bohemian one, in Paris—her response catches him completely off guard. There are two quite distinct things that may have happened to him "given the wonderful place he's in," she suggests: "One is that he may have got brutalized. The other is that he may have got refined" (53). Strether can only stare. He begins to see, and the reader with him, that his mission may be more complex than had been foreseen. Again, when his confidante inquired ever so delicately what kind of woman Mrs. Newsome really is, he evades with generalizations like "wonderful" and "magnificent." Yet on the basis of the Woollett background Miss Gostrey has elicited from him, she declares, and the reader is convinced: "How intensely you make me see her!" (50).

Even more revealing than the scenic treatment of Strether's past is the symbolic presentation of it in contrast with his present adventure on the evening in London with Maria Gostrey. He had invited her to dine with him at his hotel before the play:

> He had been to the theatre, even to the opera, in Boston, with Mrs. Newsome, more than once acting as her only escort; but there had been no little confronted dinner, no pink lights, no whiff of vague sweetness, as a preliminary.... There was much the same difference in his impression of the noticed state of his companion, whose dress was "cut down," as he believed the term to be, in respect to shoulders and bosom, in a manner quite other than Mrs. Newsome's, and who wore round her throat a broad red velvet band with an antique jewel—he was rather complacently sure it was antique—attached to it in front. Mrs. Newsome's dress was never in any degree "cut down," and she never wore round her throat a broad red velvet band.... Mrs. Newsome wore, at operatic hours, a black silk dress—very handsome, he knew it was "handsome"—and an ornament that his memory was able further to identify as a ruche. (42–43)

He had once said to the dowager of Woollett "that she looked, with her ruff and other matters, like Queen Elizabeth." Now it came over him "that Miss Gostrey looked perhaps like Mary Stuart." Strether, whose "candour of fancy ...could rest for an instant gratified in such an antithesis," was of course drawing on legend rather than history—the virginally austere queen, who dominated men, in contrast with the Parisian-bred claimant who had a reputation, at least among her enemies, for using all possible feminine wiles to lure men to her side. At any rate the antithesis created in his eyes a "positive high picture," provided him with a starting point "for fresh backward, fresh forward, fresh lateral flights."

The second part of the evening was just as full of symbolic suggestiveness. Like the scene-setting at dinner all we are given is what takes place entirely in the hero's mind, except for the opening exchange. "Oh, yes, they're types!" Miss Gostrey said with a sweeping gesture, in answer to his inquiring look at the people about him in the theater. "It was an evening, it was a world of types, and this was a connexion above all in which the figures and faces in the stalls were interchangeable with those on the stage." He felt as if the play itself was penetrating him "with the naked elbow of his neighbor, a great stripped handsome redhaired lady." Then he recognized by the same law, "beyond the footlights, what he was pleased to take for the very flush of English life. He . . . couldn't have said if it were actors or auditors who were most true" (43–44). James is here using the mirror device to double effect. The proscenium arch serves as a frame holding a reflecting glass between stage and stalls that seems to work both ways.

One is reminded inevitably of those numerous pictures of fashionable London life by George Du Maurier, the novelist-illustrator praised by James in an essay of 1883 for holding up "a singularly polished and lucid mirror to the drama of English society." Though he makes no mention of theater scenes (and I have found none among the voluminous *Society Pictures from Punch* that correspond exactly to Strether's description of stalls and stage), James has a great deal to say about his pictures of drawing rooms, dinner parties, and musical evenings of the upper classes; and much of this is repeated in a second essay, on the occasion of his friend Du Maurier's death in 1897, about the time *The Ambassadors* was germinating. This tentative suggestion of similarity between verbal picture and contemporary art—here a slight vignette compared with mere line drawings—gives but a foretaste of the striking analogues with Impressionist paintings that James's scene-settings in Paris will afford.

The paradox about actors and audience—which is the reality? which the appearance?—is a very genuine one, to be sure. In order to create the illusion that the characters in a play are "real life" people, it is necessary for actors to give the appearance of being something quite different from what they themselves are. On the other hand, when upper-class English auditors in the stalls are behaving quite naturally, they may seem to an American newcomer to be "acting," because he recognizes them as types he has first known in novels and plays.

The young Henry James, in an essay entitled "The London Theatres" written during the first year of his taking up permanent residence in England (1877), had commented on this ambiguous phenomenon in similar language. For the "newcomer" in a foreign city, he wrote, the theatres offer a good deal of interesting evidence on "the manners and customs," the ways of "thinking, feeling, and behaving" of the civilization around him: "It is furnished not by the stage alone, but by the theatre in a larger sense of the word: by the audience, the attendants, the arrangements." As such an ingenuous newcomer, Strether took the stageplay not only for "the very flush of English life" but also for a prophetic representation of the reality he might find when he got to Paris. "It befell that in the drama precisely there was a bad woman in a yellow frock who made a pleasant weak good-looking young man in perpetual evening dress do the most dreadful things"—which prompted Strether to wonder quite absurdly: "Would Chad also be in a perpetual evening dress?" (43–44).

During the intermission another view as to the "reality" of this play is expressed by Miss Gostrey, in a casual aside. They had been talking about the Newsomes' vast business enterprise in Woollett, and Strether had refused to name the article of manufacture because it was so trivial, so really vulgar. "But surely not vulgarer than this," she replied: "This dreadful London theatre? It's impossible, if you really want to know" (48). Her more sophisticated judgment echoes that of James himself in the essay already quoted as to the "newcomer," whose reaction was corrected by the author's own opinion, as an old experienced playgoer and critic in Paris as well as London. "The English stage of today," he declared, "holds the mirror as little as possible up to nature—to any nature, at least, usually recognized in the British Islands." Most of the plays are actually French originals bowdlerized to fit the requirements of British morality, he said: "They cease to have any representative value as regards French manners, and they acquire none as regards English." Although James endowed Strether with some of his potentialities, he did not attribute to him his own knowledge of European civilization. By keeping his hero thus innocent, the author achieved the distance needed for presiding over his initiation. The ability to distinguish between reality and appearances, of course, is not a simple matter of being experienced rather than innocent. Human behavior by its very nature involves a certain amount of acting. Gesture, posture, inflection, even the phrasing chosen—all are necessary elements in every effort to communicate the truth, or to create a special effect, or to achieve any combination of the two.

Where would the interweaving of reality and appearances be more subtle than in Paris, the most sophisticated city in the world? In his first Notebook entry James had said that he did not like "the *banal* side" of making Paris the vision that opens Strether's eyes, only to conclude: "I'm afraid it *must* be Paris; if he's an American." Then in his late Preface he justified his choice. Negatively, the revolution that takes place in his hero under the influence of this great city "was to have nothing to do with any *bêtise* of the imputably 'tempted' state." Affirmatively, Paris had the great merit of sparing the author any preparations. It was the most likely place for Chad to have developed such an "interesting complexity of relations"; and it was the place where Strether's "whole analytic faculty would be led such a wonderful dance."

[236]

Paris

Before he began his ambassadorial mission, feeling that he had "Paris to reckon with" for himself as well as for Mrs. Newsome, Strether determined to give himself up to an exploration of the city, "a single day to feel his feet" as he had already done at Chester and in London. The starting point for his walk was the banking establishment in the rue Scribe where all American tourists came for mail and money (even as they still do today at the American Express). Here Waymarsh preferred to spend the morning reading his letters, convinced that this was "a post of superior observation." Strether, in sharp contrast, stuffed in his pocket the letters he found waiting for him and set off down the rue de la Paix, strolled through the gardens of the Tuileries, crossed the bridge over the famous river, paused before the bookstalls of the opposite quay, then went on up the rue de Seine as far as the Luxembourg. The route is a fairly obvious one for the newly arrived sightseer, but it also had a special meaning for Henry James. It had been one of the memorable walks of his life, taken repeatedly with his brother William when they were living in Paris during their early teens, 1856–57. As he recalled in the first volume of his autobiography, *A Small Boy and Others*: "That particular walk was not prescribed us, yet we appear to have hugged it . . . as the finest, which could only mean the most Parisian, adventure." The itinerary of the young Jameses differs from that of Strether at the outset, but they are alike in their emphasis on the focal points of the Tuileries, the Seine, and the Luxembourg.

The two accounts also part company at the end since they were written to serve different purposes. In the *Autobiography* James was writing of himself as the embryonic novelist so that his early walks in Paris, which seemed to hold the secret of his future, conclude with incidents relating to art and style. With regard to the Luxembourg, most of his space is given over to the exhibition of contemporary paintings in the old palace there and his youthful admiration of the pre-Impressionists, including Delacroix, Rousseau, Daubigny, and Lambinet. The last named is to play a climactic role in the great final scene of *The Ambassadors*, but the hero of that novel in his first Parisian walk confines himself to the gardens at the Luxembourg without setting foot inside the palace. Again, what follows in the *Autobiography* is an account of the future author's discovery at the Louvre of a "bridge over to Style constituted by the wondrous Galerie d'Apollon," as restored under Napoleon I. Later in the novel when Strether pays a crucial visit to Mme de Vionnet he finds in the furnishings of her apartment the same glamour of Empire style; but since he is not an embryonic artist he is nowhere represented as haunting the museums and galleries. Still, by having him retake the same walk that had meant so much to the young Henry James, according to the *Autobi-*

ography, his creator may be suggesting (at least for the reader of both books) one more important point of identification. The adequacy of Paris as a symbol of what the hero has *missed* may be spelled out in the words of what it had *meant* to the "small boy" and future novelist, as epitomized in the Louvre: "a general sense of *glory*, ... not only beauty and art and supreme design, but history and fame and power, the world in fine raised to the richest and noblest expression."

Strether's first walk in the French capital, at any rate, added a new dimension to the picture of Europe that was opening out for him. Medieval towns like Chester might conjure up the vision of "Europe" as old, complex, and devious. But the great cities of the Continent offered something quite different for the American visitor, as James had noted in an early travel essay: "The greater part of the life about you goes on in the streets; and for an observer fresh from a country in which town scenery is at the least monotonous, incident and character and picture seem to abound." The Parisian scene reminds Strether once again that "Europe" is complex. But the emphasis now, in the flood of images that assault his eyes, is on the variety of color and movement. The brilliance is such that he is content, for the moment at least, with mere surface appearances.

For readers of the novel, the most memorable impression produced by Strether's walk is a new kind of picture, new that is in the fiction of Henry James:

> In the garden of the Tuileries he had lingered, on two or three spots, to look; it was as if the wonderful Paris spring had stayed him as he roamed. The prompt Paris morning struck its cheerful notes—in a soft breeze and a sprinkled smell, in the light flit, over the garden-floor, of bareheaded girls with the buckled strap of oblong boxes, in the type of ancient thrifty persons basking betimes where terrace-walls were warm, in the blue-frocked, brass-labelled officialism of humble rakers and scrapers, in the deep references of a straight-pacing priest or the sharp ones of a white-gaitered red-legged soldier. He watched brisk little figures, figures whose movement was as the tick of the great Paris clock, take their smooth diagonal from point to point; the air had a taste as of *something mixed with art....*
> In the Luxembourg Gardens he pulled up; here at last he found his nook, and here, on a penny chair from which terraces, alleys, vistas, fountains, little trees in green tubs, little women in white caps and shrill little girls at play all sunnily *"composed" together*, he passed an hour in which *the cup of his impressions* seemed truly to overflow. (58–59; italics added)

The picture Strether paints brings to mind Pissarro's many views of Paris dating from the 1890s, with their whirling brushstrokes and dabs of delicate broken colors, echoed here in the flitting movements and in the patches of blue-brass-white-red-green that emphasize the brightness of this Parisian scene for the hero. In particular one is reminded of that series of *Les Tuileries* painted by Pissarro in 1899–1900 when his studio was on the rue de Rivoli overlooking these famous gardens, with the great central fountain and radiating paths traversed by all of Paris. *Jardin des Tuileries, Matinée de Printemps, Soleil* (1899) is so strikingly like the verbal picture above that one feels certain James must have seen it during his visit to Paris that very spring. (It is true that Pissarro's painting of the Tuileries is an aerial view, from his studio window, but Strether is shown later in the novel looking down on these gardens at a similar angle from the balcony of a hotel on the rue de Rivoli, as noted on p. 265, below.)

This is the first of a half-dozen major scenes in *The Ambassadors* that are described in language that increasingly suggests the mode of the Impressionist painters. The external evidence that James was consciously so influenced is only fragmentary, but the internal evidence is such as to make it worthwhile to point out similarities between these scenes and certain paintings of the French school that flourished in the quarter-century prior to the composition of this novel.

The young James had written an unfavorable review of a notable exhibition of Impressionist painters in Paris as early as 1876—including Renoir, Monet, Sisley, Pissarro, Degas, and others. But most contemporary critics had reacted in the same way. During the next two decades, through the influence of Whistler and Sargent whom he took to be Impressionists of a sort, the conservative representationalist James gradually came to appreciate the new French school. As late as 1887, in an essay on Sargent, while agreeing that the American painter had been deservedly hailed as "a recruit of high value to the camp of the Impressionists," he warned of the dangers of following that school too closely. By 1894 he had come around to a more favorable attitude; in a Notebook entry for that year he concluded that the only way to limit one of his stories to the desired length was "to make it an Impression—as one of Sargent's pictures is an impression." Though the steps by which James revised his early attitude can only be sketchily retraced, his final favorable judgment is clearly stated. During a long stay in America, shortly after *The Ambassadors* was published, he tells of a visit in 1904 to a great new house in Connecticut where he saw with unfeigned delight "an array of modern 'impressionistic' pictures, mainly French, wondrous examples of Manet, of Degas, of Claude Monet, of Whistler." His comment follows: "No

proof of the sovereign power of art could have been for the moment, sharper."
The phrasing suggests that he had held this favorable opinion for a number
of years.

Actually there is plenty of indirect evidence why such a conversion should
have been expected. All the earliest autobiographical records show James to
have begun with what he himself described as a "picturesque" vision, responsive to the play of light and shadow, color and movement. Then in his late
teens he came under the influence of William Hunt and John LaFarge, painters with whom William James studied seriously and Henry in a desultory
manner, during the Newport years (1858–62). Though their tutors did not
practice the techniques of the impressionists they had something of the same
attitude, the belief that one should be alive to the "crowding impressions of
life" instead of trying to arrange one's ideas in any schematic way. "To La-
Farge...air and light and space was most important," according to one
commentator: "This was a sort of Impressionism long before Claude Monet."
As the best critic of James's use of the visual arts has put it, his "response to
reality" was in many ways similar to that of the Impressionist painters—citing
his view of consciousness as something not fixed and stable but as ever in
flux, and his emphasis on the subjective aspects of experience. But there is a
limit to what the critic may hope to show in the way of Impressionist influence on James. It is more likely to be found in a similarity of subjects than
of techniques. This does not mean that the novelist tries to reproduce exactly
the subject of an individual work of art so much as the type of subject characteristic of a particular painter; nor does it rule out the possibility of some
aspects of the mode of rendering in prose having been suggested by the rendering in pigment.

Actually what is presented by Strether's first Parisian walk is not a scene
but a dramatized picture, the setting for a scene-without-dialogue that takes
place entirely in the hero's mind. With the present picture of Paris in his eye
and the vision of Woollett, Massachusetts, brought back by Mrs. Newsome's
letters, which he read slowly sitting on his penny chair in the Luxembourg,
"the cup of his impressions seemed truly to overflow." What came back to
him first was his own past: the abortive wedding trip to Paris, the "lemon-
colored volumes" he had bought from the bookstalls on the quay, the "pale
figure" of his youth and the paler presences of wife and son who died so long
ago, the "grey shadow" of his solitude during the long grind that had followed, the gradual fading of a cherished dream of coming back to Europe.
"Buried for long years in dark corners at any rate these few germs had
sprouted again under forty-eight hours of Paris" (62). As his vision of the
past shifts forward again to the present picture, these somber colors begin to
glow in the Parisian light, which finally culminates in a dazzling image: "It

hung before him this morning, the vast bright babylon, like some huge iridescent object, a jewel brilliant and hard, in which parts were not to be discriminated nor differences comfortably marked. It twinkled and trembled and
melted together, and what seemed all surface one moment seemed all depth
the next" (64).

This is the perfect metaphor for the inextricable fusion of appearance and
reality. The brillance of the jewel is the result of both its carved surfaces and
its reflecting depths. One of Strether's problems will be to distinguish between the two. James himself had noted this same paradox in a letter written
to an architect friend during a visit to Paris a year or so before the composition
of the novel:

> This extraordinary Paris, with its new—I mean more and more multiplied
> manifestations of luxurious and extravagant extension, grandeur and
> general chronic *expositionism*.... It strikes me as a monstrous massive
> flower of national decadence, the biggest temple ever built to material
> joys and the lust of eyes.... It is a strange phenomenon—with a deal of
> beauty still in its great expansive symmetries and perspectives—and such
> a beauty of light.

Such are the rough field notes of even so mature an artist—the discourse on
decadence to be condensed into "Babylon," the apostrophe to "light" expanded into the jewel image, when transposed to the novel.

The ambivalence of Paris is still there for Strether too, but the Woollett
view has shrunk to an epithet while his own vision of a possible personal adventure in "the most brilliant city in the world" gleams before him. "He had
never expected—that was the truth of it—again to find himself young" (60).
Yet even by allowing himself this little leap of the heart he might be be-
traying his trust. The only merit in being young, as Woollett saw it, was to
be preparing to take one's proper place in the adult world as soon as possible.
And if that is exactly what Chad Newsome is not doing, then he must certainly be wasting his substance in a foreign land, like a veritable prodigal
son. In the Parisian context it could only mean that at best he was leading
the life of a Bohemian on the Left Bank.

Woollett had only the most melodramatic notions of what such a life would
be like. Strether, on his youthful trip to Paris, had bought and read Mürger's
Scènes de la vie de Bohême, the stories on which Puccini had based his great
popular success *La Bohême* in 1896. And since Mrs. Newsome frequently
went to the opera in Boston escorted by Strether, one can easily picture them
attending a performance of it. He sat now in the Luxembourg gardens reflecting on all this: "Old imaginations of the Latin Quarter had played their
part for him, and he had duly recalled its having been with this scene of

rather ominous legend that, like so many young men in fiction as well as in fact, Chad had begun" (65). Strether, who is secretly beginning to envy the young man his freedom, turns the reflection to himself. "Was it at all possible," he wondered, "to like Paris enough without liking it too much? ... Surely it was a privilege to have been young and happy just there" (65, 68).

The second half of the day brings a second revelatory picture. Knowing that it was time to begin his "campaign," Strether transferred himself to the Right Bank, following Chad's migration of several years before when he had moved to the boulevard Malesherbes, in a quietly fashionable section of Paris. The hero lingered for a few minutes across the street, looking up at the third floor apartment whose windows opened onto "a fine continuous balcony":

> What call had he, at such a juncture, ... to admire Chad's very house? High broad clear—he was expert enough to make out in a moment that it was admirably built—... the quality produced by measure and balance, the fine relation of part to part and space to space, was probably—aided by the presence of ornament as positive as it was discreet, and by the complexion of the stone, a cold fair grey, warmed and polished a little by life—neither more nor less than a case of distinction. (69)

The dignified façade, and the sense of style, bring to mind the paintings of Parisian town houses by Bonnard and Vuillard.

Almost instantly the picture comes to life when a young man, "light, bright and alert," appears on the balcony and leans over it, observing Strether observing him. The hero quickly realized that this was not Chad, but since he was a gentleman in appearance and behavior, it was sufficient that he should be Chad's friend. There was "youth" in all of this, enough to give a quick life to everything: "The balcony, the distinguished front, testified suddenly, for Strether's fancy to something that was up and up; ... a perched privacy appeared to him the last of luxuries" (69-70). Chad's quarters were high up in more than the literal sense, being the very opposite of a Bohemian garret. The elegant exterior alone presented a picture strongly suggesting a transformed Chad, but Strether would not be convinced of that without an inside view of both his residence and his way of life in the French capital. As everyone knows, a façade may be a false front as well as a true indication of what is behind it. Strether crossed the boulevard Malesherbes and entered the porte cochere of Chad's apartment building, but the reader is left outside.

What went on in the apartment is merely reported to Waymarsh that evening by Strether. He had been received by a Mr. John Little Bilham, an American art student, who is occupying the rooms of his good friend Chad while he is spending the month at a fashionable resort on the Riviera. And Strether had been so pleased with "little Bilham" that he had accepted an invitation to breakfast at noon on the morrow for himself and Waymarsh. The latter growled, in the voice of Woollett, "Does he live there with a woman?" and "Why don't he go home?" But he went along to the Boulevard Malesherbes the next day anyhow.

What the reader gets from this second occasion is, in the first place, a sketch of the interior to show that it does go with the façade, rendered in a few brush strokes—Chad's mahogany table, the gilded surrounding objects, the richly furnished little salon that opened onto the balcony. James is saving his scenes until Chad's return, confining himself to revelation by pictures until then. He even justifies himself for not rendering any of this breakfast party in dialogue by implying that the talk, mostly between little Bilham and his co-host Miss Barrace, is too sophisticated for Strether to follow. So the impact of the characters as well as the setting on the hero is given to us by authorial exposition. The young lady, who is a friend of both the young men, is described as "eminently gay, highly adorned, perfectly familiar, freely contradictious," and the fact that she smoked cigarettes was the least of her freedoms. Waymarsh simply glowered, but Strether was as charmed as he was baffled: "It was interesting to him to feel that he was in the presence of new measures, other standards, a different scale of relations, and that evidently here were a happy pair who didn't think of things at all as he and Waymarsh thought.... It was the way the irregular life sat upon Bilham and Miss Barrace that was the insidious, the delicate marvel" (77, 79). He was still trying to convince himself of "the fundamental impropriety of Chad's situation," though all Strether had seen of his house and his friends painted a very different picture.

With the arrival of young Newsome himself on the Parisian scene about a week later, the complications of appearance and reality multiplied for poor Strether. During the days in between, with Miss Gostrey's return, he had his confidante once again to help him sort out his impressions. That Chad had a lovely house and remarkable friends didn't prove anything, she said. But when she was introduced to little Bilham she approved of him even more highly than Strether did. In fact, when a friend loaned her a box at the Comédie Française for an evening, she included him along with Waymarsh and Strether as one of her guests. Yet by the time the play was half over he had not arrived, so that they decided the message of invitation must have miscarried. Miss Gostrey, during the entr'acte, was setting before Strether her theory that everything that was being done for him by little Bilham was on daily instructions from Chad in telegrams sent from Cannes. When asked why young Newsome didn't come back to Paris and function in his own right, her reply ("That's what we shall see!") was cut off by the beginning of the last act:

> Quite as she spoke she turned, and Strether turned; for the door of the box had opened, with the click of the ouvreuse, from the lobby, and a gentleman, a stranger to them, had come in with a quick step. The door closed behind him, and, though their faces showed him his mistake, his air, which was striking, was all good confidence. The curtain had just again arisen, and, in the hush of the general attention, Strether's challenge was tacit, as was also the greeting, with a quickly deprecating hand and smile, of the unannounced visitor. He discreetly signed that he would wait, would stand.... The gentleman indeed, at the same time, though sounding for Strether a very short name, did practically as much to explain. Strether gasped the name back.... They were in the presence of Chad himself. (89)

For readers of novels who also care for the visual arts James's picture evokes those pastels of Degas which depict the real world of the theater and are yet rendered in full enjoyment of the paradox that what it offers after all is only illusions. Though this highly individualistic painter liked to call himself an anti-Impressionist, his handling of light and space differentiates him from the older masters he admired and brings him very close to Impressionism. This is particularly true of his later scenes from the theater with their sharp contrast between the large dark close-ups of spectators and the distant lighted stage. Such a one is *La Loge* (1877), in which a small, bright part of the stage is visible, upper left, and all the rest of this intriguing pastel is taken up with the foreground of a darkened box, containing two ladies and a gentleman. Though this reverses the situation described in the novel (two gentlemen and one lady), the gentleman in the painting does have a luxurious moustache like Strether's! Degas' art fascinated not only painters but also writers, as Paul Valéry has testified, and as may be inferred as to James.

This picture of the box party at the Comédie Française presents an inextricable fusion of reality and appearance, the real life situation engulfed in shadow and the stage play focussing all eyes beyond the footlights. The impact on Strether was such that for days afterwards he felt that everything happening since was comparatively a minor development. "He had never in his life seen a young man come into a box at ten o'clock at night," and it would never have occurred to him that there were different ways of doing so; but it was now clear to him that "Chad had had a way that was wonderful:... he knew, he had learned, how" (91). The transformation was so complete it surpassed anything Strether had imagined. "[He] had faced every contingency but that Chad should not *be* Chad," he reflected: "You could deal with a man as himself—you couldn't deal with him as somebody else" (90). Everything on this occasion takes place in the hero's mind, since none of them can talk until the play is over without disturbing the other spectators. By creating a situation in which dialogue is ruled out, James has once again postponed his great scene until later, happy enough during the meantime with revelation by pictures.

The critic's whole concern, and the author's principal one, is with the theme of *The Ambassadors*—Strether's unfolding awareness of the richer and more varied opportunities for living afforded by Europe as contrasted with America, or rather by Paris as contrasted with Woollett, since the picture-and-scene mode of this novel like that of poetry calls for the concrete. This is "the story of the story," emphasized by James in his initial Notebook *donnée* and in his final comment in the late Preface. The story itself—Chad's desire to cling to his life abroad and his mother's desire to bring him home (through the agency of her ambassador)—is interesting in its own right. But the reader needs no help in following the development of this story line, which is worked out in the traditional type of scene used to advance the plot, like the one that follows immediately after the play is over.

At a small table in a café on the Avenue de l'Opéra the confrontation takes place between ambassador and prodigal. Though Strether comes out forthrightly with the purpose of his mission ("to make you break with everything ... and take you straight home"), Chad parries every thrust with consummate skill. He admits nothing and denies nothing; instead, he answers Strether's questions with rhetorical questions of his own. To the central challenge (is it some entanglement with a woman that is keeping him so long in Paris?) he replied: "Do you think one's kept only by women? ... Don't you know how I like Paris itself?" (100–101). Both points apply equally well to the older man, so that he begins to feel that his every weapon is a boomerang. The double-entendre of "*kept*" made him wince, brought out as it was by the "verbal emphasis" of young Newsome, who had already asked if Strether's engagement to his mother was a *fait accompli*. But Chad's behavior throughout is genial as well as sophisticated. He had not only manners but style.

During the next week or two the plot continues to develop without need of scenes even in the conventional sense. As Strether reports in letters to Mrs. Newsome his somewhat baffled view of everything, he constructs for himself an imaginary scene in which the family back home react to the news—one of the many touches by which James brings Woollett across the ocean to Europe without violating his unity of place. This recall of Chad's background makes his transformed state stand out in sharp contrast for Strether on each renewal of contact with him. There are strolls over Paris together, evenings in the lovely apartment on boulevard Malesherbes with Chad's circle of friends, whose endless opinions on such a variety of subjects is a revelation for Strether of "the taste of talk." The freedom achieved by these young cosmopolites, their talent for living, comes from their being open to experience, in contrast to the people he had known in New England who keep themselves closed. If Chad's friends seem to indulge in double-talk it is not from any wish to deceive but because they see experience as fluid, shifting from moment to moment, so that to pin things down to precise and definite statements is to be false to life. None of this is acted out in scenes, merely reported by the author.

The nearest James comes to a rendering in dialogue is in the exchanges between Strether and little Bilham as they walk away together from one of these gatherings. Chad really wants to go back and take up a career, his best friend suggests, but he does not feel free to make the break. Asked why he is not free, Bilham replies: "Because it's a virtuous attachment." The phrase is not so much ambiguous as it is evasive of Woollett's determination to define things as right or wrong according to a conventional code of sexual morality. It is given a particular reference when, a few days later, Chad himself says that his two best friends, a mother and daughter, are about to return to Paris after their long holiday, and he does not want to give any answer about going back to Woollett until Strether has come to know them well. The hero at last has something specific to discuss with his confidante. When he uses Maria Gostrey as a sounding board for this word "virtuous," it comes back not only with the denotation of "chaste" but with a suggested reference to the general quality of the attachment, its merit or value.

James's own style in this novel is similarly complex, indirect, suggestive—confusing to readers who want a straightforward story. The great advantage of using the mode of picture alternating with scene, therefore, is that it enables him to clarify meanings, to bring into focus the double vision of appearance and reality, without resorting to anything "so abject as to 'state'" —to quote his own condemnatory words for the expository mode. Best of all, James said in his Preface to *The Wings of the Dove*, are those rare occasions "when the boundary line between picture and scene bears a little the weight of the double pressure." There are two such picture-scenes in *The Ambassadors*, one of which comes at this point.

The Garden Party

They were all invited next Sunday afternoon to a party being given by the celebrated sculptor Gloriani in his "queer old garden," Chad had announced. Madame de Vionnet and her daughter would probably be "on view." Apprehensive at first that his clever young friend was trying to win him over by a climactic dispensing of bread and circuses, Strether checked himself with the reminder that he would never arrive at the truth until he got rid of "his odious ascetic suspicion of any form of beauty"—that is, the Woollett point of view. By the time Sunday came he had surrendered himself to the expectation of something special:

> The place itself was a great impression—a small pavilion, clear-faced and sequestered, an effect of polished parquet, of fine white panel and spare sallow gilt, of decoration delicate and rare, in the heart of the Faubourg Saint-Germain and on the edge of a cluster of gardens attached to old noble houses.... It was in the garden, a spacious cherished remnant, out of which a dozen persons had already passed, that Chad's host presently met them; while the tall bird-haunted trees, all of a twitter with the spring and the weather, and the high party-walls, on the other side of which grave *hôtels* stood off for privacy, spoke of survival, transmission, association, a strong indifferent persistent order. The day was so soft that the little party had practically adjourned to the open air, but the open air was in such conditions all a chamber of state. (119)

The distinguishing characteristic of the Impressionists was a passion for painting out-of-doors, *en plein air*, whether their landscapes were of field and stream or gardens in the city. Concerned as they were with contemporary life and with the visible world, they were convinced of the basic importance of sunlight and air in the rendering of reality. Devotees of this school of painting will each, quite naturally, prefer his own candidate as the model for Gloriani's garden party. Of all the French Impressionists Monet was the most subtle in handling the nuances of light, to heighten the sensuous beauty of such a canvas as *Femmes au Jardin* (1866). This subject is only tangential to that of James's climactic scene, but the overall effect is similar to the general tone he intended. "Monet's theme is the real theme of Impressionist painting —light as the element of life, and the atmosphere as its medium," according to one authority: "never before had individual objects and individual beings been so completely fused in the vibrating light, never had they become to such an extent patches of colour in a complex of impressions of light and colour." Then there is Renoir, with his love of sunlit places and the shifting tracery of trees rendered in bold brushstrokes of color. *Le Moulin de la Galette* (1876), for example, though inspired by a dancehall for the bourgeoisie, is transmitted by the artist into an elegant scene of youth and beauty, of silks and velvets glittering in pink and blue patches of sunlight and shade, not too different from that depicted in Gloriani's garden.

The painting closest to James's verbal picture in both subject and manner, it seems to me, is Manet's *La Musique aux Tuileries* (1862), a festive occasion representing ladies and gentlemen of the artistic society of Paris during the Second Empire, inspired by his friend Baudelaire who, along with Gautier and the composer Offenbach and several of Manet's fellow artists, can be recognized among the figures in the garden. In his "Project," one may recall, James had described his setting succinctly as a place "consecrated to artistic and literary talk," a notation that is duly expanded in the novel. Manet's canvas may be a bit more crowded with people than Gloriani's garden, but it gives the effect of an open air scene in which the purpose of the composition is "to render the total high-pitched gaiety of the spectacle as a banquet of sunlight and colour rather than a collection of separate dramatic groups," as one art critic expressed it.

James could have seen all three of these paintings, though there is no way of proving that he was really influenced by any one of them. Just for the fun of it he claims for himself authorship of the "picture" in his novel, by a clever device. As Strether stands there in Gloriani's garden and looks up at the houses rising above the high party-walls in the background, he has "the sense of names in the air, of ghosts at the windows." The reader who knows the author's life as well as his fiction recognizes one of these ghosts as the young Henry James, looking down into the garden from the third floor apartment of Mme Mohl during one of his visits in the spring of 1876. This is his "signature" to the picture—creator peering out at spectator—similar to the practice of those Renaissance painters who included a small self-portrait, usually comic, in one corner of their canvas. Readers of *The Ambassadors* need not concern themselves with this ghostly figure, of course, there being enough "real" figures in the foreground of the author's picture to hold their attention.

In his first Notebook entry James had envisioned the elderly man's declaration for life as taking place "in the presence of some great human spectacle, some great organization for the Immediate, the Agreeable, for curiosity, and experiment and perception, for Enjoyment, in a word." Half a dozen years later when he came to write the novel, he filled out his canvas for the garden party with the same kind of crowding life that so delighted the Impressionists in their city-scapes. Since Strether is less a participant than a spectator, we see through his eyes the whole gala spectacle of host and guests:

> This assault of images became for a moment, in the address of the distinguished sculptor, almost formidable.... With his genius in his eyes, his manners on his lips, his long career behind him and his honours and rewards all round, the great artist, in the course of a single sustained look and a few words of delight at receiving him, affected our friend as a dazzling prodigy of type. (120)

[248]

As Strether looked round him at Gloriani's guests he saw faces he knew not what to make of: "Were they charming or were they only strange?" Little Bilham at his side helped to identify these types that were so alien to Woollett. There are "*gros bonnets* of many kinds—ambassadors, cabinet ministers, bankers, generals," he pointed out; also, quite probably, "an actress, an artist, a great performer, ... and in particular the right *femmes du monde*." The ladies seemed even more unlike those of Woollett than the gentlemen, to our wondering hero.

Had Chad's particular friends, the mother and daughter, arrived he asked, and were they really "the virtuous attachment"? Bilham replied with his customary ambiguity that this is what they pass for: "What more than a vain appearance does the wisest of us know? I commend you ... the vain appearance" (122–124). Strether, groping for some sense of reality in this illusional world, broke out with a challenge: "You've all of you here so much visual sense that you've somehow all 'run' to it. There are moments when it strikes me that you haven't any other." He was answered by Miss Barrace, who had joined them, that people here do have a moral sense also; but she quickly dropped her serious tone: "We all do here run too much to mere eye. But how can it be helped? We're all looking at each other—and in the light of Paris one sees what things resemble. That's what the light of Paris always seems to show." This little exchange sounds as if they were discussing an Impressionist painting. But Strether makes a desperate attempt to bring them back to the real world. "Does Madame de Vionnet do that? I mean really show for what she is?" he demanded. "She's wonderful," Miss Barrace replied. "Judge for yourself," Bilham added, pointing to Chad who was coming to make the introduction (126–127).

As they approached, Strether recalled how Chad had impressed him on that first night as knowing how to enter a box: "Well, he impressed him scarce less now as knowing how to make a presentation":

Her air of youth, for Strether, was at first almost disconcerting, while his second impression was [that] ... she had spoken to him, very simply and gently, in an English clearly of the easiest to her, yet unlike any other he had ever heard. ... She was dressed in black, but in black that struck him as light and transparent; she was exceedingly fair, and, though she was as markedly slim, her face had a roundness, with eyes far apart and a little strange. Her smile was natural and dim; her hat not extravagant; he had only perhaps a sense of the clink, beneath her fine black sleeves, of more gold bracelets and bangles than he had ever seen a lady wear. (127–128)

Mme de Vionnet did not show for as "vividly alien" as he had expected, "but what *was* there in her . . . that would have made it impossible he should meet her at Woollett?" (129). Chad left them seated on a bench where they got on together well enough, but with a minimum of conversation. After a very short while she was led away by a duchess and an ambassador who, as a professional, turned a little trick of social art that left Strether the amateur bemused and alone, but content to be so.

In spite of these small movements and light exchanges, what we have had down to this point is still essentially picture; indeed the Impressionists, in paintings such as the three described above, create the illusion of figures in motion so successfully we feel that by listening closely we can overhear scraps of their talk. When at last setting comes to life as scene, in Gloriani's garden, it is by dialogue between Strether and Little Bilham—not Madame de Vionnet nor Chad nor Gloriani. His young confidant has come back to introduce him to other guests, but he declines, wishing instead to deliver himself of something that has been welling up inside and has now gathered to a head. Strether's climactic declaration—"Oh, you are young, . . . be glad of it and *live*"—is almost identical with the original *donnée* that Jonathan Sturges had reported of W. D. Howells, at least through the first half. But beginning at the point where the latter had said, "This place makes it all come over me," the novelist adds a highly significant extension of his initial notation:

> This place and these impressions—mild as you may find them to wind a man up so; all my impressions of Chad and of people I've seen at *his* place—well, have had their abundant message for me, have just dropped *that* into my mind. I see it now. I haven't done so enough before—and now I'm old; too old at any rate for what I see. Oh I *do* see at least; and more than you'd believe or I can express. It's too late. . . . you're, as I say, damn you, so happily and hatefully young. . . . Do what you like so long as you don't make *my* mistake. For it was a mistake. Live! (132)

James drives home here with repeated emphasis the importance of the visual sense in his novel: the use of picture-setting as indispensable to "action," such as that which takes place in this crucial scene.

Bilham's attempt at consolation—"I don't know that I want to be, at your age, too different from you!"—is of no avail. Strether's eye has already fixed on another picture, in the middle of the garden, where the duchess is awaiting Gloriani's eager approach: "Were they, this pair, of the 'great world'?— and was he himself, for the moment and thus related to them by his observation, *in* it?" (133). (That is, can one *live* simply by *seeing*?) "Yet it made him admire most of the two, made him envy, the glossy male tiger, magnificently marked." For the sculptor had *lived*. According to Bilham his past with *femmes du monde* had been "fabulous"; and Strether had seen enough for himself, when he was "held by the sculptor's eyes" at their first introduction: "The deep human expertness in Gloriani's charming smile—oh the terrible life behind it!—was flashed upon him as a test of his [own] stuff" (121).

Now, near the end of the party, "another impression had been superimposed," obscuring even the vision of his dazzling host: "A young girl in a white dress and a softly plumed white hat had suddenly come into view." Chad was bringing Mademoiselle de Vionnet to present to him:

> She stood there quite pink, a little frightened, prettier and prettier and not a bit like her mother. There was ... no resemblance but that of youth to youth.... So slim and fresh and fair, [Mme de Vionnet] had yet put forth this perfection.... What was in the girl was indeed too soft, too unknown for direct dealing; so that one could only gaze at it as at a picture.

Strether now shifts his envy to a third object. To Little Bilham's query if it were Gloriani, he replies: " 'Oh Chad!'—it was that rare youth he should have enjoyed being 'like.' " Jeanne de Vionnet, this charming creature, she would be *his* "virtuous attachment" (133–135).

As scene lapses back into picture, James's camera-eye singles out one aspect of it after another for a close-up, as if he were labelling each one: "Garden Party. A Detail." The picture as a whole gets its effect from carefully chosen patches of color and a few suggestive details, after the manner of the Impressionists, with no attempt at pictorial completeness as in the representational paintings of the preceding century. The impression carried away by Strether (and the reader) is created by the faded gilt of the rococo pavilion, the tawny mane and "medal-like Italian face" of Gloriani the "bold high look" of the duchess as she strolls off on the arm of the ambassador in his fastidiously buttoned frock coat and hat "with a wonderful wide curl to its brim," the vision of "gold bangles" beneath the sleeves of Madame de Vionnet's transparent black dress, contrasted with the soft pink perfection of her daughter—all seen in the luminous spring air against the dark green of "tall bird-haunted trees," as the spectator-hero surrenders to the sensuous beauty surrounding him, "letting his rather grey interior drink in for once the sun of a clime not marked in his old geography."

This is Paris, to be sure, but Paris heightened by the esthetic imagination. As for the scene itself, we have James's own clear statement that it contained no action; its sole purpose was the establishment of relations among the characters. When Strether asked himself afterwards "what really *had* happened," he had to admit that for a gentleman taken into the "great world" for the first time, "the items made a meagre total." But it was not a surprise to him to discover that "a man might have—at all events such a man as he—

an amount of experience out of any proportion to his adventures" (137). Lambert Strether's education has taken a considerable stride, but it still has a long way to go.

Portraits of Madame de Vionnet

How could Strether establish relations with people he had not really communicated with, other than through his eyes? He had scarcely exchanged a word with Madame de Vionnet or her daughter; his conversations with Bilham and Miss Barrace had been little more than verbal skirmishings; in spite of many friendly talks with Chad he had learned from that sophisticated young man nothing of the "truth" he came out to discover. The only person with whom the hero had been able to establish a candid relationship through words was Maria Gostrey. But his confidante was even more an outsider to the whole situation than he, so that she had been able to serve only as a sounding board for his speculations and whatever scraps of information he could bring to their endless colloquies.

After the garden party, however, she had some facts of the first importance to contribute. Three-and-twenty years before in school at Geneva, it turned out, she had been a close friend of Madame de Vionnet, and now she was able to fill in for Strether the background of that charming lady. The daughter of a French father and an English mother, she had been "dazzlingly clever" in languages and in playing leading parts in all the school theatricals. After that she had been married quite young to the Comte de Vionnet, "a high distinguished polished impertinent reprobate"; though they had been separated since an early period, divorce was out of the question. She had been left in this "horrid position" with a lovely daughter to bring up alone and a new life to work out for herself. Today she could not be a day less than thirty-eight, hence ten years older than Chad. It was now clear to Maria Gostrey what role that rich young American was to play in the *ménage de Vionnet*: "She has brought him up for her daughter" (139).

It was with this happy resolution of his problem hovering in the back of his head as a possibility that Strether found himself in Madame de Vionnet's drawing room a few days later, paying the visit Chad had urged upon him. She occupied the first floor of an old house in the rue de Bellechasse, in the same part of the Faubourg St. Germain where he had met her at Gloriani's garden party:

> The [entrance] court was large and open, full of revelations, for our
> friend, of the habit of privacy; ... the house, to his restless sense, was in

the high homely style of an elder day, and the ancient Paris he was always looking for—sometimes intensely felt, sometimes more acutely missed—was in the immemorial polish of the wide waxed staircase and in the fine *boiseries*, the medallions, mouldings, mirrors, great clear spaces, of the greyish-white salon into which he had been shown.... He found himself making out, as a background of the occupant, some glory, some prosperity of the First Empire, some Napoleonic glamour, some dim lustre of the great legend; elements clinging still to all the consular chairs and mythological brasses and sphinxes' heads and faded surfaces of satin striped with alternate silk....

She was seated, near the fire,... with her hands clasped in her lap and no movement, in all her person, but the fine prompt play of her deep young face. The fire, under the low white marble, undraped and academic, had burnt down to the silver ashes of light wood; one of the windows, at a distance, stood open to the mildness and stillness of the court. (145, 147)

This scene-setting owes less to the Impressionists (who were not much given to painting interiors) than to pictures by some of the representational painters of a half-century before, whom James had admired in the Luxembourg Gallery during his boyhood residence in Paris. One of them, Ernest Meissonier, had made quite a reputation about this time for his genre paintings, characterized by minuteness of detail; and James had referred to him in one of his letters to the New York *Tribune* in 1876 as a painter he admired for his realism (though chiefly with reference to his many canvases glorifying Napoleon). Much closer to the verbal picture of Madame de Vionnet's salon are some of the detailed elegant interiors by a slightly younger painter, J. J. Tissot, notably in his *Eugene Coppens de Fontenay*, the portrait of a gentleman with mustache and cane, standing by a marble mantlepiece with mirrors, clocks, and other *objets* above; or *Mlle Reisener*, showing an aristocratic lady seated beside an open window in her drawing room.

On the other hand, James may have been drawing on his memory of the actual old house near the Place Vendôme where he had written *The American*, that early novel so filled with Paris. His apartment there could have furnished a partial model for Madame de Vionnet's drawing room. As he recalled years later, it had been a place "where a black-framed Empire portrait-medallion, suspended in the centre of each white panel of my almost noble old salon, made the coolest, discreetest, most measured decoration," and where the "light of high, narrowish French windows in old rooms" seemed like the light "of 'style' itself." It would have been easy enough to transfer this picture to the Left Bank and the rue de Bellechasse, which James knew well, having spent

evenings there in the winter of 1875–76 with one of the French novelists most
influential on him, Alphonse Daudet, in whose home the memory of the Im-
peratrice was still cherished.

Whatever the model, whether an interior by Meissonier or Tissot or an
actual one remembered by James, the setting in *The Ambassadors* is worked
out in full pictorial detail. Beyond what has already been described, Strether
at the end of a quarter of an hour made out in the glass cases that lined the
room "swords and epaulettes of ancient colonels and generals; medals and
orders once pinned over hearts that had long since ceased to beat; snuff boxes
bestowed on ministers and envoys; copies of works presented, with inscrip-
tions, by authors now classic" (146). From his first days in Paris, during
visits to his confidante's apartment, he had become increasingly aware of "the
empire of 'things,' " of how possessions seem to symbolize the owner (80).
But it comes over him now how different Miss Gostrey's "little museum of
bargains" is from Madame de Vionnet's possessions, "not vulgarly numerous,
but hereditary cherished charming" (145–146). His adventure had now
brought him to break his nose unexpectedly against the strange blank wall
of supreme respectability.

After the minimum of talk in such surroundings, the merest exchange of
civilities, Madame de Vionnet had somehow managed to turn their encounter
into a relation. It was a relation that profited by a great many things that were
only tangential to it: "by the very air in which they sat, by the high cold
delicate room, by the world outside and the little plash in the court, by the
First Empire and the relics in the stiff cabinets" (148). On his final visit
to this apartment, at the end of the novel, Strether felt once again how the
objects surrounding this lady would help him to understand her: "things from
far back—tyrannies of history, facts of type, values, as the painters said, of
expression" (318). There could hardly be a clearer statement of the impact
of setting on scene, of place and thing on character.

A great deal of dialogue follows during Strether's first memorable visit, but
it chiefly goes to show that the fountainhead of all the *double-entente* of the
young American expatriates is simply the high Parisian talent for conversation
—for talk that seems to conceal as much as it reveals, but can more properly
be described as talk that assumes the complexity of human relations and so
cuts across the dogmatic assumptions of Woollett. Madame de Vionnet is
ambiguous in her inquiries about Strether's relations with Mrs. Newsome,
and equally so in her answers to his queries about her own relations with
Chad. When the Ambassador pleads his dilemma, that he does not have any
facts to report to the Home Office, she replies: "Simply tell her the truth . . . ,
any truth—about us all—that you see yourself." He answers that the simple

truth is exactly what he is trying to discover, but this only makes her shift ground: "Tell her ... you like us." Then, when Strether braces himself to ask if Chad is to marry her daughter, she shakes her head: "No—not that. ... He likes her too much" (150–151). So his hoped-for solution disappears in a paradox. It will be evident from these samples that what the hero learns from this scene comes through the visual rather than the verbal medium. He has seen Chad's "best friend" in the setting of her own home, and the impression made on him is to have decisive consequences. As he takes leave he is surprised to hear himself promising, "I'll save you if I can," without quite knowing what he means. "At bottom of it all for him was the sense of her rare unlikeness to the women he had known" (146).

One of the rarest things about Madame de Vionnet was her infinite variety. Simple in one sense, in another she was more complex than her conversation. This was the first of several sittings for portraits by Strether, and each of the ensuing ones brings out another nuance as surprising as it is charming. For the sake of contrast, and because both situations are tête-à-tête (with an implied self-portrait of the hero), we turn from the most formal to the most informal. Some three weeks after his visit to the rue de Bellechasse, he invited her to lunch, quite as unexpectedly as he seemed to be doing everything now that he was "living almost disgracefully from hand to mouth." There is a preliminary sketch for this portrait.

Strether had gone one morning to the famous cathedral of Notre Dame, a sanctuary from anxieties he had resorted to on several occasions recently. As an observer rather than a worshipper, his attention soon fixed on a lady who was sitting before a lighted altar, not prostrate but quite serious about the need that had brought her there. Having imagined her as the "heroine of an old story, something he had heard, read, something that, had he a hand for drama, he might himself have written," he was brought back to reality by recognizing her as Madame de Vionnet, when she passed him on her way out of church. What set them at ease was her tact, on finding him there, which took for granted in him a love of beautiful places. What set the luncheon invitation in motion was his awareness of her perfect taste, as proved by her choosing such a subdued and discreet toilet to suit her special mission this morning: "her grey-gloved hands, ... her slightly thicker veil, ... the composed gravity of her dress, in which, here and there, a dull wine-colour seemed to gleam faintly through black" (173). Everything about her impressed him —her attitude before the glimmering altar, the dignity and ease of her posture as she sat with him in the dim nave, looking back at the vastness and mystery of the great monument and talking in low tones of its history and beauty:

[255]

"She was romantic for him far beyond what she could have guessed." And everything confirmed what he had already decided about her relation with Chad: "If it wasn't innocent why did she haunt the churches?" (174).

As soon as they were outside the cathedral, in the open air, he took the plunge and invited her to come to *déjeuner* with him. (One suspects that James's setting is the most famous restaurant in Paris, La Tour d'Argent, on the Quai de la Tournelle, overlooking Notre Dame; in the novel it is simply described as "a place of pilgrimage for the knowing, ... who come for its great renown," an "easy walk" from the great cathedral.)

> The end of it was that half an hour later they were seated together for an early luncheon at a wonderful, a delightful house of entertainment on the left bank ... seated on either side of a small table, at a window adjusted to the busy quay and the shining barge-burdened Seine; where, for an hour, in the matter of letting himself go, of diving deep, Strether was to feel he had touched bottom. He was to feel many things on this occasion, [but he saw reasons enough for keeping them to himself], ... in the mere way the bright clean ordered water-side life came in at the window—the mere way Madame de Vionnet, opposite him over their intensely white table-linen, their *omelette aux tomates*, their bottle of straw-coloured Chablis, thanked him for everything almost with the smile of a child, while her grey eyes moved in and out of their talk, back to the quarter of the warm spring air, in which early summer had already begun to throb, and then back again to his face and their human questions. ... Ancient proverbs sounded, for his memory, in the tone of their words and the clink of their glasses, in the hum of the town and the plash of the river. ... She was a woman who, between courses, could be graceful with her elbows on the table. It was a posture unknown to Mrs. Newsome, but it was easy for a *femme du monde*. (175–178)

This is Impressionism at its highest pitch: "the doctrine that the pictorial rendering of the real is possible only through the medium of atmosphere filled with light," according to one of the principal historians of the movement. Besides being obsessed with sunlight the painters of this school were dedicated to depicting contemporary life, being especially fond of joyous occasions, so that several of them found favorite subjects in picnics and luncheons in the open air, or in situations that give the effect of being *en plein air*.

Once again, choosing the possible inspiration for James's picture is largely an expression of personal preference. Among the Impressionists Monet in particular was concerned with capturing in paint the fugitive effect of light falling on materials and three-dimensional objects, with the play of reflections, and with the illusionism of variegated coloring—using the warm colors in which yellows predominate for the fully lit areas. Though none of his pictures have a subject matter corresponding to James's picture of the luncheon at the Seine-side restaurant, the general attributes of his painting style are suggestive. Manet's *Chez le Père Lathuille* (1879), one of the crowning works of his career, is very close indeed as a subject: a gentleman and a lady are seated tête-à-tête at a small table covered with a white cloth, the waiter hovering attentively in the background; her dress is dark but with a kind of wine-color gleaming through, like that of Madame de Vionnet; a glass of wine and a plate of fruit mark the end of a luncheon; the gentleman's earnest posture bending forward and her arms resting informally on the table emphasize the intimacy of their conversation. But thought the setting is spring-like and fully *en plein air*—a garden restaurant with their table at the edge of a roofed terrace—the play of light and color is on the whole subdued.

These all-important qualities in conjunction with a comparable subject, thus combining the effects of Monet and Manet, can be found in Renoir's well-known *Déjeuner des Canotiers* (1881). Here, to be sure, instead of a middle-aged couple in earnest though happy conversation, there are a dozen young people in animated talk over their festal table; but everything else is just right. The setting is the terrace of a restaurant at the Île de la Grenouillère, on the Seine near Paris; the light flows in under an orange-striped awning, turning the fruit, bottles, and glasses on the gleaming white linen into a sparkling still-life; the colors of the whole picture, iridescent as mother-of-pearl, make a harmony suggestive of music or poetry. The *Déjeuner des Canotiers* was painted at the height of Renoir's Impressionist period. Whether or not James saw it and was influenced by it, this masterpiece offers a brilliant analogue to the setting of Strether's luncheon with Madame de Vionnet on the bank of the Seine.

The characters in James's fictions are frequently pictured as sitting down to lunch, to dinner, to breakfast (there are a half-dozen such scenes in *The Ambassadors*), but this is one of the few times when he deigns to mention what they had to eat. Even here the description is more for the palette than for the palate. The sunshine on the river is filtered through the window in order to light up the colors on the table—white, crystal, pale-to-deep yellows, orange-shading-to-red, and the brown-crusted loaf that the reader supplies—and in order to symbolize for the hero the beauty that may fall to the lot of anyone lucky enough to live in Paris, the poetry that may characterize human relations there. The relevance of picture to scene is made explicit by James: Strether's whole adventure on this occasion is conditioned by "their déjeuner, their omelette, the Chablis, the place, the view." What follows immediately is "their present talk, his present pleasure in it—to say nothing, wonder of wonders, of her own" (177).

For the reader the real wonder is that at last, under the influence of this most propitious setting, they achieve some lucidity of communication through words. Their exchanges deal quite explicitly with the "problem" they have all been circling around for weeks. Strether declares that he has carried out his mission and it is high time for him to go back home; he has put Woollett's "case" before Chad and it is now up to that young man to make up his mind. But he also tells her, somewhat inconsistently, that he has written a letter to Mrs. Newsome "all about you." This takes him back to a question Madame de Vionnet had asked him at Chad's dinner some ten days before. "The question," he recalls, "was *how* I should save you. Well, I'm trying it by thus letting her know that I consider you worth saving." When he adds that the best way to prove that would be for Chad's mother to see for herself what Madame de Vionnet has done for him, the latter comes right out with her deepest fear: if they get him back in Woollett they'll keep him there, holding out the lure of riches offered by the family business and pinning him down by marriage to a local girl.

"The question will come up, of course, of the future that you yourself offer him," Strether reminds her (both of them aware that *she* is not free to marry), but Madame de Vionnet declares her willingness to face up to that and her hopes that Chad will do so too. "Stay with us—stay with us!" she exclaims. "That's your only way to make sure...that he doesn't break up." When Strether promises that he will see them both through, she rises from the luncheon table. "Thank you!" she says quite simply, but with no less meaning than she had given to the same two words after Chad's dinner. "The golden nail she had then driven in pierced a good inch deeper" (178–181). To get the full meaning of this metaphor it is necessary now to revert briefly to the former occasion, which took place about mid-point of the three weeks between Strether's visit to Madame de Vionnet's apartment and his luncheon invitation to her.

Chad's dinner party for a dozen friends was a full-dress affair. It is presented at great length and altogether scenically, though only in the sense of a theatre-in-the-round, that is, a play without stage scenery. But it is acted out like a comedy of manners at the Théâtre Français, with entrances and exits, groupings and re-groupings of characters, and almost entirely in dialogue—of the Parisian sort that left poor Strether guessing. "He was moving verily in a strange air and on ground not of the firmest" (158). Only twice did meanings come through to him with any clarity, both times when he stopped listening to the talk and created portraits for himself of the two guests who particularly caught his eye. The first of these was Jeanne de Vionnet, whom Chad had urged him to get acquainted with, as a perfect type of the *jeune fille*. "She was fairly beautiful to him—a faint pastel in an oval frame: he thought of her already as of some lurking image in a long gallery, the portrait of a small old-time princess of whom nothing was known but that she died young" (154). This was simply Strether's metaphorical way of convincing himself that young Mlle de Vionnet had died out of the picture as the possible lady holding Chad in Paris. But it gave him a better clue to the problem he was trying to solve than he got from the riddling talk of Little Bilham: how could Chad be in love with the daughter after being in love with the mother? how could they hope to marry since the Comte de Vionnet might live forever? maybe Madame de Vionnet cares more now for Chad than he for her?

Strether felt himself "in a maze of mystic allusions" (165). His brief exchange with that charming lady was scarcely more enlightening. For she asked him to find out if her daughter had "any sentiment for Mr. Newsome." But he refused, saying that the lovely Jeanne should not be pressed to reveal her shy secret. The mother's reply ("I shan't know then—never. Thank you") gave him nothing but a metaphor, the full meaning of which was not clarified until their luncheon, ten days later. With her incomparable subtlety "she had driven in by a single word a little golden nail," turning his bid for independence into a commitment to serve her.

Strether's attempts at conversation with the other guests at Chad's dinner met with even less success. With Miss Barrace he expected only enigmas, which is what he got when he asked her about Chad's real relation with Madame de Vionnet, or persiflage, as when he asked how that magnificent lady could manage to be so different from one time to another. The response seemed double-edged, at first: "She's various. She's fifty women" (157). But, inadvertently, it gave him the cue for his final portrait of Madame de Vionnet, the most important revelation that came to him at Chad's party:

She had struck our friend, from the first of her appearing, as dressed for a great occasion.... Her bare shoulders and arms were white and beautiful; the materials of her dress, a mixture, as he supposed, of silk and crape, were of a silvery grey so artfully composed as to give an impression of warm splendour; and round her neck she wore a collar of large old emeralds, the green note of which was more dimly repeated, at other points of her apparel, in embroidery, in enamel, in satin, in substances and textures vaguely rich. Her head, extremely fair and exquisitely festal, was like a happy fancy, a notion of the antique, on an old precious medal, some silver coin of the Renaissance; while her slim lightness and brightness, her gaiety, her expression, her decision, contributed to an effect that might have been felt by a poet as half mythological and half conventional. He could have compared her to a goddess still partly engaged in a morning cloud, or to a sea-nymph waist-high in the summer surge. Above all she suggested to him the reflexion that the *femme du monde* —in these finest developments of the type—was, like Cleopatra in the play, indeed various and multifold. (160)

Madame de Vionnet's special talent, first revealed by her taking leading parts in all the plays at boarding school, had developed over the years. One is tempted to press the drama reference as far as possible, since the Egyptian queen (in history though not in the play) also held two men enthralled, one older and one younger. But James limits his allusion to one aspect of the heroine of *Antony and Cleopatra*, and he expects the literate reader to be able to supply Shakespeare's well-known lines: "Age cannot wither her, nor custom stale / Her infinite variety." Strether found Marie de Vionnet a fascinating actress, who could play the role of "an obscure person, a muffled person one day, and a showy person...the next." James, as master of the wardrobe, found great delight in supplying costumes appropriate to her performances. Or, to change the metaphor, he shared the painter's great concern for color and texture in choosing the proper dress for his sitter.

The picture of Madame de Vionnet presented above brings to mind some of the portraits of elegant ladies by Manet or by Renoir, especially the latter's *Jeanne Samary*, a glamorous actress who was the toast of Paris in the late 1870s. This portrait shows a brightly bejewelled young woman with an exquisitely fair and festal head, in an extremely décolleté evening gown that suggests the tone colors of old emeralds. Or, since James likened Marie de Vionnet to "a sea-nymph waist-high in the summer surge," one may dare to suggest Renoir's *Nude in the Sunlight*, who is waist-high in the green and gold of midsummer air. Strether was really plunging: "He thought of Madame de Vionnet tonight as showy and uncovered" (161).

It is not until their next meeting, when she accepts his luncheon invitation in the same "subdued and discreet" toilette she had groomed herself in for church, that Strether is sufficiently composed to ask himself just where he really *is*. As he sits with her at the small table by the river, conversing intimately and aware that he is "diving deep," he takes stock by recalling the setting where his European education had first consciously begun: "He had travelled far since that evening in London, before the theatre, when his dinner with Maria Gostrey, between the pink-shaded candles, had struck him as requiring so many explanations" (176). That earlier scene had its retrospective aspect too. His confidante's dress, "cut down in respect to shoulders and bosom," not only made him think of her as Mary Stuart but brought back his pictured memory of Mrs. Newsome as always, on similar occasions, dressed in black silk with a high ruche like that of Queen Elizabeth. It was indeed a great leap forward to find that the third woman who had come into his life reminded him of Cleopatra.

At their luncheon meeting, happily, she is no longer an exotic Egyptian but simply French—and, though clearly a *femme du monde*, sufficiently "muffled" as to her attire to make him quite at ease during their tête-à-tête. The candid talk that flows between them on this occasion has already been reported. What can be added now is a final meaning for the "golden nail" metaphor. Strether's chivalric offer at the end of the luncheon "to see them both through"—like a troubadour in the tradition of Courtly Love—makes clear enough how he has come to feel about Madame de Vionnet: it would be the easiest thing in the world to fall in love with that extraordinary lady! This explains Chad's "problem," but poses another for himself. Even while he thumbs through his portfolio of Impressionist portraits of Madame de Vionnet—at the garden party, at home, at Chad's dinner, at Notre Dame, at the Seine-side restaurant—the first step is being taken by the Home Office to relieve him of his other portfolio, the one with which he had come out to Paris in the first place as minister plenipotentiary.

Comic Interlude

"If I can't bring you I'm to leave you; I'm to come at any rate myself," Strether tells Chad, holding the cable in his hand: "If I don't immediately sail the Pococks will immediately come out" (185). He had written to Mrs. Newsome his full and favorable impressions of Madame de Vionnet, and he knew that the reply to his letter would be crucial. It arrived three days after the luncheon, in the form of an ultimatum.

James has provided amusement for his readers all along by treating this family affair as a diplomatic venture—Woollett as the Home Office, Mrs. Newsome as Secretary of State, reports and cables sent back and forth, the danger of Ambassador Strether going over to the enemy, and so on. When the daughter, Sarah Pocock, is sent out to replace him the plural of the title, *The Ambassadors*, is filled out and the note of comedy is heightened. Further, with the bustling entrance of Sarah, accompanied by her husband Jim and his young sister Mamie, Woollett is brought onto the Parisian stage. Previously scene has been used to reveal character. Now by his virtuosity James has done the reverse and made characters represent scene, the requirements of unity of place having kept him from presenting the New England town directly. The Pococks embody it, make it real, and in doing so they perform a third function of great importance for the author. They take on the burden of the international theme, in the sense of a contrast of two cultures—two sets

[261]

of manners, values, attitudes. Down to this point the contrast has been only sketchily worked in through the minor figure of Waymarsh, Strether's foil, but he is off-center; and through the absent figure of Mrs. Newsome, conjured up by Strether's recalls, but she is never present in the flesh. The Pococks were indispensable to the author's strategy in this particular novel.

The international theme was one of James's great discoveries. But when it is too explicit in his fictions, overtly involving major characters, the contrast tends to be too extreme and painted in brushstrokes so broad as to run the risk of caricature in people and melodrama in plot—even the argument of a thesis. This was the problem he was wrestling with in *The American* (1877). When he returned to the international theme in *The Ambassadors*, another novel set entirely in Paris but written a quarter-century later, he avoided these dangers by assigning the major weight of contrast to minor characters, the Pococks, and by having no French aristocrats who are romantically overdone. Madame de Vionnet is much more subtly handled than the Bellegardes (antagonists of the early novel), and the American expatriates in Chad's circle as well as the hero's confidante are cosmopolitan enough to pass for Parisians.

Above all, with Strether the emphasis is not on the international contrast as such, but on his initiation into an understanding of the richer life he has missed. With his esthetic sensibility and responsiveness to all aspects of French civilization, his differences melt away at each new experience in Paris. No European tricks him or "does him in." And his revised status as pure spectator, once he is relieved of his mission as ambassador, saves him from any clashes; it might have been otherwise if he had tried actively to drag Chad home or to win Madame de Vionnet for himself. The Pococks, whose substitute ambassadorial mission is carried off in the key of high comedy, take the burden of the sociological contrast off the hero's shoulders. At the same time they offer readers momentary relief from any possible overemphasis on the seriousness of Strether's esthetic education.

Jim Pocock's only talent was for farce, for the most exaggerated and ridiculous kind of comedy. "Small and fat and facetious, straw-coloured and destitute of marks, he would have been practically indistinguishable hadn't his constant preference for light-grey clothes, for white hats, for very big cigars and very little stories, done what it could for his identity" (213–214). From the moment of his arrival he was clowning, proud of being a comedian but unaware that he was really a fool. He insisted he was not on the "official" side represented by his wife but quite absurdly because for all the wrong reasons, on that of Chad and Strether. He did not blame them in the least for staying put in Paris, the best place in the world for having a good time. Waking up in mid-career to what *he* had missed, he had come over for some fun himself before it was too late. His first inquiry, with a salacious wink and an aggressive elbow in Strether's side, was "if there were anything new at the Varieties, which he pronounced in the American manner" (216). Jim Pocock was the type of American male, philistine and sex-starved, for whom the Parisian panderers invented "feelthy" pictures and peep shows. The circumspect James leaves it to our imagination what his activities were—"[sniffing] up what he supposes to be Paris from morning till night"—other than going to the French version of a burlesque show, the *Variétés*.

The rest of what we learn about Jim comes indirectly, as Strether reports it to his confidante. First, in reply to Maria Gostrey's question as to how well Mrs. Newsome's substitute ambassador is succeeding with Chad. "She's sounding the note of home," he says: "The difficulty's Jim. Jim's the note of home ...—the home of the business...and Jim *is*, frankly speaking, extremely awful" (245). Second, Strether gives Madame de Vionnet Jim's view of her: "He sees you as awful. A regular bad one—.... Dreadful, delightful, irresistible.... Your wickedness and the charms with which, in such a degree as yours, he associates it" (232). Seizing on that as her cue, this versatile actress plays up to Jim and before it's all over leads him such a dance as fairly to bewilder him—the final farcical skit that emerges from the Pocock's month-long visit to Paris, though once again it comes to the reader indirectly.

Sarah Newsome Pocock, the surrogate who takes over Strether's forfeited portfolio, is funny in a very different way. The kind of comedy she unconsciously provides, less obvious and more complex than Jim's, can best be suggested by likening her to the *alazon* of classical tradition. That comic type was characterized by hypocrisy, moralizing, the conventionality of the stolid citizen, and a tendency to posturing that borders on pomposity. The first and last of these qualities—the ones most productive of comedy—are strikingly illustrated in the behavior of the new ambassador. Though her avowed purpose in coming out was to protest against the immorality of Chad's affaire with a "low" French woman and to save him from it by dragging him home, she promptly falls into an affair of her own with, of all people, Waymarsh. She admires him as the only one in this Parisian circle who has the proper suspicion of Europe as decadent, and at the same time she despises her husband for yielding to the corrupting influence of Paris. Waymarsh on his side, despairing of Strether who now seems to him as Europeanized as Chad and his group of cosmopolitan friends, turns eagerly to Sarah as the only proper embodiment of the American point of view, so that their "romance" comes about naturally.

If this strange pair had been capable of passion, and possessed of sufficient courage, they also might have enjoyed an adulterous affaire. Being still adolescent, despite their age, it remained merely comic. In his role as romantic lover, Waymarsh becomes a vivid part of the international contrast. After a month of this innocent courtship, he loomed one morning in his new guise before the eyes of Strether, who had come down to a late breakfast at their hotel: "He wore a straw hat such as his friend hadn't yet seen in Paris, and he showed a buttonhole freshly adorned with a magnificent rose.... He was fairly panting with the pulse of adventure and had been with Mrs. Pocock, unmistakeably, to the Marché aux Fleurs." With his "wide panama" and his "bulging white waistcoat" he reminded Strether of "a Southern planter of the great days" (268). Such is the transformation of Waymarsh, struck by the arrows of Eros. He also had come a long way during the three months in Paris. The first lady who had tried to lift him out of his anti-European gloom, Miss Barrace, had during the early weeks rendered a portrait of him as Sitting Bull, wrapt in his blanket and glowering from a corner of her carriage (125, 158). Southern Colonel or Indian Chief? Both are celebrated American types, picturesque but subject to humorous jibes, and in sharp contrast to the characteristic Parisian gentleman.

In spite of the diversions offered by Waymarsh and Jim Pocock, Sarah occupies the center of the stage. The word is quite justified, incidentally, by James's constant use of theater references during this comic interlude. On one of the first evenings, Strether reports to his confidante that Jim is dragging him to the Variétés, Chad is escorting Mamie to the Comédie Française, Waymarsh is taking Mrs. Pocock to dinner at the Café Riche and then to the *cirque*. Miss Gostrey's response is to the point: "We're abysmal—...all of us: Woollett, Milrose, and their products" (240–241). When Madame de Vionnett offers her services as guide, Sarah declines with proud self-assurance, "I *know* Paris." And she proves it by dining at all the expensive restaurants, making extravagant purchases of all sorts, and employing a dressmaker to create her new wardrobe—just as her husband has been proving that he knows *his* Paris.

All of the Pococks spend their month in the French capital doing nothing but the superficial round of things traditionally associated with American visitors. James had gently satirized this national trait a quarter-century before in the first of his "Parisian Sketches" written for the New York *Tribune*. During the high tourist season, there is a "classic region" in the center of the great city where one hears more "American" spoken than French, he reported—that square mile bounded on the north by the rue Scribe and on the south by the rue de Rivoli, of which "the most sacred spot" is the Grand Hotel. "The ladies, week after week, are treading the devious ways of the great shops," he quipped: "the gentlemen are treading other ways, sometimes also, doubtless, a trifle devious." These observations on the comedy of the American-in-Paris in 1875, at the time James was composing his early novel *The American*, fit so perfectly the behavior of the Pococks in *The Ambas-*

sadors as to suggest that this comic aspect of the international contrast had not changed much by 1900.

When Chad himself put on a performance at his apartment for the Woollett contingent, with fifteen or twenty for dinner and a large concourse of others coming in at midnight for a concert by several famous singers, Sarah Pocock stood in the forefront of the listening circle "dressed in a splendour of crimson which affected Strether as the sound of a fall through a skylight." The hero himself took refuge in a small room next to the salon, where he was joined by Miss Barrace, who had "forsaken the music, dropped out of the play, abandoned, in a word, the stage itself, that she might stand a minute behind the scenes with Strether," to taunt him for shrinking from his part as the real "hero of the drama" (256, 262, 265). In fact he refused to play any role in the Pocock comedy except once, when for a moment he took on the character of the *eiron*, the sophisticated and immensely clever fellow who makes sport of the pompous *alazon*. This was at the first meeting of Mrs. Pocock and Madame de Vionnet, when the former was backed up in her New England hauteur by Waymarsh, and Strether came to the support of the latter; these two, with their Parisian chic and mastery of *double entente* talked rings around the stolid Americans: "It was indeed as if they were gathered for a performance, the performance of 'Europe' by his confederate and himself" (226).

Sarah's high-handed game throughout their whole stay, until the very end, was to pretend that there was no problem, no ambassadorial mission to be carried out. In this way she kept everyone hanging fire, waiting for the impending confrontations. She ignored Madame de Vionnet's charm and distinction as though they did not exist, and refused to recognize that any transformation had taken place in her brother Chad. She even closed her eyes to the beauty and wonder of Paris that had been such an important part of Strether's education, though it lay all about her. The gaudy splendor of the salon in her hotel suite took her eye more than what could be seen through its windows:

> The glazed and gilded room, all red damask, ormolu, mirrors, clocks, looked south, and the shutters were bowed upon the summer morning; but the Tuileries garden and what was beyond it, over which the whole place hung, were things visible through gaps; so that the far-spreading presence of Paris came up in coolness, dimness and invitation, in the twinkle of gilt-tipped palings, the crunch of gravel, the click of hoofs, the crack of whips, things that suggested some parade of the circus. (221)

It was not Sarah but Strether who saw this—an aerial view of the same scene that had so fascinated him on his first day in Paris, like the Impressionist picture cited above as an analogue to it. Indeed, just like the studio from whose window Pissarro had painted *Le Jardin des Tuileries*, Sarah's hotel was on the rue de Rivoli. (James himself sometimes stayed at the Hotel Continental, on the same street, which also had windows overlooking the Tuileries.) Sarah Pocock had the opportunity of looking at practically all the persons, places, and things in Paris that had brought about Lambert Strether's transformation, but she saw nothing. In terms of *The Ambassadors*, seeing is understanding; the visual sense is the chief instrument for perceiving values and meanings. But eyes conditioned by Woollett, Massachusetts—myopia? astigmatism?—are likely to see Europe in a limited and distorted way.

When Mrs. Pocock decided that the time had arrived for acting, she conducted herself in the dictatorial manner of an emperor or a pope—rather, since she lacked such absolute power, with the pomposity of an *alazon*. On the last day before her departure from Paris she waited upon Strether in the reading room of his hotel with an ultimatum:

> Her appearance was really indeed funnier than anything else—the spirit in which he felt her to be there.... Her calculation was sharp in the immobility with which she held her tall parasol-stick upright and at arm's length, quite as if she had struck the place to plant her flag; in the aggressive repose in which she did quite nothing but wait for him.... She had come to receive his submission. (274-275)

Chad had promised on his honor that he would go straight home if Strether gave him the word, she declared; her demand was that he should do so within the next twenty-four hours. When he parried by asking if she had no appreciation for her brother's "fortunate development," she retorted: "I call it hideous." When he spoke of the charm and distinction of Madame de Vionnet, her comment rang out sufficiently loud: "Do you consider her even an apology for a decent woman?" Strether suddenly realized that he was hearing the very words of Mrs. Newsome, spoken through her daughter's mouth. But if the mother had the excuse of ignorance, Sarah, who had come out precisely to see for herself, had no excuse for her arrogance in refusing to admit the truth of what was before her eyes: "She wasn't at all funny at last—... she was nobly and appointedly officious" (275-280).

The break was sharp. Ambassador Pocock departed the next day for a month in the Alps, taking in her entourage Waymarsh to counterbalance Jim, and Little Bilham for her young sister-in-law Mamie, who realized she had lost Chad as a prospective husband. But they would not sail for America until the end of July, so that Chad and Strether had another month in which to change their minds and join the party at Liverpool—the former to retrieve his place in the family business and family fortune, the latter the hand of the rich widow in marriage. What Strether's decision will be seems forecast by the new image that has come to his mind. Seeing the mother reflected in Sarah's hard bright coldness, Mrs. Newsome now looms for him as "some particularly large iceberg in a cool blue northern sea" (298).

The comic interlude has been wholly concerned with the outer plot, and though it takes up one-third of the book it calls for only such minimal treatment here. The critic whose sole concern is the hero's education is now ready to move on to the final picture which completes it (in the last two chapters of Book Eleventh).

Landscape with Figures

Strether took advantage of his freedom, after the Pococks's departure, by treating himself to a day-long excursion into the countryside just out of Paris. He not only wanted to be alone, but after several months of doing everything for the sake of everybody else he resolved, for once, to indulge his own pleasure. His destination was not some particular place geographically determined, but the "right" place esthetically. He would devote the whole of one day to "that French ruralism, with its cool special green, into which he had hitherto looked only through the little oblong window of the picture-frame." This odd motivation is then specified as "the chance of seeing something somewhere that would remind him of a certain small Lambinet"—a landscape that had charmed him long years before at a dealer's in Tremont Street, Boston, but that he could not afford to buy in spite of its ridiculously low price. It would be some compensation now "to assist at the restoration to nature" of that whole faraway hour (301).

Two of James's fictional techniques in this passage are noteworthy, the simplest being his complication of the time scheme. The intensity of Strether's present experience of Europe has been constantly enhanced by reminiscences of past experiences, chiefly marked by what he had missed; the "lost" Lambinet of his early manhood is an especially poignant example of this heightening. It is interesting also that James as autobiographer singled out this landscapist as the one who, during his own youth, "summed up for the American collector and in the New York and Boston markets the idea of the modern in the masterly." And in 1872—just about the date when Strether missed out at the Boston dealer's sale—he had reviewed an exhibition of privately owned paintings of the Barbizon School, including Rousseau, Daubigny, and others (possibly Lambinet, though he is not named), that was held in the rooms of Messrs. Doll and Richards on the same Tremont Street. The second technical device in the passage quoted above is even more significant—James's inverted use of the mirror image, as in the incident at the London theater near the beginning of the novel. The normal purpose in comparing a representational painting with the landscape the artist was looking at is to see if the painting is "correct," that is, properly faithful to nature. Here Strether has gone out to test the actual landscape against the Lambinet painting to see if the French countryside is "correct," that is, properly picturesque.

Once more, in reference to this mirror technique, there is striking evidence of a link between author and hero. In 1873 Henry James himself had played the same game with Claude Lorraine, taking horseback rides out in the Roman Campagna to see the locales where the classic French landscapist had painted those pictures that the young American had admired in the Doria Gallery. The travel essay in which this is recorded concludes with a detailed example of the inverted mirror image. An American artist, who owned a small sketch by Claude, told James how an hour's ride out of the Porta Caval-legieri would bring him to the very "Arcadia" that had inspired this painting two centuries before:

> The exquisite correspondence in this case altogether revived its faded bloom; here veritably the oaten pipe must have stirred the windless air and the satyrs have laughed among the brookside reeds. Three or four grassy dells stretch away in a chain between low hills over which delicate trees are so discreetly scattered that each one is a resting place for a shepherd. The elements of the scene are simple enough, but the composition has extraordinary refinement. By one of those happy chances which keep observation in Italy always in her best humour a shepherd had thrown himself down under one of the trees in the very attitude of Meli-boeus. . . . The poor fellow, lying there in rustic weariness and ignorance, little fancied that he was a symbol of old-world meanings to new-world eyes.

It seems more than likely that James had this early essay before him when he began his account of Strether's day in the country. His fictional counter-part now selected a train out of Paris with only one requirement, that it should make several stops well after getting beyond the suburbs. After little more than an hour it pulled up at just the right spot. Strether alighted and began his rural walk with as much confidence "as if to keep an appointment" —an appointment, indeed, with himself as a young man and with the painter whose landscape he had not been able to afford:

> The oblong gilt frame disposed its enclosing lines; the poplars and wil-lows, the reeds and river, . . . fell into a composition, full of felicity, with-in them; the sky was silver and turquoise and varnish; the village on the left was white and the church on the right was grey; it was all there, in

short—it was what he wanted; it was Tremont Street, it was France, it was Lambinet. Moreover he was freely walking about in it. (302)

James's skill in choosing one of the Barbizon School was unerring. They carried on the traditional idealizing of the older French landscapists, like Claude Lorraine, yet at the same time they were harbingers of Impressionism; but in comparison, today they appear much more romantic than naturalistic —which befits Strether's initial mood. Again, though the Barbizon painters may have discovered the value of actual native landscapes as subjects, their ambition to achieve generalization kept their pictures from seeming like portraits of particular places. This, plus the fact that Lambinet is one of the lesser talents of the school, saved James from having to specify some well-known painting, as would have been called for had he named a master such as Corot. Also, it gave Strether the freedom of discovering one Lambinet-like landscape after another as he walked: "He really continued in the picture...all the rest of this rambling day;...and had meanwhile not once overstepped the oblong gilt frame" (305). There are two paintings by Lambinet that seem typical of the landscapes Strether saw. One pictures a river (with a rustic fisherman in a boat), with reedy banks and a green meadow, a cluster of thatched cottages in the distance on the left, trees in the foreground on the right, a cloud-flecked sky with patches of delicate blue. The second shows a pond in the foreground, reeds and a grassy bank beyond, a peasant with scythe walking toward a small stand of wheat, rolling countryside with trees on the near horizon, an overcast but pearly sky—all in muted tones of gray and shades of green-brown-beige. (Both are small untitled canvases.) It was all just as picturesque as it should be—except that Lambinet's peasants, the only figures in his landscapes, "struck him perhaps a little more as men of the world than he had expected."

Strether was relaxed and happy. But though he was alone all day he had never before seemed to himself so much engaged with others "and in midstream of his drama." For at bottom "the spell of the picture" had been all morning "that it was essentially more than anything else a scene and a stage, that the very air of the play was in the rustle of the willows and the tone of the sky." Something was beginning to happen, in subtle stages, to the romantic rural landscape he had been "freely walking about in." He had been most at peace, most "lost in Lambinet," when stretched out on his back for the better part of the summer afternoon on a grassy slope. After that he had found his way down to the principal village, the one right on the river, to pick out the inn where he would have dinner before returning to Paris. Everything now conspired to draw him out of his idyllic reverie of the past into the troubled present again.

As the experiences of the last three months crowded back on his consciousness, he began to make comparisons that heightened the "drama" of his still unsolved problem: "The conditions had nowhere so asserted their difference from those of Woollett as they appeared to him to assert it in the little court of the Cheval Blanc while he arranged with his hostess for a comfortable climax." His day in the country would conclude with a very Parisian dish for dinner, *cotelette de veau à l'oseille*. Simple and few as were the elements composing his present situation at the riverside inn, it struck him as being *"the thing*, as he would have called it, even to a greater degree than Madame de Vionnet's old high salon where the ghost of the Empire walked." Still more interesting is a third comparison, implied by the picture that the village aspect as a whole presented, "whiteness, crookedness, and blueness set in coppery green" (306). This is a fusion of two previous pictures that had sounded the note of Europe for Strether from the very beginning: the medieval walled town of Chester, suggesting all that was old, complex, and devious; the light and color that had dazzled him on his first walk in Paris, revealing the beauty of this modern Babylon.

One is even tempted to pinpoint a single color as symbolizing the shift from one school of landscapists to another that took place at the end of his rural adventure—green, the indispensable color for all painters who aim to represent nature. James himself emphasizes it with five references in as many pages: twice to that "special-green vision" so distinctive of Lambinet; three times to "coppery green," a pigment that brings to mind Manet, Renoir, Monet and the others. One of the leading historians of the transition period in French art of the 1860s and 1870s has seized upon the treatment of this particular color as one way of differentiating between two schools. The muted tonality of the Barbizon painters was achieved by using the many gradations from emerald to greyish moss-green, he says; the brilliant effects of light and atmosphere achieved by the Impressionists is the result of their radical theory that the green of nature is not green at all but a combination of other colors. And "coppery green" suggests the blues and yellows into which they broke it down.

When Strether strolls down into the riverside garden of the Cheval Blanc, to pass the time until dinner, he steps through a very different picture frame from the oblong gilt one that had enclosed the Lambinet. He is now really *en plein air*, in the sense made famous by the new school of landscapists who revolutionized European painting in the last quarter of the nineteenth century:

For the next twenty minutes [he sat in] a small and primitive pavilion that, at the garden's edge, almost overhung the water.... It consisted of little more than a platform, slightly raised, with a couple of benches and a table, a protecting rail and a projecting roof; but it raked the full grey-blue stream ... ; and it was clearly in esteemed requisition for Sundays and other feasts. Strether sat there and, though hungry, felt at peace; ... with the lap of the water, the ripple of the surface, the rustle of the reeds on the opposite bank, the faint diffused coolness and the slight rock of a couple of small boats attached to a rough landing-place hard by. The valley on the further side was all copper-green level and glazed pearly sky, a sky hatched across with screens of trimmed trees ... ; and though the rest of the village straggled away in the near quarter the view had an emptiness that made one of the boats suggestive. (307)

This river-view (and its sequel) has struck more readers as being like an Impressionist painting than any of the other verbal pictures in *The Ambassadors*. Previous commentators have been divided between Renoir and Manet as the likely influence on James in the scene above. But before attempting to identify the particular painter, there is a general similarity to the Impressionists to be noted.

In the most detailed study of James and the visual arts, the author has suggested a shift in the mode of his verbal pictures at this point corresponding to the difference in technique between the Barbizon painters and the Impressionists, a suggestion that deserves full quotation here:

A comparison of descriptive phrases in the first part of this chapter with those of the latter part and the opening of the next reveals a significant change in Strether's vision: "sunny, silvery sky, the shady, woody horizon," ... "the village on the left was white and the church on the right was grey"—this is how Strether "sees" initially. Color is presented through adjectives, and the light is represented as concentrated in the sky, not diffused throughout. That the horizon is "shady, woody" suggests a traditional perspective in which objects at a distance appear blurred. In contrast, the primary emphasis in the description of the village where he stops for dinner is not on the thing modified by the adjective; instead, adjectives are converted into substantives, a grammatical shift which places the emphasis on the sensory quality of the visual experience rather than on the thing itself. "The village aspect" affects him "as whiteness, crookedness and blueness set in coppery green. . . ." Color details are rendered with greater precision: the church is a "dim slate-colour" on the outside; the stream is "grey-blue". Distant objects are not described as if the perspective were conventional.

This verbal and syntactical analysis is indeed convincing, though the particular paintings cited in conclusion are not the ones I would have chosen. "What we have here," this art critic says of the two superimposed river-views at the chapter's end, "is no longer, say, Lambinet's 'Le Passeur sur La Seine, près Bougival' but Renoir's 'Canotiers à Chatou' or Manet's 'En Bâteau'." If one is looking for similarity in subject as well as in the technique for conveying Strether's vision, however, there are two canvases by Monet that are more strikingly relevant.

In James's first notation for this episode (in the preliminary "Project" sent to his publisher) he conceived it as taking place "in a surburban village by the river, a place where people come out from Paris to boat, to dine, to dance, to make love, to do anything they like." In the novel this blunt expository statement is subtly transformed by being rendered scenically in a pair of overlapping "pictures." The first of these (quoted two pages above) could easily have been modelled on one of a series of paintings by Renoir and Monet depicting a restaurant and riverside resort on the Seine near Bougival, about twenty kilometers downstream from Paris, frequented by young men and women who came there to enjoy the popular pastime of boating. (James was well acquainted with Bougival, having visited Turgenev at his châlet there in the early 1880s.) "It was a perpetual holiday—and what an assortment of people!" Renoir said many years later: "You could still enjoy yourself in those days! ... I found as many magnificent girls to paint as I wanted." His biographer adds a significant comment: "There are grounds for claiming this spot as the birthplace of Impressionism, because the first works which clearly exhibited this entirely new conception of painting are Monet's *La Grenouillère* ... and *La Grenouillère* by Renoir, ... both painted there in 1869." At this period Renoir was very much under the influence of Monet, learning from him the free style, broad brushstrokes, and atmospheric effects that were to characterize the new mode.

The best of Monet's paintings of *La Grenouillère*—distinguished by "the scintillating brilliance and movement of the sun, the water, and the gay costumes," in the words of his biographer—was included in the second Impressionists' Exhibition held in Paris, 1876, the show that was briefly reviewed by Henry James for the New York *Tribune*. It is remarkably close in subject matter to what Strether first sees from his riverside garden. Here also is a simple pavilion hanging over the water, two small boats pulled up at the reedy bank, trees and a suggestion of village stretching beyond. The only difference is that there are a dozen ladies and gentlemen in evidence—but these may be said to appear in Strether's conjuring up of holiday-makers that frequent the Cheval Blanc "on Sundays and other feasts." Even more remarkable is the similarity in painterly effects: the bold contrasts of value and color, the luminous sky and shifting tracery of leaves, the dancing light and shade on the lapping water achieved by patches of blue-yellow-grey. "Such a river set one afloat almost before one could take up the oars," Strether reflected.

This perception, and something he saw a moment later that gave him a sharp arrest, brought him to his feet:

What he saw was exactly the right things—a boat advancing round the bend and containing a man who held the paddles and a lady, at the stern, with a pink parasol. It was suddenly as if these figures, or something like them, had been wanted in the picture, had been wanted more or less all day, and had now drifted into sight, with the slow current, on purpose to fill up the measure.... For two very happy persons he found himself straightway taking them—a young man in his shirt-sleeves, a young woman easy and fair, who...had known what this particular retreat could offer them.... They were expert, familiar, frequent—this wouldn't at all events be the first time—and it made them but the more idyllic, though at the very moment of the impression, as happened, their boat seemed to have begun to drift wide, the oarsman letting it go. [It was suddenly as if they had recognized him.] ... He too had within the minute taken in something, taken in that he knew the lady whose parasol, shifting as if to hide her face, made so fine a pink point in the shining scene. It was too prodigious, a chance in a million, but, if he knew the lady,...the coatless hero of the idyll, was, to match the marvel, none other than Chad. (307–308)

Strether's hostess at the inn had told him she was expecting two other persons for dinner, but he was taken completely by surprise at what now loomed before his eyes. This completes the shift from the romantic landscapes of Lambinet, with their muted tones, to the gay colors and sensuous suggestiveness of the pleasure-trip that the Impressionists were so fond of painting.

Thumbing through the large collection of reproductions of Monet, Manet, Renoir, and the others at the Courtauld Institute (London), I too was brought to my feet—just like Strether—when I stumbled on *La Seine à Vétheuil*, painted in 1880 by Claude Monet. The similarity in subject and technique to James's picture is so startling as "to match the marvel" again. Monet had spent some months at Vétheuil, a village on the Seine about sixty kilometers north-west of Paris (Strether's trip into the country was about one hour out by train), where he made several versions of the painting referred to above. They all show a stretch of the river with reeds on the bank, willows and poplars beyond, and a church tower rising above them; around the bend there is a glimpse of the village, with a prominent white building that could be the Cheval Blanc; in the distance a valley with rolling hills can be seen; in the foreground is a rowboat, headed downstream toward the concealed landing-place, with a man at the oars and a lady in the stern. The coloring and atmospheric effects are just right also: a sky that is glazed and pearly, the gentle slope of the distant valley all coppery green, the rippling surface of the river full of reflected light and color. In the version of this painting that bears the title *La Seine à Vétheuil* there is one more surprisingly exact point of resemblance to James's scene, not found in Monet's other variants: the lady in the stern of the boat is holding a parasol, and it is pink! (James might well have seen this painting on visits to Paris. If he did not, its similarity to the verbal picture at the climax of *The Ambassadors* is a fabulous coincidence.)

Consciously or not, James made dramatic use of a special Impressionist technique, the color-spot to focus the eye of the beholder. In his own words, Madame de Vionnet's parasol "made so fine a pink point in the shining scene." The color is exactly what it should be, retaining a touch of the romantic—like the pink candle shades at the dinner with Maria Gostrey in London—even though this is the "revelation" scene. (Red would not do at all for a lady's parasol, besides being too crude a suggestion of adultery.) The whole weight of meaning for Strether has to be borne by this symbolic object, as transpires when the three of them sit down to dinner at the Cheval Blanc. For they cannot really communicate; they can only, with all their tact, cover the truth of the situation with exclamations about the extraordinary chance that had brought them together on their day's outing: "it was as queer as fiction, as farce, that *their* country could happen to be exactly *his*." Madame de Vionnet's surprise and amusement overflows wholly into French, though she had never fallen back on her native language with him before. True, Strether had felt all afternoon that he had suddenly acquired "a fearless facility in French" and had tried to talk with the rustics he met, hoping to find out "what the French people were thinking" (302). But her conversation at the dinner table that evening is a different matter altogether, consisting as it does of "unprecedented idiomatic turns ... [and] little brilliant jumps that he could but lamely match."

What little he can understand tells him that there is "a charming lie" behind the whole affair: "It was with the lie that they had eaten and drunk and talked and laughed." The revealing picture on the river has been replaced by a concealing farce in the dining room of the inn. Madame de Vionnet keeps up her "performance" all evening, her elaborate pretence that they had left Paris that morning being "the essence of her comedy." It is only when their little play is replaced for Strether by the Impressionistic picture coming back again into his mind that he is sure of the truth: they have been spending the past twenty-four hours at a quiet retreat nearby, to which they had fully meant to return this evening. He is convinced now by "the too evident fact ... that she hadn't started out for the day dressed and hatted and shod, and even, for that matter, pink parasol'd, as she had been in the boat" (308–312). Such is the subtle transformation of James's first notation: that Chad and Madame de Vionnet were to be discovered at a rendezvous where people come out from Paris "to make love, to do anything they like." The movement from a rural idyll to a landscape with figures (not peasants but sophisticated city people) parallels Strether's development from innocence to experience. The couple in the boat are not "right" for Lambinet, because there is no intrigue in his paintings to damage their picturesqueness. But they are just right for Monet, who made the pleasures of contemporary life a special province of his painting. And just right for Strether too. They "correct" his romantic vision.

Throughout his experience of Europe Strether has learned primarily by what he sees, entirely so at this climax. The hypothesis of a "virtuous attachment" has now vanished before his eyes, just as the earlier theory that Chad was being held in Paris by a romantic attachment to Madame de Vionnet's lovely daughter had vanished—both delusions being dissipated by something that he *saw*. The revelation on the river removes the last veil from his eyes: the young man is involved in a mature and passionate love affair with the *jeune fille's* charming mother! Strether's first reaction was to be shocked at his discovery, then shocked at himself for being shocked: "He was mixed up in a typical tale of Paris, and so were they, poor things—how could they all together help being?" Mrs. Newsome had been right, after all, but her Ambassador has left her censorious judgment of such affaires far behind. The final lesson in his education has shown him, however, that passion and deceit may lie hidden beneath the beauty and charm of Paris—a paradox that he realizes may be characteristic of Europe in general, as contrasted with America.

Book Twelfth serves the purpose of winding up the loose ends of the outer plot—full of interest in its own right and rendered with the master's consummate skill. In these final chapters the reader learns what "happens" at the conclusion, as far as each of the principal characters is concerned. But, because of James's new conception of the novelist's obligation to truth, the reader learns only as much as one learns in real life about motivations and meanings. Why does Chad at long last decide to go back to Woollett? (For weeks he has been wavering between the certain fortune awaiting him there, as head of the family business, and the uncertain future for him here, as Madame de Vionnet's lover.) Why does Strether not stay on in Paris and marry Miss Gostrey? (It seems quite clear that this alternative is open to him.) Most intriguing of all is the third permutation among these four characters. How does Strether himself feel, at the end, toward Madame de Vionnet?—"the finest and subtlest creature, the happiest apparition, it had been given him, in all his years, to meet." Coming to know her, more than anything else, had made him feel that life had gone past him—that it was "too late" (323). Such ambiguities, unresolved motivation, and unfinished business are a deliberate part of James's later manner—though some readers would prefer a more explicit conclusion to the story line. But these matters lie beyond the province of the critic whose sole concern is with the novel's inner theme, "the story of the story." With the Monet-like picture of the revelation-on-the-river (one of the most brilliant scenes in all of James's fictions), Lambert Strether's education has been brought to completion, his awareness that there could have been another kind of life for him.

The Ambassadors is a supreme illustration of James's mature statement as to what we can expect of the great creators. In a late essay, casting himself for the moment as a reader, he declares of novelists: "They offer us another world, another consciousness, another experience that . . . makes us face, in the return to the inevitable, a combination that may at least have changed." Here James certainly means a "combination" of our experience with that of the fictional world so as to change us into something different from what we were. This describes, exactly, the effect of *The Ambassadors* on many readers, and makes them satisfied with its conclusion. Since the reader tends to identify with Strether, it also describes what happens to the hero. He returns to "the inevitable" (Woollett, Massachusetts) to face a "combination" (his experience of Paris added to his previous experience of life) that suggests a "change" in store for him. The final dialogue with Miss Gostrey supports this interpretation:

> "To what do you go home?"
> "I don't know. There will always be something."
> "To a great difference?". . .
> "A great difference no doubt. Yet I shall see what I can make of it."

The last clause is spoken with the "voice of the true high comic hero," according to a recent critic. His interpretation of *The Ambassadors* as a comedy of manners throughout—in its form and in the hero's final vision—confirms my opinion that the novel's ending is just what it should be.

Literary Impressionist

The close similarity of so many major scenes in *The Ambassadors* to paintings by the French Impressionists is extraordinary indeed. Without more external evidence, of course, it cannot be proved that they were conscious influences on Henry James. But at the very least they are illuminating analogies that emphasize the pictorial effects he intended. James had expressed himself clearly and emphatically on this point twenty years before in "The Art of Fiction," his key statement of literary theory. There, ranging himself on the side of the artist rather than the moralist, he declared: "[The novelist] competes with his brother the painter in *his* attempt to render the look of things, the look that conveys their meaning, to catch the color, the relief, the expression, the surface, the substance of the human spectacle." In making comparisons of this sort one must bear in mind the limitations inherent in treating the relation of one art form to another, here painting to prose fiction. A previous critic has put it succinctly: "The technique of *describing* a scene as a picture is intrinsically different from that of *painting* it." Although Impressionist paintings may have furnished the inspiration for James's scene-settings in *The Ambassadors*, it was the French "literary impressionists" who influenced the compositional mode and descriptive style of his last great novels. The evidence for this is full and explicit.

A younger generation of writers—Daudet, Maupassant, Loti—were carrying on the fictional experiments of Flaubert and the other "sons of Balzac." James had met the first two at Flaubert's Sunday afternoons in the winter of 1875–76; later he met Loti at Daudet's house, 1884. His essays on all three reveal his indebtedness to their techniques. Since these novelists were themselves close friends of Renoir, Manet, Monet, and the rest—whose paintings confessedly affected their prose—the influence of French Impressionist painters may have reached Henry James in this indirect but logically literary way. An adequate discussion of the style of his "major phase," including these important influences, would call for another full-length study. But a few quotations from his essays on the French Impressionist writers will point the way, and at the same time add a valuable coda to my preceding chapter.

Pierre Loti was the least influential, both the man and his works coming to James's attention somewhat late in his career. In an essay of 1888 he declares that the "master-sign of the novel in France today," linking Loti with

Daudet and Maupassant, is "an extraordinary development of the external perceptions—those of the appearance, the sound, the taste, the feeling, the general physical sense of things." Pierre Loti he ranks among the very first of sea-painters, "all the poetry of association, all the touching aspects and suggestions in persons, places and objects connected with it." Deficient in composition and in psychological depth though he may be, his surface is always magnificent, suggesting "how long and how far impressionism will yet go."

The American novelist's delight in Loti's landscapes and coloring, his "moments and pictures," is testified to a decade later by the eulogistic introduction for a slender volume of shorter pieces which he translated into English and published in 1898 under the title *Impressions*. Their special charm lies in "the fine vibrations in Loti of what he sees and what he makes us see," according to James, whose preference was for the early works that dealt with the sea and with the village scenery of his native Brittany—not his erotic fictions. "He uses all his impressions," the introduction concludes, "never misses them on the wing nor shirks the catching; and of the lightest, loosest, yet cunningest interweaving of these his curious prose mainly consists." One of Loti's vignettes, "Cathedral Impressions," describing the great Spanish church at Burgos, is suggestive of Monet's paintings of Rouen Cathedral; and when Loti shifts to the interior, with a lady in black kneeling before a lighted altar, it reminds one of the scene in Notre Dame de Paris when Strether discovered Mme de Vionnet at her devotions. Another, an impressionistic French landscape with sea, mountains, village, and church, entitled "A Reflective Moment," is reminiscent of the climactic revelation scene in *The Ambassadors* inspired by *La Seine à Vétheuil*. The similarity of Loti's verbal pictures to the paintings of Monet is marked, so that James may have been drawn to them by a double attraction.

The case for Guy de Maupassant is much stronger. James had known him since his own seminal year in Paris; the twenty-five-year-old Frenchman was not then a published author but an athletic young man full of talk about swimming, boating on the Seine, and the conquest of women. A decade later in the summer of 1886 he visited London, where James did his best to serve as host, but the irrepressible Maupassant, though at the peak of his literary fame, still cared more for women than for talk about books. The Anglo-American novelist greatly preferred the French artist to the man. His intimate knowledge of the works is recorded in a full-scale critical estimate published two years later, which remains the classic on Maupassant in English. This fifty-page essay, along with a comparable one on Daudet, forms the centerpiece of *Partial Portraits* (1888), a volume that marks a turning point in James's career (his new direction being staked out in the concluding essay, "The Art of Fiction").

His genuine admiration for Maupassant was subject to two serious qualifications. The first of these was a disapproval of his emphasis on sex, something that James felt was overdone by all French novelists and that had reached its culmination in the flagrant eroticism of Flaubert's young disciple. The second was his reaction to Maupassant's rejection of any concern with the psychological or moral motivation of human behavior, his determination to limit himself to visible things and to render objectively only what he had seen. This is close to the theory held by some of the Impressionist painters—though it was hard to adhere to in practice. "However much Degas tried to confine to the phenomenon itself his determination to be truthful, he could not help producing criticisms of life," according to a distinguished art historian, who concludes with an explicit comparison: "In other words, feeling could not be eliminated, and the result is somewhat reminiscent of Maupassant."

Although James likewise doubted that such complete objectivity was possible, he admitted that what made Maupassant the supreme observer was his dedication to the axiom that a writer produces "the effect of truth better by painting people from the outside than from the inside." Yet it was clear that Maupassant had broken away not only from the naturalism of Zola but also from the new generic realism of Daudet. He avoids the "analytic fashion of telling a story," James declares, and confines his mode "to making persons and events pass before our eyes." His great gift is the vividness of his five senses, most powerful of all being his visual sense. "His eye selects unerringly, unscrupulously, almost impudently—catches the particular thing in which the character of the object or the scene resides, and, by expressing it with the artful brevity of a master, leaves a convincing, original picture," James concludes: "[In all his descriptions] the whole thing is an impression, as painters say nowadays."

The relationship of Maupassant to the Impressionist school has frequently been commented on, with the suggestion that the influence flowed both ways. Degas' similarity to the novelist has already been pointed out. Perhaps his best friend among these painters was Manet, whose biographer says specifically of *Chez Père Lathuille* (the painting I suggested as one of the models for James's Seine-side restaurant scene) that it was a brilliant vignette of contemporary French life "like one of Maupassant's verbal pictures." On the other hand the charm of Renoir's and Monet's canvases entitled *La Grenouillère* (cited as models for the first part of James's revelation scene in the French countryside) may well have inspired Maupassant, the ardent boatsman, to set several of his stories at this popular riverside resort. His translator has singled out one of the late tales, "Mouche," as a particular example of this similarity: "It conjures up as perfectly as the contemporary Renoir painting of a riverside restaurant a vanished world of mustachioed young men in boaters and striped jerseys and laughing girls in flowered bonnets." The reference here is to Renoir's *Déjeuner des Canotiers* rather than *La Grenouillère*, though both depict the same resort at Bougival on the Seine.

As a matter of fact, "Mouche" does not include a luncheon scene though it does embody the theme of gaiety and the carefree life of boating parties on the river, as immortalized by Renoir. Pictorially Maupassant's tale conjures up a painting much more interesting to readers of *The Ambassadors*—Monet's *La Seine à Vétheuil*, cited as a model for the second part of James's revelation scene on the river. In "Mouche" the five roistering blades put the finishing touch on their fun by finding a cocotte who fills the double role of sitting in the stern "to take the tiller" and serving as mistress to all of them during their weekend parties. "A woman is an indispensable adjunct to a boat like ours," the autobiographical narrator says, "indispensable because she keeps minds and hearts awake, because she provides excitement, amusement and distraction, and because she gives a spice to life and, with a red parasol gliding past green banks, decoration too." Madame de Vionnet's romantic "pink parasol" has been replaced in Maupassant's tale by one with a more realistic hue, symbolizing adultery! At this point, in an authorial aside, Henry James himself enters the picture. It is clearly the stories of promiscuous love-making like "Mouche" that he has in mind when he says in *The Ambassadors*—just before the boat with Chad and Madame de Vionnet appears round the bend of the river—that all of Strether's experiences in the countryside earlier that day "remind him, as indeed the whole episode would incidentally do, of Maupassant" (302). This vague hint has now been made specific.

Alphonse Daudet more than anyone else influenced the style and mode of rendering in James's last great novels. Of all the writers he met in 1875–76 at Flaubert's literary gatherings only two became intimate friends. One was Turgenev, old enough to be his father; the other Daudet, about his own age. One reason for the warmth of his response to this young French novelist was his Provençal expansiveness, another their mutual attachment to the older Russian writer. In the years that followed James paid a number of visits to the home of Daudet—notably during long stays in Paris in 1884, 1889, and 1893. And near the end of the Frenchman's life he served as attentive host to him during his month-long visit to London.

More pertinent to the present inquiry is his admiration of Daudet's art, as reflected in several essays. Two of them came early: a short one in 1882 prompted by the appearance of a memoir by the French novelist's brother, and the next year a fifty-page appraisal of his fictions down to 1883. In the longer essay, which undertakes to place Daudet among his contemporaries, James indicates some of the reasons for his own preference. "The new school of fiction in France is based very much on the taking of notes," he says, citing Zola and Flaubert; but though his favorite probably takes them too, he needs them less: "Daudet proceeds by quick, instantaneous vision." All these novelists are less concerned with the moral and metaphysical world than with the sensible, "conceiving everything in the visible form." Like them, what Daudet mainly sees is the great surface of life. But he has feeling, and the "inveterate poetical touch"; this is what distinguishes him from Flaubert and Zola, who by comparison seem "hard and dry." Yet Daudet is very modern, "he has all the newly developed, the newly invented, perceptions." As applied to this school, "modern" means "a more analytic consideration of appearances," James explains: "It is known by its tendencies to resolve its discoveries into pictorial form.... The magic of the arts of representation lies in their appeal to the associations awakened by *things*" (italics added).

It is inevitable that one should talk about Daudet's writings in terms of Impressionist paintings. He was a friend of several of that school, closest perhaps to Renoir, who visited the novelist in 1877 and made a portrait of his wife. Did James ever meet the painter at his house? At any rate, his general commentary on Daudet in the earlier short essay could apply equally well to Renoir:

> No one has such an eye for a subject; such a perception of "bits," as the painters in water-colors say. It is indeed as if he worked in water-colors, from a rich and liquid palette; his style is not so much a literary form as a plastic form. He is a wonderful observer of all external things—of appearances, objects, surfaces, circumstances; but what makes his peculiarity is that the ray of fancy, the tremor of feeling, always lights up the picture.... The new fashion of realism has indeed taught us all that in any description of life the description of places and things is half the battle. But to describe them, we must see them, and some people see, on the same occasion, infinitely more than others. Alphonse Daudet is one of those who see most.... Ah, the things he sees,—the various fleeting, lurking, delicate, nameless human things! ... What could be more modern than his style, from which every shred of classicism has been stripped, and which moves in a glitter of images, of discoveries, of verbal gymnastics, animated always by the same passion for the concrete.

Especially pertinent to my own thesis is James's assertion here that "in any description of life the description of places and things is half the battle."

If this general commentary makes a strong case for the similarity of Daudet to the Impressionist painters, a specific comment on *Le Nabab* and *Les Rois en Exil,* in James's longer essay, points to a striking similarity between *The Ambassadors* and the French novelist's pictorial mode. In these works of his maturity Daudet, the native of Provence, has "conquered" Paris, and it is for these that the American novelist reserves his greatest admiration. "He has made of it a Paris of his own—a Paris like a vast crisp water-color":

> To Daudet...the familiar aspects of Paris are endlessly pictorial, and part of the charm of his novels (for those who share his relish for that huge flower of civilization) is the way in which he recalls it, evokes it, suddenly presents it, in parts or as a whole, to our senses. The light, the sky, the feeling of the air, the odours of the streets, the look of certain vistas, the silvery, muddy Seine, the cool, grey tone of color, the physiognomy of particular quarters, the whole Parisian expression, meet you suddenly in his pages, and remind you again and again that if he paints with a pen he writes with a brush.

James could hardly have realized in 1883 how aptly he was anticipating his own verbal pictures of Paris in the novel he was to publish two decades later. And it may be added that his final comment on the pictorial aspects of *Le Nabab* and *Les Rois en Exil*—"these books have their full value only for minds more or less Parisianized"—applies equally well to readers of *The Ambassadors.*

Such a reader, turning the pages of either of Daudet's novels as if it were merely a picture book of Paris, with little regard to plot, might easily get the illusion that he was leafing through James's masterpiece. To take a random example, here is the vignette of a leading lady in *Le Nabab* as she appears in the sculpture gallery at the International Exhibition of 1855:

> The first person whom he saw, on arriving, was Felicia Ruys, standing, leaning against the pedestal of a statue, surrounded with congratulations and homage.... She was simply dressed, clothed in a black costume, embroidered and trimmed with jade, tempering the severity of the dress with a scintillation of reflections and the splendor of a ravishing little hat of pheasant plumes, of which her curly hair, coming together on the forehead, dividing at the nape of the neck in large waves, seemed to continue and soften the play of colors.
>
> A crowd of artists, of worldlings [*gens du monde*], pressed forward, eager to meet such genius combined with such beauty.

This lady, said to have been modelled on Sarah Bernhardt, could have inspired the portraits of Madame de Vionnet at Gloriani's garden party and at Chad's dinner.

James's relations with Daudet remained active right down to the time when *The Ambassadors* was germinating. In 1890 he translated the last part of the Tartarin trilogy, at the author's request, and published it in New York under the title of *Port Tarascon*, with an introduction expressing his delight in these gay chronicles of Provence, these "light and bright and irresistible" specimens of Daudet's "perfect art." Then, after friendly exchanges of visits across the Channel in 1893 and 1895, he wrote the final tribute to his *cher confrère* in a memorial essay on the occasion of his death in December 1897. "To think of one of his books is to see a little gilded gallery with small modern master-pieces," James summed up his quarter-century of admiration for Daudet's art: "His style is impressionism carried to the last point." In the three mas-terpieces of his own major phase, it may be argued that Henry James carried it one point further.

Like Lambert Strether, his creator had come a long way since his first commitment to the profession of letters in 1865. During a prolific writing ca-reer of over forty years he had published thirty-six volumes of fiction and a dozen more of literary criticism. This great shelf of books offers a brilliant commentary on the whole development of the novel from early Victorian times into the twentieth century. James shaped his own art by learning from many masters. Chief among them were Hawthorne and Balzac, Turgenev, Flaubert and George Eliot. Less important but still interesting were his debts to Dumas and George Sand, Dickens and Thackeray, even to such unlikely writers as Mark Twain and Zola. Finally there were the literary impressionists: Daudet, Maupassant, Loti—all told, an impressive list of nineteenth-century novelists. What James borrowed from them, as indicated in the preceding chapters, was almost exclusively their fictional techniques. One measure of his greatness, continuing down to the very end, was his insatiable desire to learn. Another and more important measure is that his integrity was such as to give everything that he borrowed the stamp of his own genius. No novelist has ever been less derivative, more original. And what he learned from the past pales by comparison with what he projected into the future.

The modern novel, with all its brilliant technical flowering, begins with Henry James. One could not make a finer claim than that staked out by his official biographer for *The Ambassadors*—"the first authentic masterpiece of the 'modern movement'"—in his concluding volume, *Henry James: The Master*. "It is a Stendhalian mirror in the roadway, past which Marcel Proust, James Joyce, Virginia Woolf, William Faulkner and so many others have since travelled," Edel declares: "Its pattern-structure pre-figured *Ulysses*; its long river-like sentences anticipated the reflective novel of Proust. Its quest for 'auras' of feeling foreshadowed the experiments of Virginia Woolf." The list can be extended, of course. One may add Conrad, Lawrence, Hemingway, who continued experimenting with a narrator or other center of consciousness as the controlling point of view; such diverse writers as Kafka, Camus, Nabokov, Murdoch, who discovered new worlds of psychological realism by following James's emphasis on the experiences of consciousness instead of outward adventures; many other disciples such as Wharton, Fitzgerald, R. P. Warren, Welty, and K. A. Porter, who explored further uses of place and thing to symbolize people. The range and variety of fictions represented by even this small sampling make it clear that the influence of James has nothing to do with plot, character, setting, or other subject matter. He was the great inheritor of the nineteenth-century tradition because he assimilated all it had to teach him of the art of fiction, then turned it in a new direction. In like manner, Henry James may be called the father of the modern novel because its rich flowering resulted from following the new paths he first opened up.

Notes and Index

Abbreviations

AE	*The American Essays of HJ* (Vintage, 1956)
Autobiography	F. W. Dupee, ed., *The Autobiography of HJ* (1956)
Cargill	Oscar Cargill, *The Novels of Henry James* (1961)
Edel, I–V	Leon Edel's biography of HJ: I, *The Untried Years* (1953); II, *The Conquest of London* (1962); III, *The Middle Years* (1962); IV, *The Treacherous Years* (1969); V, *The Master* (1972)
EH	*English Hours* (1905)
FN	*The Future of the Novel* (Vintage, 1956)
FPN	*French Poets and Novelists* (Grosset, 1964 [1878])
Hawthorne	*Hawthorne* (English Men of Letters, 1879)
IH	*Italian Hours* (1909)
Letters, I–II	Leon Edel, ed., *HJ Letters*, Vol. I (1974); Vol. II (1975)
Lubbock, I–II	Percy Lubbock, ed., *The Letters of HJ* (1920), 2 vols.
LRE	*Literary Reviews and Essays* (1957)
Notebooks	Matthiessen and Murdock, eds., *The Notebooks of HJ* (1947)
Novotny	Fritz Novotny, *Painting and Sculpture in Europe, 1780–1880* (1960)
PE	J. L. Sweeney, ed., *The Painter's Eye* (1956)
PP(1)	*Partial Portraits* (1888)
PP(2)	*Portraits of Places* (1948 [1883])
Prefaces	R. P. Blackmur, ed., *The Art of the Novel: Critical Prefaces* (1934)
PS	*Parisian Sketches* (1957)
SA	*The Scenic Art* (1948)
SL	Leon Edel, ed., *Selected Letters of HJ* (1955)
SLC	*Selected Literary Criticism* (1964)
Story, I–II	*William Wetmore Story and His Friends* (1903), 2 vols.
TS	*Transatlantic Sketches* (1875)
Winner	Viola Hopkins Winner, *HJ and the Visual Arts* (1970)

Notes

References to James's novels will be found in the text, in parentheses, immediately following the quotation or citation; the edition used for each of the novels is indicated in an end-note cued back to the first quotation. All other references will be found in these notes. In the interests of conciseness I have used a shortened form for books in the list of abbreviations; also, I have omitted the publisher and place, except when necessary to identify a particular edition; and the author is only named if other than Henry James.

The notes that follow are cued back to the text by page number and key phrase (the last words of quotations, several important words for other than quoted matter). No superscript numerals are used in the text, since in a book of this sort there are few annotations that will be of concern to any but the specialist, and the quotations and other matters that do call for annotation will be readily apparent.

Experimenter

3 *"satisfaction from it"* Letters, I, 427–428.
4 *"part of the action"* FPN, 90, 92, 96.
6 *"superstitious valuation of Europe"* Letters, I, 274.
8 *James's list of novels* Lubbock, II, 333. One purpose of my study being to trace HJ's development as a novelist, I have used the first editions of *Roderick Hudson, The American,* and *The Portrait of a Lady,* since they were elaborately revised in the New York Edition. For the other three, which were only slightly revised, I have used the text of the collected edition, since it is most readily available.

The Heady Wine of Rome · RODERICK HUDSON

9 *"operation on the senses"* Letters, I, 159–160.
"sober practical tourist" Letters, I, 162.
"I shall have written" Edel, I, 313.
10 *"the* Italian *feeling"* Letters, I, 142–143.
"color and style" TS, 120.
"from the foreground" Story, I, 93–95, 108–109.
11 *"criticized and rhapsodized"* Roderick Hudson: all references are to the first American edition, 1875.
12 *"business to be idle"* Edel, I, 299.
"art should demand them" TS, 211.
"with extraordinary gusto" Letters, I, 460.
"it was priceless" Letters, I, 397.
13 *William on Rome* F. O. Matthiessen, *The James Family* (1947), 291.
"things go on famously" Letters, I, 443–444.
14 *"great shadow of Balzac"* Prefaces, 9.
"appear to do so" Prefaces, 5.
15 *"evocation of localities"* FPN, 31–56; Edel, II, 195.
16 *"silvery column . . . the Bolognese"* TS, 183–185; 207–208.
17 *The vanished Villa Ludovisi* See *Roma: Città e Piani* (Torino, n.d.), 118–119, for three maps of the villa before its destruction, an aerial photograph of the modern

area around Via Veneto, and an engraving of the gardens as originally laid out by G. B. Falda. The villa comprised an area extending in an arc bounded by the Aurelian Wall from Porta Pia to Porta Pinciana, then downhill almost to Via Sistina, then eastward to Via XX Settembre, and back to Porta Pia.

18 *The tortuous Roman street*   This was Via dei Coronari, opened up by Sistus IV in the fifteenth century as a main pilgrim route to Saint Peter's. One can follow it today under its varying names beginning at the Corso near Piazza Colonna: Via del Collegio Capricana, Via delle Copelle, Via dei Coronari, Vicolo del Curato, and Via del Banco di Santo Spirito—ending at Ponte Sant'Angelo.

19 *"large still studio"*   Letters, I, 335.
   "roof, not a ceiling"   Letters, I, 332.

20 *"to hold the play"*   Prefaces, 15–16.

21 *"to him greater"*   Letters, I, 362; Edel, II, 91–96.
   "into the picture"   Hawthorne, 134 (Margaret Fuller as model for Zenobia).

22 *"what has been revealed"*   Spender, *The Destructive Element* (1935), 191–192.

24 *"at table to the end"*   Story, I, 82–84, 329–331.

25 *"Balzac would have known"*   Prefaces, 12–13.

28 *"the Dramatist's intensity"*   Prefaces, 15.

29 *"carry you wonderfully near"*   TS, 178–179.

31 *"the new government"*   TS, 120–121.

32 *"regardless of expense"*   TS, 83–84, 250–251.
   James's travel writings   His essays are superior to most contemporary ones, whether in standard guidebooks like Augustus Hare's *Walks in Rome* (1878), or more literary volumes like those of his fellow Americans—C. E. Norton's *Notes of Travel and Study in Italy* (1859), Story's *Roba di Roma* (1863), Lowell's *Fireside Travels* (1864), and Howells's *Italian Journeys* (1867)—close friends all.
   "Roman sights and impressions"   AE, 20.

33 *"pictorial aspects of Rome"*   Hawthorne, 165, 160.
   "as we turn the page"   AE, 21.
   "finest background in the world"   Letters, I, 401.

34 *Influence of Turgenev*   FPN, 223, 227. HJ says that the hero of *Rudin* is "one of those fatally complex natures who cost their friends so many pleasures and pains; who might, and evidently might not, do great things; nature strong in impulse, in talk, in responsive emotion, but weak in will"; and of the young man in love with the heroine of *On the Eve*, "Schubin, the young sculptor, with his moods and his theories, his exaltations and depressions, his endless talk and his disjointed action, is a deeply ingenious image of the artistic temperament."
   Sources for Roderick Hudson   See Cargill, 19–24.

35 *Eliot on James*   Little Review (Aug. 1918), 49.
   "wreck everyone near him"   Astarte, by the Earl of Lovelace, quoted by Praz in *The Romantic Agony* (Oxford, 1970), 64; see chap. 3, "The Metamorphoses of Satan."

36 *"La Belle Dame Sans Merci"*   Praz, *Romantic Agony*, chaps. 1 and 4.

37 *"dramatic and eventful"*   Letters, I, 460.
   Forster's "tapeworm"   Aspects of the Novel (1927), 26–28.

38 *Christina and Mary*   Prefaces, 18. Mary is "on stage," pp. 1–76, 292–482; Christina, pp. 86–382. Though they overlap for about 100 pages, Christina is all but absent from that part, and they meet only once, briefly.

Walls of Separation · THE AMERICAN

42 *"more to my imagination"*   Letters, II, 104–106.
   "Salon Carré of the Louvre"   Prefaces, 23–24.

(42 cont.)

"an aesthetic headache"   *The American*: all references are to the first American edition, 1877, as reprinted in the Rinehart paperback.

43 *"Combien?"*   See John Goode, *The Air of Reality: New Essays on Henry James* (1972), 17.

44 *"immense overhanging presence"*   *Prefaces*, 23, 26–27.

45 *"in perfect security"*   PS, 3, 5.

46 *"American greenness abroad"*   W. D. Howells, *Italian Journeys* (1867), 166.

"but they are not now"   *The Innocents Abroad* (1869), 190–191. The initial scene in HJ's early story "Travelling Companions" (1870) is close to MT's. The narrator, an American tourist with his "Murray," is standing in front of the famous fresco but intently watching a copyist, while his daughter gazes in awe at the original.

47 *"new gilding of the frame"*   Hawthorne, 160–161; *AE*, 9.

48 *"their ancient individuality"*   PP (2), 120.

50 *"germination process"*   *Prefaces*, 24.

51 *"common travelling Americans"*   Letters, I, 152.

"ill-mannered, ill-dressed"   "Americans Abroad," *Nation*, 3 Oct. 1878.

52 *"when I was abroad"*   F. O. Matthiessen, *The James Family* (1947), 323.

"fairly termed aristocratic"   "Travelling Companions," *Atlantic Monthly*, Nov. 1870.

"account in small ones"   AE, 79–81, 95.

53 *"provincial" overused and abused*   Albert Mordell, *Discovery of a Genius: WDH and HJ* (1961), 92–97.

"the company of Balzac"   Letters, II, 267; Mordell, ibid., 120–121.

54 *Newman and Western Humorists*   The concurrence in time and place of HJ's hero and the leading humorist cannot be accidental: Newman went West in 1865, with mining interests in Nevada, and wound up his career in San Francisco in 1868. Twain was in Nevada in 1862–64, and 1867, and in San Francisco in 1864–68.

55 *"through having remained free"*   *Prefaces*, 129–130.

"fixed" and "free" characters   Richard Poirier, *The Comic Sense of Henry James* (1962), 44–47.

60 *Newman meets the marquise*   See Poirier, ibid., 71–74, for illuminating comments on this scene.

63 *The Duke d'Aumale's reception*   Letters, II, 20: "All the Orleans family was there, except the Comte de Paris; and I was presented to the Duke and to a Princess of Saxe Coburg—the latter old, corpulent and deaf, . . . yet in spite of these drawbacks so gracious and 'chatty' as to give me a realistic sense of what princesses are trained to."

64 *Peter Garrett*   *Scene and Symbol from George Eliot to James Joyce* (1969), 76–159; Spender, *The Destructive Element*, passim.

67 *"figure out of Balzac"*   Letters, II, 61–62 (*Notebooks*, 26–27). See also PP (2), 167, for an essay of 1876 with an account of his visit to several old places in this area: "The châteaux are extremely different, but both as pictures and as dwellings each has its point." One was Varennes, which he describes in a single sentence; another was certainly Renard, but he makes no further comment.

"Nullement . . . Château-Renard"   Letters, II, 96.

"à peintes raides"   Henri Soulange-Bodin, *Châteaux Anciens de France: Connus et Inconnus* (Paris, n.d.), 309.

68 *Château Bellegarde*   HJ had known the Childe family in Paris since Jan. 1876, and may have heard from them there of the Marquis de Bellegarde and his château.

"adjusted their pride to it"   *Prefaces*, 34–36.

69 *"without our detecting him"*   *Prefaces*, 30–34.

"my reader's suspecting it"   *Prefaces*, 25, 35; also 21–22.

70 *"your memory of it"*   Letters, II, 22.

71 *"making up as you go"* PS, 183, 184.
"*superior Mrs. Radcliffe*" FPN, 155, 156, 168.
"*as wine unto water*" SL, 49.
72 *Essays on the Théâtre Français* SA, 3–4, 11, 68. All ten of HJ's theater critiques of 1875–76 are reprinted in *SA*, 32–92.
73 "*plates of smaller people*" SA, 265, 268. HJ had written a short critique of Dumas fils twenty years before, at the end of "Paris Revisited," reprinted in *PP(2)*.
"*elimination of the intruder*" G. B. Fitch, *Publications of the Modern Language Association*, 63 (March 1949): 274–280. Cargill, 42–43, points out that Fitch's formula fits *The American*, but he misses the evidence in the rest of my paragraph. His thesis that HJ wrote *The American* to refute Dumas' satire in *L'Étrangère* is not convincing.
"*mercenary wiles*" SA, 116, 117.
"*Dumas, Augier, Sardou*" Letters, II, 171.
74 "*a concentrated patriot*" PP (2), 115–116 (under a new title, "Occasional Paris").
75 "*exclusively commercial ... his revenge*" "Americans Abroad," *Nation* (3 Oct. 1878), 208–209—never reprinted.
"*an eternal outsider*" Notebooks, 26.
"*the fancy picture*" IH, 116.
"*I see absolutely nothing*" Letters, II, 51, 59. Edel, V, 348, 352, gives evidence that it was not until a long visit to Edith Wharton in the spring of 1907 that HJ at last penetrated the aristocratic society of the faubourg St. Germain: "I have had a very interesting time, one of the most agreeable I have ever had in Paris," he reported to a friend, "a great many social impressions ...—some of them of a more or less intimate French sort that I had never had."
76 *Flaubert's salon* FN, 130–132. This is HJ's introduction to his translation of *Madame Bovary* (1902). It contains a detailed portrait of Flaubert surrounded by his *cénacle*: distinguished philosophers and men of affairs and "most of the novelists of the Balzac tradition."
Influence of Turgenev Cargill, 42, summarizes the claims of two source-hunters that *A Nest of Noblemen* served as a model for *The American*: the hero there also doesn't "belong" but he falls in love with an aristocrat, the family interferes, and the conflict is resolved by the heroine entering a convent. But a reading of Turgenev's novel does not bear this out. The hero is not an "outsider" but an aristocrat; his marriage to Lisa fails to come off because he is already married and cannot get a divorce, *not* because of family interference. The only real similarity is that Lisa does retire to a convent, but all the circumstances surrounding this action are different from those in *The American*.
Zhukovsky, model for Valentin Letters, II, 46. HJ wrote on 8 May 1876: "He lacks vigor, but has a very amiable and interesting nature, and, on the artistic side, very fine perceptions, ... but I am afraid will never be anything but a rather curious and delicate dilettante. He is one of the flowers of civilization. ... He has here a most enchanting studio and apartment, a treasury of Italian relics." See also Edel, II, 261.
Aristocrats drawn from Balzac Edel, II, 249.
77 "*vividness of his imagination*" FPN, 66–118; quotations from pp. 80, 73, 74.
"*the weakest in talk*" FPN, 103–104.
78 "*Frenchmen and Italians*" HJ's introduction to *Odd Number: 13 Tales by De Maupassant* (1899).

Vistas Opening and Closing · THE PORTRAIT OF A LADY

80 "*freshness of his theme*" Hawthorne, 110. During the long germination of *The Portrait* HJ's conception of it underwent radical changes, as revealed in a sequence

(80 *cont.*)
of newly published letters. To Howells, 24 Oct. 1876: "My novel is to be an *Americana*—the adventures in Europe of a female Newman." To the same, 2 Feb. 1877: "It is the portrait of the character and recital of the adventures of a woman —a great swell, psychologically; a *grande nature*—accompanied with many 'developments.' " By the following summer he declares it will be as superior to *The American* "as wine unto water." During the next two years he cleared his desk of lesser projects, three novelettes and two short novels. In 1879 he answered his brother's complaint that these were all too slight as subjects, giving the reasons for postponing composition of his "great novel": "I have a constant impulse to try experiments of form, in which I wish not to run the risk of wasting or gratuitously using big situations. But to these I am coming now. It is something to have learned how to write" (*Letters*, II, 72, 97, 179, 193–194; *SL*, 49). He began *The Portrait* in Florence in the spring of 1880.
"the picture hung"   *Prefaces*, 58.

81 *"things are all expressive"*   *The Portrait of a Lady*: all references are to the first English edition in three volumes (it appeared one week before the American edition). The importance HJ attributed to imagery in this novel is indicated by the extensive revisions he made in the New York Edition; for example, the image for Stackpole, quoted in my next paragraph, was changed to read: "Ralph saw at a glance that she was as crisp and new and comprehensive as a first issue before the folding. From top to toe she probably had no misprint." Most interesting of all are the newly added images that clarify our understanding of the four men in Isabel's life; they are given later on in my notes.

83 *"all my measure"*   *Prefaces*, 42–43. Next quotes are from pp. 47–53.
"seem most fruitful"   Morris Roberts, ed., *The Art of Fiction* (1948), 111–112.

84 *"Puritan angularity"*   *FPN*, 286–287, 293. *On the Eve* does have a country house for a setting and an unhappy marriage for theme, it is true. But the heroine, though she chooses against the wishes of family and friends, is not trapped by exploiters. The marriage is all for love, and is only unhappy because of the tragic early death of her husband, and he is a revolutionary hero, not a dilettantish egotist.
Madame Bovary not a model for Isabel   Emma has no fortune; she marries, without opposition and without trickery, a dull country doctor. Bored with her drab life in a provincial town she tries to escape through an adulterous affaire, and when this romance collapses she commits suicide.
"any novel we can recall"   *FPN*, 201–202, 206. Philip Grover's *HJ and the French Novel* (1975) is a thorough account of his relations with Flaubert and the others, his reading of their novels, and his comments on them. But Grover's approach is quite different from mine, my sole purpose being a study of their impact on HJ's own fictional techniques.

85 *"the embrace of thought"*   *SLC*, 152, 153.
"classic ideally done"   *FN*, 137–138.
"step-by-step evolution"   Lubbock, I, 66.
"plunge and plunge again"   *SLC*, 151.
Reading George Eliot in 1876   Edel, II, 220–222.

86 *Claims of indebtedness to G. E.*   See F. R. Leavis, *The Great Tradition* (1948), 85–153; George Levine in *English Literary History*, 30 (1963): 244–257.
"its full capacity"   *FN*, 82, 83.

87 *"very bad logic"*   *SLC*, 44–46.
HJ and GE   HJ visited her in London in 1877; referred favorably to *Middlemarch* in a travel essay of 1878; was deeply moved by her death in the summer of 1880, just a few months after her marriage to his friend John Cross (Edel, II, 371; *Letters*, II, 289–290, 332; "Very Modern Rome," 1878, first published in the *Harvard Library Bulletin*, Spring 1954).

(87 *cont.*)
"*the greatest novels to produce*"   FN, 86.
88 "*is a poor affair*"   FN, 81, 89; *SLC*, 43, 44.
"*the amount of felt life*"   *Prefaces*, 45.
"*to pass for an impressionist*"   Lyon Richardson, ed., *HJ: Representative Selections*, (American Writer's Series 1941), 106–107, 113.
"*chief exemplar in Mr. James*"   *Century Magazine*, 3 (Nov. 1882): 25–29.
89 *Realistic novel transformed*   Peter Garrett, *Scene and Symbol* (1969); his chaps. on Eliot, Flaubert, and HJ have proved helpful here.
90 *To foreshorten at the end*   *Notebooks*, 15.
91 *Imagery in the midnight vigil*   J. T. Frederick in the *Arizona Quarterly*, 25 (1969): 150–156, analyzes the imagery in chap. 42, with special emphasis on the "prison" image, but does not show how it echoes throughout the book, thus serving reader and critic as a unique instrument for exploring the full meaning of the novel. My analysis of "Person, Place, and Thing in James's *Portrait of a Lady*," the year before, does just that (*Essays in Honor of Jay B. Hubbell*, 1968); and it serves as a basis for my extended analysis in the present chapter.
92 *Model for Gardencourt*   See Edel, II, 421; Virginia Harlow, *Thomas Sergeant Perry* (1950), 307–308; Julian Sturgis, *From Books and Papers of Russell Sturgis* (Oxford, 1893), 258, 260, 261; Nicolaus Pevsner, *Surrey* (1962), 496–497. HJ wrote a letter to another American friend during this same visit "under the genial roof of Russell Sturgis" in which he said: "R. S. is a dear delightful old fellow and Mrs. S. the kindest, easiest and handsomest of hostesses" (*Letters*, II, 301).
Model for Isabel's Albany home   See *Autobiography*, chap. 1.
95 "*what strange gardens*"   This phrase was added in the New York Edition.
98 "*of privacy and of study*"—"Recent Florence," *Atlantic Monthly*, May 1878, 587–588 (reprinted, revised, in *IH*, 123–124).
Model for Osmond and Villa   *Autobiography*, 521–522. Villa Castellani, renamed Villa Mercede, corresponds strikingly even today to HJ's description in *The Portrait*.
100 *Image of an antique coin*   In the New York Edition HJ added a similar image for Osmond earlier in the novel: "He suggested, fine gold coin as he was, no stamp nor emblem of the common mintage that provides for general circulation; he was the elegant complicated medal struck off for a special occasion" (I, 329).
103 "*the pain is the same*"   *TS*, 118.
104 "*incrustation of marble*"   *TS*, 130–132.
107 *Image of light for Ralph*   In the New York Edition HJ added one of his most moving images for the invalid Ralph: "Blighted and battered, but still responsive and still ironic, his face was like a lighted lantern patched with paper and unsteadily held" (II, 59).
109 *Source for vista-alley image?*   HJ may have found a possible hint for this complex image in chap. 20 of GE's *Middlemarch*: "How was it that in the weeks since her marriage, Dorothea had not distinctly observed but felt with a stifling depression, that the large vistas and wide fresh air which she had dreamed of finding in her husband's mind were replaced by anterooms and winding passages that seemed to lead nowhither?" (Riverside Ed., 1956, p. 145; this text follows that of 1874, the last one corrected by GE.) But besides being quite different, these images for Dorothea and Casaubon are used only this once and are not part of a structure of imagery pervading the novel.
Model for Palazzo Roccanera   Murray's *Handbook for Rome and the Campagna* (London, 1908, 17th ed.), 242: "Palazzo Mattei, built on the site of the Circus Flaminius by Asdrubale Mattei (1615).... The court and staircase are decorated with reliefs from sarcophagi and other fragments of ancient sculpture, the only relics of the once famous Monumenta Matheiana." See also Georgina Masson, *Italian Villas and Palaces* (1959), 219; and *Companion Guide to Rome* (1963), 108–

109. Palazzo Antici-Mattei belongs to the Italian State and is used for cultural purposes; in 1953, as visiting Fulbright Professor, I gave my lectures there. Prof. Mario Praz ("Ritratto di Signora," in the Roman newspaper *Il Tempo*, 30 June 1965) thinks that Palazzo Ricci on Via Giulia, where he once lived, may have been a partial model since it does have frescoes by Caravaggio (though they are on the façade) whereas the frescoes at Mattei (in the *piano nobile*) are by Domenichino; in *The Portrait* HJ speaks of frescoes by Caravaggio in the *piano nobile* of Palazzo Roccanera. In all other ways Mattei is much nearer to the description of Isabel's Roman house than Ricci is.

116 *Conversation Galante*   Watteau in the first edition is corrected to Lancret in the New York Edition. See George Wildenstein, *Lancret: Biographie et Catalogues Critiques* (Paris, 1924), Item 285, Fig. 73, and Item 271, Fig. 67, for other possible originals for HJ's picture.

119 *Image of Goodwood as knight-errant*   See the New York Edition for a revision of this scene, prepared for by an added image that occurred to Isabel on two earlier occasions: (1) Goodwood as one of those "armoured warriors—in plates of steel handsomely inlaid with gold ... seen in museums and portraits"; (2) his eyes on her "seemed to shine through the vizard of a helmet" (I, 165, 218). In the climactic scene after the "kiss like white lightning," Isabel's submission to his embrace is given a suggestive extension: "she felt each thing in his hard manhood that had least pleased her, each aggressive fact of his face, his figure, his presence, justified of its intense identity and made one with this act of possession" (II, 436).

121 *"complete in itself"*   Notebooks, 18. See *Prefaces*, 5, for fuller statement of the same doctrine.

122 *"take my stand"*   Letter quoted by Edel, II, 405.
"without leaving her chair"   *Prefaces*, 57.

Lost Between Two Worlds · The Princess Casamassima

125 *"the plates of glass"*   *The Princess*: all references are to the paperback Torchbooks Edition (reprint of the revised edition, Macmillan, 1922, very few changes having been made from the first edition).

127 *"privation ... the question"*   *Autobiography*, 101. The image of the "confectioner's window" was almost obsessive with HJ. In 1897 he used it in *What Maisie Knew* to describe the little heroine's only way of getting at experience (I, 137; N.Y. Ed.). In 1915 he applied it to himself again, in a letter, to describe his sense of exclusion from the inner circle of political life (*SL*, 215).

128 *"the book ... was born"*   *Prefaces*, 59–60.
"London pavement ... doors that opened"   *Prefaces*, 60–61.

129 *"the gaping barbarian"*   EH, 16, 18. The essay, though not written until spring 1886, was based on HJ's London walks in the late 1870s. HJ's "Du Maurier and London Society," *Century Magazine* (May 1883), praised the novelist-illustrator for holding up "a singularly polished and lucid mirror to the drama of English society." Du Maurier, on his side, said of *The Princess*: "The background of London is ever there, treated ... as it has not been treated before" (Edel, III, 190, quoting his letter of 1 Nov. 1886).

Consciousness of the hero   Though the point of view is not strictly limited to Hyacinth, he is present and dominant throughout 36 of the novel's 46 chapters; in the others he either appears or is the chief subject of conversation (absent in chaps. 2, 4, 18, 36, 37, 39, 46; partially absent in chaps. 1, 16, 40). The effect is that everything comes to us through his consciousness.

131 *"it was erected to punish"*   EH, 38.
"quite the Naturalist"   Virginia Harlow, *Thomas Sergeant Perry* (1950), 319. The

(131 *cont.*)

letter contains no further reference to Millbank, nor is the prison mentioned in any of HJ's other published letters. See *SL*, 80, for an account of his meeting with Zola et al. in 1884.

"weight of one's accumulations" Prefaces, 76–77. HJ's Notebooks, 68–69, contain only two brief entries relating to *The Princess* (dated 10 and 22 Aug. 1885), totalling a bare twenty lines. There is nothing to suggest Zolaesque note-taking.

144 *"produced a reality"* FN, 13.

148 *"no ray of sun ever shone"* Oliver Twist (Penguin Ed.), 152; chap. 15.
  "in his hand" Ibid., 236–237; Chap. 26.

151 *"wants blood-letting"* Lubbock, I, 124.

152 Factual basis of HJ's "Underground" W. H. Tilley, *The Background of* The Princess Casamassima (1960), provides a statistical and documentary supplement to Lionel Trilling's thesis of the complete accuracy of HJ's account of anarchism in the 1880s. (See his introduction to the 1948 Macmillan edition of the novel.) Internal evidence indicates that the setting of *The Princess* covers the years 1881–84—from Hyacinth's renewal of friendship with Milly, age 20, until his suicide less than three years later.
  "the vast smug surface" Prefaces, 77–78.

153 *"in a high degree"* LRE, 190–196.
  Virgin Soil, *model for* Princess? Cargill, 146–173, summarizes the most extreme claims of indebtedness by two source-hunters. The most moderate view is expressed by Tilley, *Background of* The Princess Casamassima.
  "the game of life" FPN, 212–213; PP (*1*); LRE, 190.

154 Keats as model for Hyacinth The miniature of Keats by Joseph Severn (water color on ivory?) is in the Fitzwilliam Museum, Cambridge, U.K.—a gift from the collection of Sir Charles Dilke in 1911. Since Dilke had been a friend of HJ since 1877, he may well have seen the Keats miniature. The same museum owns a MS of Keats's "Ode to a Nightingale."

161 *"attuned to a different pitch"* PP (*2*), 118.
  "dreariest, stodgiest commonness" EH, 15.

164 *"don't make a scene"* Autobiography, 107.

166 *"company as you go"* EH, 160–161 (next quote from 163). This essay, first published in 1877, was reprinted in 1883, in *PP (2)*, shortly before HJ began writing *The Princess*.

169 *"the right place"* Notebooks, 27–28.

171 *"pillars of the Empire"* EH, 162.

172 Hyacinth's suicide The ending has been the subject of much controversy. Sister Jane Luecke, *Modern Philology*, 60 (1963): 274–280, says the suicide is the choice of a weak character and does not resolve his problem; Trilling in *The Liberal Imagination* calls it an "act of heroism," the response to a withdrawal of love; Elizabeth Stevenson, *The Crooked Corridor* (1949), 67, says he was the victim of a triple betrayal; Cargill, 160, says it was quadruple; Irene Samuel, *Bull. New York Public Library*, 69 (1965): 117–130, fixes on Muniment as the real betrayer.

For Love or Money · THE WINGS OF THE DOVE

173 *"clings to it with passion"* Notebooks, 169, 3 Nov. 1894. When HJ returns to the subject on 14 Feb. 1895, he also takes up again his donnée for *The Golden Bowl* (first noted on 28 Nov. 1892). On 31 Oct. 1895 occurs the first entry for *The Ambassadors*.
  "the passionate things" Notebooks, 166.

(*173 cont.*)
"*given anything to live*"   *Autobiography*, 544 (504–544).
174 *Biographer rather than critic*   See F. O. Matthiessen, *HJ: The Major Phase* (1944), 43-53; Edel, I, 226 ff.
"*marches like a drama*"   *Notebooks*, 111, 113, 133, 135, 187.
175 "*the work of my life*"   *Notebooks*, 179.
"*principle of the Scenario*"   *Notebooks*, 188.
Experiments in the 1890s   See Walter Isle, *Experiments in Form* (1968), 35–37 and passim.
176 *Scenarios for the novels*   HJ wrote to H. G. Wells, 15 Nov. 1902, declining his request to see early drafts of his novels: "A plan for *myself*, as copious and developed as possible, I always draw up— ... a preliminary *private* outpouring. But this voluminous effusion is, ever, so extremely familiar, confidential and intimate— in the form of an interminable garrulous letter to my own fond fancy—that though I always for ready reference have it carefully typed, it isn't a thing I would willingly expose to any eye but my own" (Lubbock, I, 405).
177 "*synthesis of picture*"   *Prefaces*, 298; 322-323.
"*the double pressure*"   *Prefaces*, 300-301.
178 "*as if I were alive*"   *The Wings of the Dove*: all references are to the revised edition (Macmillan, 1922); down to p. 201 the references are to Vol. I, and from there to the end they are to Vol. II.
187 *Bronzino portrait, previous critics*   Miriam Allott, *Modern Language Notes* (Jan. 1953) made the identification. Bernard Berenson in *Italian Painters* (1948), 118, singles out this portrait for special praise as "a fine example of dignified rendering of character." See Winner, 81–85, for commentary on the Bronzino; Laurence Holland, *The Expense of Vision* (1964), 78 ff., for HJ's interest in Mannerist painting.
"*grand Watteau-composition*"   PE, 76–77 (HJ's essay "The Wallace Collection," first published in 1873).
189 "*becomes their drama*"   *Prefaces*, 288–290.
194 *Problem of form in* The Wings   J. A. Ward, *The Search for Form* (1967), 166, calls this "structurally the most difficult of all James's novels." His commentary in that book and in *The Imagination of Disaster* (1961) has proved helpful.
"*what is truncated*"   Lubbock, I, 403.
"*foreshortening at any cost*"   *Prefaces*, 306, 302.
"*narrowing circumvallations*"   *Prefaces*, 291–292, 294.
195 "*some abysmal trap*"   *Prefaces*, 393.
"*novel of relations*"   Ward, *Search for Form*, 75, 191.
196 "*the possibilities of Milly Theale*"   *Prefaces*, 303–304.
200 *The lamb and the lion*   Isaiah 11:6—"The wolf also shall dwell with the lamb, and the leopard shall lie down with the kid; and the calf and the young lion ... together; and a little child shall lead them."
201 *Hallmarks of sterling*   See Judith Banister, *English Silver* (1969), 145, 152.
"*brilliant if brief career*"   Page references in parentheses from here to the end of this chapter are to Vol. II, Macmillan Ed., 1922.
206 "*just the very last*"   *IH*, 67–68, "Two Old Houses." The palace is not named in the essay but is identified by Edel, IV, 284. With the kind guidance of the owner, Mr. Ralph Curtis, I made a detailed comparison of Palazzo Barbaro with "Palazzo Leporelli" on a visit to Venice.
207 "*waters had overtaken them*"   *IH*, 47–48.
209 *Composite of Veronese paintings*   *The Marriage at Cana* is commented on in *IH*, 58, and is admired by the hero of *The American* in the opening chapter. Though *The Feast in the House of Levi* is not specifically named in HJ's essays on Venice,

they indicate numerous visits to the Accademia, where it hangs. *The Supper in the House of Simon* he certainly saw during his visit to Torino in 1877 (*IH*, 108–111). It is noteworthy that two Veronese canvases, though quite unlike the above, hung in the grand sala at Palazzo Barbaro at the end of the 19th century (Winner, 84; see 81–85 for her comments on the scene in *The Wings*).

210 *Analogy or Allegory?*   See Holland, *Expense of Vision*, 306–310, for as persuasive a reading by strict analogy as can be made. My own reading (which adds a third source-painting) agrees inevitably with his in some details but stops far short of his Christian interpretation. Similarly, his point that the four Gospel writers seem to be invoked strikes me as more fortuitous than meaningful.

"prose of corresponding color"   For the letter to LaFarge see *New England Quarterly*, 22: 178–180. See also *IH*, 59, and *Letters*, I, 138–140.

211 *"kind of breezy festival"*   *IH*, 19, 23. Berenson, *Italian Painters*, 47–48, praises Veronese for similar reasons.

213 *"wings and wondrous flights"*   Psalm 55 has often been cited as the source of HJ's image. Verse 6, "O that I had wings like a dove, / For then I would fly away and be at rest," may have suggested the title for his novel. But the rest of the text of this Psalm I find alien to HJ's heroine and to his theme, in spite of the eloquent argument by Holland, *Expense of Vision*, 303–304.

216 *"remedy for her despair"*   *Notebooks*, 170.

Through the Picture Frame · The Ambassadors

220 *"the best all round"*   *Prefaces*, 308.

221 *Strether as point of view*   *Prefaces*, 317–318. Percy Lubbock was the first to emphasize the crucial value of this technique of HJ's, notably in *The Ambassadors*, making it the touchstone of his *Craft of Fiction* (1921), 156–171. Edel, V, 77, (1973) is the first important writer to take issue with this consensus.

222 *"his thought unexplored"*   Lubbock, *Craft*, 167.

223 *"but nowhere seen"*   HJ is quoting from one of Flaubert's letters, in a review of his *Correspondence*, reprinted in *Essays in London* (1893).

Photo of HJ by Boughton   See *PE*, frontispiece.

Imagery, places, and things   Of the many studies of imagery in *The Ambassadors* the best seems to me that of W. M. Gibson, *New England Quarterly*, (Sept. 1951). But none of them touches on my method of person-place-and-thing as a way of understanding HJ's symbolic structure.

224 *"I can hear him"*   *Notebooks*, 225–226.

225 *"scene of my friend's anecdote"*   *Notebooks*, 372–373. See 372–415 for the full text of HJ's "Project."

226 *"Oh, you're young"*   *Notebooks*, 373–374.

The actual house and garden   Edel, II, 230–231; III, 336.

"this process of vision"   *Prefaces*, 308–309.

227 *"too like W.D.H."*   *Notebooks*, 226–227.

"any range of possibilities"   *Prefaces*, 311. After the novel was finished but before publication, HJ wrote to Howells: "The mere point of a start" had come when young Sturges "repeated to me five words you said to him one day at Whistler's." Immediately after this "germ [went] to work in my imagination," HJ concluded, "it got away from you or anything like you" (Lubbock, I, 376–377). Howells's limitations as a possible further model for Strether are revealed in his own letter to a son whom he had left in Paris to study architecture, written on 27 July 1894, shortly after his return to America: "Perhaps it was as well I was called home. The poison of Europe was getting into my soul. You must look out for that. They live much more fully than we do.... When I think of the Whistler garden!"

(*227 cont.*)
(Mildred Howells, ed., *Life in Letters of WDH*, 1928, II, 52). HJ didn't know of this confession, of course, but he did know Howells. Perhaps some aspects of his resistance to European civilization are incorporated in Waymarsh, created by HJ as a foil to Strether.

"*resemblance to . . . Henry James*" *SL*, 198.

"*the reader of his record*" *Notebooks*, 374.

228 "*round*" *and* "*flat*" *characters* E. M. Forster, *Aspects of the Novel* (1927), 67 ff.

"*Project*" *compared with novel* The editor at Harpers, H. M. Alden, who had only the "Project" to go by, can almost be excused for rejecting it as "too subtly fine for general appreciation, . . . fold within fold of a complex mental web, in which the reader is lost" (quoted by the editor of *Notebooks*, 372).

"*for present feeling*" *The Ambassadors* (Norton Critical Edition), 24; all references are to this reprint, a "corrected text" of the revised New York Edition.

229 *HJ and Strether at Chester* HJ planned to go there early in 1869; he actually went on the next trip, after arrival at Liverpool in May 1872 (Edel, I, 287–288; II, 63–64). Strether's first European trip was between 1865 (end of the Civil War) and 1871 (burning of the Tuileries)—from internal evidence in the novel, pp. 24, 59, 62–63.

"*the use of his eyes*" *EH*, 51.

230 "*by dramatic projection*" Lubbock, II, 245.

"*cheap infatuations*" *EH*, 51. That this complaining gentleman was an invention is proved by the fact that HJ's sister Alice and his Aunt Kate were his only companions on the 1872 visit to Chester.

231 "*her smelling salts*" *Prefaces*, 320–323.

232 "*a psychological commentary*" *EH*, 63.

"*romantic city in the world*" *EH*, 56.

233 "*question of Strether's past*" *Prefaces*, 323.

The novel's inner theme *Prefaces*, 313.

235 *HJ's essays on Du Maurier* *PP* (*1*), 341; and *Harpers' Magazine* (Sept. 1897).

Paradox of appearance and reality One of HJ's finest treatments of this is in his short story "The Real Thing" (1893), in which a fashionable artist (Du Maurier?) who is making illustrations for a magazine fiction dealing with high society employs as models a husband and wife who, as impoverished gentry, seem like "the right real thing"—but it turns out otherwise.

"*the audience, the attendants*" *SA*, 93.

236 "*none as regards English*" *SA*, 95.

"*such a wonderful dance*" *Notebooks*, 226–227; *Prefaces*, 316–317.

237 "*the most Parisian adventure*" *Autobiography*, 190–191. The James's residence in 1856–57 was in the rue Montaigne, so that the boys began their walk about one kilometer west of Strether's starting point, but joined his route in the garden of the Tuileries.

238 "*richest and noblest expression*" *Autobiography*, 196.

"*picture seems to abound*" *IH*, 149. The comment is about Rome, but it applies equally well to HJ's response to Paris.

239 *Jardin des Tuileries* It is reproduced in *Masterpieces of Impressionist and Post-Impressionist Painting* (Washington; National Gallery of Art, 1959), 13. See L. R. Pissarro and L. Venturi, *Camille Pissarro* (1939), No. 1099; see also No. 1129, *Jardin des Tuileries, Matin, Printemps, 1900*. Monet's *Jardin des Tuileries*, three views, were included in the Impressionists' Exhibition of 1877, which HJ may well have seen; the one looking toward the Louvre fits Strether's picture almost as well as Pissarro's does.

HJ's changing opinion of Impressionists See *PE*, 114–115 (review of 1876 Exhibition); 143, 165, 209, 258–259 (comments on Whistler); 217 (comment on Sargent); 29-30 (quotation of HJ's comment in 1904). For the period of change in between see *PE*, 217; *Notebooks*, 160; and the summary by Winner, 50-51.

240 *HJ's affinity with the Impressionists*   See E. E. Hale in *Faculty Papers of Union College*, II, 14-17 (Jan. 1931). But my chief debt in all this is to Winner, 15 (LaFarge); 32-35 (HJ on the "picturesque"); 89 (influence of the Impressionists).

241 *"beauty of light"*   Letter to Edward Warren, 13 Mar. 1899 (quoted in *New Statesman & Nation*, 17 Apr. 1943, 25: 255).

244 *James, Degas, Valéry*   "La Loge" is in the Corcoran Gallery, Washington, D.C. See also the favorable reference to Degas on p. 239, above. For Valéry see *Degas, Danse, Dessin* (Paris, 1938).

246 *"the double pressure"*   *Prefaces*, 300.

247 *"light and colour"*   Novotny, 348, 351.

248 *"banquet of sunlight and colour"*   D. S. MacColl, "Impressionism," *EB*, 11th Ed., XIV, 344 (1910). See also John Rewald, *History of Impressionism* (1946), 48. The Monet and Renoir are at the Louvre, the Manet at the National Gallery in London.
HJ "a ghost at the window"   See p. 226, above; also Edel, V, 73.
"for Enjoyment, in a word"   *Notebooks*, 226.

253 *"light of style itself"*   *Prefaces*, 28.

254 *Meissonier*   *PS*, 35-37, 109.
Visits to Daudet's house   Edel, I, 72-73.

256 *"atmosphere filled with light"*   Novotny, 331.

257 *Luncheons, Manet and Renoir*   See François Fosca, *Renoir* (Thames and Hudson, 1961) 156; John Richardson, *Edouard Manet* (Thames and Hudson, 1958), 129. The Manet is in the museum at Tournai, Belgium; the Renoir is in the Phillips Gallery, Washington. A second Renoir painting, *Le Déjeuner au Bord de la Rivière* (Art Institute of Chicago) is even closer in subject matter, but the lighting effects are not.

260 *"her infinite variety"*   *Antony and Cleopatra*, II, ii, 238-239.
Two Renoir portraits   See Fosca, *Renoir*.

264 *"a trifle devious"*   *PS*, 6.

267 *HJ and Lambinet*   *Autobiography*, 193; *PE*, 43.

268 *"to new-world eyes"*   *IH*, 168-169.

269 *Lambinet and Barbizon School*   Novotny, 177-178.
Two Lambinet paintings   The first is in a private collection, Charleston, S.C. (The owner, Mr. John M. LeCato kindly let me examine it, then supplied me with a colorslide.) There is a color print of the second in the Witt Library, Courtauld Institute.

270 *"coppery green"*   Novotny, 178, 180.
Renoir and Manet   Matthiessen, *HJ*, 34-35, suggested Renoir; Edel, V, 75, picks Manet.

271 *"if perspective were conventional"*   Winner, 77-78, 88. The Renoir and Manet cited by her are similar to HJ's "picture" in colors and light effects, but the subjects are quite different. The Lambinet she cites is totally different from HJ's in colors and light effects, but fairly close in subject.

272 *"do anything they like"*   *Notebooks*, 409.
"both painted there in 1869"   Fosca, *Renoir*, 27-28; Rewald, *History of Impressionism*, 191.
Monet's La Grenouillère   This painting is in the Metropolitan Museum, New York. See Wm. C. Seitz, *Claude Monet* (1960).

273 *La Seine à Vétheuil*   This painting was owned by the Durand-Ruel Galérie from 1888 until some time in the 1890s when it was bought by the Louvre. (HJ was in Paris in 1893 and 1899.) It is now in the Metropolitan, N.Y.

276 *"combination that may have changed"*   "London Notes" (1897), quoted in J. E. Miller, Jr., ed., *Theory of Fiction: Henry James* (1972), 23.

(*276 cont.*)

"*true high comic hero*"   Ronald Wallace, *Henry James and the Comic Form* (1975), 131. The novel's structure is that of comedy, he argues, "with its opposition of conflicting societies, its mock-heroic tone, its doublings and triplings"— moralistic Woollett versus romantically imagined Paris; the ironic use of diplomatic language; the double ambassadorial mission; the three "virtuous attachments" (Chad-Vionnet, Strether-Gostrey, Waymarsh-Pocock). "Within this framework Lambert Strether progresses slowly toward a great comic vision.... Strether finally discovers that he has been a fool all along, and, at the close, he perceives that the real is no less wonderful than the imaginary" (126, 132).

Literary Impressionist

277   "*the human spectacle*"   FN, 14.
"*of painting it*"   Winner, 88 (italics added).

278   "*impressionism will yet go*"   *Fortnightly Review*, 49 (Apr. 1888): 647–664.
Loti and Monet   Loti, *Impressions* (London, 1898), 43–46; 93–99.

279   *Reminiscent of Maupassant*   Novotny, 360.
"*impressionism, as painters say nowadays*"   PP (*1*), 251–252, 256, 259. See also HJ's introduction to a translation of Maupassant's tales entitled *The Odd Number* (New York, 1889), p. xv.
"*Maupassant's verbal picture*"   Richardson, *Manet*, 129.

280   "*girls in flowered bonnets*"   Roger Colet, trans., *Maupassant: Selected Short Stories* (Penguin, 1971), 9; cf. Fosca, *Renoir*, 27–28.
"*green banks, a decoration too*"   Colet, *Maupassant*, 359.
HJ's relations with Daudet   A detailed account of an evening at Daudet's in February 1884, with Goncourt and Zola and Loti present, was recorded by Theodore Child in the "Contributor's Club," *Atlantic Monthly*, 53 (May 1884): 724–727. For Daudet's visit to London see Edel, IV, 132 ff.

281   "*associations awakened by things*"   PP (*1*), 206–207.
"*passion for the concrete*"   LRE, 183–184.

282   "*he writes with a brush*"   PP (*1*), 213–214.
"*genius combined with beauty*"   Daudet, *Le Nabab* (Boston, 1895), 82–83; my translation.

283   "*carried to the last point*"   HJ, "Alphonse Daudet," *Literature*, I: 306–307 (25 Dec. 1897); uncollected.
"*experiments of Virginia Woolf*"   Edel, V, 77.

Index

Index

Index

James, William, 9, 12, 13, 51–52, 53, 72–73, 75, 85, 240
Joyce, James, 21, 39, 89, 283; *Ulysses,* 123, 283

Kafka, Franz, 284
Keats, John, 158, 165, 169, 187, 294; "La Belle Dame Sans Merci," 36; "Ode to a Nightingale," 154–160

LaFarge, John, 210, 240, 296
Lambinet, Émile, 237, 267–270, 272, 275, 298
Lancret, Nicolas, 116, 293
Lawrence, D. H., 283
Leavis, F. R., *The Great Tradition,* 291
Leonardo da Vinci, 46, 289
Levine, George, 291
London, 5, 75, 102, 124–154, 161, 163–172, 178–183, 190–194, 219, 229, 233–236, 291, 299
Lorraine, Claude, 268, 269
Loti, Pierre, 277–278, 283, 299; *Impressions,* 278
Lovelace, Earl of, *Astarte,* 35, 288
Lowell, J. R., 52–53; *Fireside Travels,* 288
Lubbock, Percy, *The Craft of Fiction,* 222, 296. See also *Letters*
Luecke, Sister Jane, 294

MacColl, D. S., 298
Manet, Edouard, 239, 247–248, 257–258, 270–273, 277, 279, 298
Masson, Georgina, *Italian Villas and Palaces, Companion Guide to Rome,* 292
Masterpieces of Impressionist and Post-Impressionist Painting, 297
Matthiessen, F. O., *The James Family,* 289; *HJ: the Major Phase,* 295, 298
Maupassant, Guy de, 7, 277, 278–280, 283, 299; "Mouche," 280; *Odd Number,* 279, 290, 299
Meissonier, Ernest, 253, 298
Melodrama, 9, 12–13, 23–25, 28, 31, 36, 38, 57, 65–74, 77, 79, 132–133, 144, 147–150
Miller, James E., *Theory of Fiction: HJ,* 298
Milton, John, *Paradise Lost,* 95
Models for characters: Valentin Bellegarde, 76, 290; Christopher Newman, 50–53; Hyacinth Robinson, 126–129, 162, 164; Lambert Strether, 221, 227, 229, 237–238, 248, 268; Milly Theale, 173–175, 187, 190
Models for houses: Château Fleurières, 67–68, 289; Gardencourt, 92–93; Gloriani's, 225–226, 239, 296; Osmond's villa, 97–98, 292; Palazzo Leporelli, 206–207, 295; Palazzo Roccanera, 110, 292–293
Modern novel, 3, 21–22, 23, 34–40, 64, 80, 85, 123, 222–223, 283–284
Mohl, Mme Jules, 226
Monet, Claude, 239–240, 247, 256, 270–275, 277, 278, 279–280, 297–298
Money theme, 43–49, 50, 56, 60, 68, 96, 100–101, 107, 115–117, 174, 180–186, 196, 219, 233, 252, 258, 266–267, 276
Mordell, Albert, *Discovery of a Genius: W. D. Howells and HJ,* 289
Murdoch, Iris, 284
Murger, Henry, *Scènes de la Vie de Bohème,* 241
Murillo, Estéban, 46, 47–48
Murray's *Handbook for Rome,* 109–110, 292

Nabokov, Vladimir, 284
Nation, 73, 74, 289–290
New Statesman and Nation, 298

Index